The Anthropology of Performance

Wiley-Blackwell Anthologies in Social and Cultural Anthropology

Series Editor: Parker Shipton, Boston University

Drawing from some of the most significant scholarly work of the nineteenth and twentieth centuries, the *Wiley-Blackwell Anthologies in Social and Cultural Anthropology* series offers a comprehensive and unique perspective on the ever-changing field of anthropology. It represents both a collection of classic readers and an exciting challenge to the norms that have shaped this discipline over the past century.

Each edited volume is devoted to a traditional subdiscipline of the field such as the anthropology of religion, linguistic anthropology, or medical anthropology; and provides a foundation in the canonical readings of the selected area. Aware that such subdisciplinary definitions are still widely recognized and useful – but increasingly problematic – these volumes are crafted to include a rare and invaluable perspective on social and cultural anthropology at the onset of the twenty-first century. Each text provides a selection of classic readings together with contemporary works that underscore the artificiality of subdisciplinary definitions and point students, researchers, and general readers in the new directions in which anthropology is moving.

Series Advisory Editorial Board:

1. *Linguistic Anthropology: A Reader, 2nd Edition*
   Edited by Alessandro Duranti
2. *A Reader in the Anthropology of Religion, 2nd Edition*
   Edited by Michael Lambek
3. *The Anthropology of Politics: A Reader in Ethnography, Theory, and Critique*
   Edited by Joan Vincent
4. *Kinship and Family: An Anthropological Reader*
   Edited by Robert Parkin and Linda Stone
5. *Law and Anthropology: A Reader*
   Edited by Sally Falk Moore
6. *The Anthropology of Development and Globalization: From Classical Political Economy to Contemporary Neoliberalism*
   Edited by Marc Edelman and Angelique Haugerud
7. *The Anthropology of Art: A Reader*
   Edited by Howard Morphy and Morgan Perkins
8. *Feminist Anthropology: A Reader*
   Edited by Ellen Lewin
9. *Ethnographic Fieldwork: An Anthropological Reader, 2nd Edition*
   Edited by Antonius C.G.M. Robben and Jeffrey A. Sluka
10. *Environmental Anthropology*
    Edited by Michael R. Dove and Carol Carpenter
11. *Anthropology and Child Development: A Cross-Cultural Reader*
    Edited by Robert A. LeVine and Rebecca S. New
12. *Foundations of Anthropological Theory: From Classical Antiquity to Early Modern Europe*
    Edited by Robert Launay
13. *Psychological Anthropology: A Reader on Self in Culture*
    Edited by Robert A. LeVine
14. *A Reader in Medical Anthropology: Theoretical Trajectories, Emergent Realities*
    Edited by Byron J. Good, Michael M.J. Fischer, Sarah S. Willen, and Mary-Jo DelVecchio Good
15. *Sexualities in Anthropology*
    Edited by Andrew Lyons and Harriet Lyons
16. *The Anthropology of Performance: A Reader*
    Edited by Frank J. Korom

The Anthropology of Performance

A Reader

Edited by

Frank J. Korom

A John Wiley & Sons, Ltd., Publication

This edition first published 2013
Editorial material and organization © 2013 John Wiley & Sons, Inc.

Wiley-Blackwell is an imprint of John Wiley & Sons, formed by the merger of Wiley's global Scientific, Technical and Medical business with Blackwell Publishing.

Registered Office
John Wiley & Sons Ltd, The Atrium, Southern Gate, Chichester,
West Sussex, PO19 8SQ, UK

Editorial Offices
350 Main Street, Malden, MA 02148-5020, USA
9600 Garsington Road, Oxford, OX4 2DQ, UK
The Atrium, Southern Gate, Chichester, West Sussex, PO19 8SQ, UK

For details of our global editorial offices, for customer services, and for information about how to apply for permission to reuse the copyright material in this book please see our website at www.wiley.com/wiley-blackwell.

The right of Frank J. Korom to be identified as the author of the editorial material in this work has been asserted in accordance with the UK Copyright, Designs and Patents Act 1988.

Library of Congress Cataloging-in-Publication Data

The anthropology of performance : a reader / edited by Frank J. Korom.
    p. cm.
Includes bibliographical references and index.
ISBN 978-1-118-32398-4 (cloth) – ISBN 978-1-118-32399-1 (pbk.) 1. Anthropology. 2. Performance.
    I. Korom, Frank J.
GN27.A683 2013
301–dc23
                                                                    2012039879

A catalogue record for this book is available from the British Library.

Cover image: Pobi Chitrakar, a Bengali narrative scroll painter showing his scroll about the peasant uprising in the village of Singur against the West Bengal state government. Photo taken in the village of Naya, Medinipur District, West Bengal, India. Photo taken by Frank J. Korom.
Cover design by Nicki Averill Design & Illustration.

Set in 9/11 pt Sabon by Thomson Digital, Noida, India
Printed in Malaysia by Ho Printing (M) Sdn Bhd
1   2013

Contents

Acknowledgments to Sources

The editors and publishers gratefully acknowledge the permission granted to reproduce the copyright material in this book:

1   Anthony Tuck, "Singing the Rug: Patterned Textiles and the Origins of Indo-European Metrical Poetry," pp. 539–550 from *American Journal of Archaeology* 110 (4), 2006. Reprinted with permission of Archaeological Institute of America via CCC.

2   Rosalind Thomas, "Performance and Written Literature in Classical Greece: Envisaging Performance from Written Literature and Comparative Contexts," pp. 348–357 from *Bulletin of the School of Oriental African Studies* 66(3), 2003. Reprinted with permission of Cambridge University Press.

3   Roger D. Abrahams, "Playing the Dozens," pp. 209–220 from *Journal of American Folklore* 75(297), 1962. Reprinted with permission of American Folklore Society.

4   Richard Bauman, "The La Have Island General Store: Sociability and Verbal Art in a Nova Scotia Community," pp. 330–343 from *Journal of American Folklore* 85 (338): 330–343, 1972. Reprinted with permission of American Folklore Society.

5   E. Ojo Arewa and Alan Dundes, "Proverbs and the Ethnography of Speaking Folklore," pp. 70–85 from *American Anthropologist* 66(6), 1964.

6   Philip A. Noss, "Gbaya Riddles in Changing Times," pp. 34–42 from *Research in African Literatures* 37(2), 2006. Reprinted with permission of Indiana University Press.

7   Fiona Magowan, "Shadows of Song: Exploring Research and Performance Strategies in Yolngu Women's Crying-songs," pp. 89–104 from *Oceania* 72(2), 2001. Reprinted with permission.

8   Sam D. Gill, "Prayer as Person: The Performative Force in Navajo Prayer Acts," pp. 143–157 from *History of Religions* 17(2), 1977. Reprinted with permission of the University of Chicago Press.

9   Edward L. Schieffelin, "Performance and the Cultural Construction of Reality," pp. 707–724 from *American Ethnologist* 12(4), 1985. Reproduced with permission of the American Anthropological Association. Not for sale or further reproduction.

10   Joyce Burkhalter Flueckiger, "'He Should Have Worn a Sari': A 'Failed' Performance of a Central Indian Oral Epic," pp. 159–169 from *Tisch Drama Review*

32(1), 1988. © 1988 by New York University and the Massachusetts Institute of Technology. Permission granted.

11 Rosemarie K. Bank, "Representing History: Performing the Columbian Exposition," pp. 589–606 from *Theatre Journal* 54(4), 2002. Reprinted with permission of The Johns Hopkins University Press.

12 Alice Pomponio Logan, "The Palio of Siena: Performance and Process," pp. 45–65 from *Urban Anthropology* 7(1), 1978. Reprinted with permission of *Urban Anthropology*.

13 Gail Kligman, "Poetry and Politics in a Transylvanian Village," pp. 83–89 from *Anthropological Quarterly* 56(2), 1983. Reprinted with permission of *Anthropological Quarterly*.

14 Donald Brenneis, "The Matter of Talk: Political Performances in Bhatgaon," pp. 159–170 from *Language in Society* 7(2), 1978. Reprinted with permission of Cambridge University Press.

15 Frank E. Manning, "Celebrating Cricket: The Symbolic Construction of Caribbean Politics," pp. 616–632 from *American Ethnologist* 8(3), 1981. Reproduced by permission of the American Anthropological Association. Not for sale or further reproduction.

16 T.E. Woronov, "Performing the Nation: China's Children as Little Red Pioneers," pp. 647–672 from *Anthropological Quarterly* 80(3) 2007. Reprinted with permission of *Anthropological Quarterly*.

17 Deborah A. Kapchan, "The Promise of Sonic Translation: Performing the Festive Sacred in Morocco," pp. 467–483 from *American Anthropologist* 110(4), 2008. Reproduced by permission of the American Anthropological Association. Not for sale or further reproduction.

18 Lisa Hiwasaki, "Ethnic Tourism in Hokkaidô and the Shaping of Ainu Identity," pp. 393–412 from *Pacific Affairs* 73(3), 2000. Reprinted with permission of *Pacific Affairs* (The University of British Columbia).

19 Esiaba Irobi, "What They Came With: Carnival and the Persistence of African Performance Aesthetics in the Diaspora," pp. 896–913 from *Journal of Black Studies* 37(6), 2007. Reprinted with permission of SAGE.

20 Halifu Osumare, "Global Breakdancing and the Intercultural Body," pp. 30–45 from *Dance Research Journal* 34(2), 2002. © Halifu Osumare 2002. Reprinted with kind permission of the author.

The Anthropology of Performance: An Introduction

Frank J. Korom

When William Shakespeare's character Jacques declares that "all the world's a stage" in the play *As You Like It*, he wasn't kidding. The idea that life is a stage and that we are all actors performing our selves in a routine way on a daily basis is nothing new, but it provides a valuable way to think about how human beings expressively and aesthetically create their cultural worlds through interaction with others. This sort of artistic interaction employed in everyday communication requires us to use all of our abilities, both kinetic and verbal, in a competent fashion to convey meaningful messages to those around us. Indeed, although controversial, some evolutionary linguists have argued that our very first expressive acts that led to the emergence of language as a communicative medium were performative in nature.

Charles Darwin had already pointed out in 1872 that the strongest emotions expressed by animals were lust and hostility, which may have developed as the first verbal threats voiced by humans, especially the male of the species. Yet, while most contemporary biolinguists (e.g., Newmeyer, 2003) would agree that it is extremely difficult to derive human speech from lower primate grunts, groans, yelps, and howls, there is some evidence to suggest that the aggressive oral displays of male apes might be linked to the early development of the human male propensity to use ritual insults and other forms of expletives (see Van Lancker and Cummings, 1999). Indeed, insulting, teasing, and dueling with words (i.e., agonistic verbal behavior) are some of the earliest verbal traits demonstrated by male children, which later in life provide them the skills to function competitively in society (see Gossen, 1976; Eckett and Newmark, 1980). Linguistic evidence suggests that these expressive forms were predominantly male centered at first, functioning to release aggression, compete for status, and increase mating opportunities in a non-violent fashion (Progovac and Locke, 2009), where words replaced weapons, such as in modern-day Yemen, where they replace bullets in the oral poetry of men (e.g., Caton, 1993). From this perspective, performative utterances (see Austin, 1962) are extremely important for the study of human behavior. While another way of thinking about primate

The Anthropology of Performance: A Reader, First Edition. Edited by Frank J. Korom.
© 2013 John Wiley & Sons, Inc. Published 2013 by John Wiley & Sons, Inc.

behavior among ethologists has developed that emphasizes cooperation and altruism over aggression (e.g., de Waal, 1989, 1998), it is still not surprising that one of the perspectives for studying culture that emerged from the discipline of anthropology focused on the role of cultural performances, be they verbal or paralinguistic in nature.

Any history of performance studies could choose to begin a chronological survey of its development at different points in time and in different places in space, since the very nature of this field of study is interdisciplinary. Moreover, precisely because of its interdisciplinary nature, very few theorists would achieve a consensus on where to begin such a survey. Since a variety of other texts already exist that attempt to do precisely what I cannot do in this brief introduction (e.g., Schechner, 1985, 1988; Turner, 1986; Striff, 2003; Carlson, 2004; Madison and Hamera, 2006; Bial, 2007; Bell, 2008; Davis, 2008; McKenzie, Roms, and Wee, 2010), I have chosen to focus instead on a particular set of themes that have been important for the way that anthropology as a discipline explores the variegated roles of performance in culture.

As mentioned above, the study of performance is an interdisciplinary area of research that is essentially grounded in three distinct approaches to society and culture. I take my cue here from a valuable survey of the field of performance in folklore studies authored by Limón and Young (1986), in which they identify three major strands of thinking that coalesced into a common body of concerns over the decades leading up to the publication of their article. The first draws on Marxist notions of praxis, life as situated, ordinary practice – a stone mason building a wall, for example (Limón, 1983, 1984); the second emphasizes cultural display or enactment, when a community presents itself publicly in spectacular events such as the many forms of carnivals celebrated publicly throughout the world (Harris, 2003); while the third focuses on verbal art or oral poetics (Hymes, 1981; Tedlock, 1983), which often highlights what the folklorist Dan Ben-Amos (1972) once called "artistic communication in small groups" – an individual or group of performers, such as a lone ballad singer or the gospel choir of a Baptist church and their audiences. These three streams, developed in sociology, anthropology, and folkloristics respectively (but with a good bit of overlap), have drawn on a repertoire of theories that are further derived from a variety of disciplines ranging from theater studies and classics to political science and linguistics (Fine, 1984). The study of performance is thus a convergent field of inquiry that bridges the humanities and the social sciences, which is where I understand anthropology to be situated.

The purpose of this book is to provide readers with a selection of readings that includes examples of all three of the strands mentioned above from a variety of locations around the world, but situates such case studies within the discipline of anthropology, where key figures such as Milton Singer (1972), Clifford Geertz (1980), Victor Turner (1974, 1982), and James Peacock (1968) have utilized performance as a trope for studying culture writ large. The approach, however, is by no means new, since it builds on earlier precedents set by Bronislaw Malinowski (1992) in anthropology, Américo Paredes (1958) in folklore studies, Erving Goffman (1955, 1956, 1974, 1981) in sociology, and Albert Lord (2000) in classics. The essays included herein will therefore draw on a wide variety of sources that are not limited to anthropology but are extremely relevant to it.

Before presenting the contents of each thematic section, it may be useful to ask what exactly we mean by "performance" in the study of human culture. As one contributor to this volume describes it elsewhere, "performances are aesthetic practices – patterns of behavior, ways of speaking, manners of bodily comportment – whose repetitions situate actors in time and space, structuring individual and group identities" (Kapchan, 1995: 479). Yet while performance is based on repetition, mimicry, and reproduction to form ethnic, linguistic, and national traditions, it also varies to a great extent, even from performance to performance of the same play, song, or epic, which is often referred to as the emergent quality of performance (Lord, 2000). "Emergence" here refers to the dynamic quality of performance that allows each expressive event to be shaped by the interactions between performers and audiences. Due to its emergent quality, variation in performance is inevitable, thus making the comparative study of variation an important factor in understanding performances as agents of social change.

The dynamic and creative tension between continuity and innovation is precisely why the study of culture as performance is so fascinating. Because performances by competent individuals are most often enacted in front of an audience, which also has the right and responsibility to interact with performers, making them "co-performers," the context of performance is central to understanding and appreciating its emergent quality (Georges, 1969, 1979). For this insight, we are most indebted to the aforementioned Bronislaw Malinowski (1884–1942), the Polish-born anthropologist who is often referred to as one of the fathers of ethnographic fieldwork, along with such other prominent figures as Franz Boas (1858–1942), Frank Cushing (1857–1900), Alice Fletcher (1838–1923), and Ivan Veniaminov (1797–1879).

In describing the genres of oral tradition prevalent among the Trobriand Islanders, among whom he conducted extensive fieldwork, Malinowski famously stated that simply recording the spoken word verbatim is not enough, for it misses the sociological and cultural milieu in which the utterance achieves communicative meaning and significance. Writing words down, he argues, without evoking the atmosphere of the performance, gives us nothing more than a "mutilated bit of reality" (Malinowski, 1992: 104). Indeed, in this oft-repeated statement, an anthropologist who insisted that the audience is as much a part of the performance context as the performers themselves signaled a movement away from the text (e.g., studying the history of a ballad and its patterns of diffusion; see Brown, 2011) and toward the context (e.g., the singer of the ballad and the people who hear it; see Buchan, 1972).

By the late 1950s and early 1960s, this approach was taking root in anthropology. Milton Singer (1961), for example, emphasized the importance of describing and analyzing context in the study of religion, and then went on to develop the idea of what he called "cultural performances," in which members of a community put themselves on public display for others to see and hear (Singer, 1972). This sort of multi-sensorial engagement with our ethnographic subjects and their cultural productions would become one of the hallmarks of experiential and phenomenological approaches to fieldwork (see Stoller, 1989). Yet it was not until the 1970s that a convergence of approaches that focused on the texts being performed as well as on the contexts in which they were performed coalesced into a new and distinct interdisciplinary approach strongly allied to the field of anthropology. The new approach came to be known as the ethnography of communication, and it had strong sociolinguistic components embedded in it (Gumperz and Hymes, 1972; Hymes, 1974).

It is within the ethnography of communication literature that some of the most interesting studies of performances began to appear, which influenced a number of other scholars in a variety of fields to turn their attention to the symbolic and communicative dimensions of performance (e.g., Bauman and Sherzer, 1974). By the 1980s, performance had become an integral component in the contextual study of expressive culture in North America. From then onward, a steady stream of studies has been emerging that deals with the dramaturgical dimensions of everyday life, which has given birth to a distinct field of performance studies that is situated at the crossroads of theater and anthropology, thanks to the collaborations of Victor Turner in anthropology and Richard Schechner in theater studies (e.g., Turner, 1982, 1986; Schechner, 1985).

One of the shortcomings of the performance approach that was pointed out by Limón and Young, however, was that it was too micro-ethnographic, focusing on what sociologists referred to as "ethnomethodology," which often analyzed an unprecedented amount of indigenous detail that some would call the minutiae of everyday life. Responding partly to such critiques of hypersensitivity to context and an overemphasis on ethnographic detail, from the mid-1980s onward anthropology began to question the bounded notion of culture in a world that was caught up in complicated processes of deterritorialization caused by the increasingly rapid flow of people, ideas, and things across national borders in the postcolonial era, which gave birth to transnational anthropology by the 1990s (e.g., Appadurai, 1996; Hannerz, 1996). This theoretical and methodological move now requires anthropologists and other ethnographers to engage in what has come to be known as multi-sited fieldwork (Marcus, 1998), resulting in the enrichment of the anthropological vocabulary with

Figure 0.1 *An anthropologist performing an interview with a bard and his audience in India. (Photo courtesy of Frank J. Korom)*

terms such as "hybridity" (e.g., Kraidy, 2005) to describe the new forms of "mixed" traditions that emerged from global flows. Moreover, it has also opened up anthropology to a greater amount of reflexivity, which gave birth to what some have called dialogical anthropology (e.g., Bakhtin, 1981; Tedlock, 1987), a trend that had been growing within the discipline since the 1970s (Babcock, 1980; Ruby, 1982; Fischer and Marcus, 1986), but became an issue of extreme concern in the postmodern period. It also opened up new avenues of thinking that interrogated the role of the ethnographer in the field, an idea which forces us to wonder who is performing for whom. From this perspective, the very doing of anthropology becomes an act of performance (Turner and Turner, 1982; Stoller, 1994; Herzfeld, 2001) (Figure 0.1). A bibliography of further readings is included at the end of this volume to complement the essays included and to facilitate deeper and more thorough research.

It is with these trends in mind that the essays in this volume were selected. In an ideal world, the number and scope of selections would have been greater, but difficult decisions had to be made at the production stage concerning length and other such issues that often delimit the range of possibilities. Nonetheless, it is hoped that the selections chosen will prove tantalizing for readers in coursework or on their own, as they begin to explore the fascinating cultural worlds of performance.

The Layout of the Book

The first section is titled "Performance in Prehistory and Antiquity." It consists of two articles: the first focuses on the role of verbal performance as it relates to work and material culture; the second analyzes the relationship between performance and written texts in classical Greece. As suggested above, the Harvard classicist Albert Lord made significant contributions to performance studies in his quest to understand Homeric epic poetry. His numerous studies of Yugoslavian bards addressed such seminal questions as memory, compositional techniques, and the dynamics of orality and literacy, as well as the impact that cultural encounter and nation building have had on thematic content and technique over the centuries. To open up discussions about such topics in the context of premodern societies, I have included these two examples, which explore the relationship of singing to rug weaving, and orality to literacy.

The second section, "Verbal Genres of Performance," draws mostly on the contribution of folkloristics to the study of performance by exploring specific genres such as African American dozens; Nova Scotian yarns; African proverbs and riddles; and the female songs of an indigenous Australian community. This section draws heavily on the "ethnography of speaking" approach advocated by linguistic anthropologists such as John Gumperz and Dell Hymes, whose combined influence on the study of genres of performance has been significant.

The third section is titled "Ritual, Drama, and Public Spectacle." This section addresses ritual acts such as praying and healing, as well as a dramatic form from India that blends the sacred and the secular, dominant themes that were central to the early debates among the Cambridge School of myth-ritualists (Segal, 1998), and which continued in the theoretical works of Turner and Schechner mentioned above. The closing public spectacle portion of this section, which is indebted to the influential early work of Milton Singer on cultural performances, includes two essays on large-scale events that put cultures on display for others to see, interpret, and interrogate. Because such large-scale events are public, they rely heavily on audience–performer interaction for their success (or failure), and for the multiple meanings that may be conveyed by and taken away from such grandiose affairs.

The fourth section, "Performance and Politics in the Making of Communities," consists of four chapters, all of which offer a look at how performances of various sorts enable identities to be constructed, be it through poetry recitation in a Transylvanian village, the use of oratory in Fiji, the playing of a Commonwealth sport in the Caribbean, or an entire nation performing itself as part of a nationalization process in China.

The last section, "Tourist Performances and the Global Ecumene," explores the way that music, dance, pageantry, and ethnic enactments convey state ideologies or counter-ideologies to a larger public, but also how such ideologies can be contested through individual and small-group agency to shape identities on the local and transnational levels. This final section also looks at the inevitable phenomena of globalization and transnationalism, and how the flow of people, ideas, and practices across national borders due to mass media and quicker movement have affected such things as economic livelihood, agricultural practices, dress, ethnic identity, and even religious practices in such far-flung geographic regions as Hokkaidô, Morocco, the Caribbean, and elsewhere. Equally important, however, is to keep in mind that the local often responds resiliently to such global interventions in symbolically coded modes of resistance (Scott, 1985, 1990; Korom, 1999).

Taken together, this collection of essays should stimulate discussions about the performative dimensions of culture making on a global scale, without ignoring the local intricacies of the cultures presented, nor the specific histories that mold and shape each one.

In short, the essays selected for inclusion in this volume provide a broad range of topics all related to the performance of everyday life. The grouping of some essays may seem rather arbitrary in certain places, but this is inevitable, since culture itself is not easily divisible into vacuum-sealed compartments, such as economics, politics, aesthetics, and so forth. Instead, the divisions are heuristic in nature, intended to create a dialogue between chapters and sections. In the hands of curious, engaging readers, they may provide springboards for lively debate and future research.

REFERENCES

Appadurai, A. 1996. *Modernity at Large: Cultural Dimensions of Globalization*. Minneapolis: University of Minnesota Press.
Austin, J.L. 1962. *How to Do Things with Words*. Oxford: Clarendon Press.
Babcock, B.A. 1980. Reflexivity: Definitions and Discriminations. *Semiotics* 30: 1–14.
Bakhtin, M.M. 1981. *The Dialogical Imagination*. Austin: University of Texas Press.
Bauman, R.& J. Sherzer, eds., 1974. *Explorations in the Ethnography of Speaking*. New York: Cambridge University Press.

Bell, E. 2008. *Theories of Performance*. Thousand Oaks, CA: Sage.

Ben-Amos, D. 1972. Toward a Definition of Folklore in Context. In: *Toward New Perspectives in, Folklore*, A. Peredes and R. Bauman, eds. pp. 2–15. Austin: University of Texas Press.

Bial, H., ed. 2007. *The Performance Studies Reader*. 2nd edn. New York: Routledge.

Brown, M.E. 2011. *Child's Unfinished Masterpiece: The English and Scottish Popular Ballads*. Urbana: University of Illinois Press.

Buchan, D. 1972. *The Ballad and the Folk*. London: Routledge.

Carlson, M. 2004. *Performance: A Critical Introduction*. 2nd edn. New York: Routledge.

Caton, S. 1993. *"Peaks of Yemon I Summon:" Poetry as Cultural Practice in a North Yemeni Tribe*. Berkeley: University of California Press.

Darwin, C. 1872. *The Expression of the Emotions in Man and Animals*. London: John Murray.

Davis, T.C., ed. 2008. *The Cambridge Companion to Performance Studies*. New York: Cambridge University Press.

Eckett, P. and R. Newmark 1980. Central Eskimo Song Duels: A Contextual Analysis of Ritual Ambiguity. *Ethnology* 19(2): 191–211.

Fine, E.C. 1984. *The Folklore Text: From Performance to Print*. Bloomington: Indiana University Press.

Fischer, M.J. and G. Marcus 1986. *Anthropology as Cultural Critique: An Experimental Moment in the Human Sciences*. Chicago: University of Chicago Press.

Geertz, C. 1980. *Negara: The Theatre State in Nineteenth-Century Bali*. Princeton, NJ: Princeton University Press.

Georges, R. 1969. Toward an Understanding of Storytelling in Context. *Journal of American Folklore* 82(326): 313–328.

Georges, R. 1979. Feedback and Response in Storytelling. *Western Folklore* 38(2): 104–110.

Goffman, E. 1955. On Facework. *Psychiatry* 18: 213–231.

Goffman, E. 1956. *Presentation of Self in Everyday Life*. Edinburgh: University of Edinburgh, Social Sciences Research Centre.

Goffman, E. 1974. *Frame Analysis: An Essay on the Organization of Experience*. Cambridge, MA: Harvard University Press.

Goffman, E. 1981. *Forms of Talk*. Philadelphia: University of Pennsylvania Press.

Gossen, G.H. 1976. Verbal Dueling in Chamula. In: *Speech Play: Research and Resources for the Study of Linguistic Creativity*. B. Kirshenblatt-Gimblett, ed., pp. 21–46. Philadelphia: University of Pennsylvania Press.

Gumperz, J.& D. Hymes, eds. 1972. *Directions in Sociolinguistics: The Ethnography of Communication*. New York: Holt, Rinehart, and Winston.

Hannerz, U. 1996. *Transnational Connections: Culture, People, Places*. New York: Routledge.

Harris, M. 2003. *Carnival and Other Christian Festivals: Folk Theology and Folk Performance*. Austin: University of Texas Press.

Herzfeld, M. 2001. Performing Comparisons: Ethnography, Globetrotting, and the Spaces of Social Knowledge. *Journal of Anthropological Research* 57(3): 259–276.

Hymes, D.H. 1974. *Foundations in Sociolinguistics: An Ethnographic Approach*. Philadelphia: University of Pennsylvania Press.

Hymes, D.H. 1981. *"In Vain I Tried to Tell You:" Essays in Native American Ethnopoetics*. Philadelphia: University of Pennsylvania Press.

Kapchan, D.A. 1995. Performance. *Journal of American Folklore* 108(430): 479–508.

Korom, F.J. 1999. Reconciling the Local and the Global: The Ritual Space of Shi'i Islam in Trinidad. *Journal of Ritual Studies* 13(1): 21–36.

Kraidy, M.M. 2005. *Hybridity: The Cultural Logic of Globalization*. Philadelphia: Temple University Press.

Limón, J.E. 1983. Western Marxism and Folklore: A Critical Introduction. *Journal of American Folklore* 96(379): 34–52.

Limón, J.E. 1984. Marxism and Folklore: A Critical Reintroduction. *Journal of American Folklore* 97(385): 337–344.

Limón, J.E. and M.J. Young 1986. Frontiers, Settlements, and Development in Folklore Studies, 1972–1985. *Annual Review of Anthropology* 15: 437–460.

Lord, A.B. 2000. *The Singer of Tales*. 2nd edn. Cambridge, MA: Harvard University Press.

Madison, D.S. and J. Hamera, eds. 2006. *The Sage Handbook of Performance Studies*. Thousand Oaks, CA: Sage Publications.

Malinowski, B. 1992[1948]. Myth in Primitive Psychology. In: *Magic, Science and Religion And Other Essays*. B. Malinowski, ed., pp. 93–148. Prospect Heights, IL: Waveland Press.

Marcus, G. 1998. *Ethnography through Thick and Thin*. Princeton, NJ: Princeton University Press.

McKenzie, J., H. Roms, and C.J.W.-L. Wee, eds. 2010. *Contesting Performance: Global Sites of Research*. New York: Palgrave Macmillan.

Newmeyer, F.J. 2003. What Can the Field of Linguistics Tell Us About the Origins of Language? In: *Language, Evolution*, M.H. Christiansen and S. Kirby, eds., pp. 58–76. Oxford: Oxford University Press.

Paredes, A. 1958. *"With His Pistol in His Hand:" A Border Ballad and Its Hero*. Austin: University of Texas Press.

Peacock, J.L. 1968. *Rites of Modernization: Symbolic and Social Aspects of Indonesian Proletarian Drama*. Chicago: University of Chicago Press.

Progovac, L. and J. L. Locke 2009. The Urge to Merge: Ritual Insult and the Evolution of Syntax. *Biolinguistics* 3(2–3): 337–354.

Ruby, J. 1982. *Crack in the Mirror: Reflexive Perspectives in Anthropology*. Philadelphia: University of Pennsylvania Press.

Schechner, R. 1985. *Between Theater and Anthropology*. Philadelphia: University of Pennsylvania Press.

Schechner, R. 1988. *Performance Theory*. Revised and expanded edn. New York: Routledge.

Scott, J.C. 1985. *Weapons of the Weak: Everyday Forms of Peasant Resistance*. New Haven, CT: Yale University Press.

Scott, J.C. 1990. *Domination and the Arts of Resistance: Hidden Transcripts*. New Haven, CT: Yale University Press.

Segal, R.A., ed. 1998. *The Myth and Ritual Theory: A Reader*. Malden, MA: Blackwell Publishers.

Singer, M. 1961. Text and Context in the Study of Contemporary Hinduism. *Adyar Library Bulletin* 25: 274–303.

Singer, M. 1972. *When a Great Tradition Modernizes: An Anthropological Approach to Indian Civilization*. New York: Praeger Publishers.

Stoller, P. 1989. *The Taste of Ethnographic Things: The Senses in Anthropology*. Philadelphia: University of Pennsylvania Press.

Stoller, P. 1994. Ethnographies as Texts/Ethnographers as Griots. *American Ethnologist* 21(2): 353–366.

Striff, E. 2003. *Performance Studies*. New York: Palgrave Macmillan.

Tedlock, D. 1983. *The Spoken Word and the Work of Interpretation*. Philadelphia: University of Pennsylvania Press.

Tedlock, D. 1987. Questions Concerning Dialogical Anthropology. *Journal of Anthropological Research* 43(4): 325–337.

Turner, V. 1974. *Dramas, Fields, and Metaphors: Symbolic Action in Human Society*. Ithaca, NY: Cornell University Press.

Turner, V. 1982. *From Ritual to Theatre: The Human Seriousness of Play*. New York: PAJ Publications.

Turner, V. 1986. *The Anthropology of Performance*. New York: PAJ Publications.

Turner, V. and E. Turner 1982. Performing Ethnography. *The Drama Review* 26(2): 33–50.

Van Lancker, D. and J.L. Cummings 1999. Expletives: Neurolinguistic and Neurobehavioral Perspectives on Swearing. *Brain Research Reviews* 31: 83–104.

de Waal, F.B.M. 1989. *Peacemaking among Primates*. Cambridge, MA: Harvard University Press.

de Waal, F.B.M. 1998. *Chimpanzee Politics*. Baltimore, MA: Johns Hopkins University Press.

Part I

Performance in Prehistory and Antiquity

1

Singing the Rug: Patterned Textiles and the Origins of Indo-European Metrical Poetry

Anthony Tuck

They stood there in the forecourt of the goddess with the glorious hair, and heard Circe inside singing in a sweet voice as she went up and down a great design on a loom, immortal such as goddess have, delicate and lovely and glorious their work. Now Polites leader of men, who was best and dearest to me of my friends, began the discussion: "Friends someone inside going up and down a great piece of weaving is singing sweetly, and the whole place murmurs to the echo of it, whether she is woman or goddess. Come, let us call her our."[1]

But in the more remote sections, and among the nomads, women do all the weaving. They are the designers, too. They invent from year to year all the modifications of the old patterns. The head woman, the traveler Vámbéry relates, makes a tracing upon the earth, doles out the wool, and in some of the tribes chants in a weird sing-song the number of stitches and the color in which they are to be filled, as the work goes on.[2]

Although these passages are separated by considerable distances of time and literary purpose, the common element of singing while weaving is immediately curious. Indeed, the association between the two activities is by no means limited to the texts above, suggesting something more than merely a casual relationship. Throughout the text of the *Odyssey*, passages describing women observed in the act of weaving contain this notable detail. For example, Calypso also sings while she weaves. As Hermes speeds down from Olympus to inform Calypso of Zeus' plan for Odysseus, the text describes her while weaving.[3]

This consistent pairing of weaving and singing in the *Odyssey* has not garnered much academic

Anthony Tuck, "Singing the Rug: Patterned Textiles and the Origins of Indo-European Metrical Poetry," pp. 539–550 from *American Journal of Archaeology* 110(4), 2006.

attention. However, observation of modern-day weaving and rug production in nonmechanized households in Central Asia, Anatolia, and India suggests a greater significance to the songs Homer's nymphs sing while they weave.

John Mumford's quote above describes a "weird sing-song" related to the number of threads and colors of a given rug's design. In this case, the textiles Mumford discusses are knotted pile rugs, with knots tied onto neighboring pairs of warp threads between successive rows of the weft. Groupings of knots of the same color, organized according to the grid system of the warp and weft, form the various traditional designs of this type of textile. The traveler Mumford alludes to is Arminius Vámbéry, a Hungarian adventurer and Central Asian spy for the British during the early decades of the 19th century. Vámbéry's description of rug manufacture in Turkmenistan illustrates that specific designs of a carpet are reduced to numeric code once the overall compositional plan is complete: "An old woman places herself at their head as directress. She first traces, with points, the pattern of the figures in the sand. Glancing at this, she gives out the number of different threads required to produce the desired figures."[4]

Such 19th-century descriptions of textile manufacture indicate that traditional weaving practices in some regions of Central Asia and Persia involved the repetition of songs that communicate to a group of weavers specific information regarding thread or knot color and its relevant count position on the warp of a loom. Indeed, virtually any pattern or design that is incorporated into the weave of a textile can be reduced to numeric sequences, given the gridlike structure of warp and weft threads of a piece of cloth. Recent analysis of Caucasian textiles demonstrates how such designs are structured as count sequences.

For example, the design motif called the *balagyvrym* (small scroll) is not produced from memory as an overall design but rather as a count sequence. The weaver, traditionally a girl or woman, would knot once in the outline color, pass over seven warp threads, and knot again in the outline color. Further along the weft of the same register, the sequence is continued. On the next register, the knot sequence begins with one knot opening forward and another opening backward in conjunction with the knots of the previous register. However, the weaver could produce the *balagyvrym* only by a counting system based on the design's original starting position. Once the design turns at a right angle, the count sequence is changed. As a result, the ornamental components of traditional Caucasian carpets are woven exclusively in one position.[5]

In regions of Central Asia and rural northern India, these count sequences still take the form of songs, committed to memory by women of any given household where patterned textiles are produced. Even the nontraditional designs of an enigmatic group of Afghan carpets called *aksi*, or picture, rugs utilize coded rhythmic structures to translate images into woven patterns. *Aksi* rugs, which first came to a broader audience in the 1980s, are often called Afghan "war rugs." This class of textiles responds to the environment surrounding them, incorporating designs of Soviet weaponry, including helicopters, MiG jets, rifles, and hand grenades. While some of these weapon motifs appear to be based on traditional design elements, other types clearly are not. For example, since 2002 several weavers in the region outside of Kabul have been producing rugs that may be loosely termed "War on Terror" rugs. Many of the design elements of this new class are also present in earlier forms of war rugs, but others are obviously patterned after specific elements from an altogether different iconographic source – propaganda leaflets dropped from American planes during the course of military action in that country.[6] In the conversion from a new image on paper to a woven pattern, weavers reduce images to numerical grids that are then remembered and communicated throughout the course of production in the form of a chantlike song, perhaps akin to the one Mumford mentions.[7] Similar means of pattern reproduction are still used in rural areas of northern India.[8] However, in these regions, design traditions appear much more static than the Afghan *aksi* rug phenomenon, suggesting the specific numerical sequences and the songlike structures used to remember and communicate them can be equally static.[9]

These modern examples of women weavers in India and Central Asia suggest that the nymphs in the *Odyssey* sing because the cloths they produce are patterned textiles. In fact, the passage from Book 10 quoted above states specifically that Circe weaves a "great design." Moreover, this passage also indicates that Polites is outside Circe's house when he speaks, yet he knows that she is weaving. In fact, he seems to recognize that she is weaving not from what he sees but rather from what he hears – her singing.[10]

The study of the relationship between this phenomenon and The processes of manufacture of patterned cloth in antiquity, especially from the Mediterranean, is somewhat limited by the scarcity of surviving examples of ancient textiles and the fundamentally oral nature of such mnemonic devices for recording pattern information. While the climate of the African and Levantine deserts, the salt mines of Austria, and the bogs of northern Europe are considerably more forgiving to cloth, scholars of the Mediterranean basin can usually only speculate on the form and design of textiles from that region. Linear B documents from the Late Bronze Age palace of Knossos report an annual tally of almost 100,000 castrated male sheep, animals primarily useful in the wool industry.[11] The earliest example of a well-preserved patterned textile yet recovered in Greece comes from the "Heroon" structure and its associated burial at Lefkandi, which may be dated to ca. 1050 BCE.[12] The preserved belt of this garment displays patterned decoration similar to depictions of textiles on ceramics as early as 1450 BCE.[13] Examples of figurines in garments of patterned decoration may push such a manufacturing tradition in the Aegean well into the Greek Middle Bronze Age, perhaps even earlier.[14] Certainly, numerous Archaic and Classical Greek images of weaving, standing looms, as well as patterned textiles, reflect a thriving and remarkably longstanding tradition of the fabrication of patterned, woven cloth.[15]

Perhaps the most famous textile of the *Odyssey* is woven on the loom of Penelope. To delay her suitors, Penelope promises to choose one to marry after she completes the funeral cloth for Odysseus' father Laertes. She begins the work, only to unravel her efforts every evening.[16] Three years pass before the suitors question the pace of her progress, yet the archaeological evidence for looms associated with the Greek

Archaic period suggests that were Penelope fashioning a simple, unadorned winding sheet, little more than a few months would be needed to complete such work.[17] Yet, clearly the cloth is intended for public display. It is part of the publicly visible, ostentatious expense of burial expected of aristocrats. Penelope says:

Young men, my suitors since divine Odysseus has died, wait, although you are pressing for marriage with me, until this cloth I have finished – lest my yarns perish, wasted. This funeral cloth for the hero Laertes, which is for whenever deadly fate shall bring him low – lest any of the Achaian women in the province should fault me, that one who has acquired so much lies without his cloth.[18]

Concern for the public display of the funeral cloth is also reflected in the prothesis scenes characteristic of Geometric-period vase painting. In these scenes, the cloth, which is depicted as a patterned textile, is lifted to display the body to the collected mourners. Moreover, if the time and industry required of women producing such luxurious textiles were the expectation of aristocratic funerals, it stands to reason that elite members of such communities would also seek to memorialize the design of the impermanent cloth on some other publicly visible and lasting medium. As a result, the emergence of complex geometric designs covering the entirety of burial kraters and amphoras, which often have been thought to represent woven patterns, seems to reflect the desire to display such a prestige item in a more durable form.[19] Indeed, elaborate patterned textiles used as funeral cloths may have been the norm for elite burials throughout the Early Archaic period. However, an oral tradition of mnemonic devices for textile designs recorded in songs such as those of the *Odyssey's* nymphs would likely end with the passage of anti-sumptuary laws designed to curtail such, public displays of wealth in burial.[20]

Considering that the *balagyvrytm* design described above is merely one of the simplest in the repertoire of motifs available to the Caucasian textile worker, a song associated with both the number of "stitches" and knot color for an entire rug might be complicated indeed.[21] Presumably, traditional designs of increased complexity required count sequences of substantially greater nuance, all of which, in the absence of some other form of recording, would need to be committed to memory by the weaver.[22]

For example, a hypothetical design of a lozenge similar to, although simpler than, the design preserved on a fragment of cloth from the Phrygian city of Gordion demonstrates the numerical complexity of this process.[23] The design element of the single lozenge is created by passing over or under the warp threads in a specific sequence. Therefore, the individual strings of the warp are represented in groups according to the numerical values associated with portions of the design. The particular design and all its surrounding elements must be numerically deduced prior to initiating the weaving process, since the symmetry of the design is entirely dependent on the number of threads of the loom's warp.[24] The graphic depiction of the lozenge (Figure 1.1), therefore,

can be reproduced through the following numerical code:

7, 2, 7
6, 4, 6
5, 2, 2, 2, 5
4, 2, 4, 2, 4
3, 2, 6, 2, 3
2, 2, 8, 2, 2
2, 2, 8, 2, 2
3, 2, 6, 2, 3
4, 2, 4, 2, 4
5, 2, 2, 2, 5
6, 4, 6
7, 2, 7

While the technical processes of manufacturing a textile pattern on a warp-weighted loom vary somewhat from that of a knotted pile rug, such a numerical sequence could still be applied for either technique. Rather than counting threads on the warp and passing weft threads over or under the warp, a knotted pile carpet would require distinctions of color as knots are tied onto successive pairs of warp threads. Regardless, the result as illustrated reflects a pattern that is both visually and numerically symmetrical.

Another example of such a pattern is the traditional fret (Figure 1.2). Here, again, the pattern can be reduced to a numerical sequence:

2, 4, 8, 4, 8, 4, 8, 4, 8, 4, 2
2, 4, 8, 4, 8, 4, 8, 4, 8, 4, 2
2, 4, 2, 4, 2, 4, 2, 4, 2, 4, 2, 4, 2, 4, 2, 4, 2, 4, 2
2, 4, 2, 4, 2, 4, 2, 4, 2, 4, 2, 4, 2, 4, 2, 4, 2, 4, 2
2, 4, 2, 4, 2, 4, 2, 4, 2, 4, 2, 4, 2, 4, 2, 4, 2,4, 2
2, 4, 2, 4, 2, 4, 2, 4, 2, 4, 2, 4, 2, 4, 2, 4, 2, 4, 2
8, 4, 8, 4, 8, 4, 8, 4, 8
8, 4, 8, 4, 8, 4, 8, 4, 8

Theoretically, the elements of the pattern break *down* into repeating phrases, as demonstrated in Figure 1.3. However, the weaver could not numerically express the textile design in such independent units, since the design is not composed of separate vertical elements but rather through the positional interrelationship

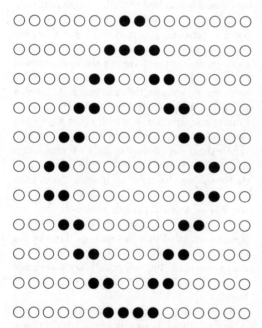

Figure 1.1 *Design of a lozenge similar to that on a cloth fragment from Gordion.*

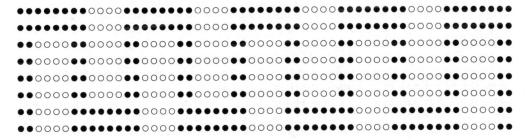

Figure 1.2 *A traditional fret pattern.*

of each entire horizontal line of the textile's weft. Therefore, the successful representation of a simple fret or meander design extending the length of a textile would require that the correct numerical sequence be expressed in its entirety and horizontally across the length of the loom's warp.

The potential complexity of numerical sequences for such designs is not limited to repetitive numerical counts, changing according to shifts in woven patterns with each register of the textile's weft. Textiles manufactured with bichrome threads might necessitate the memorization of such sequences, but the additional element of threads of variable colors would likewise require that further pieces of information be recorded within the overall numerical framework of the textile's manufacture. Complex patterned textiles would call for long strings of number sequences, all of which would require not only memorization of repeating patterns of numbers along the horizontal axis of a loom's warp but also the correct relationship of a given line of numbers

to that which proceeds and follows it in sequence.[25] The songs thus appear to be mnemonic devices communicating this information. Without further study it is difficult to know precisely how these songs fully record such designs.[26] However, information embedded within narrative structures, tonal shifts, or rhythmic changes, all in association with song, could conceivably provide the framework whereby the memorization and, equally important, the organization of numerical count sequences and color codes that are repeated each time a pattern is reproduced.[27]

But why would the characters of nymphs in Homeric Greek and modern weavers from Anatolia and Central Asia, separated as they are by vast gulfs of time and space, share this tradition? Perhaps these women sing as they weave because they share, however remotely, a textile tradition that stems from a time and region associated with the earliest roots of the Indo-European family of languages. In spite of the limitations of evidence, it is well established that patterned textiles do not originate in Greece,

Figure 1.3 *Example of the repeating phrases of a fret pattern.*

nor, it would seem, do the songlike structures used to record and communicate pattern-related information in textile manufacture.

The oldest preserved example of a knotted pile carpet with figural designs was recovered from the permafrost of a kurgan burial in modern-day Kazakhstan and survives in the Hermitage Museum.[28] This elegant carpet is knotted with 32 symmetrical, or "Gordian" style, knots per cm^2 and displays polychrome designs of mounted figures and parading animals framing a central field of star-shaped floral patterns, notable sophistication of this rug surely reflects a well-developed tradition of such production.[29] Additional fragmentary knotted pile textiles come from these same kurgan burials, although most are thoroughly published.[30]

Numerous examples of proto-Celtic patterned textiles survive from the salt mines of Hallstatt Hallein and generally date to ca. 1000–400 BCE.[31] This group of cloth frequently displays plaid twills similar to the tartans manufactured in the regions of Europe where communities of Celtic descent survive today, further underscoring the tenacity of many textile traditions.[32]

While there is little direct evidence of similarly ornate and intact textiles of earlier dates, an Assyrian archival document of the late 13th century BCE. from the reign of Tukuld-Ninurta describes the gift of two multicolored textiles, one of which is described as covered with designs of people, towns, and animals. This first textile is described as the work of a weaver, while the second cloth is noted as the work of a "knotter."[33]

Slightly earlier still are numerous examples of curved blades recovered from female burials in southern Turkmenistan dating to between ca. 2100 and 2000 BCE. According to their excavator, these blades are identical in form to knives used today in the same region to trim the excess wool threads of knotted carpets.[34] Fragments, impressions, and representations of twills and weft-faced weaves[35] displaying design elements suggest such fabrics developed in the Levant and the Caucasus at least as early as 2600 BCE.[36] Although highly fragmentary, traces of Majkop culture textiles preserving elements of patterning are known from the

region between the Black and Caspian Seas and date to ca. 3700–3200 BCE., an area and time frame curiously coincident with the region many scholars prefer for the first emergence of speakers of the proto-Indo-European language.[37]

At a minimum, these surviving examples illustrate that complex patterned textiles were manufactured as early as the third or fourth millennium BCE. While we can say very little about how these surviving specimens were manufactured, the numerical elements of their designs, dependent on prescribed intervals of warp and weft threads, remain consistent from their earliest manufacture onward. Even so, a relationship between weaving and song may be found in a text considerably older than the *Odyssey*: the Sanskrit *Rig Veda*. No consensus has emerged as to an absolute date for the composition of the *Rig Veda*, with scholars positing a long tradition of fixed oral transmission prior to the final written form of the hymns.[38] In spite of this chronological uncertainty, several instances of the pairing of song and weaving are found throughout the text. For example, "[t]he Man stretches the warp and draws the weft; the Man has spread it out upon this dome of the sky. These are the pegs, that are fastened in place; they made the melodies into the shuttles for weaving."[39]

Regardless of the difficulties associated with the date of the *Rig Veda*, there is scholarly agreement that the hymns were fully memorized, without significant revision, before ultimately being transcribed.[40] For the purposes of this discussion, it seems significant that the "melodies" appear to be the active agent of this element of the creation myth, suggesting once again that the relationship is significantly more than casual.

In Book 2 of the *Rig Veda*, another instance of the pairing of song and weaving appears: "Loose me from sin as from a bond that binds me: may we swell, Varuna, thy spring of Order. Let not my thread, while I weave song, be severed, nor my work's sum, before the time, be shattered."[41] And, once again, in Book 9 we have the following: "They for the Bold and Lovely One ply manly vigour like a bow: joyous, in front of songs they weave bright raiment for the Lord Divine."[42]

In all three of these instances, the association between weaving and song appears to be more than metaphorical, with song an expected and active element in the production of textiles. Even the "bright raiment for the Lord Divine" hints at the idea of design or patterning. Therefore, although the absolute date of the *Rig Veda* is unclear, ancient examples of the pairing of patterned textiles and songlike structures is not limited to the world of Homer but instead appears to have a far wider orbit. While the evidence of that orbit ranges across Europe, Anatolia, and Central Asia, the examples of this phenomenon share a significant feature: all are associated with regions where the dominant population speaks or spoke languages of the Indo-European family. In fact, Barber has noted that the striking similarity between Bronze Age twill-weave wool fabrics of the Indo-European-speaking proto-Tocharian or Iranian populations of the Tarim Basin in western China and proto-Hallstatt twills of Late Bronze Age Europe are sufficiently similar as to suggest that both populations, upon migrating from the region between the Black and Caspian Seas, carried with them culturally shared technologies associated with weaving such patterned textiles.[43] It is inviting to speculate that the Indo-European population migration, regardless of the exact dates of the various movements, brought not only technologies associated with patterned textile production but also the tradition of mnemonic devices used to record design information in the form of song.[44] As a result, women in the traditional and highly conservative communities in Afghanistan, Anatolia, Iran, and northern India retained this system of textile design production, in some cases to the present day.[45]

Suggestions of similar traditions are also found outside the Indo-European linguistic sphere. For example, one of the taboos associated with the Navajo traditions of weaving states, "Don't weave if you don't know a weaving song. It won't be any good."[46] This directive does not make clear the relationship between the song and the woven pattern and may be more closely associated with religious and medical rituals related to sand painting, a graphic form closely tied to Navajo rug manufacture.[47] Nonetheless, the relationship between song and textile suggested in the Navajo as well as some African cultures might suggest the independent evolution of similar strategies of mnemonic devices in weaving traditions.[48]

Song or chant systems designed around prescribed and repetitive numerical structures to convey coded, pattern-related textile information is a curious phenomenon in its own right. However, such systems certainly invite comparison with another form of numerically derived recitation: metrical poetry. For this reason, it is all the more remarkable that the process of reciting early Greek epic poetry is frequently associated with weaving.[49] The recitation, specifically of Homeric epic, by individuals known as rhapsodes hints at a relationship to textiles. The name appears to develop into a compound word derived from ῥάπτεινἀοιδήν (ῥάπτειν = to stitch or to sew; ἀοιδήν = song), a phrase that suggests that the recitation of an element of Homeric epic was to "stitch" or "sew" a song.[50]

The relationship between traditional Greek recitation of metrical poetry and weaving in particular is expressed elsewhere. For example, Callimachus (fr. 26.5) refers to the recited poem itself as "[t]he word that was woven upon the staff," which, as West notes, "suggests an analogy between the [rhapsode's] staff and the cross bar of a loom."[51] The theme of poetry as a woven phenomenon also occurs in Pindar (*Nem.* 4.44–6): "Weave out, weave out forthwith, sweet lyre, the web of lovely song with Lydian harmony, in honor of Oenone and of Cyprus, where Teucer, son of Telamon, reigneth afar."[52]

Again, a similar metaphor is used twice by Bacchylides (Odes 5 and 19):

Blessed war-lord of the chariot whirling Syracusans, you if any mortal now alive will rightly assess the sweet gift of the violet-crowned Muses sent for your adornment: rest your righteous mind in ease from its cares and come! Turn your thoughts this way: with the help of the slim-wasted Graces your guest friend, the famous servant of Urania with her golden headband, has woven a song of praise and sends it from the sacred island to your distinguished city.[53]

Countless paths of ambrosial verses lie open for him who obtains gifts from Pierian Muses and whose songs are clothed with honour by the violet-eyed maidens, the garland-bearing Graces. Weave, then, in lovely, blessed Athens a new fabric, renowned Cean fantasy.[54]

One might argue that the thematic relationship between singing and weaving is merely an effect of the casual similarity of a loom and a lyre, both of which consist of frames for the tension of strings.[55] However, the idea of poetry and song as something woven is not limited to Greek; it has earlier, proto-Indo-European roots, suggesting that the thematic relationship between poetry and weaving existed well before the development of the lyre as an instrument to accompany poetic recitation.[56]

Another historical anecdote seems to underscore the relationship of European and Central Asian patterned textiles and songlike mnemonic devices to populations of Indo-European language speakers. The long history of the manufacture of textiles in Egypt was generally limited to the production of white linen.[57] However, the 18th-Dynasty invasion of the Levant, led by Thutmose III, culminated with the destruction of the city of Meggido. Among the war booty captured in the victory were artisan slaves. Patterned textiles, as opposed to embroidered or beaded cloth, are largely unknown from Egypt prior to the 18th Dynasty but appear at this time.[58] One wonders if the emergent production of patterned textiles in Egypt might not be related to this group of weavers conquered at Meggido and brought back to Egypt as captives. Moreover, a 19th-Dynasty Egyptian lament records the following:

Lo, citizens are put to the grindstones,
Wearers of fine linen are beaten with [sticks]
Ladies suffer like maidservants,
Singers are at the looms in weaving rooms,
What they sing to the goddess are dirges.[59]

Although the precise date of the composition of this lament is debatable, the association between weavers and singing once again raises speculation that such weavers, perhaps descendents of the survivors of Thutmose's Syrian campaign, sing as a means of transmitting designs into woven fabric.

Indeed, the origin of pattern-weave textiles, although difficult to place with great precision due to the scarcity of surviving examples, appears to be centered in regions of Europe and Asia where Indo-European language groups are also predominant.[60] The presence of wool as a primary fiber in the regions of Syria and the Caucasus also gave rise to the opportunity to experiment with dyes, thus opening the path to color as a means of pattern production. Such an option was not available to the Neolithic and Early Bronze Age Egyptian weaver, who was limited to flax fibers, and linen is notoriously difficult to dye.[61]

As mentioned above, the similarity of twill-pattern weaves between Austrian Iron Age Hallstatt cloth and specimens from western China of Bronze Age Tarim Basin cloth appears to be due to a common tradition of twill manufacture among the proto-Indo-European language speakers ancestral to both the Celtic and Tocharian/Iranian populations.[62] Apparently, communities of the proto-Indo-European homeland already possessed developed systems of patterned textile production prior to the periods of migration associated with the spread of the Indo-European languages.[63] As these populations settled in regions of Anatolia, Central Asia, India, and western Europe, they could well have preserved a custom associated with textile production whereby numerically organized design information was retained by weavers through number-based systems of chant or songlike mnemonic devices ancestral to the singing of Homer's nymphs and the songs of Central Asia and northern India witnessed in the modern era.

Conceivably, these numerically organized songs, utilized by populations descended from proto-Indo-European speakers to convey information related to patterning in textile manufacture, may also explain why the notion of reciting metrical poetry is so often expressed through the metaphor of weaving in Indo-European languages.[64] Meillet's reconstruction of a system of meter common, and therefore ancestral, to both Greek and Sanskrit serves to explain poetic metrical constructions shared across a wide range of Indo-European languages.[65] Nagy, in challenging Parry's definition of formula as word groupings regularly employed under the same metrical conditions, sees traditional phraseology, whether in the form of prayers, incantations, or the like, containing its own rhythms. Over time, the strength of tradition contributes to a preference for phrases with some of those rhythms over others that do not possess similar characteristics. Eventually, Nagy concludes, "the preferred rhythms have their own dynamics and become regulators of any incoming non-traditional phraseology."[66]

For Nagy, "traditional phraseology . . . generated meter rather than vice versa."[67] With respect to language, this is entirely convincing, but it is also true that the strings of a loom's warp would provide count sequences limited to and bound by the number of vertical threads associated with a given element of an overall pattern, not unlike a poetic metrical system with lines of a prescribed number of prominent positions. While pattern- and color-related information could be transmitted through many different elements of song (e.g., narration, tonal values of music, rhythmic shifts, etc.), the development of metrical systems of recitation would be another possible way to encode weaving-related information in song. Therefore, Nagy's reconstruction of metrical formulation could be applied in equal measure to specific design elements as they evolved in the development of patterned textiles among speakers of proto-Indo-European. In considering Nagy, Foley argues, "even if the habitual groupings originally generated the abstract pattern, later on (as Nagy suggests) the abstract pattern came to govern the deployment of phraseology."[68] In the same manner, the development of rhythmic cadences and song associated with particular patterns, such as those memorized by Caucasian weavers or Mumford's "weird sing-song," would both control and be controlled by the pattern to which they conform. Therefore, it seems possible that the relationship between metrical structures in proto-Indo-European poetry and the rhythmically communicated number sequences associated with the development of patterned

textiles by members of that same population is more than merely accidental. Instead, counting systems and sing-songs associated with the production of patterns in textiles may have been an extremely early influence on, if not source of, rhythmic or metrically constructed narratives. Given the vast area where this phenomenon is seen, the mechanisms controlling such patterning certainly evolved along differing paths; but modern observation of weaving songs would suggest that some combination of cadence and narrative played roles in this process of pattern communication. Both the region associated with the origin of patterned textiles and the fact that many Indo-European languages preserve suggestions of a relationship between weaving and poetics seem to indicate that this association developed within the chronological orbit of a spoken form of proto-Indo-European.

Finally, it seems worth noting that the *Iliad* and the *Odyssey* begin with exhortations of the Muse, who inspires the poet through the gift of poetic ability as well as with assistance in composition.[69] However, the opening lines of both the *Iliad* and the *Odyssey* appear to reflect the idea that the Muse sings not to the poet but rather through the poet.

Rage-Goddess, sing the rage of Peleus' son Achilles, murderous, doomed, that cost the Achaeans countless losses, hurling down to the House of Death so many sturdy souls, great fighters souls, but made their bodies carrion, feast for the dogs and birds, and the will of Zeus was moving toward its end. Begin, Muse, when the two first broke and clashed, Agamemnon, lord of men and brilliant Achilles.[70]

And again at the beginning of the *Odyssey:* "Sing to me of the man, Muse, the man of twists and turns driven time and again off course, once he had plundered the hallowed heights of Troy."[71] In both cases, it appears that the poet does not identify himself as the composer of the poem but rather the agent of its performance.[72] Instead, the origin of the poem itself is entirely outside of the poet; it is from the female Muse herself.[73] Given the ancient world's traditional association of women with weaving, one wonders if perhaps the characterization of the female Muse might be something akin to a mythological memory, already ancient by Homeric standards, of a source of rhythmic, perhaps even metrically structured narratives developed around weaving patterned textiles.[74]

A related element of traditional Greek poetic inspiration is the appeal to Memory, the mother of the Muses and another obvious example of a feminine mythological construct related to the otherwise masculine world of epic poetry and its recitation.[75] It is again inviting to see a relationship between such a concept and the mnemonic devices of metrical narrative songs used to create patterned textiles.[76]

Further inquiry is needed to better understand the possible relationships between the phenomena of traditional forms of song or chant that communicate woven design and the ancient association of weaving with poetry. Conceivably, a close examination of modern, surviving songs associated with the production of traditional textiles might better explain how cadence, narrative, and possibly meter function as conveyors of coded information. Moreover, the discussion of the relationship between ancient patterned textiles and the origins of proto-Indo-European metrical poetry is hindered by a scarcity of surviving examples of the former and the conjecture required to study the latter. And yet, both Circe and Calypso sing as they work at their looms, a detail that holds immediate and recognizable importance to modern observers of traditional textile production. Perhaps the notion of the rhapsode of Iron Age Greece as a "sewer of songs" was originally something surpassing mere metaphor, at a time when song and cloth were more fully intertwined.

NOTES

1 Od. 10.220–28; Lattimore 1967, 158.
2 Mumford 1900, 25. Mumford fails to offer any further information as to where this specific tradition is found other than to describe the regions as "remote sections," but based on the text, he appears to refer to regions in Anatolia and Persia. He is,

however, quite clear in contrasting this activity with the "more progressive" modes of manufacture found in developed areas. These modes are probably pattern books or printed templates for designs, although he does not specify his meaning on this point.
3 Od. 5.59–62: "A great fire blazed on the hearth and the smell of cedar cleanly split and sweet wood burning bright wafted a cloud of fragrance down the island. Deep inside she sang, the goddess Calypso, lifting her breathtaking voice as she guided back and forth before her loom, her golden shuttle weaving" (Lattimore 1967, 89).
4 Vámbéry 1970, 474.
5 Kerimov et al. 1984, 12. Seiler-Baldinger (1994, 57) indicates that this technique of rug manufacture is a version of weft wrapping, often referred to as soumak.
6 Designs such as the border element of many of these rugs are often taken from the leaflets, as are fragmented elements of English they frequently include.
7 In a correspondence with an Afghan weaver based near Kabul, the author asked her how she transformed images into rug patterns. Her response, through a translator, was: "I don't see it as a picture. I see it as numbers and I make it a song."
8 While traveling in northern India, the author witnessed weavers chanting while tying knotted pile rugs. In the town of Sari Bawadi, several households had set up large looms in their forecourts. Younger members of each family worked knotting rugs while one woman sat to the loom's side chanting. When asked about the chanting, the guide replied, "She is singing the rug."
9 The rug designs typical of this region are primarily Moghul style, suggesting the specific mnemonic means of reproducing such patterns may be as much as five centuries old.
10 I am grateful to Mahoney for this observation.
11 Killin 1964, 1–15; Barber 1992, 104.
12 Popham et al. 1982, 173.
13 Barber 1991, 312–13; 1992, 104.
14 Pekridou-Gorecki 1989, 56–71; Barber 1991, 311–57.
15 An important and informative depiction of operational looms is found in the work of the Amasis Painter, a black-figure lekythos currently in New York (see von Bothmer

1985, 185–87). For the Chiusi Painter image of Penelope at her loom, see Geijer 1977. Consider as well the described complexity of a woven garment such as the peplos of Athena, woven on the occasion of the Panathenaic festival (Barber 1992, 103–17).

16 The text never describes Penelope in the act of weaving but rather has her reporting her stratagem only after the fact.

17 *Od.* 2.96–102; Barber 1991, 358–59.

18 Barber 1991, 358.

19 Barber 1991, 365–72. Such densely packed designs are characteristic of the weft float technique wherein weavers take weft threads over a specific number of differently colored warp threads at varying intervals to produce designs. However, such a technique necessarily produces design elements spaced very close together, since long weft threads jumping over warp threads create the possibility of snagging.

20 Gagarin 1986, 67.

21 Since Mumford's (supra n. 2) commentary is concerned with pile carpets, his use of the term "stitches" must refer to knots rather than some form of embroidery.

22 In modern, mechanized workshops in India and Anatolia, designs are reproduced through a color chart, rendered on paper and attached to the lower portion of the loom. This, however, is a relatively recent development designed to increase the number of workers capable of producing rugs of traditional design. However, even Mumford's (1900) description of the "weird sing-song" contrasts this phenomenon with the rug production techniques of the more developed regions of Anatolia and Persia. Levine (1977, 212) describes the creation of pile rugs in Kurdistan as a simple copying process from the back of an older rug and makes no mention of any other associated activity in the process of design or production of such rugs.

23 The cloth fragment from Gordion was preserved in a destruction horizon dateable to ca. 690 BCE. (see Ellis 1981, 294–310, pl, 101C–D).

24 This type of design construction is also characteristic of Anatolian kilims.

25 It is, however, quite easy to imagine the full memorization of such design-related chants.

Texts of substantial length and complexity, such as the Sanskrit Rig Vedic hymns, appear to have been fully memorized and preserved through sets of mnemonic devices (Nagy 1974, 15–16).

26 A full forensic analysis of a weaving song will require recording such a work in its entirety and analyzing the mnemonic device in relation to the pattern it produces. In the process of researching this study, several attempts were made to acquire visas for study in northern Iran and southern Turkmenistan, where reports suggest a surviving tradition of this practice somewhat more nuanced than that witnessed in northern India. However, the political instability in Central Asia currently makes such travel difficult to negotiate.

27 According to the author's translator in Sari Bawadi, India, the "singing the rug" chant communicated some form of story that served both the purpose of the textile design and to entertain the weavers as they worked. Unfortunately, time constraints and barriers of language prohibited further inquiry.

28 Rudenko 1953, pl. CXV.

29 Rugs of remarkably similar designs are made in Kazakhstan today.

30 Rudenko 1970, 302.

31 Barber 1991, 186.

32 Barber 1991, 138; 1996, 348; 1999, 138.

33 Barrelet 1977, 56–62. This description implies that ornate figural designs such as those seen on the Pazyrk carpet were not limited to knotted pile rugs but were incorporated into different forms of woven cloth as well.

34 Khlopin 1982, 116–18. Khlopin dates these blades to 1600 to 1400 BCE., but Thomas (1967, Chart 11.5b) places the burials from which they were recovered to the late third millennium. Barber (1991, 171 n. 10) prefers Thomas' date and points to ceramic fourth- and third-millennium ceramics from the same region that appear to reflect decorative textile patterns.

35 Seiler-Baldinger (1994, 89) defines a twill weave: "The main feature of the twill weave is a looser binding of the two yarn systems. Each weft thread passes over/under at least two warp threads and only under/over one warp thread." The weft-faced weave is a variant of plain weave in which only one

system of threads, the weft, is visible. Weft-faced and warp-faced weaves are also sometimes called rib waves (Seiler-Baldinger 1994, 88).

36 Barber 1996, 348; 1999, 144.

37 Shishlina et al. 2003. For commentary on the complex arguments of the proto-Indo-European homeland, see D'Iakonov 1985; Gamkrelidze and Ivanov 1985a, 1985b; Gimbutas 1985; Mallory 1989.

38 The oral composition of the *Rig Veda* is generally thought to be considerably older than the date of its first transmission into written form. E.g., Raju (Chan et al. 1969, 13) suggests a date of composition sometime prior to 2000 BCE. Alternatively, O'Flaherty (1988, 1) suggests a date of ca. 1000 BCE. for the hymn's composition. Davis (Lopez 2002, 7) writes that the compilation of verses into a single collection occurs ca. 1200–1000 BCE., but that the original, memorized, and oral transmission, of the hymns may have earlier stages of development, as much as 3,000 years earlier than the date of the *Rig Veda*'s transmission into written form.

39 *Rig Veda* 10.130.2; O'Flaherty 1981, 33. I am grateful to Mahoney for directing me to these Sanskrit passages.

40 Nagy 1974, 15–16; Jamison 1991, 10–12. Jamison argues that Books 1 and 10 of the *Rig Veda* are later than Books 2 through 9. However, for the purposes of this argument, the association between singing and weaving is found in both chronological groupings of books.

41 Griffith 1896, 2.28.5.

42 Griffith 1896, 9.99.1.

43 Barber 1991, 131–45; 1996, 354–55.

44 Barber (1975; 1989; esp. 1991, 260–82) details the linguistic evidence for textile technology among speakers of proto-Indo-European.

45 It is curious that the Sanskrit examples cited appear to suggest men involved in the weaving process. In India, weaving is traditionally performed by women, and a preference for male children and a general social disdain for female children metastasizes into a widely held belief that the difficulty of weaving is punishment for being born female (Parikh et al. 1991, 68–9). However, while it is certainly not impossible to imagine men weaving in this environment, it is likely

that the masculine cast to these passages related to the Vedic hymns' primary function as religious texts. Certainly, throughout prehistoric Europe and later, weaving is largely an activity performed by women (Ehrenberg 1989,102–3).

46 Bulow 1972, 58. I am grateful to Edmunds for these observations concerning weaving and song-related rituals in Native American and African cultures.

47 Armer 1931, 6.

48 Ghersi and Basile 2003. E.g., in the village of Klikor, Ghana, a close relationship between ritual song and textile is seen during an event to honor an Italian diplomatic mission. "They bring along their best cloths and instruments, both textile and musical. To the accompaniment of a sacred weaving song, they weave and dance before their traditional kings, before the diplomatic representatives and a delegation from the Italian government."

49 West 1981, 124–25. See Nagy (2002, 70–98) for a comprehensive treatment of this association.

50 Burkert 1987, 48; Scheid and Svenbro 1996, 111–13.

51 West 1981, 125. West's "cross bar" presumably refers to the heddle bar of a loom.

52 Sandys 1915, 349–51.

53 Campbell 1992, 139.

54 Campbell 1992, 233.

55 Synder 1981, 193–94.

56 Schmitt 1973, 272–74. E.g., the same metaphor is present in the Sanskrit *Rig Veda* (Griffith 1896, 10.53.6): "Spinning the thread, follow the region's splendid light: guard thou the path ways well which wisdom hath prepared. Weave ye the knotless labour of the bards who sing: be Manu thou, and bring the Heavenly People forth."

57 Barber 1982, 442; 1991, 351–53. Barber argues that the rare and unusual evidence for patterned wool textiles in Egypt reflects the presence or influence of non-Egyptians in the region.

58 Reifstahl 1944, 1.

59 Simpson 2003, 194–95. This passage, from a text known as *The Admonitions of Ipuwer*, is highly problematic. The papyrus on which the lament is recorded dates to the 19th Dynasty, but some scholars date the original text as early as the 12th Dynasty. However,

the surviving papyrus appears to record numerous errors and omissions in transcription (Simpson 2003, 188). As a result, its value for the purposes of this argument is somewhat diminished. I am grateful to Peter Der Manuelian for his insights on this text.

60　Barber 1991, 211.
61　Barber 1991, 211.
62　Barber 1991, 144; 1996.
63　For a general survey of the various difficulties associated with the questions of the proto-Indo-European homeland and the period of migrations, see Renfrew 1988; Mallory 1989; Jones-Bley and Huld 1996, 1–22. For a summary of evidence and previous bibliography concerning the archaeological evidence for Indo-European origins, see Anthony 1991.
64　Schmitt 1973, 272–74.
65　Meillet 1923. See Thieme (1953) for a discussion of the evidence of metrical poetics in proto-Indo-European. For a review of recent scholarship regarding early forms of metrics, see Watkins 1995, 19–21; Gasparov 1996, esp. chs. 1, 4.
66　Nagy 1974, 145.
67　Nagy 1974, 145.
68　Foley 1981, 263.
69　Murray, 1981, 89.
70　*Il.* 1, 1–7; Fagles 1990, 77.
71　*Od.* 1, 1–2; Fagles 1996, 77.
72　Grube 1931, 2. Cf. Murray (1981, 97), who argues for a less dependent and substantially more balanced relationship between poet and Muse.
73　Harriot (1969, 50–1) says, "The Greeks expressed the belief that poetry is in some mysterious way 'given,' and that gift comes from an external source to the poet and is other than he is."
74　Scholarly opinion seems to have coalesced around the conclusion that both the texts of the *Iliad* and the *Odyssey* are Archaic in date (Dickie 1995, 51). However, as both West (1988) and Morris (1989) have conclusively demonstrated, fragmentary elements of similar poetic constructs are present in the Aegean as early as the 17th century BCE.
75　Murray 1981, 92–4.
76　Curiously, the necessary rigidity and inflexibility of such weaving-related mnemonic devices runs counter to much

scholarship positing the spontaneity of oral poetry and its recitation. However, it could be argued that the flexibility of composition is still limited and guided by the inflexible meta-structure provided by the meter of the poem, a phenomenon common to Germanic poetry as well. In the context of weaving, such minor variation and individual creativity could allow for developments of design without compromising the geometric composition as a whole (Parry 1930, 77–8; Lord 1960, 13–29; Parry 1971, 269–70; Nagler 1974, 20–1).

REFERENCES

Anthony, D. 1991. "The Archaeology of Indo-European Origins." *JIES* 19: 193–222.
Armer, L. 1931. *Sand-Painting of the Navajos.* New York: The Exposition of Indian Tribal Arts.
Barber, E. 1975. "The Proto Indo-European Notion of Cloth and Clothing." *JIES* 3/4: 294–320.
Barber, E. 1982. "New Kingdom Textiles: Embroidery vs. Weaving." *AJA* 86(3): 442–45.
Barber, E. 1989. "Archaeolinguistics and the Borrowing of Old European Technology." *JIES* 17: 239–50.
Barber, E. 1991. *Prehistoric Textiles: The Development of Cloth in the Neolithic and Bronze Ages.* Princeton: Princeton University Press.
Barber, E. 1992. "The Peplos of Athena." In *Goddess and Polis*, edited by J. Neils, 103–117. Princeton: Princeton University Press.
Barber, E. 1996. "A Weaver's-eye View of the Second Millennium Tarim Basin Finds." *JIES* 23: 347–56.
Barber, E. 1999. *The Mummies of Ürümchi.* New York: W.W. Norton & Company.
Barrelet, M.T. 1977. "Un Inventaire de Kar-Tukulti-Ninurta: Textiles décorés assyriens et autres." *RAssyr* 71: 51–92.
Bulow, E.L. 1972. *Navajo Taboos.* Window Rock, Ariz.: Navajo Tribal Museum.
Burkert, W. 1987. "The Making of Homer in the Sixth Century BC: Rhapsodes Versus Stesichoros." In *Papers on the Amasis Painter and His World*, edited by D.Von Bothmer, 43–62. Los Angeles: J. Paul Getty Museum.
Campbell, D., trans. 1992. *Greek Lyric IV: Bacchylides, Corinna, andOthers.* Loeb Classical

Library. Cambridge, Mass.: Harvard University Press.

Chan, W.T. R. al Faruqi, J.I. Kitagawa, and P.T. Raju. 1969. *The Great Asian Religions: An Anthology.* London: Macmillan.

D'Iakonov, I.M. 1985. "On the Original Home of the Speakers of Indo-European." *JIES* 13: 92–174.

Dickie, M. 1995. "The Geography of Homer's World." In *Homer's World: Fiction, Tradition, Reality,* edited by Ø. Andersen and M. Dickie, 29–56. Bergen: Norwegian Institute at Athens.

Ehrenberg, M. 1989. *Women in Prehistory.* Norman: University of Oklahoma Press.

Ellis, R. 1981. "Appendix V: Textiles." In *Gordion Excavations: Final Reports I,* edited by R. Young. Philadelphia: University of Pennsylvania Press.

Fagles, R., trans. 1990. *The Iliad.* New York: Viking Press.

Fagles, R., trans. 1996. *The Odyssey.* New York: Viking Press.

Foley, J.M. 1981. "Tradition-Dependent and -Independent Features in Oral Literature: A Comparative View of the Formula. " In *Oral Traditional Literature: A Festschrift for Albert Bates Lord,* edited by M. Foley, 262–81. Columbus, Ind.: Slavica Publishers.

Gagarin, M. 1986. *Early Greek Law.* Berkeley: University of California Press.

Gamkrelidze, T. V., and V.V. Ivanov. 1985a. "The Ancient Near East and the Indo-European Question: Temporal and Territorial Characteristics of Proto-Indo-European Based on Linguistics and Historico-Cultural Data." *JIES* 13: 3–48.

Gamkrelidze, T. V., and V.V. Ivanov. 1985b. "The Problem of the Original Homeland of the Speakers of Indo-European Languages in Response to I. M. D'Iakonoffs Article." *JIES* 13: 175–84.

Gasparov, M.L. 1996. *A History of European Versification.* Oxford: Clarendon Press.

Geijer, A. 1977. "The Loom on the Chiusi Vase." In *Studies in Textile History: In Memory of Harold B. Burnham,* edited by V. Gervers, 52–5. Toronto: Royal Ontario Museum.

Ghersi, L., and E. Basile. 2003. *Hand-in-Hand Weaving.* http://www.hypertextile.net/hih/english/intro.htm (26 March 2006).

Gimbutas, M. 1985. "Primary and Secondary Homeland of the Indo-Europeans: Comments on the Gamkrelidze-Ivanov Articles." *JIES* 13: 185–202.

Griffith, R.T.H., trans. 1896. *The Rig Veda.* http://www.sacred-texts.com/hin/rigveda/index.htm (28 March 2006)

Grube, G.M.A. 1931. *The Greek and Roman Critics.* Toronto: University of Toronto Press.

Harriot, R., 1969. *Poetry and Criticism. Before Plato.* London: Methuen.

Jamison, S.W. 1991. *The Ravenous Hyenas and the Wounded Sun.* Ithaca, N.Y.: Cornell University Press.

Jones-Bley, K., and M. Huld. 1996. *The Indo-Europeanization of Northern Europe.* Washington, D.C.: Institute for the Study of Man.

Kerimov, L., N. Stepanian, T. Grigoliya, and D. Tsitishvili. 1984. *Rugs and Carpets from the Caucasus: The Russian Collections.* Leningrad: Aurora Art Publishers.

Khlopin, I.N. 1982. "The Manufacture of Pile Carpets in Bronze Age Central Asia." *Hali* 5(2): 116–18.

Killin J.T. 1964. "The Wool Industry of Crete in the Late Bronze Age." *BSA* 59: 1–15.

Lattimore, R., trans. 1967. *The Odyssey of Homer.* New York: Harper & Row.

Levine, L. 1977. "Notes on Felt-Making and the Production of Other Textiles at She Gabi, a Kurdish Village." In *Studies in Textile History: In Memory of Harold B. Burnham,* edited by V. Gervers, 202–13. Toronto: Royal Ontario Museum.

Lopez, D.S., ed. 2002. *Religions of Asia in Practice: An Anthology.* Princeton: Princeton University Press.

Lord, A.B. 1960. *The Singer of Tales.* Cambridge, Mass.: Harvard University Press.

Mallory J.P. 1989. *In Search of the Indo-Europeans: Language, Archaeology and Myth.* London: Thames and Hudson.

Meillet, A. 1923. *Les origins indo-européennes des mètres grecs.* Paris: Les presses universitaires de France.

Morris, S. 1989. "A Tale of Two Cities: The Miniature Frescoes from Thera and the Origins of Greek Poetry." *AJA* 93(4): 511–35.

Mumford, J.K. 1900. *Oriental Rugs.* New York: Scribner.

Murray, P. 1981. "Poetic Inspiration in Early Greece." *JHS* 101: 87–100.

Nagler, M.N. 1974. *Spontaneity and Tradition: A Study in the Oral Art of Homer*. Berkeley: University of California Press.

Nagy, G. 1974. *Comparative Studies in Greek and Indic Meter*. Cambridge, Mass.: Harvard University Press.

Nagy, G. 2002. *Plato's Rhapsody and Homer's Muse: The Poetics of the Panathenaic Festival in Classical Athens*. Cambridge, Mass.: Harvard University Press.

O'Flaherty, W.D., trans. 1981. *The Rig Veda*. London. Penguin Classics Press.

O'Flaherty, W.D., ed. 1988. *Textual, Sources for the Study of Hinduism*. Chicago: University of Chicago Press.

Parikh, I., P.K. Garg, and I. Menon. 1991. *Women Weavers*. Center for Management in Agriculture Monograph 149. New Delhi: Oxford and IBH Publishing Co.

Parry, A., ed. 1971. *The Making of Homeric Verse: The Collated Papers of Milman Parry*. Oxford: Clarendon Press.

Parry. M. 1930. "Studies in the Epic Technique of Oral Verse-Marking." *HSCP* 41: 73–147.

Pekridou-Gorecki, A. 1989. *Mode im antiken Griechenland: Textile Fertigung und Kleidung*. Munich: C.H. Beck.

Popham M.R., E. Touloupa, and L.H. Sackett. 1982. "The Hero of Lefkandi." *Antiquity* 56: 169–74.

Reifstahl, F., 1944. *Patterned Textiles in Pharaonu: Egypt*. Brooklyn: Brooklyn Institute of Arts and Sciences.

Renfrew, C. 1988. *Archaeology and Language: The Puzzle of Indo-European Origins*. Cambridge: Cambridge University Press.

Rudenko, S.I. 1953. *Kul'tura naselenila gornogo Altja v Skifskoe vremja*. Moscow: Izdvo Akademii nauk SSSR.

Rudenko, S.I. 1970. *Frozen Tombs of Siberia: The Pazyryk Burials of Iron Age Horsemen*, translated by MW. Thompson. Berkeley and Los Angeles: University of California Press.

Sandys, J., trans. 1915. *Pindar*. Loeb Classical Library. Cambridge, Mass.: Harvard University Press.

Scheid J., and J. Svenbro. 1996. *The Craft of Zeus: Myths of Weaving and Fabric*. Cambridge, Mass.: Harvard University Press.

Schmitt, R., ed. 1973. *Indogermanische Dichtersprache*. Darmstadt: Wissenschaftliche Buchgesellschaft.

Seiler-Baldinger. A. 1994. *Textiles: A Classification of Techniques*. Washington, D. C.: Smithsonian Institution Press.

Shishlina, N.I., O.V. Orfinskaya, and V.P. Golikov. 2003. "Bronze Age Textiles from the North Caucasus' New Evidence of Fourth Millennium Fibres and Fabrics." *OJA* 22(41): 331–44.

Simpson, W.K., ed. 2003. *The Literature of Ancient Egypt*. 3rd ed. New Haven: Yale University Press.

Snyder, J.N. 1981. "The Web of Song: Weaving Imagery in Homer and the Lyric Poets." *CJ* 76: 193–96.

Thieme, P. 1953. *Die Heimat der indogermanischen Gemeinsprache*. Mainz: Verlag der Akademie derWissenschaften und der Literatur.

Thomas, H. 1967. *Near Eastern, Mediterranean, and European Chronology*. Stockholm: Paul Åströms Förlag.

Vámbéry, A. 1970. *Travels in Central Asia: Being the Account of a Journey from Teheran Across the Turkoman Desert on the Eastern Shore of the Caspian to Khiva, Bokhara and Samarcand, Performed in the Year 1863*. New York: Arno Press.

von Bothmer, D. 1985. *The Amasis Painter and His World: Vase Painting in Sixth Century Athens*. Los Angeles: J. Paul Getty Museum.

Watkins, C. 1995. *How to Kill a Dragon*. Oxford: Oxford University Press.

West, M.L. 1981. "The Singing of Homer and the Modes of Early Greek Music." *JHS* 101: 113–29.

West, M.L. 1988. "The Rise of the Greek Epic." *JHS* 107: 151–72.

2

Performance and Written Literature in Classical Greece: Envisaging Performance from Written Literature and Comparative Contexts

Rosalind Thomas

The many different and possible relations between text and performance have been one of the main concerns of the AHRB Centre for Asian and African Literatures Workshops on Literature and Performance, whether we are talking of written text and performance or of performances which have no basis in writing but which still seem to demand some conception of fixity, an oral 'text'. For a society in the distant past, the only literature we still possess is inevitably preserved in written texts, and in the case of Classical Greece, in what rapidly became a canon of written texts. However, it is clear that most of the written literature from the archaic and classical periods (c. 8th–4th centuries BC) was heard rather than read silently or aloud from the page, and that much was meant to be experienced in performance. To what extent can we understand the significance and nature of these performances? What difference do they (or should they) make to our understanding of the written texts, when we are left with only the written texts themselves along with some secondary descriptions, artistic representations and theoretical discussions relating to the performance of literature? To what extent can comparative examples of performance literature shed light on this?

Scholars have recently become far more attentive to the importance of performance in Ancient Greece and the possible social, religious and cultural significance of these per-

Rosalind Thomas, "Performance and Written Literature in Classical Greece: Envisaging Performance from Written Literature and Comparative Contexts," pp. 348–357 from *Bulletin of the School of Oriental African Studies* 66(3), 2003.

formance occasions. Following the revolutionary work of Milman Parry and Albert Lord on orally composed epic, and an increasingly 'anthropological' approach to Greek culture, this further sub-revolution in classical studies has involved a growing interest in the performance and context of Greek literature which *was* written down, and which existed once written texts of literature became common. To generalize very broadly, there was a tendency until recently to concentrate upon the performance of oral poetry, particularly the oral composition of the Homeric epic, and pay less attention to the performance of poetry composed in a literate context (either composed in writing or composed orally by a literate poet who then wrote down the text). The comparative study of performance literature in other fairly traditional societies opens up a host of questions about the many possible relations of written text to performance, and the body of material discussed can help ease the understandable anxiety with which classical scholars view the problem of re-imagining these ancient performances. Conversely, the performance literature of the Greek world may also be illuminating for its differences from other performance literatures, with all the questions those raise, and for other highly articulate past cultures which are now understood primarily through their written texts.

Performance, then, is at the centre of Archaic and Classical Greece. Plato criticized the Athenians of the Classical period for being a 'theatocracy', literally a place where spectacle rules: where the people, the democratic mob to a fastidious critic like Plato, are envisaged *en masse* in the theatre judging, and thinking they have the right and ability to do so (*Laws* 701a). Plato was revealing his anti-democratic stance here, but it reminds us forcefully of the fact that in Classical Athens (5th–4th centuries BC) performance – and performance of many different kinds and genres – was fundamental to the life of the city, so much so that an anti-democratic critic like Plato could couch his dislike partly in terms of the breakdown of the traditional laws of music.[1] This might seem paradoxical. The classical world is preserved and studied primarily through its great literary texts, alongside the archaeological remains and inscriptions, it

therefore at first looks like a textual culture, one dominated by the written texts of high culture and highly literate. Yet the paradox is that these literary texts were in the main meant to be heard rather than read silently, particularly in the Archaic and Classical Greek world, and certain types of poetic text were sung with accompanying musical instruments. Our texts of Greek lyric poetry and choral poetry, silent on the written page, were originally accompanied by the lyre and other instruments, and choral poetry was sung by a group, a chorus, accompanied by dance. For this reason Greek poetry was essentially public, and concerned social and political life as Gentili has stressed.[2] The culture of Archaic Greece (*c.* 750–480 BC) has even been called a song culture, so ubiquitous are the sung poems and music in everyday life and special occasions.[3]

Most obvious in the case of the performances of tragedy and comedy at Athens, the 'performance culture' of Classical Greece rapidly expands for any observer who starts to look for it. The Athenian democracy relied on a 'direct democracy', in which the politically ambitious had to speak to a large audience in the Assembly (and sometimes in the jury courts) and persuade them to vote for their proposals. At religious festivals, which were extraordinarily frequent in this polytheistic system, the deity would usually be honoured by one or several kinds of competition, plus processions, themselves performances. Such competitions could be athletic (Olympic Games), recitations of Homer (the Panathenaia), or other poetic events at which new work was performed. Athenian tragedy grew out of poetic competitions, which gradually developed into competitions between dramas in verse and were staged in the massive public theatre of the god Dionysus to mass audiences (possibly half the citizen body), and judged by a panel of democratically elected judges. At private dinner parties or *symposia*, the mainly rich or aristocratic participants often engaged in competitions in improvising or repeating poetry; Plato's *Symposium*, with its competing speeches about love, shows a competition in prose, but a competition based on a similar model none the less. We could add to this numerous other occasions on which there was a staging of poetry, hymns or, for that matter, non-literary performances of rituals, processions, rites of passage and contests. A full understanding of this Greek literature would in theory, then, involve not simply the written texts, but also how those texts related to their performances, and what elements (to put it simply) stood outside the written texts we have; there has been much recent work seeking to understand the performance contexts of much of Greek literature.[4] This increased awareness of performance greatly enriches our image of Greek society and culture precisely because it gives more social and cultural background to the written texts which became crystallized as great literature relatively early and often lost their original performative meaning.

The Literature and Performance workshops have been particularly interesting for the study of this aspect of Greek culture and performance literature generally. Firstly, most of the literatures under discussion are 'traditional' in the sense that they are more embedded in their societies than much modern Western literature. Secondly, the workshop has focused attention upon literature which is performed even when some kind of written text exists, as well as solely oral literature, and this has enabled participants to raise numerous questions specific to performance and performance literature which are highly relevant to the case of Greek literature. Classical scholars, with their silent written texts, perhaps have most to learn about the possible dynamics of performance elsewhere, the different attitudes to the written text, and the relation of various performative elements to the written text (to which we shall return). The case of Greek performance literature, however, also pushes to the fore certain elements which seem less prominent in many other performance literatures, and which may prompt some explanation:

1. The frequent religious context and status of the performance of literature in Greece, which may have much to do with what makes a particular performance special, worthwhile, exciting and worth reproducing.
2. The competitiveness of the Greek world: much of its performance literature, and

not just political rhetoric, takes place in situations of contest or antagonistic exchange. This is by no means the case in many other performance literatures, as has been made clear by the Workshop, and it undermines the view that performance literature binds a community together. Certainly the audience present is bound by the occasion and by common acceptance of the rules of competition, but the competition is divisive in other ways. The element of contest (or *agon*) could be said to be a fundamentally Greek characteristic of oral performance.
3. The development of elaborately articulated ideas about the ethics and educational qualities of certain performances over others: debates occur about performance literature or the implications of certain aspects of performance which are important for evaluating the status of performance in Greece and raise questions about the existence or role of similar discussions in other societies.

In pursuing these three elements, I concentrate here primarily on song culture and the particular difficulties connected with the performance of complex choral lyric poetry, and upon occasions where competition is central.

Song Culture

In Archaic and Classical Greece (7th–4th centuries BC) poetry was usually performed to audiences in specific social, cultural or religious contexts and occasions and this has enhanced understanding of the way different genres would be associated with specific occasions – genres had not yet become separated from occasion and context.[5] Thus funerals and weddings had their own specific types of song: *threnoi* or dirges for funerals, and the *hymenaios* (wedding song) and *epithalamia* (song before the bridal chamber) for weddings. Elegiac poetry, which was recited rather than sung to the accompaniment of an instrument, was loosely associated with occasions giving public advice, but more specifically with military exhortations, and serious political reflections in some public gatherings (Solon, Tyrtaios).

Choral poetry on the other hand needed a trained chorus and would therefore involve groups of citizens, or of young girls or boys. It was common in festivities directly associated with religious cults, and generally centred upon the community and community celebration. Choral odes of praise for victors in the games were a development of choral lyric for the celebration of individuals, and belonged to the specific genre of the 'epinician' or victory ode, which followed its own set of conventions.

Trying to imagine such occasions contributes much towards our understanding of the original resonances of a given song – which would have been obvious to the original audiences. Thus a striking example discussed by Edith Hall concerns the type of speech attributed to the defeated Persian king Xerxes, in Aeschylus' tragedy *The Persians*. Extraordinarily, the defeated king is given no ordinary speech at all during the play (the iambic trimeter represents the 'spoken' word in tragedy); his only direct speech is in fact in song, and a particular kind of song at that – a dirge or lament. Yet in Greece, as any audience would have known, it was women who sang the laments (*threnoi*). The oddity of Xerxes singing in this way should have been very striking to the fifth-century BC audience. It might imply that Xerxes was rather effeminate, or an emotionally disturbed barbarian very different from the (idealized) Greek men who had just defeated him.[6]

The nuances and social or moral implications of certain aspects of performance are often articulated by political thinkers. The *aulos* or clarinet, for instance, was widely used and loved in Athens, but it was undignified, puffing up the cheeks, and much disliked by moralizing critics: unsuitable and demeaning for the male citizen, it should be left to slaves and women.[7] Aristotle said the *aulos* was too exciting, and besides it was impossible to sing along with it, therefore 'the ancients' were quite right to forbid youths and free men from playing it (*Politics* VIII 1341a). Similarly, different forms of music were thought to encourage different levels of moral fibre and of energy and courage, if we are to believe Aristotle, who claimed that certain music enfeebled the mind, while the Phrygian mode stimulated enthusiasm (*Politics* VIII 1340b). The fact that political thinkers like Aristotle and Plato (*Republic* and *Laws*) could devote considerable time to the kinds of music that should be encouraged enables us to look beyond the written words to some of the nuances and resonances of the performance occasion.[8]

Yet there are limits to the usefulness of this kind of moralizing, especially when we confront the performance of highly acceptable but very complex genres. Here I would like to turn to the early to mid-fifth-century poet Pindar, poet *par excellence* of the victory ode, and probably Greece's greatest lyric poet. Victory odes were choral lyrics composed on the victor's commission and performed in honour of the victors at the great games at the religious festivals at Delphi, Olympia, Nemea and Isthmia. Pindar's odes are striking in the complexity and unusual nature of metre and language, and the allusiveness of their references. Far from simply telling the audience about the victor, they combine celebration of the occasion with general gnomic or moralizing utterances about life, victory, divinity, and with a myth usually connected with the home city of the victor. There are often abrupt, surprising transitions, for instance from gnomic utterance to the myth, or from the myth back to the victory itself (each ode has a myth, often told allusively or partially). The Greek is often syntactically complex, for instance with words postponed or separated from those with which they agree, making the audience wait for the final meaning of the sentence to become apparent. Such density may generate many pages of modern commentary.[9] Yet as with other choral poetry, victory odes were commissioned to be performed originally at a specific, probably rather formal, public occasion, and for this the poet trained the chorus. They can thus only have been performed some time after the victory itself. They were poetic celebrations of the victor, the victor's family, his city and, over and above all, the deity and the festival in honour of that deity in which the victory was won. In some cases, where the victor was a ruler, the whole city seems to have shared in the celebrations.[10] A niggling question for classical scholars interested in performance is how a listening audience could possibly grasp the whole meaning of the ode as it was performed. If it is hard enough to follow on the page, how could they possibly follow its twists and turns when only listening? Moreover, it was sung not by a soloist but by a chorus, and accompanied by dancing (there has been a lively controversy about whether the victory ode could have been sung by a soloist, and, related, who is the 'I' of the poems, but this has been laid to rest in favour of the old view that it was sung by a chorus: later Hellenistic scholars had no difficulty in accepting that the victory odes were sung by a chorus[11]). At some point the musical accompaniment was lost and these odes were preserved purely as written texts, which is of course all we now have: the originals were considerably more elaborate.

This is an area which invites some comparison with other performance literatures, literatures which might provide other questions and perspectives. A pervasive, and understandable, assumption in classical scholarship is that a complex written text can only be fully appreciated by multiple re-readings. This is surely correct, but it goes hand-in-hand with considerable unease about the viability of oral performance of any such complex poetry.[12] It has to be said that scholars of Pindar have concentrated mainly on elucidating Pindar's difficulty as a written text, rather than its difficulty when heard in performance. One of the striking results of the SOAS workshop is to emphasize the variety of possible responses to having a written text of a performance. Texts may be quite deliberately kept secret and released only partially or not at all in order to protect the actors' craft;[13] texts may simply remind one partially of the performance, or form an *aide-memoire* for the poet; or texts, particularly those produced by anthropologists, may aim at re-creating a performance as accurately as possible. In addition, it is worth mentioning that some textual traditions can record in the text a great deal more of the performance than the simple words; as for instance in Japanese texts of performance literature this underlines the different levels on which writing can replicate a performance.[14]

The case of Pindar's odes is all the more puzzling from this point of view because individual victors commissioned odes as one-off poetic commemorations. We are not dealing with a frequently repeated piece (as for example in commercial theatre) and there would be few occasions for new odes. Pindar and his lesser contemporaries were creating poems for a tiny, very special athletic and often aristocratic elite. Moreover, for each victor celebrating in his community, the chorus would be a group of friends and fellow citizens (we presume) who would have to be trained for that one piece, and who might never again sing a victory ode: quite different from the systematic training of a chorus for the Athenian publicly sponsored performances of tragedy. Later performances of Pindaric odes certainly occurred, but from the point of view of the individual victor and his community, there might be only one victor in decades. There were written texts, and texts of the odes must have circulated beyond the victor's family to be performed elsewhere because Pindar's poetry was quite well known in elite circles in the fifth and fourth centuries BC., but these texts were presumably *aides-memoires* for performance.

What of the nature of the performance itself – performance of this very complex poetry by an amateur choir with dancing as well as singing? This is extremely hard to discern or envisage and, as I have stated above, most discussion has been preoccupied with the difficulty on the page (see references in n. 9). Perhaps we should embrace this complexity as essential to the performance, rather than being concerned about its effect on performance. A continuing theme of the papers presented to the AHRB Centre Workshops has been to ask what it is about a performance that makes it separate, special, and an offering of far more than the words on the written page. Literature which is both complex and meant to be performed and heard occurs all over the world: Persian court poetry of the Middle Ages was exceedingly complex and experienced in performance. In Nigeria, Yoruba praise poetry, consisting of tight and allusive name-epithets, is deliberately and powerfully obscure, and sets a premium on lack of clarity.[15] Similarly, in a European context, there are medieval French polyphonic motets which combine multiple texts and melodies. These consist of three separate musical chants with two or three separate texts, sometimes in different languages, e.g. a French text and a Latin: all are sung simultaneously.[16] There has been some discussion as to whether this meant that the words were meant to be experienced as meaningless sounds ('sheer babble', as Ardis Butterfield puts it), yet the simultaneously sung texts sometimes have contrasting meanings, in a way which suggested that singers and audience could enjoy the contrast and complexity of meanings as well as of sounds. It is also possible that the very music helps the audience follow the meaning of the words, 'giving the texts a meaning they could not possess on their own'.[17]

With these thirteenth-century motets the complexity is not so much in the wording, the texts themselves, as in the combinations of texts and music. With the Greek victory ode, we may perhaps imagine that it is precisely the complexity of combining the choral singing and dance, the 'difficulty' of language and sentiments, the allusiveness, the way even the telling of a myth breaks off or is sometimes only alluded to, that did so much to make the performance an event on quite a different level from real life, that separated the victor and his achievement from his fellow men, and in short made him a hero. It was this elaboration and grandeur that marked off the ode from ordinary life and – of course – from ordinary praise and the noisy celebrations that occurred immediately after the victory, and which gave the whole celebration a heightened atmosphere; the difficulty was a characteristic to be embraced as part of what made the victory special. But in any case the allusiveness and abrupt transitions may have been less bemusing to the original audiences, who were used to the genre and could recognize the traditional elements as they heard them, as several researchers familiar with live performance poetry have pointed out. An audience brought up to have at least some familiarity with the conventions of choral lyric (widely used for hymns), if not the victory ode, would know what elements were likely to occur and would be better able to grasp the elements and movement of the victory ode than a modern reader troubled with modern conceptions and modern questions of unity.

If such audiences expected some allusiveness, it might be teasing, certainly, but far less tantalizing than it would be to a modern reader who might not understand the allusion in any case. But perhaps we should add that, even given these conventions, the audience still does not know quite when the transition (to myth, to victor) is going to occur, and Chris Carey has pointed out that the poet would be able to surprise the audience and keep them on their toes with unexpected transitions, 'mock spontaneity' and elaborate constructions of thought. Pindar was composing at the end of this tradition and was able to exploit this element of surprise to perfection.[18]

It is perhaps worth dwelling on the deliberate obscurity of Yoruba praise poetry or *oriki*, and indeed of other praise poetry of sub-Saharan Africa. Karin Barber has described and analysed the habit in oriki performance of creating name-epithets which allude in a highly compressed and enigmatic way to a specific happening, activity or characteristic of the man being praised: *oriki* are 'essentially assemblages of elaborated epithets', apparently composed of unrelated fragments, variable in length and assembled for oral performance by the praise singer in such a way as to create maximum intensity.[19] She also points out the way the audience would be teased and egged on to try some kind of exegesis of these compressed epithets. I have no intention of suggesting any detailed stylistic or social comparison between these very different types of praise poetry and societies, but would merely point out how striking it is that a highly allusive, difficult genre is enthusiastically cultivated, whose fragmentary nature defies European conceptions of literary unity, and which only really makes sense – and indeed has particular force – as a performance in a particular context and occasion (the 'unity' of Pindar's odes has also been seen as problematic). One might also wonder if there is some cultural value in both Greece and Africa in allusiveness and implicitness for a praise genre which might be particularly useful because, among other things, it enabled the singer to avoid the pitfalls of the commonplace and obvious, and by thus avoiding platitudes to elevate the object of praise still more above the everyday level of commonality. This, however, is mere speculation.

The atmosphere of the original and subsequent performances of Pindar's victory odes is also elusive, since we have only the written text: scholars imagine a glorious Olympic victor, feted immediately after the victory with friends and an impromptu victory song, now returning to his home city where he will become the local hero, with the city turning out to celebrate, the ode a celebration of the city as well as of the victor, with perhaps a special banquet laid on by the city or perhaps only a celebration amongst the wealthy of the community. The odes themselves convey scenes of communal happiness and song: thus the beginning of *Nemean* 3 opens with an invitation to the Muse to visit them in their poetic performance on the island of Aigina, home of the victor Aristocleidas:

O mistress Muse, our mother, I beg you,
come in the Nemean sacred month to this
welcoming Dorian island of Aigina, for by the
  water
of Asopos are waiting the builders of honey-
  sounding
revels, young men who desire your voice.
Different deeds thirst for different rewards,
but victory in the games loves song most of all,
the fittest companion for crowned
  achievements.
                              (*Nemean* 3, 1–8, trans. Race,
                                        Loeb edition, adapted)

He continues to wish for skill from the Muse and 'I shall impart it [the song] to their voices and the lyre' (lines 11–12).[20] As implied here, the chorus does indeed seem to consist of the victor's friends, and the celebration is portrayed as being in the heart of the victor's community.

Another element is the religious, and here we return to more general points about the cultural context and power of performance literature. The victory occurred at a festival in honour of a particular deity (Zeus at Olympia, Apollo at Delphi), and it was regarded as the ultimate sign of divine favour. Religious festivals in Ancient Greece were occasions for celebration, merry-making,

social gatherings, feasting on the sacrificial meat, and general joy – certainly not the subdued, possibly ascetic, reverential occasions of many modern religious traditions. If we are looking for the elements of performance which are not, which cannot be, replicated in the bare representations of the words, then this religious context is one further area to explore. It is possible that the atmosphere of religious celebration, of spectacle and religious ritual, might have been particularly important, part of what made the occasion of the performance special, heightened, something quite different from the silent reading of the words. This has been little discussed in the literature relating to Greece or more generally.[21] Greece, with its peculiarly polis-oriented manner of worshipping the gods, may have been unusual in the extent to which its literature was performed at religious festivals. Yet if performance is about audience, and the impact of performance related to the context, occasion, and audience, we have to remember how much Greek poetry was performed or reperformed in Greece at festivals. Tragedy and comedy were written for and performed at the great city festival in honour of the god Dionysus at Athens: the audience was a massive citizen audience, and it was a competition judged democratically, with prizes for the best plays. Other cities had performances at festivals. One may imagine at least an air of reverent excitement, the prospect of celebration and festival, sacrificial meat, processions, something, perhaps, of a carnival atmosphere. Add to this the frequency of competition: performers and poets were often in competition, a further Greek peculiarity in the way they honoured the gods. The festival of the Dionysia is the most famous, but there were also musical and rhapsode contests at the Great Panathenaia in honour of Athena at Athens, a music festival on the island of Delos for Apollo, musical events at Argos, Sparta (Karneia, Gymnopaidiai), Sicyon, Epidauros and elsewhere.[22] While we do not have detailed verbal descriptions of such competitions, we can perhaps imagine something of the striving for excellence and ultimately victory, that is repeatedly held up in the victory odes for *athletic* victory as representing the pinnacle of human achievement.

One of the dangers created by victors at the games, especially those in the most costly events, was that they might become self-important and above the community: winners of the four-horse chariot race in particular were regarded as potential tyrants. This brings to the fore the dominance in Greek performance of firstly, the competitive element at every level (i.e. not simply competition in the performance of poetry as above); and secondly, the potential for setting the individual above and even outside his community. We do not hear of victors in musical events (as opposed to athletic or equestrian) having such political ambitions, yet this competitive element is striking: sometimes the contest is between choirs from different cities, or between individual performers or poets/composers. Emphasis is often laid on the character of performed literature in bringing together a group or community, expressing or reflecting some form of group identity. This would probably apply to the performance of hymns, processional songs, many songs sung simply for entertainment, songs in honour of deities at various festivals or other gatherings. But it is undeniable that for many arenas where performance literature is heard in Greece, there is a strong element of competition, whether between the original authors or performers of previously written work. For the odes for victorious athletes, the competition is between the victor and all his peers (Pindar frequently speaks of envy), and the performance of the victory ode has much to do with celebrating his excellence and, with varying degrees, attempting to integrate him back into his community.[23] Perhaps in elevating the victor's city and the gods, as well as the victor, the performed victory ode was trying to keep the victor in his place.

Conclusion

Much could be said about these themes in the competitive political atmosphere of Athens in the period of radical democracy (c. 450–320s BC). In Athens the need for skills in speaking to a mass democratic audience in the open-air Assembly drove forward the elaboration of rhetoric as a genre and meant that ambitious

politicians had to learn the techniques of speaking. In the latter part of the fifth century BC contests were also staged between different thinkers, sophists, natural philosophers, philosophers and doctors, and there was a wide range of different types of sophistic performances, from extempore display pieces to polished and repeatable speeches.[24] This was the atmosphere which the philosopher Plato so disliked when he accused Athens of being a theatocracy. But there was also a certain anxiety and tension even within the democratic institutions. While the dynamics of democratic decision making required good speakers, there was at the same time an ambivalence towards and distrust of the trained speaker in this democratic system and such speakers, both in the Assembly and the law-courts (which had mass democratic juries), sometimes tried to mask their training, insisted they had never been in a law-court before, or cultivated a more 'oral style' rather than a style associated with written composition in order to give the impression of unstudied spontaneity. Democracy assumed every citizen had equal ability to judge and participate, and that would include speaking, yet the richer citizens obviously had easier access to the skills of persuasion and might hoodwink the less educated 'ordinary man'.[25] The Athenian equivalent of hiring a clever lawyer to deal with your court case was to get a speechwriter to write your defence speech, which you would then learn and deliver orally in the court yourself.

However, this complex relationship between ideology, critique and reality, would be a separate study. It suffices here to stress how important the competitive context of performance is in Greek politics; and the paradox of the Athenian democracy which put a premium on oral performance from its citizens and yet which inevitably encouraged both the art of rhetoric and the use of written texts of speeches written by professionals but performed orally by the Athenian citizen. This highly competitive element was also present in Greece's earlier 'song culture'. It is the live performance of the texts in their particular religious context or social grouping that gives these surviving written texts their full cultural force. Victory odes are particularly good examples of this. They are also examples of performed poetry for which comparative performance literatures can offer revealing alternative perspectives and questions.

NOTES

1 See further Robert Wallace, 'Poet, public and "theatocracy": audience performance in classical Athens', in Lowell Edmunds and R. Wallace, (ed.), *Poet, public and perform-ance in ancient Greece* (Baltimore: Johns Hopkins University Press, 1997), 97 ff.; S. von Reden and S. Goldhill, in S. Goldhill and R. Osborne (ed.), *Performance culture and Athenian democracy* (Cambridge: Cambridge University Press, 1999), esp. 261–4.

2 B. Gentili, *Poetry and its public in Ancient Greece* (Baltimore: Johns Hopkins University Press, 1988).

3 J. Herrington, *Poetry into drama. Early tragedy and the Greek poetic tradition* (Berkeley and Los Angeles: California University Press, 1985).

4 Gentili, *Poetry and its public*; Herrington, *Poetry into drama*; Rösier, *Dichter und Groupe* (Munich, 1980); L. Edmunds and R. Wallace, *Poet, public and performance* (1997); E. Stehle, *Performance and gender in ancient Greece. Nondramatic poetry in its setting* (Princeton: Princeton University Press, 1997); O. Murray (ed.), *Sympotica: a symposium on the Symposium* (Oxford: Clarendon, 1990).

5 See M. L. West, *Studies in Greek elegy and iambus* (Berlin: De Gruyter, 1974); G. Most, 'Greek lyric poets' in T. J. Luce (ed.), *Ancient writers: Greece and Rome* (New York: Scribner, 1982), 75–98; R. L. Fowler, *The nature of early Greek lyric* (Toronto: University of Toronto Press, 1987); for an introduction, R. Thomas, *Literacy and orality in Ancient Greece* (Cambridge: Cambridge University Press, 1992).

6 E. Hall, 'Actor's song in tragedy', in S. Goldhill and R. Osborne, *Performance culture*, 100.

7 See P. Wilson, 'The *aulos* in Athens', in Goldhill and Osborne, *Performance culture*, ch. 3.

8 See further, *Politics* VIII 5 ff., 1339a; Plato, *Republic*, esp. 376–412 (on education), 424; *Laws*, 2.

9 Pindar is most easily accessible in the new Loeb translation by William H. Race (Harvard, vol. I–II, 1997). cf. Glen Most, *The measure of praise. Structure and Epinician in Pindar's second Pythian and seventh Nemean odes* (Göttingen: vol. 83, 1985, ch. 1a), for instance, for succinct discussion of Pindar's difficulty.

10 *Olympian* 3, and *Pythian* 5: C. Carey, 'Pindar and the victory ode', in Lewis Ayres (ed.), *The passionate intellect: essays on the transformation of classical traditions presented to Professor I. G. Kidd* (New Brunswick: Transaction, 1995), 85–103, at p. 95.

11 See esp. C. Carey, 'The victory ode in performance: the case for the chorus', *Classical Philology* 86, 1991, 192 ff.

12 Perhaps related to the popular idea that Greek, oral epic would have died out once there was a single written text.

13 As with Kabuki theatre in Japan: C. A. Gerstle, 'Performance literature: the traditional Japanese theatre as model', *Comparative Criticism* 22, 2000, 39–62; C. A. Gerstle, 'The culture of play: kabuki and the production of texts', *Bulletin of the School of Oriental and African Studies* 66(3): 358–79.

14 Barbara Cross, 'Representing performance in pre-modern Japanese popular fiction', paper presented at the AHRB Centre for Asian and African Literature, Literature and Performance Workshop II, April 2002. For performances as stimulant to creating texts, see C. A. Gerstle, articles cited in n. 13.

15 See further below on Yoruba poetry.

16 See Ardis Butterfield, 'The language of medieval music: two thirteenth-century motets', in *Plainsong and medieval music* 2, 1993, 1–16; and for the initial controversy, Christopher Page, *Discarding images: reflections on music and culture in medieval France* (Oxford: Oxford University Press, 1993), ch. 3.

17 Butterfield, 'Language of medieval music', p. 16.

18 See C. Carey, 'Pindar and the victory ode', esp. 100–02, on the element of surprise in Pindar's odes, where he seems to be exploiting the fact of performance; and C. Carey, 'Poesia pubblica in performance', in *I lirici greci: forma della comunicazione e storia del testo: atti dell' Incontro di Studi, Messina,*

5–6 Nov. 1999, ed. M. Cannatà Fera and G. B. D'Alessio (Messina, 2001), 11–26. I am grateful to Chris Carey for discussion on this. Cf. also Ilja Pfeijffer, *Three Aeginetan odes of Pindar. A commentary on Nemeian V, Nemean III, & Pythian VIII* (Leiden: Brill, 1999), esp. 41–6 for raising audience expectations and keeping them attentive; p. 52 for the 'fiction of spontaneity'.

19 Karin Barber, 'Text and performance in Africa', *Bulletin of the School of Oriental and African Studies* 66(3): 324–33 and Barber, *I could speak until tomorrow: oriki, women and the past in a Yoruba town* (Edinburgh: Edinburgh University Press for the International African Institute, 1991), esp. ch. 2 and 3; pp. 21ff. on lack of unity'. Cf. Barber, 'Obscurity and exegesis in African oral praise poetry', in Duncan Brown (ed.), *Oral literature and performance in Southern Africa* (Oxford: James Currey, 1999). I thank Karin Barber for discussion on this.

20 Cf. also *Olympian* 14.15 ff. *Nemean 3* featured prominently in Heath's argument that the odes were sung by a solo performer: see M. Heath and M. Lefkowitz, 'Epinician performance', *Classical Philology* 86, 1991, 173–91, at p. 186 (Carey's reply, ibid., pp. 192 ff.).

21 With the exception of Athenian tragedy, part of the Dionysia. Cf. e.g. Edmunds and Wallace, *Poet, public and performance*, Goldhill and Osborne (ed.), *Performance culture*, which has a chapter by Jameson on religious ritual, and by Kavoulaki on processional performance, but not on literature performed as part of ritual.

22 Herrington, *Poetry into drama*, Appendix 1 for references and details; Thucydides III 104 on the Delian competitions.

23 For this idea of reintegrating the victor, see L. Kurke, *The traffic in praise. Pindar and the poetics of social economy* (Ithaca, NY: Cornell University Press, 1991).

24 See R. Thomas, 'Prose performance texts. *Epideixis* and written publication in the late 5th. and early 4th.c.', in Harvey Yunis (ed.), *Written texts and the rise of literate culture in Ancient Greece* (Cambridge: Cambridge University Press, 2003), 162 ff., for details.

25 For degrees of 'oral style' or style appropriate for oral delivery, see M. Gagarin, 'The orality of Greek oratory', in E. A. Mackay (ed.). *Signs of orality: the oral tradition and its influence in the Greek and Roman world* (Leiden: Brill, 1999), 163–80. John Hesk, *Deception and democracy in classical Athens* (Cambridge: Cambridge University Press, 2000), for the 'anti-rhetoric rhetoric'.

Part II
Verbal Genres of Performance

3

Playing the Dozens

Roger D. Abrahams

"PLAYING the dozens" is one of the most interesting folkloristic phenomena found among contemporary Negroes, because in its operation it reflects so many of the cultural imperatives of the group from whom it is most often encountered, the lower class Negro adolescent. [Editor's note: for "Negro" read "African American" throughout.] Since both the forms and the culture are of importance, I will attempt to interrelate the two, while pointing.out how both function.

One of the most important aspects of folklore, and one which is too seldom investigated, is the way in which lore, both in form and substance, reflects the values and the special problems of a group and the individuals within it. Though adult lore is often a more complex and mature expression of values and problems, the lore of the child and the adolescent provides us with important indexes to a part of the group's life which we otherwise might not see. For the child and the adolescent are going through the process of identity formation, experiencing periods of pronounced anxiety different in nature and intensity from later problems. In the lore of the younger groups we are able to see the performers developing their technical resources within the confines

permitted by both their peers and adults, and at the same time attempting to find adequate release for their anxieties. Our knowledge of personality formation tells us that often the permanent techniques, values, and attitudes operative on the adult level (both conscious and unconscious) are formed during childhood and adolescence, especially if there is any kind of neurosis involved. Any folklore derives directly from the psychosocial needs of the age group which spawns it. But there is an interrelationship of lore between different age groups: a development from age to age (which is especially strong in cases of arrested development) and an effect of adult forms and attitudes upon the lore of the younger members of the group. Thus investigating the lore of the young can cast light both on the life of the young and on that of the whole group at the same time.

The process of "playing the dozens" is illustrative of these psychosocial remarks. It is an early example of the infantile fixation illustrated by the use of agonistic rhymed verbal forms, a neurotic symptom which is observable in many Negro males through much of their lives. More germane to the purposes of this study, the dozens stands as a mechanism which helps the Negro youth adapt to his changing world and trains

Roger D. Abrahams, "Playing the Dozens," pp. 209–220 from *Journal of American Folklore* 75(297), 1962.

him for similar and more complex verbal endeavors in the years of his manhood. The dozens are commonly called "playing"[1] or "sounding,"[2] and the nature of the terms indicates the kind of procedure involved; "playing" illustrates that a game or contest is being waged, and "sounding" shows that the game is vocal. It is, in fact, a verbal contest which is an important part of the linguistic and psychosocial development of the Negroes who indulge in this verbal strategy. This discussion is based on two years of research among lower class Negroes in one neighborhood in South Philadelphia, and has been enlarged through observations of other similar groups in Texas.

"Sounding" occurs only in crowds of boys.[3] One insults a member of another's family; others in the group make disapproving sounds to spur on the coming exchange. The one who has been insulted feels at this point that he must reply with a slur on the protagonist's family which is clever enough to defend his honor (and therefore that of his family). This, of course, leads the other (once again, due more to pressure from the crowd than actual insult) to make further jabs. This can proceed until everyone is bored with the whole affair, until one hits the other (fairly rare), or until some other subject comes up that interrupts the proceedings (the usual state of affairs).

When the combatants are quite young (just entering puberty), they are obviously trying out some of the words and concepts they have overheard and are just beginning to understand. Thus, their contest is liable to be short, sweet, and uncomplicated, but the pattern is established:

"I hear your mother plays third base for the
    Phillies."
"Your mother is a bricklayer, and stronger
    than your father."
"Your mother eats s − − t."
"Your mother eats s − − t and mustard."

Here the emphasis is on a reversal of roles, with the mother playing the male role, a realization of a basic fact of lower class Negro family life.

As sexual awareness grows, the vilification of the mother is changed to sexual matters, the contests become more heated and the insults more noteworthy. Many of them take the form of rhymes or puns, signaling the beginning of the bloom of verbal dexterity which comes to fruition later in the long narrative poem called the "toast," and indicating the necessity of applying strict formal structure to highly volatile matters. A sample of a fracas involving two fourteen- or fifteen-year-olds might run as follows: Someone mentions the name of someone else's mother in the course of a joking conversation − "Constance," for instance. At this point someone in the crowd says, "Yeah, Constance was real good to me last Thursday." Then Constance's son has to reply in kind, "I heard Virginia (the other's mother) lost her titty in a poker game." "Least my mother ain't no cake; everybody get a piece." The other might reply:

I hate to talk about your mother,
She's a good old soul.
She's got a ten-ton p − − − y
And a rubber a − − − − − e.
She got hair on her p − − − y
That sweep the floor.
She got knobs on her titties
That open the door.

And this in turn elicits any of the numerous retorts which are listed in the following pages. Eventually the boys' verbal dexterity increases to the point at which they can achieve more through subtlety and innuendo than through rhymes and obvious puns.

Somewhere between the ages of sixteen and twenty-six, "playing" begins to lose its effect and passes out of frequent use as an institution. When someone indicates that he wants to start, the one who is supposed to be insulted may reply, "Oh man, don't play with me." If he needs a more clever retort, he may rely on the proverb, "I laugh, joke, and smoke, but I don't play." Yet the game is never really forgotten. Any time within the period in which the boys are still running in groups of their own sex, an argument which arises can be complicated and enlivened by some fleeting derogatory reference to a member of the other's family. It has been reported to me many times that the dozens is often invoked by Negroes in the army, under those very tense and restrictive conditions of regimentation for which the young Negro is not completely suited. When it is used under such circumstances, it almost invariably leads to a fight. Similarly, when used by older males in a verbal battle, in such places as a bar or a poolroom, it also ends in a battle. As such, the institution functions quite differently among men than among adolescents.

Among the older males the references to the family of the other are fleeting, and not necessarily directed against any specific aspect of life. Among adolescents, especially the younger ones, the insults are much more rigidly constructed and are directed toward or against certain things. Most prominently, they are concerned with sexual matters. Usually both the rhymes and the taunts are directed against the other's mother, alleging sexual wantonness:

I f – – – – d your mother on an electric wire.
I made her p – – – y rise higher and higher.

I f – – – – d your mother between two cans.
Up jumped a baby and hollered, "Superman."
At least my mother ain't no doorknob, everybody gets a turn.

Sometimes the rhymes just place the other's mother in an embarrassing position:

I saw your mother flying through the air.
I hit her on the ass with a rotten pear.

Another common subject is the effeminacy or homosexuality of father or brother:

Least my father ain't pregnant in the stomach.
Least my brother ain't no store; he takes meat in the back.

Whether the game involves rhymes or not, the language which is used is different from the everyday language of the contestants. Such linguistic (or paralinguistic) elements as changes in pitch, stress, and sometimes syntax, provide the signals of contest. Just as counting-out introduces us to the world of the children's game, with its resultant suspension of reality, or the phrase "Have you heard the one about . . . ?" leads us into the permissive world of the joke, so when someone of this group makes a dozens-type preliminary remark, it can be predicted that he is about to construct a hypothetical play field on which a verbal contest is to be played.

These contrastive linguistic features outline the rules of the game, a verbal battle. Within specific forms, the rules seem to say, "You can insult my family, but don't exceed the rules because we are dealing with something perilously close to real life." The most prominent linguistic features are (1) the reliance upon formulaic patterns, (2) the use of rhyme within these patterns, and (3) the change of speech rhythms from natural ones to ones that conform to the demands of the formula. These are the strictest boundaries imposed by this game. As the youths learn to use words more securely, any contrived witticism will supply the needed formulaic requirement. Until such an age, it is easier to be clever within the confines of the appointed rhyme form. The use of rhyme is a type of wit.

The verses used in this contest show that "sounding" is a device from a transitional period of life. The technique, length, rhyme, meter, and restriction of form are very like the verses used by children; in subject they look more toward adult attitude and expression.

Roses are red,
Violets are blue.
I f – – – – d your mama,
And now it's for you.

The rhyme

I f – – – – d your mother between two tracks.
It stung so hard, the train fell back.

is very similar to these lines from a children's rhyme:

Just before your mother died
She called you to her side.
She gave you a pair of drawers.
Before your father died.
She put 'em in the sink.
The sink begin to stink.
She put 'em on on the track.
The train backed back.
She put 'em on the fence.
Ain't seen 'em since.

Negro children use tricks, catches, and taunts which utilize much the same strategy as the dozens' rhymes:

Red, red, peed in bed,
Wiped it up with jelly-bread.

Brown, brown, go to town,
With your britches hanging down.

But the importance of the verbal contest is something closer to the agonistic structure of adult discourse.

A device which links the dozens to childhood behavior is that of "signifying." This is a technique of indirect argument or persuasion that underlies many of the strategies of children and is utilized more subtly in the dozens. The unity of approach of both "signifying" and the dozens is illustrated in a toast from an older age group, called the "The Signifying Monkey and the Lion." In this verse narrative we have a dialogue between a malicious, childlike monkey and a headstrong lion,[4] in which the monkey is trying to get the lion involved in a fight with the elephant. The monkey is a "signifier," and one of the methods he uses for inflaming the lion is to indicate that the elephant has been "sounding" on the lion.

"Now the lion came through the jungle one
   peaceful day,
When the signifying monkey stopped him, and
   this is what he started to say:
He said, "Mr. Lion," he said, "A bad-assed
   m — — — — — — — r down your way,"
He said, "Yeah! The way he talks about your
   folks is a certain shame.
"I even heard him curse when he mentioned
   your grandmother's name."
The lion's tail shot back like a forty-four
When he went down that jungle in all uproar.

It is significant in this regard that the monkey is childlike, and for his "signifying" he gets killed in most endings to this toast. "Signifying" is a children's device, and is severely "put down" by adults. They say, "Signifying is worse than dying," at the same time recognizing that they themselves easily fall into the same pattern, by saying "Signification is the nigger's occupation." Thus the dozens uses many of the techniques of childhood discourse, but places them in a context that leads directly to adult modes of expression. Both the reliance on rhyme and wit and the use of "signifying" remain as major parts of adult male expression, but in considerably mutated form. The dozens signals this mutation.

Many have commented upon the institution of playing the dozens, but few have discussed the function which it performs in the life of the young Negro.[5] John Dollard's article, "The Dozens: The Dialect of Insult," perceptively points out that the game acts as a release mechanism for the anxieties of Negro youths; his article stands as a unique document in the field. But his uncertainty as to the manner of release, and a misunderstanding of its psychosocial importance, leads me to make further remarks on the way in which the dozens function. Specifically, Dollard does not seem to differentiate between the dozens as played by youths and by adults. Further, he sees the game as a displaced aggression against the Negro's own group instead of against the real enemy, the whites, a reading which I find untenable not because it is wholly wrong, but because it is too easy.[6]

Certainly these rhymes serve as a clever expression of the growing awareness of the adolescent performers, especially of matters of sex. But "growing awareness" signals the fact that dozens are an expression of boys in transition to manhood. In fact, "sounding" is one of the major ways in which boys are enabled to become men in the limited sense in which Negro males from the lower class ever attain a sense of masculinity.

The Negro man from the lower class is confronted with a number of social and psychological impediments. Not only is he a black man in a white man's world, but he is a male in a matriarchy. The latter is his greatest burden. Family life is dominated by the mother. Often a boy grows up in a home which only sporadically has an older male in it; marriage is seldom longstanding, if it occurs at all. Casual alliances are much more the standard. Women, then, are not only the dispensers of love and care, but also of discipline and authority. Women find it easier to support themselves, either through jobs or relief, than to "worry" about any man. This tends to reinforce a matriarchal system which goes back at least to slavery days, and perhaps farther.[7] The concomitant of this system is a series of attitudes which are far-reaching in their importance in the lives of those living under it; most important of these is the absolute and divisive distrust which members of one sex have for the other. Young girls brought up by their mothers are taught early and often about how men are not to be trusted. Men learn to say the same thing about the women.

Growing up in this matriarchal system, the boys receive little guidance from older males. There are few figures about during their childhood through whom the boys can achieve any sort of positive ego identity. Thus their ideas of masculinity are slow to appear under the tutelage of their mothers. Yet when they reach puberty, they must eminently be rejected as men by the women in the matriarchy; and thus a period of intense anxiety and rootlessness is created at the beginning of adolescence. The results often are an open resorting to the apparent security of gang existence in which masculinity can be overtly expressed.

Typically, of course, the little boys who are recruited into gangs come out of matriarchal families. Often they have little or no contact with their fathers. It does not appear that they get markedly different maternal treatment from that accorded to little girls, but it seems clear that vesting all parental authority in a woman would have rather different consequences for boys and girls, and the spirit of rebellion against authority so prominent in the gang is mainly derived from this source. The matriarchs make no bones about their preference for little girls, and while they often manifest real affection for their boy children, they are clearly convinced that all little boys must inexorably and deplorably become men, with all the pathologies of that sex.[8]

Life for the boy is a mass of oppositions. He is both a part of his mother-oriented family and yet not a part of it. His emotional attachments are wholly to his mother; but as a male he must seek his masculine identity, and consequently must be rejected from his family to some extent

because of this. The rejection will occur anyhow, for with puberty comes a distrust from the female members. The result is generally a violent reaction against the world of women which has rejected him, to a life filled with expressions of virility and manliness. Femininity and weakness become the core of the despicable; the expression for these reactions is the gang.

Thus an organizational form that springs from the little boy's search for a masculinity he cannot find at home becomes first a protest against femininity and then an assertion of hypervirility. On the way it acquires a structuring in which the aspirations and goals of the matriarchy or the middle class are seen as soft, effeminate, and despicable. The gang ideology of masculine independence is formed from these perceptions, and the gang then sees its common enemy not as a class, nor even perhaps as a sex, but as the "feminine principle" in society.[9]

However, before any such metamorphosis can occur, the transition must be made by the boy from his mother-oriented to the gang-oriented values. This means a complete reversal of values, after all, and in order to achieve this changeover, a violent and wildly permissive atmosphere must be established through which the boys can express the subsequent emotions involved. The dozens evolved exactly to fit this need.

At the beginning of this stage, the boy cannot openly attack his own mother (and her values) either to himself or to his peers. His emotional stability will not allow him to do this, for his oedipal attractions fasten his affections on his mother. But his impulses are not unified in this, for his mother (or some other woman) has been the source of authority from which he must react in order to achieve manhood. And the fact that it has been a woman who has thus threatened his potential virility with her values and her authority makes the reversal of his attitudes that much more potentially explosive. Yet reverse them he must, for not to do so would be to place oneself in a vulnerable position with his peers and with the older males. So he must in some way exorcize her influence. He therefore creates a playground which enables him to attack some other person's mother, in full knowledge that that person must come back and insult his own. Thus someone else is doing the job for him, and between them they are castigating all that is feminine, frail, unmanly. (This is why the implications of homosexuality are also invoked.) By such a ritualizing of the exorcism procedure, the combatants are also beginning to build their own image of sexual superiority, for these rhymes and taunts not only free otherwise repressed aggressions against feminine values, but they also affirm their own masculine abilities. To say "I f – – – – d your mother" is not only to say that womanly weakness is ridiculous, but that the teller's virility has been exercised. In this way the youths prepare themselves for the hyper-masculine world of the gang.

But the dozens functions as more than simply a mutual exorcism society. It also serves to develop one of the devices by which the nascent man will have to defend himself – the verbal contest. Such battle in reality is much more important to the psychical growth of the Negro than actual physical battle. In fact, almost all communication among this group is basically agonistic, from the fictive experience of the narratives to the ploying of the proverbs. Though the children have maneuvers which involve a kind of verbal strategy, it is the contest of the dozens which provides the Negro youth with his first opportunity to wage verbal battle.

It is not gratuitous that this *agon* should first arise at the period of emerging sexual awareness. Through the dozens the youth has his first real chance of declaring the differences between male and female and of taking sides in the struggle. The feminine world that has gripped and yet rejected him has been rejected in kind and by a complete negation. (It is not unusual for such complete rejection to occur toward something that has so nearly seduced us to its values.) Significantly, this first "manly" step is done with a traditional manly tool, the power of words. Thus this declaration of sexual awakening and independence also provides the youth with a weapon of sexual power, one which he will have to cultivate and use often.[10]

The importance of these contests is heightened when one realizes that they are indulged in by the very ones who are most conscious of

their appearance of virility to the outside. Being bested in a verbal battle in a group of this sort has immense potential repercussions because of the terror of disapproval, of being proved ineffectual and therefore effeminate, in the eyes of peers. This leads to the apparent paradox that those who are most afraid of public humiliation have institutionalized a procedure of humiliation for the purpose of releasing aggressions and repressed instincts, while at the same time learning verbal skills.

It is astonishing to find that the same people for whom ridicule's destructive power holds such terror institutionalize it for therapeutic purposes; they turn its primary function inside out as it were, and ridicule properly conducted becomes a thing to be enjoyed for the health of society.[11]

This is only a seeming paradox, however, for the dozens situation calls for extreme permissiveness, which must apply as much to the audience as to the contestants. Beyond this, one would not play the dozens with just anyone, but someone who was safe to play it with.[12] The boys then are developing the tools of battle on their own home field.

As with so many other child and adolescent phenomena, the Negro men from this background never seem to reject "playing" completely. When men do "sound," however, it provides a very different kind of release than when adolescents do. Such maneuvers indicate flatly that the players are in some way victims of a fixation, needing a kind of release mechanism that allows them to get rid of some of their tensions. But with men, the dozens is often used as an obvious prelude to a physical fight.

As an institutionalized mechanism, the dozens is most important to the lower class Negro youth in search of his masculine identity. It represents a transition point in his life, that place at which he casts off a woman's world for a man's, and begins to develop the tools by which he is to implement his new found position, in a member of a gang existence.

The following is a group of dozens rhymes and replies collected from Negro youths in one neighborhood of South Philadelphia between September 1958 and June 1960.

1

I f – – – – d your mother in a horse and wagon.
She said, "'Scuse me, mister, my p – – – – y's
  draggin'."

2

I f – – – – d your mother between two cans.
Up jumped a baby and hollered, "Superman."

3

I f – – – – d your mother between two tracks.
It stung so hard, the train fell back.

4

I f – – – – d your mother in a bowl of rice.
Two children jumped out shootin' dice.
One shot seven and one shot eleven.
God damn, them children ain't goin' to
  Heaven.

5

I f – – – – d your mother in a car.
She hit me in the eye with a f – – – – g bar.

6

I f – – – – d your mother between two cars.
Out popped a baby shouting, "Vanguard."

7

I f – – – – d your mother on an electric wire.
I made her p – – – – y rise higher and higher.

8

I f – – – – d your mother on City Hall.
William Penn said, "Don't take it all."

9

I f – – – – d your mother on a ten-ton truck.
She said, "God damn, baby, you sure can
  f – – k."

10

I f – – – – d your mother in a bowl of piss.
She said, "Hold it, baby, I got to s – – t."
I said, "S – – t on, baby, while I f – – k you
  down."
She said, "But baby, it's supposed to be black,
  not brown."

11

I f – – – – d your mother from day to day.
Out came a baby and what did it say?
He say, "Looka here, Pop, you grind so fine.
Please give me some of that f – – – – g wine."

12

I f – – – – d your mother from hill to hill.
Up popped a baby named Mr. Sill.

13

I f – – – – d your mother from booty to booty.[13]
Out came a baby called Mr. Sanooty.

14

I f – – – – d your mother from house to house.
Out came a baby named Minnie Mouse.

15

I saw your mother last night,
She was an awful old soul.
I stuck my d – – k in her hole.
She said, "Gimme some more."

16

Your mother chased me, I chased your mother
  on a sycamore tree.
The tree split, she s – – t, all I got was a little
  bit.

17

Roses are red,
Violets are blue.
I f – – – – d your mama,
And now it's for you.

18

Yes, your mother's of the neighborhood.
She's got a rutabaga [Studebaker?] p – – – – y,
  turned up ass,
She can wiggle, she can woggle,
She can do it so good.
She got the best old hole in the neighborhood.
Some people call it the G. I. jam.
A stingin' m – – – – – – – – – r, but good god
  damn.

19

I saw your mother flying through the air.
I hit her in the ass with a rotten pear.

20

I saw your mother down by the river.
I hit her in the ass with two pounds of liver.

21

Fee, fie, fo, fum,
Your mother's a bum.

22

Ring-a-ling-a, ting, ting, tong.
Your mother's related to old King Kong.

23

Don't talk about my mother 'cause you'll make
  me mad.
Don't forget how many your mother had.
She didn't have one, she didn't have two,
She had eighty m – – – – – – rs look just like
  you.

24

I hate to talk about your mother,
She's a good old soul.
And a rubber a – – – – – e.
She got a ten-ton p – – – – – y
She got hairs on her p – – – – – y
That sweep the floor.
She got knobs on her titties
That open the door.

25
I can tell by your toes
Your mother wear brogues.
26
I can tell by your toes
Your mother drink Tiger Rose.
27
I can tell by your knees
Your mother eats surplus cheese.
28
I can tell by your knees
Your mother climbs trees.
29
I heard
Your mother drink Thunderbird.
30
I saw your mother last night,
She was a hell of a sight.
I threw her in the grass.
I stuck my d – – k in her ass.
I said, "Ooh, bop-a-doo."
Then she said, "How do you do?"

Dozens' Replies

At least my mother ain't no rope fighter.
At least my mother don't work in a coalyard.
At least my mother ain't no cake – everybody get a piece.[14]
At least my mother ain't no doorknob – everybody gets a turn.
Least my father ain't tall as a pine tree, black as coal, talk more s – – t than the radio.
Least my mother ain't no railroad track, lay all around the country.
At least when my mom f – k around,
    She don't use no Royal Crown (hair dressing oil).
Least my father ain't pregnant in the stomach.
Least my father ain't pregnant in the nose, expecting boogies.
Least my brother ain't no store; he takes meat in the back.
Least my brother ain't no store, stand on the counter tempting everybody.
Your mother lost her titty in a poker game.

NOTES

1   There has been some speculation as to the origin and history of the game under this name. John Dollard in "The Dozens: The Dialect of Insult," *American Imago*, I (1939), 3–24 (referred to as Dollard henceforth) feels that the name may have come from one of the rhymes which went from one to twelve describing the obscenities "mother" engaged in. Paul Oliver in *Blues Fell This Morning* (London, 1960, p. 128) says of its history," Tutting in the Dozens' developed as a folk game in the late nineteenth century," but he gives no documentation for this. Peter Tamony, in a letter, suggests the derivation of the name may come from "DOZEN," v., to stun, stupefy, daze, which can be used both transitively and intransitively (*OED*). If this were true, its etymology would concur with many other Negro words which come eminently from English parlance of the eighteenth century. This would attach an English name to a phenomenon possibly brought from Africa. Newbell Niles Puckett *(Folk Beliefs of the Southern Negro*, Chapel Hill, 1926, p. 23) quoting Kingsley says, "The dominant affection in the home is the intense devotion of the African for his mother, more fights being occasioned among boys by hearing something said in disparagement of their mothers than by all other causes put together." This would place the game, or something like it, quite far back historically. The first mention I have found of the game with this name is from a popular "race" record by "Speckled Red" (Rufus Perryman) as quoted in Oliver, p. 128.

2   This is the more common way of referring to the game today. "Dozens" is not even understood by some Negroes now.

3   One will occasionally find girls making dozens-type remarks, but for the most part not in the organized fashion of the boys. The boys do not generally play in front of girls, except where one boy is trying to put another down. In this case the game can lead to a physical fight. Dollard seems to have encountered more girl "players" than I have. It certainly could not perform any similar psychosocial function among females, but the mechanism does exist as an expression of potential hostility by either sex.

4   For further discussion of "signifying" in relation to Negro life and folklore, see my article "The Changing Concept of the Negro Hero," in *The Golden Log*, Number XXXI,

Publications of the Texas Folklore Society, ed. Mody C. Boatright, Wilson M. Hudson, Allen Maxwell (Dallas, 1962), 125 ff.

5   R. F. Berdie *(Journal of Abnormal and Social Psychology*, XLII, 1947, 120–121) describes the game accurately in a note. William Elton, in two notes *(American Speech*, XXV, 1950, 148–149, 230–233) indicates a number of places in which the term is to be encountered in contexts literary and scholarly. He ties the practice up with the "joking relationship," especially among the Dahomeans and the Ashanti, an attribution which is both strange and unsound, the two phenomena being similar only in the socially permissive and initiatory functions. But "joking relationships" develop their permissiveness out of a familistic structure, and the dozens do not. See also *American Notes and Queries*, I (Dec. 1941), 133; Robert C. Elliott, *The Power of Satire* (Princeton, 1960), pp. 73–74; Dollard, n. 1.

6   Dollard's arguments are tenable from an outside view, because almost any aggression committed by the underprivileged group within a society can be seen as a "substitute aggression," a principle similar to sublimation. But looking at the problem generically, the psychosocial problem of a healthy ego development exists before any sociological situation incurs itself upon the individuals, and the dislocation of the ego through the mother-dominated system will create an anxiety situation that is only aggravated by the fact that the value which grow out of such a system often produce illegal or immoral acts in the white man's eyes. The result, as many have pointed out, is a double standard of law, with acts of violence being tolerated within the Negro group to a great extent, especially in the south. For a discussion of such problems in a vein similar to Dollard's arguments, see Hortense Powdermaker, "The Channeling of Negro Aggression by the Cultural Process," *American Journal of Sociology*, XLVIII (1943), 750–758. (I am indebted to Alan Dundes for this citation.) For a corroboration of my thesis, see *The Eighth Generation*, ed. John H. Rohrer and Munro S. Edmondson (New York, 1960) pp. 158 ff., which is an excellent recent study of gang-values.

7   For an excellent, if biased, review of the scholarship, see Melville J. Herskovits, *The Myth of the Negro Past*, (Boston, 1941; rev. ed., 1958), pp. 179 ff.

8   Rohrer and Edmondson, p. 161. The preference for girls is by no means the absolute rule.

9   Ibid., p. 163.

10 This type of insult contest is not limited to this group. It is found in many groups throughout Africa and Europe, at least. Johann Huizinga in *Homo Ludens, A Study of the Play Element in Culture* (Boston, 1950), p. 65, describes it as follows:

> The nobleman demonstrates his virtue by feats of strength, skill, courage, wit wisdom, wealth, or liberality. For want of these he may yet excel in a contest of words, that is to say, he may either himself praise the virtues in which he wishes to excel his rivals, or have them praised for him by a poet or a herald. This boosting of one's own virtue as a form of contest slips over quite naturally into contumely of one's adversary, and this in its turn becomes a contest in its own right. It is remark- able how large a place these bragging and scoffing matches occupy in the most diverse civilizations.

Earlier he has equated virtue and virility, so that the sexual nature of these contests is within his plan. Elliott (cf. n. 4) devotes a major part of his book showing how satire derives from just such contests. He adds the factor of the magic quality of words and how they can have power over an adversary. Oliver, p. I28, sees the dozens as also coming from the idea of casting spells with words. He indicates that the game developed out of a contest of real enmities, with an of- fended man "putting his foot up" (jamming the door of his cabin with his foot) and singing a blues that "put the Dozens" at the expense of his enemy, "calling out his name." This would agree in many respects with Tamony's derivation of the word (cf. n. 1).

11 Elliott, p. 78.

12 As stated above, the dozens is used by older Negroes to start a fight, especially in the army and prison situations. But here we are primarily concerned with youths.

13 "Booty" is an argot term for the female organs, or for the sexual act with a female.

See Oliver, p. 189. In this sense the word may go back, as Peter Tamony has suggested in a personal letter, once again to eighteenth-century English; see "Buckinger's Boot" in Francis Grose, *Classical Dictionary of the Vulgar Tongue* (London, 1931, reprint edition, ed. Eric Partridge), p. 56.

14 The word "cake," meaning any potential female sexual partner, has probably come from this saying, and has found wide acceptance in jazz circles; see *Dictionary of American Slang*, ed. Harold Wentworth and Stuart Berg Flexner (New York, 1960), p. 84.

4

The La Have Island General Store: Sociability and Verbal Art in a Nova Scotia Community

Richard Bauman

One of the rocks on which the ethnography of speaking is built is that the role of speaking in culture and society is cross-culturally variable and diverse. For some peoples, speaking will be the focus of a high degree of interest, elaboration, and evaluation, while in other groups it will receive relatively little conscious attention. A major part of our collective ethnographic task is to establish the full range of variability in this sphere. Despite this charter, however, there has been a clear bias in our work toward the groups in which speaking is a cultural focus; either we become interested in the ethnography of speaking because language turns out to be quite important in a group we are working on, or we make our choices of groups in which to do ethnographies of speaking on the basis of the apparent importance of speaking in their culture because time for research is becoming ever more precious. Certainly both sets of fac-

tors have entered into my own decisions to work on the Quakers and the Vincentians.

To be sure, we do have a few glimpses of the other side of the coin, as in Peter Gardner's description of the Paliyans, for example,[1] but note how often this case must be cited as the one example of a group with a minimal and negative concern for language because we have no others.[2] If we are to avoid skewing the still developing field of inquiry in which we are engaged, we need to start bringing in accounts of more sociolinguistically modest groups together with their more talkative brethren, with a view toward the larger goal of constructing typologies of the role of speaking in culture and society.

The reader will have surmised by now that he is being set up for a discussion of a group that does not care very much about speaking, and he will be right. The La Have Islanders are

Richard Bauman, "The La Have Island General Store: Sociability and Verbal Art in a Nova Scotia Community," pp. 330–343 from *Journal of American Folklore* 85(338), 1972.

The Anthropology of Performance: A Reader, First Edition. Edited by Frank J. Korom.
© 2013 John Wiley & Sons, Inc. Published 2013 by John Wiley & Sons, Inc.

not Paliyans, to be sure, but they are also very far from being Vincentians, or Chamula, or Cuna. They exhibit a rather narrow range of interest and elaboration with regard to speaking, with almost all their sociolinguistic interest and attention focused on one speech situation – evening talk at the general store. Of course, as in all human societies, speaking is an aspect of a wide range of other activities, but in none of these does speaking take on any significance for its own sake as it does in this particular setting. This fact alone should be of interest on a comparative level, but one of the things I hope to demonstrate in this article is that its intracultural implications are of wider significance as well.

My interest in the general store stems from one of the principal objectives of my fieldwork in the La Have Islands, namely, to investigate the esthetic of speaking in La Have Island society. As an anthropological folklorist who has been strongly influenced by sociolinguistics, I have for some time had a general predisposition toward "verbal art" as a conceptual organizing principle for my research.[3] Yet, because of certain directions my work has taken lately, it has struck me forcefully that only a small segment of the field marked out by the term "verbal art" is ever actually exploited by the coiners of the term or those who have adopted it. Where, for instance, is the concept used to guide attention to culture-specific folk conceptions of what constitutes the domain of verbal art within particular cultures? By defining verbal art in terms of esthetic principles and genres from without, anthropological folklorists have begged the question of what might appropriately be considered verbal art from within the other cultures with which they are concerned. It was this latter consideration that guided that part of my fieldwork on which this paper is based. I wanted to determine whether there is anything within the structuring of speech behavior by the La Have Islanders that might appropriately and productively be regarded as constituting verbal art.

For the purposes of this article I am concerned ultimately with a culture-specific esthetic of speaking, not with an esthetic of those forms that folklorists have conventionally been interested in. Though the islanders'

standards for deciding what constitutes a good story, for example, will be brought out in the discussion that follows, I am really concerned with a more abstract esthetic, one organized in terms of which segment of the speech economy of a community is isolated or foregrounded from the rest, marked out for special attention, and capable of evoking pleasure in the participants. This matter will be discussed further at the end of the article, following a short presentation of some background material on the islands themselves and an extended account of the central speech situation, evening talk at the general store.[4]

The La Have Islands are located off the shore of Lunenburg County on the southwest coast of Nova Scotia, between the mouths of the La Have and Petite Rivers. The group consists of about twenty named islands, fourteen of which have been inhabited at one time or another by the forbears of the present inhabitants. The islands vary significantly in size, from little more than exposed rocks to several square miles in area, with the houses distributed around the shore in settlements ranging from one to more than thirty households per island. Local communities are not confined to single islands, for segments of some adjacent islands are tied together by the intervening channels into single communities, while various parts of other islands belong to different communities. This region has always been one where people are oriented as much to the water as they are to the land. At the height of Island prosperity, during the economic heyday between 1890 and 1925, there were approximately one hundred households on the islands; at present, a number of formerly inhabited islands are deserted, and the permanent population numbers in the neighborhood of one hundred fifty people. An increasing number of vacation residents swells the population somewhat during the summer months.

The islands were first visited by de Monts and Champlain in 1604, and they figured in a number of land grants from the British crown during the eighteenth century.[5] However, it was not until the late 1840s that a significant permanent population was established. The growth and development of the islands coincided with the development of the Lunenburg

County fishing industry; with the depletion of the inshore fishery and the mechanization of offshore fishing, the area has undergone a steady decline. Lobstering is the mainstay of the present economy, supplemented by some inshore fishing, but economic opportunity is severely lacking in the area and most of the young people are leaving. While the islanders are still very traditional in outlook, the mechanization of the fishing industry, depopulation, the advent of radio and television, compulsory education in mainland schools, and access to the automobile (two of the islands may be reached by causeway and bridge) have altered the organization of expressive behavior on the islands quite considerably in recent years. The heyday of the period represented in the present article ended thirty to thirty-five years ago.

During this earlier period, the people of the islands were served by two general stores, both located on the same island, but at opposite ends and serving different communities. The one in which I am particularly interested was located at the north end of Bell's Island, facing Bush Island across the narrow channel that separates the two. This store, called Sperry's store after the family that owned it, drew its trade from the few residents of that end of Bell's Island, as well as Bush Island, George's Island, Mosher's Island, Covey's Island, and Hirtle's Island. Most of its customers, because of its location, had to reach the store by rowing, a skill acquired early on the islands and possessed by both men and women.

The store itself was a fairly large rectangular structure about sixty feet long, built out over the water with a wharf alongside. Three of the walls were lined with counters and shelves, and in the open space outlined by the counter were four or five tables for playing cards in the evening and the inevitable stove surrounded by stools, nail kegs, and benches.

In the great tradition of the North American general store, Sperry's store was stocked with an enormous range of merchandise, including hardware, soft goods, tea, sugar, flour, canned goods, fishing supplies, kerosene, clothing, housewares, and so on. For most of their food, the islanders were self-sufficient, since fish, lobsters, other shellfish, and waterfowl were plentiful, and every household had a vegetable garden, a cow, and perhaps a pig and some chickens. In general, the store filled those needs of the people that fell between what they produced for their own subsistence and the special items that were purchased on infrequent trips to Bridgewater or Lunenburg.

Shopping at the general store was never a completely utilitarian activity, for all the islanders took a certain pleasure in the opportunities for sociability that the store afforded. If possible, no matter how small the purchase, customers stayed a while to talk with the storekeeper or those of their neighbors whose visit to the store coincided with their own. With the exception of a few old, retired men, how ever, who occasionally congregated around the store during the day or young men who sometimes gathered there on stormy days in winter, daytime visits to the store were chiefly for the purpose of buying something. On winter nights, though, the situation was otherwise, with sociability – the association with others for the sheer pleasure of the interaction – becoming the primary purpose of visiting the store.

As a people who depended upon fishing for their livelihood, the La Have Islanders had little leisure time during the spring, summer, and early fall months when the weather allowed them to be on the water. Those of the men who did not sail on the "saltbankers" from Riverport, La Have, and Lunenburg to fish the Grand Banks, or work on the "coasters," which carried saltfish to the West Indies and returned with Turk's Island salt, worked at the extremely arduous task of inshore fishery. The Island men were thus away from home for months at a time, or else occupied from before dawn until dark with the catching, cleaning, and salting of fish. It was only during the late fall and winter months, when the days were too short and the weather too cold for fishing, that they could enjoy the luxury of leisurely evenings, and it was on these fall and winter evenings that they gathered at the general store. Every night in this season, from early evening until eleven or twelve o'clock, the store was filled with anywhere from twenty-five to forty men who gathered to enjoy each other's company in cardplaying and conversation.

The gathering at the store was an exclusively male activity, although both sexes recognized it as the premier speech situation of the community. Women might come in to buy something in the evening, but they preferred to leave the store to the men, and those few women who did come did not stay. Children, too, were excluded from attendance, largely because parents did not want them out at night. Once again, however, those who did come, to make a purchase, for example, were not allowed to linger, because the language and conversation of the card-players often became too rough for their tender ears. By his early teens, a boy might be suffered to listen to the conversation from on the fringes of the group, but it was not until he reached the age of seventeen or eighteen that he would be allowed to speak, though only infrequently would he think of doing so. From the early twenties, eligibility for active participation increased roughly with age and worldly experience. The younger men did not say much, but listened with interest to the "old fellers that knowed everything" and "had it further back," who dominated the conversation.

There were two principal activities that occupied the attention of the men gathered at the store, namely, playing cards and talking. It is clear, however, that in the eyes of the participants talking was what the gathering was really about, with the cardplaying providing simply another level of recreation for those in the group who wished to play.

The conversation was organized chiefly into three genres: "news," "yarns" (sometimes called "stories"), and "arguments." News consisted of matters of general interest pertaining to the day-to-day affairs of the community, including such topics as the price of fish, local politics, or a neighbor's health. While topics of this kind might evoke considerable interest for a time, they represented a rather limited conversational resource in the final analysis, because they had not yet been fully assimilated into the individual experience of the participants, and the true focus of the gatherings at the store was the presentation of personal experiences and individualized points of view. That is, the gatherings at the store represented an occasion in which the display,

maintenance, and development of personal identity was of paramount importance, through the exploitation of a conversational resource in personal terms.[6] The chief vehicles of this personal expression were yarns and arguments.

In La Have Island parlance, a yarn was a narrative, told and accepted as true, about something that transcended common knowledge, experience, or expectation. The principal feature of a yarn was that it dealt with personal experience: "each person would tell of his own experience, whichever way it happened"; "one feller seen it, he experienced it – then he'd tell it." A second requirement, however, was that the experience be in some way special in order to be foregrounded into narrative. Although the realms of experience from which yarns were drawn were common ones, the routine experiences of one's everyday life were not recounted as yarns. Fishing, for example, constituted a heavily exploited conversational resource, but always with emphasis upon an uncommonly heavy catch or an especially big fish, like a halibut, or an especially risky venture, like harpooning tuna. Uniqueness and novelty, in fact, were the standards of excellence in judging stories and storytelling; I found no indication that the formal excellence of the narrative or the performance skill of the narrator entered into the evaluation process at any point. In fact, they seem not to have been noted at any conscious level, if at all; this will be discussed further toward the end of the article.

Because they traveled more widely and, consequently, had a wider range of novel experience, the men who fished the Grand Banks or worked the coasters were generally accounted to have better stories and thus to be better storytellers. "The ones who traveled the most could tell the most and best." The old fishermen and sea captains were full of yarns about going to sea; they had been places where "everything was new to 'em." When they returned from their voyages, "they would sit down and tell all their experience – what they went through on their trip," "places where they was and what they seen." These were stories of storms, shipwrecks, hard captains, fast ships, and remote places. Thus, in the view of one inshore fisherman, "the men that went to Labrador – how they lived there in amongst those people – that would be quite a story."

Besides fishing, the second most important conversational resource exploited in narrative form was the supernatural; every evening had its complement of yarns about ghosts, spirits, revenants, spectral apparitions, and forerunners, strange occurrences that presaged impending disaster (see Appendix, Text A). The preoccupation of the islanders of a generation ago with the supernatural is still often remarked upon by their descendants: "them times you wouldn't go out the door without seem things"; "there were so many ghost stories at those times"; "every yard of road had its ghost."[7] Nowadays, the islanders are more inclined to seek rational explanations for unaccountable occurrences, but a generation ago every one on the islands had his share of experiences with the supernatural, ranging from the sighting of fire balls or fiery ships ("all them old people seen these ships and things"), to confrontations with specters in human or animal form, hearing of ghostly voices, and experiencing of forerunners.

The last major resource out of which yarns were built was the memorable local occurrence, local happenings that were readily explainable or plausible, but nevertheless unusual. Included here were accounts of pranks, the exploits of local characters, humorous situations, and the like (see Appendix, Text B).

I have stressed the fact that yarns were fundamentally personal narratives. That is, they recounted experiences in which the narrator was personally involved, either as participant or witness. However, if an especially memorable story was markedly appropriate to a particular conversational context but its "owner" was not present, it might be told by someone else, but it would always be attributed to its source, the person with whom it was directly identified. In a sense, this practice preserved the element of personal involvement, by placing the secondary narrator in a chain of transmission that linked him through his source to the event itself. The islands were settled in the 1840s and 1850s, and the Lunenburg County fishing industry was established during the same period; since all yarns related to one

or another of these settings, no storyteller in the store was ever more than one or two generations removed from events that might figure in yarns. In general, however, the preference was overwhelmingly for yarns of immediate personal experience, and people tended not to borrow each other's yarns, familiar though they were through repeated retelling. This tendency, I believe, is related to Creighton's observation that traditional Märchen are extremely rare in Lunenburg County.[8]

A corollary of the personal nature of the yarns was that they were told and accepted as essentially true: "most of them fellers, you could believe what they said." The tendency was to give people credit for being best qualified to give an account of their own experience: "you would have to believe it the way it was in their time." Still, it was commonly recognized that storytellers tend to embellish their yarns for greater personal effect. As described by contemporary islanders, "they'd tell a story tonight and a week from tonight it would be a little better." The core of truth was insisted upon, however – "they weren't really lyin' about their stories; after a while they just got polished up a bit." "Maybe somebody would add a little bit onto it – make it sound better – but most of it was true." Those few storytellers who went beyond the limits of creative license to complete distortion or fabrication were singled out for gentle ridicule and not taken very seriously. Everyone knew who they were.

This balance between the requirement of truthfulness in telling yarns, sanctioned by the group, and the impulse toward stretching one's narratives for self-aggrandizement[9] provides an entree into the structural and functional dynamics of the larger event. It is clear from the nature of the genre that yarns were a means of organizing personal experience for presentation to others. Much of what the Island men did, they did alone or away from their home community, whether in shore fishing, offshore fishing, sailing on coasting voyages, or simply going to and from the store at night. There were, of course, numbers of communal activities, like getting together to clean the fish on shore, but these were not activities central to the definition of the male role and the establishment of individual status, like fishing or maintaining composure in the face of the super-natural. Consequently, much of what the men felt to be important about themselves could only be im parted to others by telling them about it. By the same token, these were the kinds of things each man wanted to know about others. The sessions at the store rep-resented a forum in which this information could be exchanged. They afforded the partic-ipants a continuous opportunity to engage in personal and social identity-building by pre-senting the self in personal narrative and receiv-ing like accounts about others in the same form. As Watson and Potter suggest, "sociable inter-action gives form to the image of self and the image of the other; it gives validity and conti-nuity to the identifications which are the source of an individual's self-esteem."[10]

Through sociable interaction in the store, each participant engaged in image-building in several dimensions. By recounting his personal experiences with reference to activities that constituted conversational resources for the group, a man could demonstrate his involve-ment in spheres of activity that were of impor-tance to his fellows. This contributed to establishing and validating his social identity, his membership and status within the group. That this identity building was a cumulative and progressive process is evidenced by the grading of participation in the conversation on the basis of increasing age and experience, and by the repetition on many occasions of each man's best accounts. At the same time, however, he was able to demonstrate his uniqueness as an individual by presenting only his unique and special experiences in the form of yarns, for this selection was a require-ment of the genre. Finally, he was able to maximize his self- and public image through the licensed elaboration of his narrative. Par-ticipants were willing to grant each other suffi-cient latitude to put their best image forward, in a sense, in order to be granted the same opportunity to represent themselves to best advantage in their own yarns.

It is of interest in connection with this pro-cess of image-building that, although telling yarns was an important component of the process of establishing a social identity, being a good storyteller was not itself a significant identity feature. This situation contrasts with that in other societies, the Cuna, for example, in which being a good speaker or storyteller is relevant to the definition of the ideal man. Here is a dimension in which we may be explicit about the ways that speaking is or is not impor-tant in a particular society.

When we shift our focus from the individual to the community, the sessions at the store assume another functional dimension. The islanders lived a life full of strong external forces and risks, from the natural and the supernatural world. Many of these, as noted, were confronted alone but were constantly discussed with others at the general store. The sessions at the store thus constituted a forum in which wisdom could be shared, and safe, proper, and productive reactions to situa-tions and forces that any member of the group might potentially encounter could be shared. It is here, perhaps, that the limitations on stretch-ing stories might be accounted for. While a certain amount of exaggeration might be toler-ated as an outlet for self-aggrandizement in recounting one's experiences, the community had much to gain by sanctioning relative accu-racy as well, in order that each man's experi-ence might contribute to the communal wisdom. From this perspective, telling yarns in group situations may be seen as a kind of adaptive mechanism, making available to all the benefits of individual wisdom borne of experience. By participating in the sessions at the store, an individual was able to become familiar with a wide range of situations as well as possible responses to those situations, against the day when he too might confront similar situations. Hence the preeminence of the older men in the sessions, since they had a lifetime of experience to draw upon and present to the others.

This interplay between the individual and the social dimensions of the event may be distinguished in the internal structure of the event itself. Each participant's contribution was a personal one, with emphasis upon the individuality and unique ness of his experi-ence. At the same time, however, these indi-vidual contributions were bound together by a chain of association, a process in which each yarn was elicited by association, through some sharing of a common ground, with the preceding one, each individual making his personal contribution by drawing on a common conversational resource. An informant explained the dynamic thus: "some feller would tell a yarn, and by the time he was finished the next one would have one that led off of it – something that he had heard or saw." For example, "one man would mention a port and another man would have been there and that's how the yarns came out." In this way, the tension between the individual and the communal provided the energy by which the event proceeded.

The role of arguments in the sessions at the store was consistent with, and in a sense complementary to, the use of yarns; arguments represented another, more active and aggressive, way of accomplishing the same things. For the most part, arguments exploited the same conversational resources as the exchange of yarns, with perhaps a heavier emphasis on matters having to do with fishing and the sea, such as who were the hardest captains, which were the fastest ships, what was the best kind of engine for fishing boats, and so on. Around election time, politics constituted a special focus for debate: "them older fellows, they stuck up for their parties – they was all ripe for a row."

Yarns and arguments were not mutually exclusive, for the principal means of upholding one's position in an argument was to "back it up by telling a story on it." "Always to back up an argument they'd have a local story or a personal one." It is generally agreed that those with the best stories were the ones who consistently won the arguments.

Perhaps the most useful way of comprehending the relationship between the yarns and arguments exchanged in the store is to view them as tendencies along a conversational continuum, the poles of which may be represented by Watson and Potter's distinction between "matching" and "polarization." "In matching," according to Watson and Potter, "individuals assert that they are in fact alike, because they have – or say they have – similar positions, attributes, views, or experiences. In polarization, individuals differentiate themselves from one another, exaggerating their

differences, as in teasing, baiting, or argument."[11] Arguments are thus to be placed near the polarization end of the continuum, since they clearly involve relatively greater emphasis upon individuality and the differentiation of one's position from that of one's opponent. They fall short of full polarization, however, to the extent that they draw upon a common realm of experience. A certain amount of matching was apparently at the base of most of the arguments at the store insofar as the disputants addressed themselves to problems and situations common to all parties to the argument; it was the understandings and responses that differed.

The other mode of conversation, in which yarns were exchanged more neutrally, would fall closer to the matching end of the continuum. But even here there were elements of polarization, in that each participant was concerned to establish his own individuality and place himself in the most favorable light vis-à-vis the others. It is interesting in this connection that the women of the community, from their vantage point as outsiders to the sessions at the store, picked up on the element of contest in the interaction as its most prominent feature. Whereas the men insisted on the core of truthfulness in their narratives, woman after woman told me that the organizing principle of the sessions was to see "which could tell the biggest lie," "one just tryin' to beat the other."

A final point to be made about the arguments at the store, underscoring their sociable nature, is that they were event-specific. That is, the antagonisms that manifested themselves in arguments at the store did not carry over into relations outside the store: "they'd argue a point nearly to blows, but they didn't wind up bad friends or anything"; "when it was over, that was it."

At the outset of this article, I indicated that my study of the talk at the general store grew out of an interest in the La Have Islanders' esthetic of spoken language – which segment of the whole domain of speaking in their culture is esthetically marked by the people themselves, and in what way. I saw this – and still do – as a way around a priori and ethnocentric definitions of things like folklore and verbal art, that is, a way of getting at verbal art in culture-specific terms. It remains now for me to make explicit my grounds for discussing the sessions at the store with reference to an esthetic of speaking.

When I embarked on my research I had certain preconceptions about how the islanders' esthetic might manifest itself. One possibility was that there might be a set of esthetic norms attaching to the formal features of the language and governing their manipulation for their own sake. Much of our text-oriented literary and anthropological theory concerning poetic language or verbal art is framed in these terms. For example, building upon Havranek's notion of "foregrounding" ("the use of the devices of the language in such a way that this use itself attracts attention and is perceived as uncommon"), Mukařovský writes: "In poetic language foregrounding achieves maximum intensity to the extent of pushing communication into the background as the objective of expression and of being used for its own sake."[12] But similar kinds of esthetic organizing principles have been found through ethnographic investigations of folk esthetics, as for example by Barre Toelken among the Navaho.[13]

Another possibility involved the use of a particular symbolic attribute of verbal behavior to distinguish the esthetic from the nonesthetic. In Chamula, for example, as described by Gary Gossen, heat is the esthetic organizing principle and relates to the closeness of the type of speaking to the order of the sun-deity; verbal art is speech by people whose hearts are heated.[14]

A third possibility was that an esthetic might be framed in terms of a system of genres considered by the people to be artistic forms or subject to esthetic evaluation. Here again, there are many analytical definitions of folklore or verbal art, of the kind we call enumerative, which consist of a list of genres, as for example, Melville Herskovits', "the folklore of non-literate peoples consists of their myths, tales, proverbs, riddles, and verse, together with their music."[15] However, I was concerned here with the possibility of a folk esthetic organized primarily in terms of an inventory of artistic verbal forms.

Finally, I had in mind the possibility of an esthetic framed in behavioral, or performance, terms, along the lines that Roger Abrahams and I have discussed for the Vincentians.[16] Here it seems to make the best sense to think in terms of a range of speaking behaviors or speech acts available for the exercise of behavioral stylization, that is, performance skills.

When I started in to work, however, asking questions aimed at special kinds of language or special kinds of talk or special ways of talking, people kept telling me about a place, the general store, or, rather, I came to realize, about a scene – the evening sessions at the store that I have described in this paper.

In trying to explore the esthetic dimensions of this event in terms of the factors outlined above, I soon discovered that none of my informants gave the slightest indication that they considered any kind of speech at the store in any way special in terms of formal linguistic devices. In fact, try as I might, I could not discover that they paid any conscious attention to formal features of language at all. Nor was there any symbolic feature within the domain of speaking that might have served as an esthetic organizing principle.

Genres, at least, looked more promising, since yarns figured so prominently in the sessions at the store, and yarns immediately sound like good conventional grist for the folklorist's mill. Further checking, however, revealed that yarns of precisely the same kind as were told at the store were told at other places as well, such as in homes, fish stores, wharves, and boats, and were not considered special in those contexts. Certainly, more yarns were told at the store than anywhere else, and it is possible that they tended to be longer or more elaborate in that setting, although I am not certain that this was the case. The point is, though, that a yarn was not in itself any more special than a question or a greeting or any other named speech form, and the special quality of talk at the store must therefore be sought elsewhere.

The next possibility was performance. Here again, there seemed to be no sense of awareness of performance skills possessed or displayed by those who took part in the sessions at the store. When I asked what made a good talker or a good storyteller, the answer, as noted earlier, was that the older men with the widest range of experience were the best talkers and story-tellers. But this had to do with the number and content of their yarns, not with perform-ance skills. Though telling yarns certainly had its self-reflective aspects, these did not extend to the style of storytelling; one simply and natu-rally "told it the way it happened," according to former participants. This is not to suggest that there were no features of perform ance style that distinguished storytellers on the La Have Islands, merely that such features were not noted or cultivated on a conscious level. Thus, although stories and storytellers were subjected to evaluative judgments, the stan-dards of evaluation had nothing to do with the way a story was told, and it is not therefore appropriate to consider a good story or a good storyteller within the compass of an esthetic of speaking.

At this point it may appear that we have disposed of just about everything that might serve as a significant organizing principle for any esthetic of speaking worth considering. At the very least, it is probably reasonable to suggest that an esthetic lacking in the above dimensions does not argue for a very developed sense of language. But this is the very point I raised at the beginning of the article, namely, that the La Have Islanders really did not pay very much attention to speaking. Nevertheless, I would go on to maintain that there still remains a dimension of the islanders' speech economy that is properly and productively recognizable as constituting a folk esthetic and that it allows us to add significantly to our equipment for understanding the esthetic dimensions of speaking behavior. To be explicit, I would maintain that the esthetic attaches to the speech situation itself, the talk session at the general store as a culturally defined scene. What is apparently going on in the culture of the La Have Islanders is that within the whole range of speech situations making up the speech economy of the islanders, the session at the store is singled out as special, isolated from the others and enjoyed for its own sake, because talking there may be enjoyed for its own sake and not as part of another activity or for some instrumental purpose. In other words, the fact that this situation is set aside

for sociability, pure and simple, makes it spe-cial. We might say that the islanders have singled out this speech situation and marked it with what Mukařovský calls the esthetic function, which isolates or foregrounds the activity itself, causes a maximum focusing of attention upon it, and endows it with the ability to evoke pleasure in the participants.[17] Where the esthetic function is dominant, in Mukařovský's formulation, as it is in the islander's view of talk at the general store as an event, we are in the realm of art.[18]

What we have, then, is an esthetic of speech situations, not of speaking as such, to be added to our typology of folk esthetic organizing principles, which has heretofore included poetic language, special genres, and perform-ance. Talk at the store is thus the art form of speech situations on the La Have Islands, for it is to the realm of situations that the esthetic of speaking applies. This is perhaps a rather mini-mal esthetic, reflecting the lack of focus on verbal behavior generally on the part of the islanders. Nevertheless, the same principle of an esthetic of speech situations may be devel-oped in a more wide-ranging and elaborate way in other cultures, possibly in combination with the other esthetic elements we have noted or with still others to be uncovered by further research.

It is particularly striking in this connection that the folk esthetic of the La Have Islanders corresponds with one of the most significant analytical insights ever achieved concerning sociability, by the man who first drew attention to sociability as a sociological phenomenon, Georg Simmel. Simmel identified sociability as being characterized by talking "for the sake of talking . . . talk becomes its own purpose," seeking it as the exercise of the forms of soci-ation freed of their instrumental purpose or content.[19] While he overstated this latter aspect somewhat in neglecting a whole range of per-sonal and social functions that sociability may fulfill (some of these have been dealt with in the body of the paper), he was certainly correct in terms of relative emphasis. The interesting thing is that his understanding of sociability in these terms led Simmel to speak of "the socio-logical art form of sociability,"[20] thus identify-ing sociability as an esthetically marked form of social interaction. Of course, insofar as sociability is a verbal activity, we may consider sociable events as belonging analytically to the realm of verbal art. The La Have Islanders, in singling out the sessions at the store and marking them with the esthetic function, have done precisely this on the folk level as well.[21]

APPENDIX

The following narratives are illustrative of the kinds of yarns told during the evening sessions at the general store. Both were recorded from Mr. Howard Bush of Bush Island on July 27, 1970. Mr. Bush was eighty-seven at the time of recording.

Text A is a yarn of an encounter with the supernatural experienced by the narrator's father, who was thus the original teller of the story. Text B is an account of memorable local occurrence and perhaps comes closest to the way yarns were originally related in the store, since the narrator was a direct participant in the event being recounted.

It should be noted that neither text was recorded within the context of a session at the store, since these no longer take place. The informant had participated in many such sessions in his youth, but had not been an active participant in the exchange of yarns because of his youth. Moreover, the telling of yarns of either type no longer occurs at any time under normal circumstances; these texts were called up from the informant's memory in response to my elicitation. Thus, in terms of Dell Hymes' suggestive distinction between "reporting" and "performing" traditional material,[22] these texts represent a combination of the two: the informant is performing insofar as he is attempting to make his presentation of the yarns consistent with the traditional manner of storytelling, but he is also reporting a mode of narration in which he never fully engaged and which is no longer practiced.

TEXT A

HOWARD BUSH: My father and his brother, my uncle, went gunnin'. And there was a bunch of lords [mallards], we called 'em, tending out the cellar [?] in the Green Head. And they knowed . . . they knowed they tended there, and they left one mornin', 'fore daylight for to kill some of 'em. And they took their dog – everybody had a dog at that time – they was all . . . all the young men was gunners at that time, and everybody had a dog. A dog that in . . . that went in the water, to bring a duck if you killed it. Then they went out this mornin', 'fore daylight, and they waited till it got light, and when it begin to get light, the ducks begin to come in the place they knowed. They was so used to diving there and gettin their living there, that they knowed the spots. They lived in a small place. And, uh, my father, he crawled out, he was to fire at the ducks. And my uncle, laid in the . . . just a footpath of a road went along the bank, just up clear o' the sea. He laid in back of that in the bushes so he was . . . 'nough so he was hid, a holdin' the dog, that the dog wouldn't jump out and scare the ducks. And so they laid there a little while, and, uh, my father was crawlin' out after the ducks. And, by and by, my uncle looked down the . . . down the road, down the shore a ways, and he saw a man comin', walkin' right up in open sight. Well, he thought to himself, "That's funny – the ducks don't see that man." That's 'cause when a duck see a man he'll fly right away, he'll get up right away out the way. But the ducks didn't see him. He walked up. He had on a jacket, a green short jacket, and a cap with a green glazed bill just on . . . green underneath. And he walked with his two arms right straight down, not swingin', but just hangin' straight down. And a gun under the one arm. I don't know which arm it would've been. And a strap 'round the gun and up 'round his shoulder. And he walked right straight up on 'em. And the . . . the fright struck him – when he began to get, well,, fair-handed, the fright struck him. He knowed it was no livin' man. And he jumped up, him and the dog. And the dog growled. The dog growled and his hair stuck up, well, from the back of his neck clean to his tail [laughs] – right up on end, but he wouldn't bark. Wouldn't make . . . wouldn't make a sound, but to growl. And when he jumped up, why, the ducks jumped up. And he waved for my daddy – then he knowed there was somet'in' wrong. And he came up in where they was, and they started off. They started off up the shore, the way they come. And every now and then they'd look 'round at this man, comin' behind 'em a little ways – I wouldn't know how far to say, but a little way. He followed them. And there was a little pond, at the edge was a . . . a little . . . yes, a pond, with a little rock on, laid right on the edge of . . . edge of the pond. The man followed them till he come to this rock. And the second to last time that they looked back, to see if he was comin', he was standin' on the rock, half bent. . . stooped, you know, lookin in the pond. And they looked ahead and made out maybe three or four steps, maybe not that, maybe one step. And looked 'round again, and when they looked 'round, well, he wasn't there. He was gone.

INTERVIEWER: Disappeared.

HB: Disappeared, that quick. So it wasn't livin' man. No livin' man about that. That's a true story. And that's all I can tell you about that. But the . . . but the pond now has gone shut. The sea's got everything leveled off, just right down to the edge of the sea.

INT: So it was both your father and your uncle that saw that man ?

HB: Oh, yes, yes, the two of 'em.

INT: Your father would tell about it?

HB: Oh, yes, he told it.

Text B

INTERVIEWER: One story I know you know about was Frank Bell and the eggs.

HOWARD BUSH: Right. Yes, that I know is true. That I seen him do. I sat right, right in the shop and seen him . . . seen him do that. He always used to torment Aubrey Sperry, that was the boss of the shop, 'bout he could, uh, he could suck three dozen eggs and eat the shell of the last one. Well, every time he came to the shop he'd be tormenting Aubrey. And at last, uh, Aubrey got kind of tired of it. One day he come up, startin' in, he says, "I can suck three dozen eggs and eat the shell of the last one, and I want a bet for five dollars." Aubrey goes for the till, and he lays down the five dollar bill, and he counts out three dozen eggs. And uh . . . oh, there was,

uh, I don't know, maybe seven or eight young fellers – lot though – not my age, but young, young fellers, settin' 'round, and all hands begin to laugh. Well, he thought they was laughin' at him, while he didn't take right ahold of the eggs. He was going to take back water . . . and it looked like if he was going to take back water. But we laughed at him, and then that give him . . . he went to work at it. Now, I don't know how many he sucked. He punched the holes in the ends and then. . . . I guess he must have sucked pretty near a dozen the first time. Then he lit his old pipe. He had a little smoke, not very long. He took a couple more – half a dozen or so. And that's the way . . . till he had them all down. He sucked so many and then he'd have a little smoke. And he talked a very, very short time, and he left. "I guess I'll go home." He went down the road – not very far down the road. There was a man coming up while he was going down – they passed when they was comin' up – and they seen where he stood right over there and vomit them up. He put his finger down, you see, and he vomit them up, so that they wouldn't make him sick [laughs].

INT: Did he eat the shell of the last one?

HB: But he didn't eat the shell of the last one, though it wasn't mentioned. But I don't know if Aubrey . . . if Aubrey forgot that or not. But he should have ate the shell of the last one, or not got the five dollars.

INT: He got the five dollars all right?

HB: Yes, he got the five dollars. He give him the five dollars.

NOTES

1 Peter Gardner, "Symetric Respect and Memorate Knowledge: The Structure and Ecology of Individualistic Culture," *Southwestern Journal of Anthropology*, 22 (1966), 389–415.

2 See, for example, Dell Hymes, "Models of the Interaction of Language and Social Setting," *Journal of Social Issues*, 23 (1967), 10; "Competence and Performance in Linguistic Theory" [plus Discussion], in *Language Acquisition: Models and Methods*, ed. Renira Huxley and Elisabeth Ing ram (London and New York, 1971), 27;

"Sociolinguistics and Ethnography of Speaking," in *Social Anthropology and Language*, ed. Edwin Ardener (London, 1971), 81; "The Contribution of Folklore to Sociolinguistic Research," in *Toward New Perspectives in Folklore*, ed. Americo Paredes and Richard Bauman (Austin, 1972), 44.

3 William Bascom, "Verbal Art," *Journal American Folklore*, 68 (1955), 245–252.

4 Compare William Faris, "The Dynamics of Verbal Exchange: A Newfoundland Example," *Anthropologica*, 8 (1966), 235–248.

5 Information concerning the history, population, and language of Lunenburg County may be found in Helen Creighton, *Folklore of Lunenburg County* (Ottowa, 1950); Mather Byles DesBrisay, *History of the County of Lunenburg*, 3rd ed. (Bridgewater, N.S. 1967) Murray B. Emeneau, "The Dialect of Lunenburg, Nova Scotia," *Language*, II (1935), 140–147; H. Rex Wilson, "The Dialect of Lunenburg County, Nova Scotia," PhD dissertation, University of Michigan, 1958.

6 I have been strongly influenced at various points in this analysis by the perceptive and illuminating discussion of sociability of Jeanne Watson and Robert J. Potter, "An Analytic Unit for the Study of Interaction," *Human Relations*, 15 (1962), 245–263; the term "conversational resource" is theirs.

7 An indication of the importance of the supernatural in La Have Island culture may be gained from a perusal of Creighton, chapters I-V.

8 Ibid., 139.

9 The aspect of self-aggrandizement in personal narratives is noted and labelled by William Labov and Joshua Waletzky, "Narrative Analysis: Oral Versions of Personal Experience," in *Essays on the Verbal and Visual Arts*, ed. June Helm (Seattle, 1967), Watson and Potter, 263, make a similar point concerning the combination of fact and fiction in what they call "sociable legends."

10 Watson and Potter, 246.

11 Ibid., 256.

12 Bohuslav Havránek, "The Functional Differentiation of the Standard Language," in *A Prague School Reader on Esthetics, Literary Structure, and Style*, ed. Paul L. Garvin (Washington, D.C., 1964), 10; Jan Mukarovský, "Standard Language and Poetic Language," ibid., 19.

13 J. Barre Toelken, "The 'Pretty Language' of Yellowman: Genre, Mode, and Texture in Navaho Coyote Narratives," *Genre*, 2 (1969), 211–235.

14 Gary Gossen, "To Speak with a Heated Heart: Chamula Canons of Style and Good Performance," in *Talk: Explorations in the Ethnography of Speaking*, ed. Richard Bauman and Joel Sherzer (Cambridge University Press, 1974), 389–416.

15 Melville Herskovits, *Cultural Anthropology* (New York, 1955), 267.

16 Roger Abrahams and Richard Bauman, "Sense and Nonsense in St. Vincent: Speech Behavior and Decorum in a Caribbean Community," *American Anthropologist*, 73 (1971), 762–772.

17 Jan Mukarovský, *Aesthetic Function, Norm and Value as Social Facts*, trans. Mark E. Suino (Ann Arbor, Mich., 1970), 21-22.

18 Ibid., 7.

19 Georg Simmel, *The Sociology of Georg Simmel*, ed. Kurt Wolff (Glencoe, Ill., 1950), 52.

20 Ibid., 47.

21 This paper has benefited from the critical comments of Dan Ben-Amos and Joel Sherzer, which are hereby gratefully acknowledged.

22 Dell Hymes, "Breakthrough into Performance," in *Folklore: Communication and Performance*, ed. Dan Ben-Amos and Kenneth Goldstein (The Hague, Mouton, 1975).

5

Proverbs and the Ethnography of Speaking Folklore

E. Ojo Arewa and Alan Dundes

"I know the proverbs, but I don't know how to apply them."

Introduction

Like other forms of folklore, proverbs may serve as impersonal vehicles for personal communication. A parent may well use a proverb to direct a child's action or thought, but by using a proverb, the parental imperative is externalized and removed somewhat from the individual parent. The guilt or responsibility for directing the child is projected on to the anonymous past, the anonymous folk. A child knows that the proverb used by the scolding parent was not made up by that parent. It is a proverb from the cultural past whose voice speaks truth in traditional terms. It is the "One," the "Elders," or the "They" in "They say," who direct. The parent is but the instrument through which the proverb speaks to the audience.

The impersonal power of proverbs is perhaps most apparent in the well-known African judicial processes in which the participants argue with proverbs intended to serve as past precedents for present actions. In European courtrooms, of course, lawyers cite previous cases to support the validity of their arguments. In African legal ritual, an advocate of a cause uses proverbs for the same purpose. Here clearly it is not enough to know the proverbs; it is also necessary to be expert in applying them to new situations. The case usually will be won, not by the man who knows the most proverbs, but by the man who knows best how to apply the proverbs he knows to the problem at hand.

The distinction just made is expressed succinctly in the remark of an Ibo youth, studying at the University of California at Berkeley, which we have quoted as an epigraph: "I know the proverbs, but I don't know how to apply them." He explained that his Western-oriented education in Nigeria had cut him off from the daily use of proverbs. Thus, while he did recall the texts of a great number of proverbs, he was not really certain as to precisely how and when they should be employed in particular situations.

E. Ojo Arewa and Alan Dundes, "Proverbs and the Ethnography of Speaking Folklore," pp. 70–85 from *American Anthropologist* 66(6), 1964.

The Anthropology of Performance: A Reader, First Edition. Edited by Frank J. Korom.

Studying Proverbs as Communication

The distinction between knowing and applying proverbs is of the utmost importance for folk-lore fieldwork methodology. Specifically, it makes the difference between recording texts and recording the use of texts a critical one. Folklore is used primarily as a means of com-munication, and it is as communication that it needs to be studied. Yet this is virtually impossible with the common practice of recording just the texts alone, a practice con-sistent with the mistaken emphasis in folklore upon the lore rather than upon the folk.

In 1929 Roman Jakobson, in a joint essay with P. Bogatyrev, noted that folklore and language were somewhat analogous in that both are col-lective social phenomena with definite regulari-ties of pattern. This type of conceptual frame-work permitted and in fact encouraged the study of folklore as a systematic code. If language could be studied structurally, folklore could also be so studied. Although, unlike linguists, folklorists have been slow to study their materials in this way, at least the theoretical possibility of the analysis of folklore as code was cogently stated in 1929, and it has been brought to the fore of anthropological attention by studies by such scholars as Lévi-Strauss and Sebeok.

Jakobson and Bogatyrev had suggested that in folklore there was an analogue to speech (*la parole*) as well as to language (*la langue*), inasmuch as there were particular, idiosyn-cratic, actual texts of folklore utilized by indi-viduals. Recently Hymes (1962) has urged as a general perspective that to the study of linguis-tic structures must be added the study of the structures of acts of speech. The goal is not simply the delineation of the structure of lan-guage as an isolated symbolic system or code, but rather the attempt to discover exactly how language is used in specific situations. Moreover, the conception of the structure of language is extended to include the sequential structure of forms of messages, wherever such linguistic "routines" appear. This approach to the study of language in culture Hymes terms the "ethnography of speaking." In this type of study, one is interested in not only the rules of a

language, but also the rules for the use of the language. The question is not only what is a grammatical utterance, but also when does one use one grammatical utterance rather than another. It should be obvious that the notion of the "ethnography of speaking" is extremely relevant to the study of folklore. Applied to proverbs, for example, it would be concerned with precisely the sort of rules that the Ibo youth quoted at the outset had not learned.

In order to study the enthography of the speaking of folklore (or, ethnography of speak-ing folklore, more concisely), clearly one cannot be limited to texts. One needs texts in their contexts. One needs to ask not only for proverbs, and for what counts as a proverb, but also for information as to the other components of the situations in which proverbs are used. What are the rules governing who can use proverbs, or particular proverbs, and to whom? upon what occasions? in what places? with what other persons present or absent? using what channel (e.g., speech, drumming, etc.)? Do restrictions or prescriptions as to the use of proverbs or a proverb have to do with particular topics? with the specific relationship between speaker and addressee? What exactly are the contribu-ting contextual factors which make the use of proverbs, or of a particular proverb, possible or not possible, appropriate or inappropriate?

Notice that such a study of context is not the same as the more generalized study of functions of folklore. One can say that prov-erbs sum up a situation, pass judgment, rec-ommend a course of action, or serve as secular past precedents for present action; but to say this does not tell us what the particular func-tion of a particular proverb used by a partic-ular individual in a particular setting is. There is merit in prefacing a collection of proverbs (or of any other form of folklore) with a discussion of the various general functions of the materials (cf. Turner 1960), but this does not substitute for the accurate reporting of contextual data.

In a way, it seems to be an absurdly simple request to ask that students of folklore record the contexts of their texts. Other anthropolo-gists, taking for granted the call for context that Malinowski issued in Part II of *Coral Gardens and Their Magic* (1935), may assume that this is done. But while the accuracy of the linguistic transcriptions of folklore materials has steadily improved, the situation with respect to contextual data now is very much like that deplored by Firth (1926:246) – even the best folklore field workers report only texts. If context is mentioned, it is discussed in general terms, not in terms specific to given texts. Thus, for example, in an important article on the "dozens," the characteristic form of verbal dueling among American Negroes (Abrahams 1962), 30 texts are reported and 13 replies, but there is no indication whatsoever as to which reply goes with which text; and it is not possible to guess this sort of relationship. Again, Abrahams (1964:6) has argued that it is vitally important to present with any corpus of lore some analysis of the conflicts which exist within the culture that uses it. The point is a fine one, but what is needed even more is collection of the actual use of the lore in specific conflict situations. If, for example, a folklorist wants to study verbal dueling, he should not limit himself to selected texts of insults together with a general discussion of the techniques of verbal dueling. He should, if he can, and admittedly it is not an easy task, present an accurate transcription of a verbal duel. The sequence (cf. Miller 1952) and the intensity of a series of insults represent data essential for an ethnography of speaking folklore. To report data in this way clearly would not preclude the usual presentation of texts and the standard generalized analysis of the materials and their functions. Without such faithful recording of actual events, however, future analysts are deprived of an opportunity to see how folklore works.

With particular regard to proverbs, the techniques or "rules" for applying them cannot be studied unless actual instances of individuals applying proverbs to life situations are recorded. In the absence of ideal circumstances, which would consist of recording a representative variety of such instances, together with interviewing informants as to their judgments of such instances, informants can at least be asked to construct what they consider to be the typical and appropriate contexts or situations for individual proverbs, and to recall such instances as they can. If a person does know how to apply the proverbs, the chances are good that he can report and envision situations in which the proverbs have been or could be appropriately used. Herskovits used this technique effectively (without explicitly explaining the technique at the time) in his work with Kru proverbs (1930) and was so pleased with the results that he was later led to propose the construction of hypothetical situations by informants as a generally useful methodological device for all types of ethnographic field work (1950).

In principle, the more varied the contexts of a particular proverb that can be recorded, the more likely it is that the proverb and its significance in the culture from which it comes will be understood. By the same token, one should record the informants' associations and comments with regard to the folkloristic materials. If there is oral literature, then there is oral literary criticism, that is, native, as opposed to exogenous, literary criticism. The shelves of folklorists are filled with explanations of what folklore means and what its value is, but few of these explanations and valuations come from the folk. Native literary criticism, which could be considered as an aspect of "ethno-literature," the latter being parallel to ethnobotany, ethnozoology, etc., does not eliminate the need for analytical literary criticism, but it certainly should be recorded as part of the ethnographic context of folklore, both for its own interest, and because undoubtedly native interpretations and valuations of proverbs influence the decision to employ a particular one in a particular situation. Recording the text of a proverb and the situations in which it occurs may provide sufficient data for correlating the two, but if the goal is the delineation of the rules for using folklore in a given culture, then collection of the interpretation(s) of a proverb by members of the culture is equally essential.

Like other short forms of folklore, such as riddles and jokes, proverbs could be made the subject of an ethnography of speaking folklore especially easily and profitably. For one thing, proverbs are readily used in situations in which there is close interpersonal contact, often serving to release tensions related to that contact.

Unfortunately, as we have noticed, most proverb collections consist of bare texts.

Sometimes even the versions in the original language are absent. Often the meanings are not only unclear, but misrepresented inasmuch as the collector has succumbed to the worst kind of ethnocentrism, explaining a proverb in one culture by citation of a supposedly equivalent proverb from his own. This all-too-common tendency to translate a native culture's folklore into the collector's own makes most collections of proverbs of extremely limited value to serious students. Few collections are of the caliber of those made by Firth, Herskovits, Herzog, and Messenger.

Working in limited time and apart from Yoruba society, it has not been possible for us to complete a study observing all the canons specified above. A selection of Yoruba proverbs, however, can illustrate the useful information regarding context that is quite easy to obtain, even in less than ideal circumstances. One of the most important of the many uses of Yoruba proverbs is in the training of children, and twelve examples are chosen from that sphere. The relationship between use of proverbs and channel is discussed in a separate section. The Yoruba text of each proverb is given with literal translation in an appendix.

Some Yoruba Proverbs of Child Training

1. "One should not say in jest that his mother is fainting."

    One important aspect of Yoruba child training has to do with teaching the child the proper sets of relationships to be maintained between himself and his parents, his siblings, members of his lineage, and unrelated elders. The nature of these relationships, at least in terms of ideal culture, is more often than not communicated to the child by means of proverbs. Children are expected to be obedient and subordinate to parents. The proverb "One should not say in jest that his mother is fainting" is one that a parent may use to let a child know that there are certain topics which should not be made the subjects of jokes. The proverb is usually cited immediately after a child has said something he should not have said. Among the topics a child

should avoid in jokes are the important personal events in his parents' life. If, for example, a father had quarreled with his wife at some previous time, his child is not supposed to refer to this quarrel or discuss it with anyone. Even if one of the parents alludes to the quarrel in the presence of the child, the child is still not allowed to indicate that he has knowledge of the quarrel. If the child later on becomes angry with one of his parents, he must still refrain from mentioning the event. If the child did ever refer to the quarrel, he might well receive the proverb as a reprimand. As with all proverbs, there are other possible contexts for this one. For example, if a friend joked to another by saying, "I heard you are planning to assassinate the head chief of your village," the other might reply with the proverb to convey the thought that there are some things which must not be joked about. In this event, the proverb would be used only if the person citing it believed that the original comment was intended as a joke. Literally, the proverb refers to fainting which is interpreted in Yoruba culture as a significant passage from the normal state of life to another state. Such a passage is serious business and it is one of those things one does not treat lightly. Figuratively, the proverb could refer to any event of the family's history which brought shame to the family. For example, if a child's parents were in debt, this would be a taboo topic for jokes. Thus, in a child-training context, the proverb helps teach the child at an early age to discriminate between those messages he should and those he should not utter regarding his parents, a distinction which would be of particular interest to someone doing an ethnography of speaking, or a sociolinguistic study correlating speaker and topic.

2. "Untrained and intractable children would be corrected by outsiders."

3. "If a man beats his child with his right hand, he should draw him to himself with his left."

    The role of the proverb as an agent of communication is even more apparent in an actual case in which the parents of a child disagreed as to the amount of indulgence the child should be given. The mother, who felt that her child should be given more rather than less indulgence, told her husband that the child was young and foolish, and that because of this he should be given much indulgence. The husband remained silent for a few seconds and then replied with the proverb: "Untrained and intractable children would be corrected by outsiders." At this point, the wife responded by saying, "If a man beats his child with his right hand, he should draw him to himself with his left." In the first proverb, one finds expressed several important cultural values concerning the education of children. The parents' obligation to give proper and adequate training to their child is conveyed by the word "untrained" (àbfìkóó). The child's duty to obey the instructions of his parents is suggested by the word "intractable" (àkóìgbó). If the parent or the child fails to fulfill his or her respective obligations, the community at large might take action, which would be a socially overt recognition or indication of such failure. However, the second proverb frames the cultural expectation that while parents must take active steps to discipline their child effectively, they should also feel and demonstrate parental love for the child. That is what is meant by beating a child with the right hand and drawing him close with the left.

4. "The chameleon has produced its child; the child is expected to know how to dance."

In some instances, a child's parents might have given what they considered to be good training, but nevertheless the child may have turned out to be unmanageable. In such a situation, the parents would no doubt be unhappy, but in order to assure themselves and others that they had done their part, they might say to one another, to the child, or possibly to an outsider, "The chameleon has produced its child; the child is expected to know how to dance." This means that the parents have fulfilled their obligations

in bringing the child into the world and rearing him. It is the child's responsibility to use his opportunities and abilities to the fullest extent. The proverb might be used in a situation like the following. If a child told a friend of his parents that he was foolish, the friend would be annoyed inasmuch as a child is supposed to respect all those who are his elders. The friend would almost certainly tell the parents about the incident. (It is unlikely that the child would have uttered the insult in the presence of his parents.) The parents would assure their friend that appropriate disciplinary action would be taken. Later they might address the chameleon proverb to the offending child to tell him how displeased they were with his conduct and to remind him that his behavior at that point was his, not their, responsibility.

5. "Do not be like me; a thief's child takes after its parents."

6. "The offspring of an elephant cannot become a dwarf; the offspring of an elephant is like the elephant."

Yoruba parents do have responsibility with respect to their own behavior in the child training context. They are expected to do more than simply bring up their child in accordance with cultural norms. They are supposed to be good examples for the child. As evidence for this, there is a proverb which a parent might cite whenever he felt the other parent fell short of being a good example for their child. The proverb would be used to inform the guilty spouse of his mistake. In the proverb "Do not be like me; a thief's child takes after its parents," there is an explicit indication of the importance attached to parental example in the education of a Yoruba child. Suppose a father who quarrels with his siblings strikes them when he gets angry. The child sees this and later when he becomes angry with one of his brothers or sisters, he hits him. The father, observing the child's behavior, is upset and he admonishes the boy not to do such things. When the father complains to the mother about the boy's actions, she might reply (not in front of the child) with the proverb to communicate the idea that if he is disturbed about what the child is doing, he should remember that he himself is the model for the child. It should be noted that this proverb is not limited in its use to indicating only the effects of bad parental example. It may also be used to show the effects of good parental example on the child. Essentially the proverb is an expression of the strong Yoruba belief that the parental influence to which a child has been exposed has a great deal to do with the type of person he ultimately becomes. The same concept is somewhat differently expressed in the proverb: "The offspring of an elephant cannot become a dwarf; the offspring of an elephant is like the elephant."

7. "If you talk of cutting off somebody's head in the presence of a child, he will always be staring at the man's neck."

Another type of parental responsibility which is an integral part of Yoruba child training has to do with the kind of conversation parents carry on in front of their child. On one occasion, the senior members of a Yoruba family were engaged in an evening conversation in the presence of their child. The young boy's father was talking about a neighbor in a very destructive manner. The boy was listening with unusually keen attention. The boy's mother noticed this and she became nervous and impatient as she listened to her husband. Soon, her patience ran out, and she suddenly sent her son on an errand. While the boy was away, she said to her husband, "If you talk of cutting off somebody's head in the presence of a child, he will always be staring at the man's neck." With this proverb from the wife, the destructive talk about the neighbor immediately ceased. This is an excellent example of the proverb as communication, and in fact as most effective communication. But what exactly is being communicated? If a parent expresses his bias about a person or refers to what he considers to be a fault in the person *in the presence of his child*, the child will always remember this bias or alleged fault whenever he sees the person in question. The proverb is urging that the

parent take care not to transmit his personal bias to his child.

8. "We use a closed fist for tapping our chest."

With regard to the relationship between a child and his siblings, proverbs play an important role in showing how one child should behave towards another. Yoruba parents are very anxious to have unity among their children and they believe that a lack of such unity would have a serious disruptive effect upon the family's solidarity. They are, therefore, constantly on guard to insure that sibling unity is encouraged. A situation where there has been some evidence of intersibling rivalry or conflict will probably elicit a proverbial comment from a parent or older relative. For example, suppose one of two or three brothers is courting a girl. Ordinarily the other brothers visit the girl to show their interest in their brother's life and to display commendable family unity. If, however, the brothers fail to do this and either of the parents notices this, he might urge them to visit the girl by saying, "We use a closed fist for tapping our chest." In this proverb, one finds reference to traditional gestures. Inasmuch as gestures are often functionally equivalent to proverbs (in that they summarize a situation, pass judgment, or recommend a course of action), this is not surprising. The "closed fist" is an expression of unity and strength, while tapping the chest with the fist is a characteristic gesture indicating boasting. The gestural message is that unity is a desideratum of which the family is proud and furthermore a family without it is in no position to boast.

9. "A child trying to act like an older person will find that his age gives him away."

The importance of the principle of seniority and relative age in Yoruba social structure and verbal behavior has been described in detail by Bascom (1942). These factors are definitely manifested in the relationship between a child and his younger or older sibling. A younger sibling is expected to be deferential to an older child. It should be realized that it is not just that age is crucial with respect to Yoruba interpersonal relationships, but that its influence upon a particular relationship is in some sense never-changing. A younger brother is at and by birth destined to be a younger brother. But it is not just relative age which is fixed. There is apparently a notion of absolute age, especially in regard to the cultural distinction between child and adult. The suggestion that age is an almost absolute regulator or indicator of behavior, impossible to escape, is made in a proverb: "A child trying to act like an older person will find that his age gives him away." This might be cited in a situation in which a child was trying to act like an older person, but the child because of his age was unable to act properly. Let's say a boy gets married at a relativel yearly age (e.g., under 20) or a girl (under 15) does this and the marriage does not work out well. An older person, perhaps the parent, might comment either to the child or to someone else upon the unhappy marriage by quoting the proverb which would convey the opinion that the child should have waited to get married until he was old enough.

10. "A white fowl does not know it is old."
11. "When a child acts as a child, a man should act as a man."

If a younger child is criticized for trying to act older than his years, so also is an older child criticized for acting like someone younger than his years. In a situation where an older sibling has fallen short of his obligations towards one or more younger siblings, he may be chastised for his failure. When the parents are not at home, for example, the oldest child is expected to assume the responsibility for the other children's acting properly. He is also supposed to see that the children do not hurt themselves. If for any reason he is careless, and one child goes outside to a place where he is ordinarily not permitted to go, and if the child hurts himself, the oldest child will be censured by the parents upon their return. Had the senior sibling fulfilled his responsibilities, the younger child would not have been hurt. The parents might say, "A white fowl does not know it is old," or more probably "When a child acts as a

child, a man should act as a man." Both these proverbs could also be used appropriately in contexts in which an adult does not act as an adult should. The significance of a white fowl depends upon the fact that white chickens are culturally regarded as distinct from red, black, and other color chickens. White fowl are used solely for sacrificial and ritual purposes, although the sacrificial chicken is eaten by the participants after the ceremony which has been prescribed by a diviner. The proverb suggests that the white fowl does not comprehend its higher status with respect to other chickens. Thus the proverb could be used in a situation in which an elder (not necessarily with white hair) does not appear to know, or act in accordance with, his privileged position relative to younger individuals. The second proverb is more hortatory in that it implies that a child cannot help acting as a child, which places the burden of regulatory responsibility squarely upon the shoulders of oldest sibling present.

12. "The hand of a child cannot reach the high shelf, nor can that of an older person enter a calabash."

In Yoruba culture, there is not only a principle of seniority (Bascom 1942) but also a principle of reciprocal responsibility. The young have a responsibility to the old and the old have a responsibility to the young. More concretely, the child has obligations to his parents; the parents have obligations to their child. The younger sibling has obligations to older brothers and sisters; the older sibling has obligations to his younger brothers and sisters. The interdependence between an individual and his elders is metaphorically rendered by the proverb: "The hand of a child cannot reach the high shelf, nor can that of an older person enter a calabash." For a child to reach his goal, the aid of an elder is essential. Things which children cannot do for or by themselves must be done for them by their elders. On the other hand, there are tasks which elders can perform only with difficulty if at all. For such tasks, children are expected to serve their elders. The proverb might be employed in a situation like the following. An uncle (paternal or maternal) asks a nephew, or any older individual asks a younger one to go on several errands such as fetching water from a pond. The youth does this many times. Then one day, the younger person asks the older for a favor. He sees that the older person has some pineapples and he asks to be given one to eat. The older person refuses. The following day the older person asks the younger to go on another errand, but the younger refuses to go. Later the older one is talking to another person of the same age as himself, not necessarily a relative, and he complains of the younger person's behavior. The third party responds by quoting the proverb as a means of explaining the appropriateness of the youth's conduct.

Notice how pale are the explanation of the proverb and the analytical phrase about principle in comparison with the proverb itself. Folklore is both communication and art. It has been studied as art more than as communication. Yet if it is studied as communication, its artistic qualities should not be overlooked. Even in translation, this last proverb offers proof that there is art in the communication.

Discussion

Much more might be learned about the import of each of these proverbs and the conditions governing their use through field study in an indigenous setting. Some provisional observations, however, can be made here.

Apparently the most important Yoruba rules for the use of proverbs have to do with the identity of the participants in the speech situation. It is the identity of the addressor which seems crucial for the genre to be used at all, and the identity of the addressee, or audience, which seems crucial to the appropriate use of a particular proverb.

Regarding the genre as a whole, the main consideration seems to be the age of the person speaking relative to the age of the addressee. The speaker is normally older for some proverbs, equal in age for others. Some proverbs might be appropriate to either case. Younger persons are not wholly excluded, but Yoruba etiquette dictates that a younger person's use of a proverb in the presence of an older person must be marked by a prefatory apology. The standard politeness formula runs something as follows: "I don't claim to know any proverbs in the presence of you older people, but you elders have the saying . . . ."

Of the present examples, it seems safe to say that an elder person would probably address numbers 8, 9, 10, and 11 to a younger person; e.g., a parent might say them to his child (but the elder need not be a parent). In contrast, numbers 3, 5, 6, 7, and 12 would be more likely to be addressed by an elder to another elder person, e.g., by a husband to his wife or by an adult to a friend or relative. Numbers 1 2, and 4 could be used by either seniors to juniors or by age equals.

The topics or situations which might appropriately elicit a proverb are primarily concerned with a younger person's behavioral responsibilities toward his elders and an elder's behavioral responsibilities toward younger indivduals. Numbers 1, 4, and 8 refer to a child's obligations to his family; numbers 2, 3, 5, 6 and 7 refer to a parent's obligations to his child; and numbers 9, 10, 11, and 12 refer to behavior proper to one or the other or both. It is clear that the identity of the addressee is crucial with regard to whether a particular proverb is appropriate or not. For example, a child would most probably be a suitable addressee for numbers 1 and 8, but a child would rarely, if ever, be the addressee of numbers 3 and 7. In fact it is doubtful whether number 7 would be used to any addressee if the child in question were even present. The point is that the presence or absence of individuals other than the principal addressee may be an important factor governing the use of particular proverbs in speech (but not in drumming).

The use of proverbs is not restricted by need for knowledge of any special code other than the Yoruba language itself, so far as we know. Neighboring or other foreign languages are not, for example, used, as they are among the Jabo (Herzog 1945) for purposes of concealment and mocking, so far as our data go. Nor is use of proverbs conditional upon skill in creative and adaptive change in message form. By the very nature of fixed-phrase genres of verbal art, the messages are culturally standardized in form and content. The creativity and adaptation lie rather in the successful application of these traditional materials to new situations. The relation between use of proverbs and channel, however, requires special consideration.

Proverbs and Channel

Althouth most proverbs are transmitted by speech, some on occasion are communicated by drums. The type of drum (there are more than twenty different types of Yoruba drums) which is very often used to transmit proverbs is the "dundun" described by Bascom (1953). Although drummed proverbs may be used to insult an individual (especially in struggles for political office or for coveted titles), generally drumming is a channel of communication utilized for ceremonial purposes, such as a funeral, a marriage, a naming ceremony, or the installation of a chief. Proverbs may be drummed on any of these occasions so long as the particular proverb is deemed appropriate by the drummer or by the person hiring the drummer, appropriate in terms of the particular situation and the particular addressee. It is, however, somewhat less likely that proverbs would be used as often in funeral ceremonies as in happier events such as marriages.

Certain families specialize in druming and the skill is passed on within the family (Laoye 1954). Part of the training in drumming is the accumulation of both a large store of proverbs and the knowledge of the appropriate occasions for their use. Thus drumming is a channel not equally available to all members of Yoruba culture. However, a nondrummer could ask a drummer to drum an honorific or congratulatory proverb for a friend's marriage. The drummer receives payment for this. With regard to a drummed proverb honoring a marriage, the nominal addressee is considered to be the bridegroom, not the bride. (This is related to the bias inherent in Yoruba patrilineal social organization.)

The techniques of drumming generally and drumming proverbs specifically are too complex (Bascom 1953) to be adequately treated here,

but, essentially, suprasegmental patterns are extracted from the spoken versions of the proverb and the addressee is able to recognize the proverb whether he actually articulates the segmental phonemes or not. By moving the left arm by which the drum is held, the shape of the drum is varied, hence the tone is varied. The relative pitch differences and the rhythmic sequence of the drum tones are culturally perceived as being similar to the tone sequence found in particular proverbs (as is not the case among the Jabo according to the ethno-theory of Herzog's informants [Herzog 1945]).

13. "It will in no way hurt him if it falls upon him. A tree which fails to hold up a person when he leans against it will in no way hurt him if it falls upon him."

This proverb is one of several which are possibly more often drummed than spoken. The proverb would be most appropriate in a situation in which a person dismisses the possibility of another person's being able to do him harm. For example, suppose a boy asks an older relative for money to attend school. The elder promises to support the boy. Later the elder fails to provide this support. Then the boy may bitterly complain to a friend about this relative's action or lack of it. The friend tells him that he shouldn't talk that way about this relative, because he might find out and as a result he might try to make trouble for the boy. The boy might then reply with the proverb to convey the idea that anyone who was too feeble to help another was surely too weak to be able to do that person any harm. In this context, the proverb would be spoken, not drummed. The situation, in part, determines the channel.

A situation in which the proverb would be drummed rather than spoken might be one like the following. A man is seeking a title, such as chief. A friend who has money and influence in the community promises to use them in his behalf. However, when the time comes, the wealthy man fails to honor his promise. The title-seeker is angry and he complains to many people about this breach of faith. Some of these people warn him about speaking ill of such an important person and some point out possible dangerous consequences, such as the rich person's using his influence against him. The would-be chief decides to hire a drummer, and he directs him to drum the proverb in order to tell the people of the community that in his opinion, since the man had shown himself to be too weak to live up to his pledge to support him, he was clearly in no position to hurt him, even if he did use his influence to oppose the attempt to get the title.

One extremely interesting aspect of the relation between channel and proverb concerns the effect of the former upon the form of the proverb. One might conjecture, for example, that it may be more than coincidence that the drummed proverb mentioned above has in Yoruba a clear ABA form, a form which is also common in Yoruba songs as well as in other traditional materials communicated by drum. Moreover, the ABA form is not common in spoken Yoruba proverbs.

Another proverb which is drummed more than it is spoken has the same ABA form.

14. "It is palm-oil that I carry. Person bearing rock, please don't spoil that which is mine. It is palm-oil that I carry."

This proverb is used to refer to situations in which one person has something of great value whose worth could be totally destroyed by the act of a thoughtless person. The proverb might be drummed in a situation where an important person with a good reputation is threatened by an irresponsible young man with no reputation. The latter envies the important man's position and prestige and he seeks to spread malicious rumors such as that the man has taken bribes. Thus a man who has a reputation worth little is in a position to destroy the fine reputation of an honorable man as pieces of rock can ruin palm-oil. The threatened man might hire several drummers and tell them of the situation, but in this case perhaps he might not indicate the specific proverb to use. One of the drummers decides to employ the particular proverb because he judges it to be appropriate.

If there is a definite correlation between channel and proverb form, this has important theoretical implications. For one thing, it would suggest that stylistic studies of folklore genres without taking channels into account might be misleading. What folklorists think is chance variation may in fact be a reflection of channel alternatives. The correlation could also provide a way of gleaning information from the scores of bare texts already reported. It might be possible, for example, to tell from the form alone that a particular Yoruba proverb could have been transmitted by drums.

As mentioned in the preceding section, the presence or absence of particular individuals is not important if the channel selected is drumming rather than speech. Drumming is a public, speech a private, channel. In terms of addressees, drumming is nonexclusive, speech exclusive. Spoken proverbs would normally be addressed to an individual or to a relatively small number of individuals. Drummed proverbs, in contrast, would be addressed to a larger group of individuals or to one individual in that situation where it was important that the message be made public. This latter factor suggests that situational circumstances are more crucial than addressees with respect to the selection of drumming as a channel for proverbs. In any event, the investigation of differences in a single genre of folklore as it is communicated in diverse channels represents a potentially rich area of inquiry.

Conclusion

If folklore is communication, then the ways in which it is used as communication must be taken into account. The study of folklore should include both the study of lore and the study of folk. The study of lore alone without reference to the folk by whom it is used is incomplete and may even be misleading. To borrow from a recent American indictment of the commercialism of Christmas ("Let's put the Christ back in Christmas"), we might urge: "Let's put the folk back into folklore."

APPENDIX

Proverb Texts

In the following texts, standard Yoruba orthography is employed. Two tones are indicated as: High Tone (/), and Low Tone (\\). The phonetic equivalents of Yoruba orthography include: ẹ is ɛ, ṣ is š, p is kp, and ọ is ɔ. The reader is reminded that many collections of proverbs made by folklorists and linguists consist of just what is presented in this appendix. If the reader seriously doubts the necessity of collecting context, let him ask a non-Yoruba friend what some of these proverbs mean.

a ki fí ìyá   ẹni dákú ṣeréi
we not use mother   one faint play

1. "One should not say in jest that his mother is fainting."

àbiíkó   àkoígó   ode   ni o ti
untrained intractable outside is he have
kó   ọgbón   wá   ilé
learned wisdom come home

2. "Untrained and intractable children would be corrected by outsiders."

bí a bá   fi ọwó òtún na   ọmọ
if we should use hand right beats child
ẹni a fi   ósì fa   á   móra
one we use left draw him to self

3. "If a man beats his child with his right hand, he should draw him to himself with his left."

agemọ   bí   omo ró ná
chameleon produces child his already
ài mọ   jó   di   owó rè
not know dance becomes hand his

4. "The chameleon has produced its child; the child is expected to know how to dance."

maṣe fi   ìwà   jọ   mí ọmo
do not use behavior resembles me child
olè ni olè jọ
thief is thief resembles

5. "Do not be like me: A thief's child takes after its parents."

omo àjànàkú ki ya   ràrá ọmọ
child elephant not becomes dwarf child
tí erin   bí erin   ni njọ
that elephant born elephant is resembles

6. "The offspring of an elephant cannot become a dwarf; the offspring of an elephant is like the elephant."

a ki sóró orí bíbó lójú omọdé
we not talk   head cutting before child
lórùnlórùn ní ima
at the neck is will
wo olúwaró
look the person

7. "If you talk of cutting off somebody's head in the presence of a child, he will always be staring at the man's neck."

àgbájọ owó ni a fi nsọ àyà
together fist is we use tap chest

8. "We use a closed fist for tapping our chest."

bí ọmọdé bá   fé   ṣ e ìṣe àgbà ọjó
if child   happens want do deed elder day
orí rè kò jó
head his not allow

9. "A child trying to act like an older person will find that his age gives him away."

adiẹ funfun kò mọ   ara ró ní àgbà
fowl white   not know self his as elder

10. "A white fowl does not know it is old."

bí ọmọdé bá   nṣe   ọmọdé àgbà
if child   happens doing child   elder
a ma ṣe àgbà
he will act elder

11. "When a child acts as a child, a man should act as a man."

ọwọ ọmọdé kò tó   pẹpẹ ọwọ
hand child   not reach shelf hand
àgbàlàgbà kò wọ   àkèrègbè
elder   not enter calabash

12. "The hand of a child cannot reach the high shelf, nor can that of an older person enter a calabash."

b' ó wó lu ni kò lè pa ni
if it falls hits one not can kill one
igí tí a f' èhìn tì tí ko
tree that we put back lean that not

gba ni duro
hold one stand
b' ó wó lu ni kò lè pa ni
if it falls hits one not can kill one
13. "It will in no way hurt him if it falls upon him. A tree which fails to hold up a person when he leans against it will in no way hurt him if it falls upon him."

epo   ni mo rù
palm-oil is I   carry
oníyangí   ma   ba t' emi jó
rock bearer do not — mine —
                        (ba+f-jẹ =spoil or ruin)
epo   ni mo rù
palm-oil is I   carry
14. "It is palm-oil that I carry. Person bearing rock, please don't spoil that which is mine. It is palm-oil that I carry."

NOTE

1 All the Yoruba proverbs cited in this paper were contributed by Arewa, who learned them about 1945 in his native village of Oke-agbe in Western Nigeria. He also provided the translations and explanations of the proverbs. The authors are indebted to Dell Hymes for invaluable comments and suggestions.

REFERENCES

Abrahams, Roger D. 1962. Playing the dozens. *Journal of American Folklore* 75: 209–220.

Abrahams, Roger D. 1964. Deep down in the jungle: Negro narrative folklore from the streets of Philadelphia. Hatboro, Folklore Associates.

Bascom, William R. 1942. The principle of seniority in the social structure of the Yoruba. *American Anthropologist* 44: 37–46.

Bascom, William R. 1953. *Drums of the Yoruba of Nigeria*. Ethnic Folkways Library, Album P441. New York, Folkways Records and Service Corp.

Firth, Raymond. 1926. Proverbs in native life, with special reference to those of the Maori. *Folk-Lore* 37: 134–153; 245–270.

Herskovits, Melville J. 1930. Kru proverbs. *Journal of American Folklore* 43: 225–293.

Herskovits, Melville J. 1950. The hypothetical situation: a technique of field research. *Southwestern Journal of Anthropology* 6: 32–40.

Herzog, George. 1936. *Jabo proverbs from Liberia*. London, Oxford University Press.

Herzog, George. 1945. Drum-signalling in a West African tribe. *Word* 1: 217–238.

Hymes, Dell H. 1962. The ethnography of speaking. In *Anthropology and human behavior*, Thomas Gladwin and W. C. Sturtevant, eds. Washington, Anthropological Society of Washington, pp. 13–53.

Jakobson, Roman and P. Bogatyrev. 1929. Die folklore als besondere form des schaffeni. In *Donum natalicium Schrijnen: Verzameling van opstellen door oud-leerlingen en bevriende vakgenooten opge-dragen ann Mgr. Prof. Dr. Jos. Schrijnen*. Nymegen-Utrecht, Dekker, pp. 900–913.

Laoye, H. H. 1954. Yoruba drums. *Nigeria* 45: 4–13.

Lévi-Strauss, Claude. 1963. *Structural anthropology*. New York, Basic Books.

Malinowski, Bronislaw. 1935. *Coral gardens and their magic. II.* New York, American Book Company.

Messenger, John C, Jr. 1959. The role of proverbs in a Nigerian judicial system. *Southwestern Journal of Anthropology* 15: 64–73.

Miller, Robert J. 1952. Situation and sequence in the study of folklore. *Journal of American Folklore* 65: 29–48.

Sebeok, Thomas A. 1959. Folksong viewed as code and message. *Anthropos* 54: 141–153.

Turner, Lorenzo D. 1960. The role of folklore in the life of the Yoruba of southwestern Nigeria. In *Report on the ninth annual round table meeting on linguistics and language studies: anthropology and African studies*, William M. Austin, ed. Georgetown University Monograph Series on Languages and Linguistics no. 11, Washington, D. C. Georgetown University Press, pp. 45–56.

6

Gbaya Riddles
in Changing Times

Philip A. Noss

Riddles are associated with the games of children at play in the schoolyard or in the village square.[1] In academia, riddles are accorded the status of a minor literary genre. In the spirit of the riddler, however, Harold Scheub challenges the readers of his latest book, *The Poem in the Story*, with the apparently extravagant claim "The riddle establishes a model for all oral art" (124). If this claim is true, then the evidence of changing metaphors and their dynamics in riddles is highly significant for understanding and appreciating the entire gamut of oral literary art.

Sumgba is the Gbaya term for riddle, but while this is its denotation, its connotations are those of challenge and confrontation, sometimes playful but not always.[2] A riddling session is launched with a high-pitched cry of "Sumgba!" followed by the shouted exclamation "Girimm!" This response is pronounced loudly in a low tone, for it represents the sound of the great drums of a chief announcing news of weighty import to the community, or it depicts the sound of enemy troops clashing in battle. The riddle competition may be among friends, but the challenge constitutes a sum-

mons to combat, and the opponents' response signifies that the battle is joined!

The challenger launches the attack with a riddle, "The pregnant woman doesn't leap over a gully!" to which the well-known answer is given, "The tortoise."[3] A second or a third attack may not be as easily met: "I went to visit my in-laws; no one greeted me, only the dead greeted me." Cultural norms dictate that one has many responsibilities toward the family of one's fiancée or one's wife that must be fulfilled personally. Visits to one's in-laws are therefore important social events, and one should expect to be welcomed with words of greeting. On this visit, however, the riddler was not received by the greetings of the living but of the dead.[4]

If a correct answer is given, the challenger may meekly acknowledge "Yes" or he/ she may exclaim, "You found it!" If, on the other hand, the answers offered are unacceptable, the challenger formally declines each with the archaic negative "Singkom!" If the opponents are unable to provide the correct answer, they may seek to placate the attacker by surrendering

Philip A. Noss, "Gbaya Riddles in Changing Times," pp. 34–42 from *Research in African Literatures* 37(2), 2006.

villages and towns and even cities. The challenger will reject each locality that is offered on the grounds that his or her own family members live in this one, in-laws live in that one, he or she has visited this one or lived in that one. This contest continues until at last the voracious appetite of the attacker is satisfied and he shouts his acceptance of his opponents' surrender: "I take this village and that town and that city, I execute all their inhabitants – it is dry leaves!" The correct answer to the riddle is dry leaves. When one walks in green leaves, they do not make noise; when one walks in dry leaves, they make a loud rustling or crackling sound.

The Gbaya description of the riddle is to say that it is something one "calls" for which there is a response. That is, there is an implied question of identification in the "call" to which an appropriate answer must be furnished. Without *Girimm!* there is no *Sumgba!* for the challenge dissolves into nonexistence. If there is acceptance of the challenge, there must be an answer, if not provided by the riddlee, then by the riddler. There may, of course, be more than one correct answer, but the challenger is the sole arbiter in determining the acceptability of responses that are offered.

What is "called" by the riddler is a metaphor, a description of something that is known to the cultural community. The metaphor veils the reality of the object or the event that is in focus through the expression of an apparent contradiction or ambiguity. "A little bird among the thorns" is a literal description of a small winged creature perched in a thorn bush, but the contextual framework of *sumgba* alerts the audience that another level of reference is in play. As Scheub writes, "the play is between fantasy and reality, between the figurative and the literal" (124). The answer to the riddle is one's tongue that may easily be bitten by one's teeth. Implicit in the riddle and its answer is the warning that one must be careful while eating not to bite one's tongue. To paraphrase Max Black, unraveling a riddle is to understand a metaphor (32).

Much has been written about the riddle, its form, its structure, its content, its underlying meaning, and even its social value. It is widely accepted that the riddle is a reflection and outgrowth of the culture in which it finds

expression and that it retains relevance in its cultural context. However, P. D. Beuchat in an article entitled "Riddles in Bantu," after demonstrating the widespread occurrence of certain riddles in Bantu, Africa, concluded, "Only a thorough investigation might give some clue as to the origin of some riddles" (137). Lee Haring in his article "On Knowing the Answer" noted that "no investigator has observed or recorded the creation and subsequent acceptance of an African riddle" (198). Other scholars have echoed the same theme. Ruth Finnegan only alluded to the "inventing" of riddles among the Anang-Ibibio of Nigeria (440) and C. Faïk-Njuzi made the claim that riddles could be invented, but she did not elaborate, except to assert that the tone riddles were all received from the past (29).[5] Thomas Green and W. J. Pepicello in 1984 wrote: "The cultural origins of riddles have eluded scholars and remain almost as impenetrable an enigma as the question of how riddles operate in a culture" ("The Riddle Process" 189).

The terms associated with the Gbaya riddling phenomenon are ancient terms: *sumgba* is the language of tradition and myth; *girimm* is the language of ancient warfare. The rejection of a proposed answer is marked by the fossilized negation *Singkom!* that is pronounced only in riddling contexts. Thus the form of the riddle, its tradition, its ambiguities and incongruities bring the world of tradition to the present-day world for the riddler and his or her partners, who both represent and constitute the world of the present in an immediate communicative event. As suggested by Ian Hamnett, "New and alien ideas appear to be re-classified through a transformation that brings it into relationship with familiar experience or traditional knowledge" (388), or both.

The riddle itself may be timeless or modern; yet the setting of the riddle is always direct and contemporary. In the riddles cited above, the tortoise is a timeless creature that is known today just as it was in antiquity.[6] Marriage is a present-day social institution with obligations for all concerned, just as fresh green foliage and dry leaves are features of the flora that is part of our modern environment.

It is true that it may be difficult to speak of the creation of a riddle, for this is an internal act. The coining of the riddle occurs in the creator's mind subsequent to observation and prior to the "calling" in the riddling act. It is also difficult to predict whether a riddle will be accepted and will enter the repertoire of riddles maintained and passed on through successive generations of Gbaya culture.[7] Nevertheless, even if creation and acceptance are difficult to document, it is possible both on the basis of the content of riddles and observations of riddling exchanges to make certain statements about the continuing creative presence of riddles in Gbaya aesthetic expression.

Borrowed words frequently reflect historical relationships and developments.[8] "I crossed the river here and no one saw my footprints" refers to a boat, while "I have an animal: if I tie a cord around its neck, it doesn't walk well; if I tie a cord on its rear, it walks well" describes a sewing needle. "The belt burned up leaving the trousers" depicts the savanna when the grass has been burned off and the path remains as a clear distinct line across the countryside. "The soldier wrapped his stomach when he climbed the hill" refers to the vine of the wild yam that was a staple food for the ancestors. "The paramount chief sits in his doorway playing his pencil" portrays the cicada as it perches at the entrance to its hole and produced its ear-piercing high-pitched drone.

The word for boat is *kombon*, borrowed from the neighboring Mbum people; the needle became known to the Gbaya through Hausa merchants from whose language the word is taken; the word for belt was borrowed from the forest Ewondo to the south; while trousers came from the language of the Fula through the Hausa. The soldier is called *sooza* from English and the cicada's pencil is from the French *crayon*.

Thus, cultures that have influenced the Gbaya through history are reflected in the riddles that are still remembered and called today.

References to specific peoples and places also indicate historical contacts and political pressures. "The turban of the great chief doesn't easily become unwound" refers to a road that resembles a turban but that cannot be wound or unwound. The allusion of the turban is to the Fulani emirates who established power in northern Cameroon in the nineteenth century, and the great chief alludes to the hierarchy

of the Mbum who were conquered by the Fulani. "The old boy is dressed in German clothes" describes the starling whose glossy purple feathers bring back memories of the clothing worn by German colonizers. The riddle of the soldier wrapping his stomach may be told about a slave of the Fulani or about a white person, each with reference to the wild yam.

Obviously, these riddles and many others in the corpus reflect features that were introduced in Gbaya life or influences that offered a new perspective on what the Gbaya previously knew or practiced. As A. C. Jordan wrote about Southern Bantu riddles, "Every fresh experience in life provides scope for originality" (102).[9] John Blacking has written about the social role of riddles among the Venda of South Africa, and in the Gbaya repertoire there is extensive evidence of evolving social and political practice. Through reference to emirs and slaves, to Germans and soldiers, to the French and pencils, successive eras of Gbaya history are indisputably evoked. Even the missionary era and the influence of Christianity are portrayed in the riddle "Only one thing that has spread everywhere in the world," that is, the Bible.

Like the riddles about the wild yam, other series of riddles exemplify the incorporation of content that reflects successive historical change. One such series is about a man urinating. This series is also proof of the fact that riddle variants associated with different historical epochs may exist side by side over relatively long periods of time:

- My snare caught an animal: the animal fought to another place but then came back and died where it had been caught.
- My animal that I speared, it will flee, but it will come back and die in front of me.[10]
- I shot my animal (with an arrow) and it came and died in front of me.
- If I send my slave to the distant horizon, he will come back and die in front of me.
- I have something that can run from here to Yaoundé and come back and die in front of me.

The traditional tools of the hunt were the knife, the spear, and the snare and trap as reflected in the first two riddles above. Later the Gbaya borrowed the bow and arrow from neighboring peoples for more efficient hunting in open savanna country. The early acephalous and seminomadic existence of the Gbaya came under the influence of the hierarchical structures of encroaching northwestern emirates replete with palace slaves. More recently Gbaya society has looked southward toward Yaoundé, the nation's capital where the young go in search of job opportunities and excitement.

Mutations may occur not only in the content of the riddle, but also in the answer. Old riddles may find new answers, or more precise answers. In the following pair, the answer for the first was given as the horns of an unspecified wild animal, while the answer to the second was the horns on the head of a cow. In days past, cows were uncommon in Gbaya territory and the word for "cow" is a borrowed word.

- Something of mine, they travel together from morning to evening, they never brush against each other.
- I have some things that are together, but they do not touch.

Cars, airplanes and trains have become known to the Gbaya over past decades and riddles reveal the people's observations, for example, "Car tires remained in the abandoned village." Normally when inhabitants of villages moved to new locations, often in search of new hunting territories or new farm lands, or to escape disease, they left behind clay pots that were either broken or were too heavy to carry with them. The answer to this riddle, however, was graves. "The load-carrying-millipede doesn't climb hills and doesn't go down hills" is a commentary on trains. Trains resemble millipedes; yet, while they carry loads, which the millipede does not do, they do not go up or down hills which the millipede does do. The airplane is obscured behind the mythical bird in the riddle "My great bird carries a greater load than a human being does." Even very current events may provide inspiration for riddles, as in this one told among secondary school students after the death of a national football hero: "The

Cameroon lion cub died on the battlefield." The answer to this riddle is Marc Vivien Foé, a player on the national team called the Indomitable Lions who died on the football pitch while playing in an international match in France in 2003.

The pipeline that is presently being built to transport oil from southern Chad to Kribi on the seacoast of Cameroon has become the subject of riddles as in the following:

- Our dragon has its tail in Chad, its head comes out in Kribi where it vomits clay that produces wealth.[11]
- Idris is my spring, Paul counts me, Bush looks after me.

Idris Deby, the president of Chad, is the source of the spring, the head of the stream. Paul Biya is the president of Cameroon, where money must be paid for the pipeline to pass, and George Bush is the president of the United States who is considered to oversee the oil-drilling and pipeline building exercise to make sure that all goes well for the exploitation of the oil from Chad.

The riddles about the pipeline are newly created riddles, and the Gbaya comedian Dogobadomo is the coiner.[12] The riddle about the Cameroon soccer hero is also very contemporary, but its creator is anonymous. The following series of riddles was called by the late Paul Tenmbar, a Gbaya pastor, as he challenged and entertained a group of young people who were watching a motor vehicle being loaded and prepared for a journey[13]:

- Wanto has an animal; it drinks through its nose.
- An animal of mine; it opens its eyes at night to travel.
- Wanto's nanny goat, if Wanto doesn't squeeze her ear, she doesn't bleat.
- A certain animal of mine, it doesn't go slowly.

Although no proof can be provided that these riddles were coined on the spot, the riddling exchange that took place suggested that the riddler, who was well-known during his lifetime for his folktale performances and dramatic preaching, was acting extemporane-ously. The first riddle was called as he approached the people who had gathered around the driver as he poured water into the leaky radiator. The next riddles were called successively in the order listed as though the challenger were proceeding from one observa-tion to another, from the radiator to the head-lights to the horn and finally to the vehicle itself. Each of the four riddles, although dis-playing common thematic and structural unity, was characterized by slight introductory varia-tion. By evoking Wanto, the trickster and hero of Gbaya folklore (see Noss 1971), the artist conferred the legitimacy of ancient tradition upon his riddles. The last of the four riddles, the least successful, marked the cessation of the entertainer's display of creativity and the end of the riddling session. The enthusiasm of the crowd was evidence of their appreciation for his efforts, if not proof of the ultimate accep-tance of the riddles as permanent additions to the Gbaya repertoire.

In another setting and at a later time,[14] Reverend Tenmbar embellished the headlight riddle as follows:

• I have a great big animal: in the morning it gets up here and eats all the way to the Mba River keeping its eyes tightly closed the entire distance, but in the evening when it comes back, when night falls, it opens its eyes to walk around.

On another occasion, as a group of confer-ence participants were traveling home at the end of a long journey, the conversation included much reminiscing and not a few sto-ries and anecdotes. Suddenly one of the travel-ers called out the challenge *Sumbga!* to which the reply came *Girimm!* "Its feet are bigger than its body!" The riddle was called only a moment after the travelers had driven past a front-end loader, a large earth-moving machine that was parked on the side of the road. The riddle was a spontaneous observation called to test the acuity of the fellow passengers and to introduce an element of play into the conver-sation of weary travelers.[15]

These riddles would probably be the result of what Kenneth Goldstein called "incidental"

riddling. Nevertheless, the fact that the coiner of the headlight riddle called the same riddle on two separate occasions would indicate that in his own mind it had gained acceptance as a worthy addition to the Gbaya repertoire. Had it not been accepted with appreciation by his listeners the first time, there would have been no incentive on his part to embellish and "call" it a second time for a new audience.

Scheub's asssertion that the riddle is a model for all oral art may be observed in the Gbaya repertoire of oral art forms. The riddle and the proverb are closely related as metaphorical form. Indeed, some riddles and proverbs may be distinguished only by the context in which they occur. The pronouncement "Climb a dead tree with nary a thought of death!" may be announced as a *sumgba*, in which case the response may be little ants or preferably ter-mites that often are found in dead wood. How-ever, if this expression occurs as an observation about an incident or in a conversation, it is a proverbial warning about the dangers of a thoughtless act.

Intertextuality is frequently apparent through metaphors and their allusions. The riddle describes a situation – "We beat the drum, but we never hear the sound of the drumming" – while the well-known proverb affirms, "The drummer does not hear the sound of his own drumming." The drum holds a position of supreme importance among the Gbaya as it is used to accompany music and dance. The blinking of eyes is compared to drumming that has no sound. Meanwhile, the proverb observes that the drummer cannot judge the quality of his own drumming. As George Lakoff and Mark Johnson argued in their classic work, we do indeed live by metaphors.

The folktale that is the most complex Gbaya literary genre may incorporate the riddle, the proverb, or the parable. It may include riddles or proverbs, it may be composed on riddles, and it may be summarized by a proverb, or it may be an expanded parable. But when Scheub posits the riddle as a model for all oral art, he is speaking of "The Riddle in the Story." He is seeking the "metaphorical core" that "controls expansion and development into more complex forms" (122). The riddle is more than a model.

The changing metaphors of the riddles are not merely historical allusions; they are more than simple evidence of historical data and passing eras. They are the images, ancient and modern, mythic and contemporary, that constitute the ever-changing raw material of Scheub's "Story" (4).

The riddle of the needle and thread may be called in elaborate form[16]:

- Wanto's nanny goat, when Wanto takes a cord and ties it to her neck and ties her to a tree to eat grass, she doesn't eat grass; when Wanto takes the cord and ties it to the end of her tail, she eats grass.

Through the evocation of the trickster, Wanto becomes the riddle of Gbaya life, the core of the Gbaya Story. When the riddler evokes his or her little animal, the old grandmother, the dragon, the mythical bird, or uses other stylized formulae for introducing the ancient into the contemporary, the riddle is renewed in the Gbaya Story from one generation to the next as the Gbaya create new images in the face of new challenges to their life and their culture.

From remembering and retaining out of the past, to borrowing from the present, and to creating in the midst of the new, with the ever present possibility of transforming and adapting in new ways, the Gbaya riddle endures as a prominent cultural element for entertainment and instruction. Change does not destroy and render obsolete. On the contrary, change offers the potential for the riddle to continue to provide an avenue for the Gbaya intellect to challenge reality, proving time and again that what appears to be nonsensically impossible is indeed logically true. The vicissitudes of history are made friendly through the metaphor of the riddle in the contemporary Gbaya Story.

NOTES

1   The more than 500 riddles that constitute the corpus on which this study is based were recorded during field research in Cameroon and the Central African Republic in 1966–68, while working at the Gbaya Translation Center from 1971 to 1978,

and during subsequent visits and work in Cameroon up to 2004. I would like to express appreciation to Thomas Christensen and Dogobadomo Béloko for their assistance in my research.

2   The earliest published collection of Gbaya riddles is found in Tessmann 1: 219–22. For discussion of African riddles see Finnegan 426–43, Harries 180–84, and Derive 395–96.

3   All riddles are quoted in this paper in translation from the original Gbaya text by the author.

4   A variant of this riddle is the following: "I went on a visit: living people didn't greet me; only dead people greeted me."

5   For a helpful theoretical discussion of the process of riddle formulation see Green and Pepicello, "The Riddle Process." Earlier work by Köngäs Maranda postulated the existence of "riddle-making rules" on the model of transformational generative grammar.

6   The tortoise features prominently in riddles just as it is an important character in Gbaya tales. The following are additional examples of tortoise riddles:

- Father wears armored clothing, the children wear armored clothing, the wife wears armored clothing.
- I have a very important chief: the armor that they put on him long ago, he will die still wearing it.
- My house is myself.

7   In addition to retention of traditional riddles and the coining of new ones, a frequent source of new riddles is borrowing or diffusion. "My little house, it has no door" (Egg) is a very widespread riddle in Africa. The Sphinx riddle occurs twice in the Gbaya corpus for this paper, as well as several examples of Alphabet riddles: "I went to Douala twice, to Yaoundé once, and to Madagascar four times"; "I am three in Canada, one in Paris." The answer to both riddles is the letter A (see also Green and Pepicello, "Sight and Spelling Riddles" 28).

8   David Henige in *Oral Historiography* implies that the riddle might have historical significance by his quotation from George Gomme, who in 1908 wrote, "Every single

item of folklore, every folk-tale, every tradition, had its origins in some definite fact in the history of man" (qtd. In Henige 7). In Jan Vansina's book *Oral Tradition as History*, proverbs are mentioned with some frequency, but the riddle is conspicuously absent, even when the author writes, "All art is metaphor and form" (11).

9   Godfrey Nakene in his article on Tlokwa riddles identifies one category of riddles as "Modern Articles" (137–38) and John Blacking in his collection of Venda riddles includes a section entitled "European Culture" (31–32).

10 A common practice in riddling is to expand the metaphor by adding details; for example, this riddle has been expanded as follows: "I have a certain animal, if it is speared, it will writhe over a long distance fleeing across many streams, but no matter how many streams it crosses, it will come back and die at the very spot where it was speared."

11 This may be based on analogy with other geographic riddles such as the following:

- Something of mine, if one takes one from the northern horizon or the southern horizon, they are identical. (Eggs)
- If I bring one from Paris, and if I bring one from Maroua and if I bring one from Yaounde, they are exactly the same! (Eggs)

12 Pers. comm.. 12 Mar. 2004, Ngaoundéré, Cameroon.

13 This event occurred and was recorded in Bétaré Oya, Cameroon, on 31 Oct. 1976.

14 23 Nov. 1976.

15 This riddle is analogous to the widely known "I am taller sitting down than standing," for which the answer is a dog.

16 Called by Rev. Paul Tenmbar, 23 Nov. 1976.

REFERENCES

Beuchat, P. D. "Riddles in Bantu." *African Studies* 16.3 (1957): 133–49.

Black, Max. *Models and Metaphors: Studies in Language and Philosophy.* Ithaca: Cornell University Press, 1962.

Blacking, John. "The Social Value of Venda Riddles." *African Studies* 20.1 (1961): 1–32.

Derive, Jean. "Riddles." *African Folklore: An Encyclopedia.* Ed. Philip Peak and Kwesi Yankh. New York: Routledge, 2003. 395–96.

Faïk-Njuzi, C. M. *Devinettes tonales: tusumwinu.* Paris: SELAF, 1976.

Finnegan, Ruth. *Oral Literature in Africa.* Oxford: Clarendon, 1970.

Goldstein, Kenneth. "Riddling Traditions in Northeastern Scotland." *Journal of American Folklore* 76 (1963): 330–36.

Green, Thomas A., and W. J. Pepicello. "The Riddle Process." *Journal of American Folklore* 97.384 (1984): 189–203.

Green, Thomas A., and W. J. Pepicello. "Sight and Spelling Riddles." *Journal of American Folklore* 92 (1980): 23–34.

Hamnett, Ian. "Ambiguity, Classification and Change: The Function of Riddles." *Man* New Series 2.3 (1967): 379–92.

Haring, Lee. "On Knowing the Answer." *Journal of American Folklore* 87 (1974): 197–207.

Harries, Lyndon. "The Riddle in Africa." *Journal of American Folklore* 84 (1971): 180–84.

Henige, David. *Oral Historiography.* London: Longman, 1982, 1985.

Jordan, A. C. "Towards an African Literature III: Riddles and Proverbs." *Africa South* 2.2 (1958): 101–04.

Köngäs Maranda, Elli. "A Tree Grows: Transformations of a Riddle Metaphor." *Structural Models in Folklore and Transformational Essays.* Ed. Pierre Maranda and Elli Köngäs Maranda. The Hague: Mouton, 1971. 116–39.

Lakoff, George, and Mark Johnson. *Metaphors We Live By.* Chicago: University of Chicago Press, 1980.

Nakene, Godfrey. "Tlokwa Riddles" in *African Studies* 2.3 (1943): 125–38.

Noss, Philip A. "Wanto-The Hero of Gbaya Tradition." *Journal of the Folklore Institute* 18.2 (1971): 3–16.

Scheub, Harold. *The Poem in the Story: Music, Poetry and Narrative.* Madison: University of Wisconsin Press, 2002.

Tessmann, Günter. *Die Baja, ein Negerstamm in mittleren Sudan.* 2 vols. Stuttgart: Strecker und Schröder, 1937.

Vansina, Jan. *Oral Tradition as History.* Madison: University of Wisconsin Press, 1985.

Shadows of Song: Exploring Research and Performance Strategies in Yolngu Women's Crying-Songs

Fiona Magowan

Heart-wrenched wailing suddenly pierced the night air, as a commotion of distressed voices rumbled closer in the darkness. From the house opposite, the distinctive high-pitched cry of a woman was soon joined by several more, the wailing intensifying in descending cascades of sorrowful melodies, weaving a garment of sadness that seemed to cloak the town of Gali-win'ku (Elcho Island).[1] The wailing continued, polyphonically wrapping itself around the mourners and those who stayed in their houses, waiting to hear of the death, sung by men to the community through the Ancestral Law. In waterfalls of song, poetic laments of loss, longing and ancestral belonging echoed across the street, invisible cords of kin-song weaving a web that tied the deceased to the mourners and their ancestral identities. Each melodic wave of grief served to bind singers to listeners and the family of the deceased, enveloping them in a multitude of sentiments and memories. As the dawn met the last rays of the morning star, a lone woman's voice continued the lament, her thin chords straining the tenuous links remaining between life and death. Hoarse, partly sobbing and partly singing, her lament became less and less frequent until silence reclaimed the street, awaiting the funerary proceedings to follow.

These entangled webs of song pose particular problems of meaning-making for researchers of music culture, an experience that has been identified as 'chasing shadows' (Cooley 1997:3). These shadows are elusive and as evanescent

Fiona Magowan, "Shadows of Song: Exploring Research and Performance Strategies in Yolngu Women's Crying-songs," pp. 89–104 from *Oceania* 72(2), 2001.

The Anthropology of Performance: A Reader, First Edition. Edited by Frank J. Korom.

as the multiple, ambiguous and open-ended conundrums that this performance analysis addresses. I argue that Yolngu women's crying-songs, *ngäthi-manikay*, create a shadow-dance of making meaning between performers and listeners, variously twisting and turning around a performative nexus of music making, recording and the writing of music. In this examination of one senior woman's songs a series of shadow-dances between self-reflection and strategic positionings were played out between ritual performances and research recordings. For the purposes of the analysis that follow, it must be recognised that each song is only one element of the much larger and longer series from which it comes and from the complexity of other series that interact with it.[2]

In one regard, shadow-dancing suggests an ever-mobile revelation of meaning between performers and listeners where images grow longer and fuller as they are sung, like a shadow stretching out from a person as they move in relation to the sun's rays. Just as shadows change shape depending on the position of the person and their movements to the light, so, too, do the songs change until one fades and the next begins. In another regard, shadow-dancing is also a technique within song composition. Just as shadows require light in order to create them, so singing is the medium of ancestral brightness, evoking the spiritual power of ancestral beings. As one ancestral being comes into view so another may be partially alluded to, its shadow hiding in the background, waiting to be revealed in the next part of the singing. As such, ancestral beings are always in the land and sea covered and concealed, their forms but a shadow until they are sung into vision once more.

Discursive analyses in the West have all too frequently produced hegemonic narratives about cultural others. However, it is nowhere more pertinent than in a performance context that performers should be recognised as not just having begun to write themselves back into representations of their performances but that they have always done so. The 'ground of musical knowing' has increasingly been recognised as an intersubjective ground of being and being known where performers are integral authors of their performance experiences.[3]

Writing the discursive and non-discursive practices of singers back into their songs is an embodied process of cultural performativity, not just a tool of 'knowing about' music research. This intercultural and intersubjective nexus of creativity is a highly complex one as Rabinow (1977) and Dumont (1978) recognised early on, where the fieldworker's personal relationships constitute the primary data of anthropological research and their self-reflections form the epistemological base for analytic development.

This paper explores the extent to which the effectiveness of musical anthropology (Seeger 1987) depends on how various sorts of reflexivity might be recognised and managed in relation to the performances the researcher seeks to evoke, analyse and recount. It poses questions for the discipline about how the experience of performance might change the performance of anthropology. It also seeks to show how strategies of knowing and being known can be conveyed in their immediacy, intimacy and particularity without heading over the cliffs of either romanticisation or irony.[4] Crying-song knowledge cannot be entirely separated from the learning experiences of the anthropologist or ethnomusicologist, nor from the processes of recording and interpreting because 'personal experience is neither free nor individual; it is constrained by interaction with the tradition' (Rice 1994:308). Therefore, rather than viewing song as exuding an authority whose dynamics of production remains largely unquestioned, this shadow-dance is partly a play of 'how power enters into the process of "cultural translation", seen both as a discursive and non-discursive practice' (Asad 1986:163), and about 'scanning sound energy for patterns' (Clayton 2001:4) in order that a tuning-in to the world of the performer might allow a series of reflections to flicker, grow, dance and extend into and from the singer to the researcher and back again.

In order to illustrate fluidities of consciousness within the research context, I borrow Said's (1978: 20) notions of 'strategic formation' and 'strategic location' in an analysis of a selection of one woman's ritual songs.[5] In this case, 'strategic formation' could be said to be a means of analysing the relationship between individual performances of songs and their transmission to the researcher where performances acquire a particular mass, weight and referential power among themselves in the research context, as well as through multiple performances in public gatherings. The performer comes to be situated in a strategic location between other performers and the researcher, each positioned in relation to the production of particular song meanings and their effects. I examine these performance strategies as ways of knowing and coming-to-know, manifest in a small sample of *ngäthi-manikay* to show how my understanding of the learning context changed over time. For as Sangren notes:

> 'Meaning' and 'culture' are not merely the negotiations 'between' subjects in acts of 'communication'; such acts of communication are inevitably embedded in encompassing systems of power and meaning. These encompassing systems are related dialectically in the process of social and cultural reproduction to the 'experiences' of the subjects that they encompass and that are necessary in their reproduction. (Sangren 1988:417)

Different aspects of the performer-researcher relationship were revealed and concealed over seven years of performances and recordings. By reflecting on my engagement in this field-work context, it will become apparent that the singer deconstructed and reconstructed song texts as shifting narratives of herself, simultaneously locating me as strategically as possible in her own world. In recognising these strategies, the importance of a reflexive approach to the latent, and often taken-for-granted dynamics of the research process is highlighted, as it is only 'once "informants" have begun to be considered as co-authors, and the ethnographer as scribe and archivist as well as interpreting observer, we can ask new, critical questions of all ethnographies'. (Clifford and Marcus 1986:17)

The critical questions that will be posed here are: how is the complex experience of self and other danced out in a web of mutuality, reciprocity and obligation in the process of music making and, in particular, of learning crying-songs; what dynamics of respect, power, mutuality, love and obligation are generated by discursive and non-discursive practices between the performer and researcher; and how have these song strategies of location and formation shaped our relationship over time? These questions are

situated firstly in a historical trajectory of performance research in Arnhem Land.

Arnhem Land Performance Research

The only detailed analysis of *ngäthi-manikay*, from northeast Arnhem Land in the Northern Territory of Australia is Catherine Berndt's 1950 *Oceania* article, 'Expressions of grief among Aboriginal women' which compared women's song texts from Melville and Bathurst Islands with those from northeast Arnhem Land.[6] This article discusses eight texts of four Yirritja and four Dhuwa songs; two by the same woman while the others are from women of different groups. As no tape recordings exist of these songs,[7] it is probable that Berndt transcribed the texts phonetically discussing their semantics with women afterwards.[8] Apart from Berndt's analysis, *ngäthi-manikay* have only occasionally received general mention in broader discussions of ritual genres.[9] This analytic lacuna arises from a combination of academic trajectories and cultural restrictions in the research context: firstly, apart from the ethnomusciological writings of Moyle (1974) and Stubington (1978), there were few female anthropologists in northeast Arnhem Land exploring the contexts of ritual, art and performance at that time. Since the 1990s, however, there has been an increase in research on dance, ritual art and song by female researchers (see Tamisari 1998; Slotte 1997; Hutcherson 1998; and Bonfield 1998 located primarily at Milingimbi, Ramingining, Yirrkala and Gapuwiyak, respectively);[10] secondly, although male anthropologists in this region have not always treated 'relationships which flow through women as secondary and secular' (Bell 1983:240),[11] their discussions have tended to focus less upon women's views, due to the cultural limitations of gender involvement in ritual; and thirdly, as women's crying-songs constitute a period of intense personal grief, reflection and soul-searching that conjure feelings of loss and sorrow when research discussions focus upon them, women are often reluctant to sing other than at times of deep grieving.[12]

Crying-songs are solely the domain of senior knowledgeable and respected women but northeast Arnhem Land is not the only region of Australia where women's crying-songs can be heard.[13] It is common knowledge that, prior to European contact, women would wail, sing and sometimes hurt themselves[14] to show sorrow and deep love for their kin when a death or other ritual occurred.[15] In northeast Arnhem Land, both men's songs, *manikay*[16] and women's crying-songs relate the travels and actions of the ancestors embodied in and emergent from the Arnhem Land topography. Women's *ngäthi-manikay* use the ritual words of men's songs but the texts are performed in quite a different fashion. In a broad sense, anyone may cry but *ngäthi-manikay* is a specific form of emotional release from anger or grief or loss.

Unaccompanied by clapsticks or didjeridu, women cry in long slow lines, revealing the travels of ancestral beings as a series of related ancestral events. Men perform the same ancestral subjects but in three to four repeated segments with breaks between each subject. They also sing a sequence of subjects comprising an ancestral journey of the land and the sea before the song series is finished, whereas women may focus their singing upon just one major (*yindi*) song subject. While these events speak of the creative actions of ancestral beings, they are also a commentary on the physical and spiritual nature of the singer's ties to places, to other individuals and to key groups. Each ancestral being holds the essence of individual and group identities inside their own country and waters whilst connecting groups with different ancestral beings at other places. Places are spiritual containers of human life and of the possibilities for healing, illness, conception, birth and increasing spiritual strength through invoking the power of the ancestors in song. For women it is 'an individual matter about what to cry' (Berndt 1950:308) although there are certain occasions when it is obligatory to do so, for example, immediately after death, at a funeral, during or after a circumcision, or in preparation for a Ngarra or Gunapipi ritual. A woman may also cry when she remembers loved ones far away, or particular attributes of the environment such as the morning star.[17] For women, as for men, music is power – a social, spiritual and political force. Thus performance is a means of making powerful statements by authorizing, teaching and controlling the place of the researcher within the community through song.

Seeing Musically

From 1990-1992, I sought to learn and record women's crying-songs on Galiwin'ku, working with a range of senior women from different groups. This engagement was marked by a shadow-dance of increasing trust as it took several months before senior women were willing to share these songs of sorrow. The senior Datiwuy leader had adopted me on my arrival and insisted that he must teach me men's songs first as the 'inside' knowledge of ritual songs is controlled by men.[18] Once he was confident that I could dance[19] (and I had recorded and transcribed many songs of his own group, his mother's group, his mother's mother's group and his sister's son's group) he allowed me to approach women. There were problems in this shift. Moving from the status of 'honorary male' to female was a difficult transition as women were unsure how much 'inside' knowledge I had been given. Eventually, those who kindly agreed to teach me their songs were often unable to talk in depth afterwards for the pain of the memories they caused. It was also a slow and difficult process to find women who 'felt like singing' but the word gradually spread around Galiwin'ku that I was keen to learn *ngäthi-manikay*.

Murukun Dhamarrandji was acclaimed as one of the most knowledgeable and adept performers of crying-songs in the region and it was early February 1991 when this gentle but vivacious woman knocked at my door. She said, 'I will teach you *milkarri* (crying). Yolngu know my voice. It is clean and hard, *dal*. It has a good sound, *manymak rirrakay*'. Her stress on the quality of her voice was qualification of her right to know and to pass on her knowledge. The deeper a woman's voice, the greater the respect, as the timbre of the voice is consonant with the depth of song knowledge. Young women sing in higher pitches, *garramat*, while older women and men sing in a lower pitch, *ngoy*. Pitches are identified along a continuum of relativity to the singer's voice and to others known to them. Younger women would say how ashamed, *gora*, they felt to sing in public as their voices had not deepened,[20] an indication of the 'outside' and lesser status of their knowledge and the right to sing. Murukun and I met daily and we would sing, talk and record until sunset. Our days were more than song and more than musical knowledge, they were a sharing of one another in a delight of knowing and coming-to-know. Her melodies of mourning constituted a gift of musical embodiment; a generous exchange of musical knowing for my coming-to-know, that I might be enfolded in her web of musical being-in-the-world.

Of course, many town events intervened: visits of dignitaries; graduation ceremonies for Batchelor College graduates; the regular welfare pay day rush and shopping sprees; trips to Yirrkala and other homelands; and sadly, all too frequent funerals. The latter proved constant throughout 1991 with 11 funerals during the year. On some occasions Manydjarri would often request his songs to be recorded, on others, I would ask his permission to record songs of other groups, and at times, Murukun would take me to sit with the women mourning near the funeral shade to listen to their songs.

On my first trip to Arnhem Land, I was a young, unmarried, childless woman and therefore not in a position to sing crying-songs either publicly or privately without deep embarrassment. At the start, Murukun would sing as I recorded. She worked through the crying-songs of her own Djambarrpuyngu inland and seaways song series; her three groups of mother's song series, Lamamirri, Warramirri and Wangurri; her mother's mother's song series, Golumala; and those of her sister's group, Gälpu. Her decision about what to sing was always one that related to recent events and memories. If her daughter had just called from Darwin she would sing either her mother's songs or her sister's son's songs; when she would recount her patrilineal connections she would sing her father's and father's brothers' songs. She always began by saying, 'Listen to my voice', whilst I tried to memorize the timbre, pitch, melodic line and juxtaposition of her words. My initial efforts to sing were often met with a patient silence and a kind smile as she would begin to sing again . . . She would

repeat the song tirelessly without identifying what had been wrong in my rendition. On each of her repeats there would be variation in the words or in the length of the melodic line making it difficult to perfect.

In our initial days together, Murukun would not explain songs word for word. She would give a gloss and sing them again, despite my attempts to quiz her tediously on each individual phrase. I had hoped Murukun might be concerned with my questions of accuracy: had I understood the meaning of individual words; had I created the correct images from each phrase; had I captured the essence of meaning in the long lists of names so common in crying-song structure? Instead of responding analytically, Murukun would say 'listen again', as if it would become self-evident to me. It appeared as Ewing (1990:264) has noted, 'as if the utterance and the self-representation it expressed or implied were her total experience of self and that I could automatically share this. Due to the tendency to sing alternate words on each repetition, I had taken to playing the recording back, listening to the song and then singing it with her together with the tape. After a couple of attempts Murukun cried elatedly, 'Yo, manymak dhuwali', 'Yes, that's right'. On this occasion, the only change I had made was to the placing of the breath mark, a controlling factor in making meaning in crying-song performance. Gradually, I ceased wanting to ask, instead, I wanted to hear again and in doing so, I came to *feel* how she wanted me to *see* musically, the colourful movement and detail of the bird or animal that was flying in sound.

Strategies of Formation and Location

In the initial stages of song instruction, she adopted one main strategy of formation: condensed repetition of song couplets. When I had difficulty following the text she chose which segments and sections of music should be repeated for the research context, representing them in a condensed form in comparison with their elaboration in funeral contexts. This shift in the processes of contextualisation was reflected in the songs themselves, and by focusing more on these processes, I came to recognise how Murukun used particular forms of 'poetic patterning' to interpret the structure and significance of her song narrative (Bauman and Briggs 1990:70). In the learning process, when I failed to grasp the logic behind the phrasing of the melody, she would adopt a pattern of condensed repetition in every couplet, singing each line the same way twice. However, whether I had managed to correct a line or not, each repeated couplet would only be sung once before moving to the next and if I had still failed to grasp the song she would perform all of it again. In this example, of the bar-shouldered dove, the bird cries out '*gukguk*' as it sees the shadow of a shark moving slowly in the shallow waters, warning Yolngu that danger is near:

Ngapaḻawaḻ – The Bar-Shouldered Dove

Ngapaḻawaḻ gukguktja ngäthi
Ngapaḻawaḻ gukguktja ngäthi
The bar-shouldered dove is crying

Dhatharram ngäthi gukguk
Dhatharram ngäthi gukguk
The bar-shouldered dove called Dhatharram
    and Gukguk is crying

Yimingiḏa gukguktja
Yimingiḏa gukguk
The dove, called Yimingiḏa, Gukguk

Gapu nhdngal djarrarranmirrnydja
Gapu nhdngal buwaṉaṉamirrnydja
He sees the muddy water called Djarrarran and
    Buwaṉana

Ngäthi dhatharram gukguk
Ngäthi dhatharram gukguk
The dove, Dhatharram and Gukguk cries

In 1991, Murukun's first lessons began with song instruction from the perspective of her own subgroup whose patrilineal identity comes from the King Brown snake, Ḏarrpa, at Ngurruyurrtjurr. This subgroup is one of five other subgroups that join to make the one Djambarrpuyngu group. All the subgroups speak the same dialect and share the same main ancestral being, shark, as well as having rights in other ancestral beings peculiar to their own homelands.[21] Although shark is the group's primary ancestral being, Murukun chose to teach me her own subgroup's identity first, making only passing reference to the shark. As my *märi*, grandmother, Murukun was in the kinship position of key ritual authority to hold and pass on knowledge to a granddaughter and she sought to establish a sense of order and authority, teaching respect for her ancestral King Brown snake identity. In addition to the technique of condensed repetition, Murukun cried short extracts to illustrate how crying-songs are constructed in thematic segments. In this excerpt of the text, the King Brown snake lies sleeping in the shade, the shade that is also hers, the shade of the Ngurruyurrtjurr Djambarrpuyngu clan. Just as the snake sleeps, so do the people in her shade where the snake and people are one:

Warraw' (1991): King Brown Snake Shade (Ngurruyurrtjurr Djambarrpuyngu)

Ngarraku dhuwali Walarritj Lumbilumbi
This is my snake shade called Walarritj
    Lumbilumbi

Ngalimurr dhu wanganhami dhuwal
We all talk to each other here

Wulanayngu Wurrpurrnydja Riyahya
    Mangaṉiny
We are the King Brown snake people called
    Wulanayngu Wurrpurr Riyariya Mangaṉiny
    (the deep ritual names of the subgroup that
    are the essence of their identity in the land)

Throughout the learning process, we were strategizing each other from our own self-referential viewpoints; Murukun wanting to establish a sense of authority through webs of kin-song, while I wanted to understand the elements of crying-song structure. Her strategy of location was one of 'discursive formation' (Foucault 1972:49)[22] whereby she situated my kinship to her as part of our mutual becoming. We were remaking ourselves in the process as 'cultural poesis – and politics – is the constant reconstitution of selves and others through specific exclusions, conventions, and discursive practices' (Clifford and Marcus

1986:23–24). Strategically speaking, Murukun had 'tuned-in' to my infancy in understanding Yolngu culture, locating me in techniques of Yolngu education. This was evident in the differences between her crying-songs recorded at funerals and those in our private sessions. In each mode of tuning-in different streams of consciousness emerged, for example, in the discursive formation of her own crying-song identities in relation to those of other women singing and in the personal relationship between her knowledge and remaking of the deceased through her crying-songs. Women share a lifetime of streams of song conscious-ness collated from successive funeral events where, sitting together at the funeral shade, they simultaneously create their own personal-ised narratives of the deceased through the webs of kin-song, a quite different kind of tuning-in from that which happens between the performer and researcher in the learning process. In the educational context, the layer-ing of her own or other women's personal references to the deceased are often omitted.

Murukun frequently sought to emplace her own subgroup identity as the focal point of the performance in these first lessons. Speak-ing of her authority to teach me the song, she said, 'My father was Mayamaya and his ancestral identity is Manggani Wurrpurr (snake). Another brother was Badinggu but he is Darrkamawuy [shark]'.[23] By outlining her genealogical connections, Murukun organised both the performance and the dis-cussion of her own identity as a strategic response to me as her pupil, and her grand-daughter. I was placed in the situation of not only learning to respect her, but learning to respect the importance of her clan songs in relation to my own Datiwuy shark songs. She would begin with her song of the Cloud that rises over the King Brown snake shade where people are talking.

Here, three main thematic ideas are alternated:

X   Yolngu talking at the shade.
Y   the cloud forming from the breath of the groups talking to one another.
Z   the deep ritual names bundurr of the Ngur-ruyurrtjurr subgroup.

Warraw' ga Mangan
Clouds over the Ngurruyurrtjurr Djambarr-puyngu Snake Shade

X)   Dhiyal ngalimurr wanganhamirrnydja
     Here we all talk to each other
X)   Warraw 'ngur lumbilumbingurnydja
     At the shade Lumbilumbi
Y)   Malarrmalarr gudji ngatiti
     Speaking in dhangu and dhuwal languages to the cloud
Y)   Gudji ngatiti räliyi buwangbuwangdja
     The breath from our speech rises to form the cloud called Ngatiti, Buwangbuwang
Z)   Räliyi Wurrpurrtja Wulangayngu
     It comes over to us, to the Wurrpurrtja Wulanayngu Djambarrpuyngu
Z)   Djanggadpaniny Manggani Wurrpurrdurrdu
     Our bundurr is Djanggatpani, Manggani Wurrpurrdurrdu
Z)   Djanggatpaniny Manggani Wurrpurr-durrdu
     (We are the snake people) Djanggatpaniny Manggani Wurrpurrdurrdu
Y)   Manganthinan dhäruk ngalawurr
     The language is going to the cloud called Ngalawurr
Y)   Malarrmalarr Gudji Ngatiti
     The dhangu language and the dhuwal languages called Malarrmalarr and Gudji form the cloud called Ngatiti
X)   Dhiyal ngilimurr wanganhamirrnydja
     We talk together here
X)   Walarritj'ngur Walarriffngur
     At the shade called Walarritj
X)   Lumbilumbingur warraw 'ngurnydja
     At the shade called Lumbilumbi
Y)   Ngätil ngätilma Gudij Gudji Ngatiti
     In the Gudji language to the cloud Ngatiti

In this song the alternating segments create shifting images. The image of Yolngu sitting talking in the shade is contrasted with their breath being transformed into clouds rising above the shade. In a funeral context, the cloud rising over Nurruyurrtujurr is an indi-cation to other Yolngu that a Ngurruyurrtjurr member has died. When they see the cloud travelling to Yalangbara - Rirratjingu home-land, and then to Rarrakala - Barrarrngu and Barrarrparrarr land in the Wessel Islands, they may be able to establish the identity of the deceased because of the implicit links in the song. Clouds *are* the breath of Yolngu. Their essence drifts over homelands to indicate a death in another group's land by the direction in which they are travelling. While the shapes of Dhuwa and Yirritja clouds are different, the shapes of clouds are shared between groups of the same moiety enfolding multiple identities of group members.

As both a knowledgeable senior leader and a practising Christian, Murukun would always sing these crying-songs two ways: with grieving for her lost relatives and absent loved ones and as parables of faith. She would tell of how the song of her cloud at Nurruyurrtjurr is the breath of people praising God, joining Barrarrngu and Barrarrparrarr with the different Djambarrpuyngu subgroups at her Wotjara snake shade, just as in funerals, groups come together to sing their respect and love for their deceased. Their songs rise to the cloud as they unite to form the body of the family or the church. She remarked:

I am singing about each group. This one He called Dadayana, Marawunggu, Bur-ruwalka, and this one Gululuwanga, Gadulkirri, Wadulnyikpa and this one Gulkalirrngu. Our group is Wotjara Yolngu (King Brown snake people) and those others are Gundangur from Garrata (Shark people) and Miliwurrwurr from the Wessel Islands. God made each *mala* (group) to be together so they are singing praises to Him.

Although the ritual words of the song remain as they were in the previous rendition, Murukun is seeing inside the cloud, to change its colours of meaning in a shadow-dance of Christian interpretation.[24]

Warraw' ga Mangan
Shade and Cloud
Räliyi dhu Minirringa, Baliyana Rrapudja
The cloud *Minirringa, Baliyana, Rrapudja* is coming

Miliwurrurrnydja gudji 'yunmirr
From the Wessel Islands belonging to *Barrarrparrarr* and *Barrangu* where they used to speak *gudji* language[25]

Ngatiti Banggilpanggilyurra
The cloud called *Ngatiti Banggilpanggil*

Ga räliyi Burruwalka Dadayana Letileti Marawunggu
It comes from the *Djambarrpuyngu Marapay* group called *Burruwalka, Dadayana Letileti Marawunggu*

Walarritjngur warraw 'ngurnydja
At the shade of the King Brown snake called *Walarritj*

Warraw 'ngurnydja Gumukulngur
At the shade where the *Gumuk* cloud is

Nhe raliyi Wotjangurnydja
You are coming from *Wotja*

Gulkalirriyunydja Wotjangur Banggilpanggilyun
The cloud, *Gulkalirri, Banggilpanggil* is coming from *Wotja*

Dhiyal walarritjngur
Here to the king Brown snake's shade

Thus, the process of learning the melody, pitch, timing, timbre and song semantics was a process of recognising sounds as a plurality of patterned meanings. The task of understanding was also one of accumulated absorption rather than strict interpretation: while Murukun would provide glosses on the songs and identify names of places or ancestral beings, eliciting their relationship to one another and to the broader context, her singing was like a kaleidoscopic sphere turning constantly to view changing colours providing additional glimpses of meaning into her extending song web.[26] Lists of names for each song subject would evoke a myriad of nuances of movement, colour or sound relating to the ancestral being at a particular place. Often the names would be synonyms for a place or ancestor – part of the *bundurr* (deep ritual names) of the ancestral being. The layering of names allowed multiple aspects of ancestral beings to be viewed simultaneously.[27] And as my learning progressed, a freedom of improvisation and creativity emerged that had been lacking in the early sessions. Gone were the condensed repetitive phrases and instead flowing lines emerged, pictures of vitality and intensity, mosaics of ancestral action captured in the essence of improvisation.[28]

In September 1998, I returned to work with Murukun on her song texts. Whilst Murukun

was away in Yirrkala visiting relatives, Rrika-
wuku, a teacher linguist at the school, came to
see me to say that Murukun was now involved in
a music project with the school, Shepherdson
College on Galiwin'ku, and Murukun had been
recording crying-songs for Yolngu teachers to
use in classes providing an additional body of
comparative material. When Murukun returned
she agreed to record songs with me once more.
Now, time, distance and increased familiarity
created a new set of dynamics between us, as
well as a performative continuum between the
earlier research and current performance context. With a shared understanding of Murukun's
crying-songs, our discussions about songs were
as much part of music making as the performances themselves. In this new context,
'performance provided a frame that invited critical reflection on [previous] communicative
processes' (Bauman and Briggs 1990:60).
When I had first gone to the field, I had asked
Murukun if she would teach me to sing from the
knowledge of a child to the understanding of a
senior woman. Now I could witness the early
teaching strategies of condensed repetition mir-
rored in the texts of recordings made for schoolchildren seven years later.[29]

This time, however, Murukun began with
the song of the shark shade, not the snake
shade, a shift that was determined by changing
contexts as we became more familiar with one
another, 'implicitly redefining ourselves and
each other [once again] during the course of
interaction' (Sangren 1988: 273).[30] This
change in emphasis, from singing her subgroup
identity to that of the ancestral shark identity,
reflected three new strategic responses: 1) my
welcome home as her Datiwuy granddaughter;
2) recognition that I already knew the Djambarrpuyngu subgroups joined together under
the one ancestral shark; 3) and an acknowl-
edgement that this song was of deep personal
significance to our ancestral identities.

In the text the reference to the shark, Gululuwänga, indicates that there are members of
the Gundangur Djambarrpuyngu ancestral
shark subgroup present in the shade but they
are sitting apart from Murukun's snake subgroup. With an identity that encompasses both
ancestral beings, Murukun could choose
between the song of the snake and the shark,

although on this repeat occasion, her song of
the main ancestral being bound us together in
an emotive reunion of mutual musicality:

(1998) **Warraw'**
The Gundangur Shark Shade
Warraw 'nydja ngarraku dhuwal
This is my shade

Dhawurruwurru rongiyinan
(The shark ancestor is) coming back to
    Dhawurruwurru

Gong-djalk yurr ngarraku warraw'nydja
Creator of my shade

Minitjpu dhuwal warraw'
This shade is called *Minitjpu*
Ngarraku dhuwal warraw'
This is my shade

Gadulkirri wadulnyikpanydja
The shark shade called *Gadulkirri
    Wadulnyikpa*

Dhämalamirri Gululuwänga
Dhämalamirri Gululuwänga, (the deep
    ancestral names of the shark at *Gundangu*)

Go naVyurra ngarraku warraw'nyda
Let's go to the shade
Minitjipurrnydja Dhawurrurr rongiyinan
Returning to the shade called *Minitjpu,
    Dhawurrurr*

Yä– – –

Warraw' ngarraku bilyurra
Coming back to my shade

Ga minitjpurrnydja
Called *Minitjpurr*

Go ngalyurr ngarrakuy warraw 'nydja
Let's go to my shade

Ngarra dhuwal Yolnguy
I am the Yolngu (for that shade)
Dhämalamirr dhuwal
(A person from) *Dhämalamirr*
Gadulkirri Wadulnyikpa Yolngu
A shark person called *Gadulkirri,
    Wadulnyikpa*

Nhina ngarra marrtji warraw'
I am going to sit at the shade

Nhina ngarra marrtji warraw 'nurngydja
I am going to sit at the very shade

Dhawurrurr rongiyiny ngarraku go naVyurra
   warraw'nydja
Returning to *Dhawurrurr*, let's go to my shade

Minitpurrnydja.
Called *Minitjpurr*

This time, after each crying-song, Murukun's glosses painted vivid pictures of the shark lying in the mouth of the river, its shadow just visible in the shallow water; or of it making its way along the riverbed, hollowing out the creeks. Her songs were 'tone poems' of ecology and the senses they evoked inscribed feelings of her own history and experience as well as memories of past shadow-dances reaffirmed as presently shared friendship.[31] I understood that seeing meant that Murukun might project at any particular moment what Ewing (1990:251) has identified as, 'multiple, inconsistent self-representations that are context-dependent and may shift rapidly'.

As I began to understand how her songs had been strategically formed and located, I became aware that I had not been oblivious to the technical differences between ritual and non-ritual performance contexts. I was fully aware that women cried in non-repetitive lines outside the research context, and I was equally aware that Murukun was using condensed repetition to teach me the structure of these songs. What aroused my interest latterly, however, was the extent to which the strategies that Murukun employed at that time had been consciously adopted by her and employed by other senior women also. I came to ask myself: to what extent were they tuning-in to the political and emotional weight carried by the song and its pertinence for the listener, as well as placing the song in relation to themselves and their memory or recounting of others?

Consequently, there is an intensive reflexive critique that is required in evaluating the nature of the product that we come to label song, and, in turn, a corresponding ambiguity about how we create a musical anthropology.[32] Song is more than the sounds and contexts of performance; it is a way of being musically related, feelingfully entwined by patterns of sound through strategies by which researchers attempt to experience music as a performative

process and by which performers engage with us in a reciprocal web of experiential exchange. There is the need for both critique of the experiential language of musical knowing and coming-to-know and an unravelling of the nature of power relations between performers and researcher between what is sung and what is said, and between what is expressed and what is inexpressible. As it is in the music-making process that musical knowledge exists in an uneven exchange with various kinds of power – political, intellectual, cultural and moral, there is a multivocality inherent in these power relations raising questions about 'how distinct groups . . . imagine, describe and comprehend each other' (Clifford 1988: 260).

Conclusion

In this comparative analysis of one woman's crying-songs over a six year time span, I have sought to deal with the strategies of Murukun's crying-songs in relation to my own position as a researcher allowing reflection upon her perspective, as well as to engage in a generalist discourse about one woman's principles of singing. In contrast to personal narratives, it has been argued that generalist discourse tends to be a cultural-political configuration of a kind of textual attitude, yet, for Murukun, a generalist discourse was often included in her own song narration. And though I have tried to write Murukun's empowering strategies back into the text, I acknowledge that this act is a disempowering one for her. To deconstruct and reconstruct a text is an act of control and 'in regard to the differential exercise of such control the issue of power arises' (Bauman and Briggs 1990:76).

Murukun did not always choose to start every song session in the same way or with the same song. Nor were her glosses and narratives of kin and family ties always logical and cohesive. Through generalist discourse, Murukun made sense of indeterminacy, variation and her own personal strategies in performance practice. She tended to tidy up the discrepancies between performers and song variations, constantly reordering and making sense of the unruly process of music making. Yet, her performance variations did not reflect her tidy rhetoric, leaving open the possibility for future shadow-dances of mourning for her loved ones.

In this discussion, I have attempted to avoid reducing Murukun's crying-songs to one definitive musical moment but, rather, to recognise the performative strategies that account for the researcher in the moment of performance. The disparate nature of ritual and non-ritual recording contexts offers a continuum of performative paranoramas where researching and music making are mutually evolving and constitutive processes. I have argued that we need to uncover and account for the strategies and power relations between performers and researchers that go into generating musical understanding in order to understand the nature of the musical event. By writing about music, we are inextricably involved in another performance of music making, one that comes to have a related, but different tune. Thus, the sounds in our recorders are a product and process of the anthropologist actively conducting fragments of Aboriginal music into notation and text as orchestrated by the performer. The task of translating experience into textuality when there are multiple subjectivities, strategies and political constraints operating within and beyond our control is to recognise that there is a continuous 'tacking between the 'inside' and 'outside' of events: on the one hand grasping their sense of strategic occurrences and performative positioning empathetically, on the other stepping back to situate these meanings in their wider contexts' (Clifford 1988:34).

Consequently, the production of this text is itself a reflection upon reflection. Sadly, Murukun died in March 2000 and others are now reproducing her songs in her absence.[33] The writing of this piece is a shadow-dance of a different kind and another layering of strategical positioning is being played out in the knowledge that her musical gift will raise new research questions for the future: how is her memory living on in the reproduction of her song performances by the younger generation who will learn from her recordings at the school; how much of her song technique will be adopted by these younger women; and how will the learning process feed into ritual performance as younger women take up the obligation to cry for those who have passed on?

NOTES

1 Elcho Island is known today by its Yolngu name, Galiwin'ku, and is situated six kilometres off the cost of northeast Arnhem Land. It is approximately 55kms long and 35 kms wide with a population of about 1,200 Yolngu and 100 *balanda* (non-Indigenous Australians).

2 Intersections of ancestral song tracks are beyond the scope of this paper and I cannot do justice to the incredi ble depth of all Murukun's kin-songs and their links.

3 See Clifford (1988:21–54) for a detailed discussion of the authorial presence of the 'other' in the 'experiential, interpretive, dialogical and polyphonic processes at work' in the making of ethnography. Berliner (1993) also explores the nature of knowing as privileged information in his relationship with an *mbira* musician.

4 See Kisliuk (1997: 38) for a discussion of techniques of evocation in writing about performance.

5 Said (1978:20) posits that 'strategic formation' is a way of analysing the relationship between texts, and the way in which groups of texts, types of texts, even textual genres come to shape cultural thought and therefore carry their own referential power. He also argues that 'strategic location' refers to an author's position in a text in relation to the material of production.

6 While Berndt gives the singer's group identity and relationship to the deceased, no details are provided as to where these songs were recorded, although Yirrkala is a likely location. It does not appear that Catherine Berndt made tape recordings of these songs as none exists in the Berndt collection.

7 I am grateful to Dr. John Stanton for his generous assistance in accessing the Berndt collection for the purposes of listening to the Berndt's recordings from Arnhem Land.

8 I have recorded and transcribed versions of two Dhuwa songs of the Wawilak cycle, djulwadak, friarbird and *wujal*, honey ancestral being, that were also transcribed by Berndt, although space does not permit discussion of them here.

9 For example, speaking of the Maḏayin ceremony with Gunapipi, Keen (1994: 250) notes that women had their own

interpretations of songs that were similar in form to men's.

10   In addition, there have been a significant number of women anthropologists and linguists writing on other topics, e.g. land tenure, Williams (1986); linguistic variations and dialects, Morphy, F. (1977); health and sorcery, Reid (1983).

11   Morphy, H. (1978) demonstrates the centrality of women and their circulation in a cycle of exchange and Rudder's (1993) analysis of Yolngu cosmology posits the 'inside' essence of Yolngu identity as intimately related to women.

12   They may be sung out hunting and gathering, or at home following a death, but the most common occasion on which they may be heard is at funeral rituals.

13   For some excellent recent work on Aboriginal women's music see Mackinlay (2000).

14   Bodily harm was inflicted with sticks or rocks in a desire to share in the suffering of the deceased because of the remorse and regret of not having seen or spoken to the person prior to their death; not fulfilling kin duties while the deceased was alive; or a wish for revenge or blame to be attributed to a family in order to avenge the death. In many places these practices are now extant.
    Berndt (1950:307) notes how women were criticized in the past for not showing sufficient respect by cutting themselves and received hostile comment. Today the church on Galiwin'ku dissuades women from this practice and prayers are said before the announcement of the deceased is made.

15   In the Eastern Kimberleys, Kaberry (1939:209–211) reported that women's wailing comprised mainly sobbing, and ritual words were rarely included, whereas on Melville and Bathurst Islands women's songs were composed for illness and funerals (Berndt 1950:289-305).

16   *Manikay* is the generic term for song. Ritual songs performed by men at funerals are known as *bäpurru manikay*, or funeral songs. For a detailed description of a variety of men's song genres in Arnhem Land see Anderson (1992), Knopoff (1992) and Toner (2000).

17   For a more detailed analysis of environmental memory and identity in Yolngu crying-songs see Magowan (2001).

18   As all Yolngu are related through the asymmetrical marriage system, *balanda* who work closely with Yolngu are frequently adopted by a family member and placed within a particular group, creating rights and limitations upon their knowledge and behaviour.

19   Berndt (1950:306) also reports that women should 'be well acquainted with the various steps and dances as well as the relevant songs . . .'.

20   For a discussion of women's song as one element in the relational aesthetics between singing, dancing and the processes of didjeridu production and playing in Arnhem Land, see Magowan (1998).

21   The shark is also connected to Djapu and Ngaymil because it travelled through these areas on the way to Dati-wuy and Djambarrpuyngu homelands.

22   Foucault (1972:49) notes that 'discourses . . . [are] . . . practices that systematically form the objects of which they speak'.

23   Murukun's father, Mayamaya, is recognised as an important leader because he was the son of Djumbala, as was his stepbrother, Badinggu. Djumbala was renowned for his wives, 9 in total, which gave him increased ritual importance. He was also an apical figure in the continuity of the Djambarrpuyngu clan, having produced 35 children. Mayamaya increased the snake subgroup's strength fathering 28 children from 6 wives, while Badinggu supplied the shark subgroup with 17 children from 3 wives.

24   For a fuller discussion of Christian interpretations of Yolngu ritual songs and Aboriginal theology see Magowan (1999).

25   Barrarrngu and Barrarrparr members are now deceased although the Ancestral Law of these groups is held by the Murrungun aggregate of Naymil, Datiwuy, Murrungun and Golumala.

26   For a brilliant exegesis of the complexity of language in Yolngu men's songs see Keen (1977).

27   As the allusions and significances of song names are polyvalent there are many layers of meaning that cannot be extrapolated here. Keen (1994:275) has noted that radical variability in interpretation between song meanings is possible because songs are not anchored in ordinary language. Also, for a

highly sophisticated analysis of a multiplicity of meanings in ancestral landscape, art and identity see Morphy (1991).

28   Berndt (1950:306) also identifies 'some individual modification in the form of variation on an existing rhythm, or alteration of certain words whilst the traditional basis remains relatively stable . . . '.

29   The text of the bar-shouldered dove was taken from the 1998 recording done for the school.

30   Bauman and Briggs (1990: 68) note that 'shifts in social interactions can be discerned by attending to the "contextualisation cues" that signal which features of the settings are used by interactants in producing interpretive frameworks'.

31   The concept of the 'tone poem' is borrowed from the symphonic term for compositions that conjure up images of landscape imbued with national sentiment, such as Sibelius' Finlandia.

32   Within the context of Australian Aboriginal studies of music, there have been a variety of approaches to these problems of reflexivity. Barwick (1989:12) has argued that music is capable of generating new ways of understanding Aboriginal thought and culture, whilst also pointing out that no ethnomusicologist has been able to provide a comprehensive theory of Aboriginal music due to the complex relationshp between the melody, text and spoken explanations of the song (see also Ellis and Barwick 1987).

33   NB I have been given permission to write Murukun's name but it is still not allowed to be spoken, the proper practice following a death.

REFERENCES

Anderson, G. 1992. Mularra: A Clan Song Series From Central Arnhem Land. Unpublished PhD thesis, University of Sydney.

Asad, T. 1986. The concept of cultural translation in British social anthropology. In J. Clifford and G.E.Marcus (eds.) *Writing Culture: the poetics and politics of ethnography*. Berkeley, London: University of California Press, 141–164.

Barwick, L. 1989. Creative (ir)regularities: the intermeshing of text and melody in performance of Central Australian song. *Australian Aboriginal Studies*. 1: 12–28.

Bauman, R. and C. Briggs. 1990. Poetics and performance as critical perspectives on language and social life. *Annual Review of Anthropology* 19: 59–88.

Bell, D. 1983. *Daughters of the Dreaming*, 2nd edn. Minneapolis: University of Minnesota Press.

Berliner, P. 1993. [1978] *The Soul of Mbira: Music and Traditions of the Shona People of Zimbabwe*. 2nd ed. Chicago: University of Chicago Press.

Berndt, C.H. 1950. Expressions of grief among Aboriginal women. *Oceania* XX(4): 286–332.

Bonfield, A. 1998. The Dhanbul Ritual. Unpublished PhD thesis. Manchester University.

Clayton, M. 2001. Introduction: Towards a theory of musical meaning (in India and elsewhere). *British Journal of Ethnomusicology* 10(1): 1–17.

Clifford, J. 1988. *The Predicament of Culture: Twentieth Century Ethnography, Literature. and Art*. Cambridge, Mass.: Harvard University Press.

Clifford, J. and G. Marcus. 1986. *Writing Culture: The Poetics and Politics of Ethnography*. Berkeley: University of California Press.

Cooley, T. 1997. Casting shadows in the field: an introduction. In G. Barz and T. J. Cooley (eds.) *Shadows in the Field: New Perspectives for Fieldwork in Ethnomusicology*. Oxford: Oxford University Press, 3–19.

Dumont, J.P. 1978. *The Headman and I: Ambiguity and Ambivalence in the Fieldworking Experience*. Austin: University of Texas Press.

Ellis, C. and L. Barwick 1987. Musical syntax and the problem of meaning in a Central Australian Songline. *Musicology Australia* 10: 41–57.

Ewing, K. 1990. The illusion of wholeness: culture, self and the experience of inconsistency. *Ethos*: 18: 251–78.

Foucault, M. 1972. *The Archaeology of Knowledge and Discourse on Language*. New York: Pantheon.

Hutcherson, G. 1998. *Gong-Wapitja: Women and Art from Yirrkala*. Canberra: Aboriginal Studies Press.

Kaberry, P. 1939. *Aboriginal Woman. Sacred and Profane*. London: Routledge.

Keen, I. 1977. Ambiguity in Yolngu religious language. *Canberra Anthropology* 1(1): 33–50.

1994. *Knowledge and Secrecy in an Aboriginal Religion*. Oxford: Oxford University Press.

Kisliuk, M. 1997. (Un)Doing Fieldwork: Sharing songs, sharing lives. In G. Barz and T. J. Cooley (eds.) *Shadows in the Field: New Perspectives for Fieldwork in Ethnomusicology*. Oxford: Oxford University Press, 23–44.

Knopoff, S. 1992. *YUla manikay:* Juxtaposition of ancestral and contemporary elements in the performance ot Yolngu clan songs. *Yearbook of the Illternational Council for Traditional Music*. 24: 138–53.

Mackinlay, E. 2000. Maintaining grandmothers' law: female song partners in Yanyuwa culture. In *Musicology Australia* 23: 76–98.

Magowan, F. 1998. Singing the light: sense and sensation in Yolngu performance. *RES: Anthropology and Aesthetics* 34: 192–207.

1999. The joy of mourning: Resacralizing 'the sacred' music of Yolngu Christianity and Aboriginal theology. *Anthropological Forum* 9(I): 11–36.

2001. Crying to remember: reproducing personhood and community. In B. Attwood and F. Magowan (eds.) *Indigenous Memory and History in Australia and New Zealand*. Sydney: Allen and Unwin, 41–60.

Morphy, F. 1977. Language and moiety: sociolectal variation in a Yu:lngu language of North-east Arnhem Land. *Canberra Anthropology* 1(1): 516.

Morphy, H. 1978. Rights in Painting and rights in women: A consideration of some of the basic problems posed by the asymmetry of the 'Murngin' system. In J. Specht and P. White (eds.) *Trade and Exchange in Oceania and Australia. Mankind* Special Issue 11 (3): 208–219.

1991. *Ancestral Connections: Art and an Aboriginal System of Knowledge*. Chicago: Chicago University Press.

Moyle, A. 1974. North Australian Music. Taxonomic Approach to the Study of Aboriginal Song Performances. Unpublished PhD thesis. Monash University, Victoria.

Rabinow, P. 1977. *Reflections on Fieldwork in Morocco*. Berkeley: University of California Press.

Reid, J. 1983. *Sorcerers and Healing Spirits: Continuity and Change in an Aboriginal Medical System*. Canberra: Australian National University.

Rice, T. 1994. *May it Fill Your Soul: Experiencing Bulgarian Folk Music*. Chicago: University of Chicago Press.

Rudder, J. 1993. Yolngu Cosmology. Unpublished PhD thesis. Canberra: ANU.

Said, E.W. 1978. *Orientalism: Western Conceptions of the Orient*. London: Penguin Books.

Sangren, S. 1988. Rhetoric and the authority of ethnography: 'postmodemism' and social reproduction of texts. *Current Anthropology* June 29(3): 405–425.

Seeger, A. 1987. *Why Suya Sing: A Musical Allthropology of an Amazonian People*. Cambridge: Cambridge University Press.

Slotte, I. 1997. We are Family, We are One: An Aboriginal Christian Movement in Amhem Land, Australia. Unpublished PhD thesis. Australian National University.

Stubington, J. 1978. Yolngu *manikay:* Modern Performances of Australian Aboriginal Clan Songs. Unpublished PhD thesis. Monash University.

Tamisari, F. 1998. Body, vision and movement: in the footprints of the ancestors. *Oceania* 68(4): 249–271.

Toner, P. 2000. Ideology, influence and innovation: the impact of Macassan contact on Yolngu music. *Perfect Beat*. 5(1): 22–41.

Williams, N. 1986. *The Yolngu and their Land: a system of land tenure and the fight for its recognition*. Canberra: Australian Institute of Aboriginal Studies.

Part III

Ritual, Drama, and Public Spectacle

pair w/
Film on Navchs
& Navaho white man
jolable

8

Prayer as Person: The Performative Force in Navajo Prayer Acts

Sam D. Gill

Doc White Singer, an old man knowledgeable in the traditions and ways of Navajo religion, told me about prayer. He said, "Prayer is not like you and me; it is like a Holy Person, it has a personality five times that of ours." I have heard other Navajos refer to the act of prayer variously as a person who knows everything, as a person who can take you on a journey down under the earth or up to the sky, and as a person who is all powerful. The extent of the references to prayers as active agents, or more familiarly as persons, has led me to believe that this reflects the Navajo conception that prayer acts are active forces which can render effects on the world. In other words, the Navajo conception of prayer acts is one which emphasizes their pragmatic character. In the philosophical vernacular of J. L. Austin, Navajos see their prayer acts as "performative utterances," that is, as groups of words the utterance of which is actually the doing of an action.[1]

Scholars have occasionally recognized that Navajos believe that their prayers affect the world, but their view of how that takes place has been to see prayer as magically compulsive. Gladys Reichard, in her book, *Navaho Prayer: The Compulsive Word*, analyzed the rhythmic substructure in Navajo prayers to demonstrate various repetitious patterns which, she argued, garner magical forces of compulsion.[2]

In this paper I am going to exemplify a different approach by focusing upon the semantic structure of a prayer act commonly performed in Navajo ceremonials. I want to show that it is due to the semantic structure of the prayer act, rather than to its magically compulsive character, that Navajos see it as an active agent in their world.

I will show that the uttering of the prayer plays an integral part in satisfying the needs which motivate the prayer utterance. From this point of view I think we can more accurately

Sam D. Gill, "Prayer as Person: The Performative Force in Navajo Prayer Acts," pp. 143–157 from *History of Religions* 17(2), 1977.

understand the Navajo notion of prayer as a person capable of effective actions.

An Outline of Navajo Ceremonialism

I must preface my text analysis with a brief outline of Navajo ceremonialism. The passing of seasons, the cycle of life, and the efforts to subsist seem to take a position in Navajo ceremonialism secondary to the exigencies of maintaining health. Most of Navajo ceremonies are motivated by someone's illness. The acceptance of a persistent illness triggers a process bent upon restoring health. First, a diagnosis is made upon information collected by using techniques of divination to determine the cause of the illness. Normally, there need be no physiological relationship between the cause and the symptoms felt. The diagnosis leads to a recommendation for a curing way and a specific ceremonial within that way. A figure called a "singer" maintains the traditional knowledge of the prayers, songs, and procedures of the various ceremonial ways. Singers normally specialize in only one or two of the many ceremonials because of the enormous task of learning the songs, prayers, and ritual procedures necessary to perform the ceremonial. A singer must be procured and arrangements made for the ceremonial performance, which may last from one to nine nights, including the intervening days. Singing is heard almost constantly throughout, yielding to prayer chants at focal points in ritual acts. The variety and complexity of the rites which constitute the ceremonials reflect the richness and sophistication of Navajo religious thought.

Holyway Ceremonials

The prayer act which I have chosen for analysis is found in the context of a commonly used ritual way of curing known as Holyway. Holyway is used for illnesses whose cause is directly attributed to a Holy Person. Holy People are spiritual entities which Navajos identify with the power of creation and the life force of all things. The anger of the Holy People is commonly traced to some trespass by the person suffering. Navajos say that the Holy People place a spell (*álííl*) upon or within the sufferer. The theory of curing calls for the removal of the spell and the restoration of the suffering person.

Many ceremonials may be performed within the general classification of Holyway, and each of these has an extensive associated mythology telling the story of the original performance of the ceremonial. This kind of mythology features a heroic figure who journeys into forbidden places or performs forbidden acts. Predicaments of various kinds, ranging from his illness to his complete annihilation, are the consequences of these trespasses. Holy People are brought to aid the hero in his predicament, healing and restoring him by performing a ceremonial over him. The full ritual procedures, including prayers and songs, are normally told in the myth as archetypical for the Navajo use of that ceremonial. This mythology informs the meaning of the ceremonial. Navajos maintain a close association between the ceremonial and its myth. They identify the sick person with the hero of the myth.

Holyway Prayer

The prayer act I have chosen is distinctive to Holyway. It is chanted during the prayerstick and offering ceremony, which is performed each morning of the first four days of all Holyway ceremonials. Prayersticks are usually short hollow reeds which are prepared and decorated with particular Holy People in mind. Offerings of small bits of semiprecious stone of various colors are prepared. Cycles of songs accompany the readying of these ritual materials and their placement in cloth or cornhusk bundles. The subject in the ceremony, referred to as the "one-sung-over," is given these objects to hold while he intones the prayer in litany fashion with the singer.[3] At the conclusion of the prayer the singer takes the bundles and ritually presses them several times to various parts of the one-sung-over's body. Then, as songs are sung, an assistant takes the bundles outside the ceremonial structure to deposit them in places appropriate to the Holy People.

The prayer from this ritual as performed in the Holyway ceremonial Navajo Windway is as follows:

Dark Wind youth chief, who runs along the top
   of the earth,
I have made an offering for you,
I have prepared a smoke for you!

This very day you must remake my feet for me,
This very day you must remake my legs for me,
This very day you must remake my body for me,
This very day you must remake my mind for me,
This very day you must remake my voice for me!

This very day you must take your spell out of
   me by which you are bothering me,
This very day you have removed your spell
   from me by which you were bothering me,
You have left to take it far away from me,
You have taken it far away from me.

This very day I shall recover,
This very day my body is cooling down,
This very day my pains are moving out of me!

With my body cooled off, I am walking about,
With my body light in weight, I am walking
   about,
With a feeling of ease I am walking about,
With nothing ailing me I am walking about,
Immune to every disease I am walking about,
With pleasant conditions at my front I am
   walking about,
With pleasant conditions at my rear I am
   walking about,
As one who is long life and happiness I am
   walking about,
Pleasant again it has become,
Pleasant again it has become![4]

This prayer is normally repeated several times, changing only the name of the Holy Person and his attributes. This constitutes a prayer set.

    The prayer text can be divided into constituent parts to facilitate analysis and discussion of the prayer act. First, the name of a Holy Person is mentioned along with his distinctive attributes. Next, two phrases mention the making of an offering and the preparation of a smoke. Following this a passage beseeches the Holy Person to remake the one praying, referring specifically to the feet, legs, body, mind, and voice. Next is a passage which describes the removal and dispersion of the inflicted spell. It is followed by the statement of the consequent recovery taking place. The prayer concludes with a description of an accomplished state of pleasantness.[5]

Name mention

The names of the Holy People, which are mentioned in the first prayer constituent, normally refer to those who are active characters in the corresponding ceremonial origin myth. For example, Dark Wind, who is named in this Navajo Windway prayer, appears frequently in the Navajo Windway myth. In one instance his help was sought to cure the hero, Older Brother, and his brother and two sisters when they ate a forbidden plant and became ill.

Offering/smoke

The second constituent, "I have made an offering for you,/I have prepared a smoke for you!" refers to the prayerstick and offering bundles. The hollow prayerstick reeds are cut in designated lengths and filled with tobacco. The open ends of the reeds are sealed with moistened pollen, and a rock crystal is held so that the light entering the smokehole of the ceremonial hogan is directed to the tips of the prayersticks in a symbolic lighting. The prayersticks are placed in cloth bundles containing fragments of turquoise, abalone, white shell, and jet as offerings.

    The purpose for designating the prayersticks and bundles as "offering and smoke" is illuminated by an event commonly recounted in ceremonial origin mythology. In Holyway myths a sequence of episodes describes the procurement of the help of the Holy Person who is believed to be offended by the sufferer's trespass. This help is considered essential, for only the Holy Person can relieve the situation. An intermediary is sent to the Holy Person bearing a gift of one laced bundle. He presents this gift to the Holy Person with a ritual gesture, but the Holy Person makes no acknowledgment. The intermediary returns with two laced bundles, but the response is the same. After trying three and four such bundles, without success, those seeking his help conclude that they must be approaching the Holy Person incorrectly. They seek the help of someone who, they are told, knows the right address and gift. An episode is sometimes necessary to tell how this information is obtained, but eventually forthcoming is a description of the proper gift for the sought-after Holy Person and the design of the prayerstick which must accompany it. With these prepared, the intermediary returns

to the Holy Person, who immediately acknowledges the gift and says to the messenger, "Go
ahead then, my grandchild, prepare me a
smoke." A cloth is laid down upon which the
smoking elements are prepared. Tobacco is
placed in the pipe and a rock crystal is held
up to the sun so the sunlight may be directed
to light the pipe. After the Holy Person smokes,
the messenger is given the pipe to smoke. The
Holy Person addresses the messenger, "All right
my grandchild, what can happen to him!" He
knows the desires of the messenger without ever
being asked! He continues, "I will positively
return to my grandchild! What can happen to
him? In four days I will follow you." But the
messenger is unsatisfied with a four-day delay
and implores the Holy Person to return with him
immediately. Yielding, the Holy Person says,
"All right, my grandchild, let us go then!"
And they depart to perform the cure for the
suffering hero.

The meaning of the words which name a
Holy Person and announce that an offering
and smoke have been made may be understood
at various levels. In the limited context of the
immediate ritual acts of the prayerstick rite they
are simple descriptive statements which refer to
the completed manual tasks of preparing the
prayersticks and the offering bundles. At this
level of meaning the words perform in a locutionary sense, in Austin's vernacular, in that they
refer to, or describe, an event which has taken
place.[6] This is confirmed by the perfective mode
of the Navajo verbs used to designate completed
acts.[7] Recall the phrases, "I have made" (*'ishła*)
and "I have prepared" (*nádįįhíílá*).

But when these constituents are seen in light
of Navajo religious tradition as borne in
mythology, another level of meaning is
revealed. The words of these first two prayer
constituents not only make reference to the
manual acts which precede the prayer utterance
but also to the events in sacred history which
established the Holyway procedures for getting
the help of a Holy Person. Here, the words of
the prayer, along with the ritual acts associated
with the prayersticks and offerings, constitute
the proper procedures for acquiring this helper.
The utterance of this part of the prayer in the
appropriate ritual context amounts to the acts
necessary to establish the kind of relationship

with a Holy Person which obliges him to
respond to certain requests made of him. It is
the relationship of "grandfather" to
"grandchild." It is the performance of the
speech act as conventionalized in ceremony
which seeks to establish a relationship, and
thus it carries, in Austin's terms, an
illocutionary force. The performance of this
part of the act has a certain conventional force.

Imperative to remake

The next constituent of the prayer amounts to
an imperative to remake: "This very day you
must remake my feet for me," and so on. This
passage confirms the performative effect of the
preceding passage in that it assumes that the
Holy Person is attentive and that a relationship
is established in which the Holy Person may be
addressed directly in an imperative verbal
mode. It does not humbly ask a favor of the
Holy Person, it beseeches the Holy Person to
remake the feet, legs, body, mind, and voice of
the sufferer.

The significance of the catalog of body
parts is illuminated in Navajo creation
mythology. The Navajo conception of life is
presented as a manlike form (*bii'gistíín*) which
stands within all living physical forms –
mountains, rivers, plants, and animals. The
placement of the manlike inner life form
within the outer physical form is the basic
act of creation as revealed in the study of
Navajo creation mythology.[8] This act focuses
upon the correspondence of the inner and
outer forms at these particular body parts.
The correspondence is often expressed in ritual by the manual act of pressing at the body
parts concerned, symbolizing life entering the
physical form. Thus, the act of remaking in
Holyway is an act of recreation. It is enacted in
Holyway ritual as the prayerstick and offering
bundles are pressed to the body of the one-
sung-over at these named places.

Removal and dispersion

The prayer constituent beseeching the Holy
Person to act has a pragmatic effect in that
the utterance of the words exerts a force upon

the Holy Person addressed. The constituent bears an illocutionary force of an "exercitive type" in Austin's categorization.[9] Following the utterance of words which effect an obligatory relationship between the one praying and the Holy Person addressed, a response to the beseechment should be anticipated. According to the conventional response, the Holy Person should fulfill his obligation by removing the spell and allowing the return of health. Austin reminded us that the exercitive force of beseechment invites, by convention, a response or sequel. And indeed the next constituent of the prayer describes the progressive removal and dispersion of the inflicted spell.

> This very day you must take your spell out of
>   me by which you are bothering me,
> This very day you have removed your spell
>   from me by which you are bothering me,
> You have left to take it far away from me,
> You have taken it far away from me.

The Navajo verbal modes of the constituent reveal a shift from the imperative – "you *must* take it out of me" (*shá'áádíídłííł*) – to the perfective mode – "you *have* taken it out of me" (*shạhanéinílá*) and "you *have* taken it away" (*dahnídinílá*). Beginning with an imperative, "You must take it out of me," the prayer constituent concludes in the perfective indicating the completion of the act of removal.

Recovery

The expected response to the imperative to remake is thus begun, but it is a partial one, for it only removes the bothersome object. The concluding constituents describe the recovery taking place.

> This very day I shall recover,
> This very day my body is cooling down,
> This very day my pains are moving out of me!

Again the verbal mode of this constituent is telling. The Navajo verb of the phrase "I shall recover" is in the iterative mode, indicating the repeated return to a state once held. The verb, *náádideshdááł*, would translate literally something like "I shall start right now to go again

like I went before." It indicates that the action is beginning in the immediate present. The Navajo verb translated as "is cooling" (*hodínook'eeł*) is in the progressive mode indicating that the action of cooling is taking place as the words are being uttered. Hence, the shift in verbal mode indicates that the act is initiated and is progressing as the prayer is being uttered.

Pleasantness regained

The prayer utterance closes with the repetition of the verb *naasháadoo*, rendered here as "I am walking about": "With my body cooled off, I am walking about,/With my body light in weight, I am walking about," and so on. *Naasháadoo* is a verb in the progressive mode with a continuative aspect. In other words, the form of the verb indicates that the action is in progress and that it will continue or endure. The other verbs in this passage are in the perfective mode indicating that the action has been completed. This passage maintains the correspondence between the prayer and the episode in the ceremonial origin myth. It presents in summary the curing of the hero and his recovery to a state of good health. The state of health is expressed in terms of coolness, lightness in weight, feeling of easiness, and a state of immunity to disease. These clearly refer to the physical state, but the state of health is also expressed as being surrounded by a pleasant environment, designated by the Navajo word *hózhó*. This was the condition obtained at the completion of the process of creating life on the earth's surface. When the world had been created with all of its living features, two Holy People were sent to the tops of the sacred mountains to view the new creation. From these high vantage points, they found a world which they described as *hózhó*, "simply beautiful." Thus, through the prayer act the one-sung-over regains a condition of *hózhó*, an environment fitting the pristine beauty of creation, in which he may walk about.

Finally, the words of the prayer identify the one-sung-over with "long life and happiness." "As one who is long life and happiness I am walking about." In English the terms long life and happiness have an admirable enough

character, but they are two of the most important terms in Navajo religious language –
są'ah naghái bik'eh hózhó.[10] In creation
mythology these terms are personified as a
young man and woman whose beauty was
without equal. They were among the first of
the forms to be created. They are described as
the means by which life moves through time.
They are the kinetic force of life. They are also
identified with speech and thought, which are
essential to the process of creation and the
maintenance of life through time. Hence,
from the perspective of Navajo religious traditions, the identity of the one-sung-over with
long life and happiness is the ultimate expression of health regained.

The prayer concludes with the conventional
phrase, "Pleasant again it has become," which
is repeated twice for each prayer in the set and
an additional two times after the concluding
prayer.

The Prayer as a Pragmatic Act

The pragmatic effect of uttering the prayer
must be realized in the context of the situation
motivating the act. In this case it is a part of a
ceremonial motivated to cure an individual
who is sick. The one suffering the illness is
the one who utters the prayer with the singer.
At the surface level the prayer is uttered as a
prayer of intercession by the singer and as a
prayer of petition and beseech ment by the one-
sung-over. But on the basis of my analysis of
the prayer as a ritual act in a religious tradition,
other levels of meaning have been revealed. The
semantic structure of the prayer is identical to
the effect the prayer seeks, the restoration of
health. It mentions the name and distinctive
attributes of the Holy People who are thought
to be responsible for the suffering. It reports
that an offering and smoke have been prepared
for the Holy People and it engages them in
binding relationships of reciprocity. It
beseeches these Holy People to remake the
sufferer, an act they are obliged to perform.
The subsequent removal of the spell, its dispersion to a place far away, and the return to
health are described by the prayer as they
take place.

It is clear that the significance of the prayer is
dependent not only upon the situation which
motivates its utterance but also upon the
intended pragmatic effect. But it must be
observed that the physical symptoms of the
sickness which motivate the act, and their
physiological causes, are not the primary field
which is intended to be affected by the prayer
act. It is not directed toward physical symptoms nor to their physiological causes but
rather toward the establishment of relationships with spiritual entities, the Holy People.
The illness suffered is attributed to the impair-
ment of spiritual relationships. The physical
symptoms of illness are only the manifestation
of this situation. Hence, at its core, the prayer
act is a religious act, yet it functions at one level
as a medical act. In terms of Navajo thought the
prayer act is significant as a religious act of
communicating at a spiritual level. This is what
is distinctive of any act of prayer. The effect of
this religious act is thought to be reflected in the
return of physical health. But, it is impossible to
perceive the pragmatic character of the prayer
act as curative in a physical sense without first
considering it as a religious act.

Much effort has been expended in the study
of Navajo ceremonials from the perspective of
Western scientific medical practice.[11] Theories
of psychological techniques, of physical ther-
apeutics, and folk pharmacology have been
advanced to demonstrate the pragmatic significance of these ceremonial practices. Where
these are found to be inadequate, theories of
magical control have been advanced. Still,
these explanations seem partial and
inadequate. They are burdened with a host
of insoluble problems when held against the
whole fabric of Navajo ceremonialism. In order
to realize more fully the significance these
prayer acts have for Navajo people, I believe
that Navajo ceremonials must be considered as
religious events in which Navajos participate in
the meaningful way of life revealed to them by
the Holy People at the beginning of time. The
pragmatic effects of the prayer are directed
toward the spiritual realm. But, as the prayer
text shows, there is an expected attendant
change in the physical world.

The prayer act is, therefore, not simply a
curing act, but a religious act of curing. When

seen as a total integrated act, illuminated by the religious traditions, it becomes evident that it is meaningful to those who perform it not simply because it cures physical ailments, but because it performs the acts which institute and maintain a particular way of life. Its semantic structure is comprised of a sequence of words and related actions significant in Navajo religious tradition for what they do as they are performed. In the context of a Holyway healing ceremonial, the prayer act is significant in being among those things a Navajo does in response to certain culturally recognized needs. It is the performance of an act of curing as much as is the administration of an injection of drugs by a physician in the Western scientific medical tradition.

The ritual prayer act is necessarily symbolic, because it focuses upon spiritual rather than physical conditions. Yet, Navajos recognize a correspondence between the physical and the spiritual world in much the same way that a symbol serves as the vehicle for an abstract referent. This is demonstrated in the prayer act analyzed. When the relationship with the Holy Person was reestablished and he removed the spell, the consequence was described in terms of a renewed state of physical health.

The entire prayer act, including the manual gestures and the speech utterance, operates as a performative and in the perlocutionary sense, in Austin's terms, because it attests to the generation of a force which causes something to be accomplished – generally, to bring about a change in the state of health of the one praying. We can state in simple terms the perlocution: by performing a sequence of several conventional acts which constitute the act of prayer, the one praying is cured of an illness suffered.

I have used J. L. Austin's classification of types of performative utterances not as a guide to the analysis of the prayer act but rather as a way to state more clearly the pragmatic character of the prayer act. It will be recalled that the prayer act has been seen as performative in all three of the types Austin describes – locutionary, illocutionary, and perlocutionary. It has also been shown that the type of performative is dependent upon the extent of the context allowed to inform the act. In its most limited

ritual context, the prayer act can be seen only as a performative of the locutionary type. The prayer utterance has a certain referential relationship to the manual acts performed. When considered as a religious act patterned upon an episode described in mythology, it is recognized as a performative of the illocutionary type. In performing the prayer act it is beseeching a Holy Person to respond to a given situation. Finally, when seen as a religious act of curing it is recognized as a performative of the perlocutionary type. By performing the act the Holy Person is beseeched to act so that health is restored.

"Doctrine of the Infelicities"

But these acts do not always obtain the expected results. Upon the performance of a Navajo ceremonial motivated by the need for a physical cure, it is not uncommon that the expected physiological effect is not gained. The person often remains ill or dies. In Austin's discussion, he observed that there is nothing automatic about performatives since they are not mechanical acts. He demonstrated that the failure of such an act must be accounted for in terms of contexts and intentions, rather than in terms of veracity. Austin presented six rules, all of which must be upheld for a performative to be effective. The rules amount to what he called a "doctrine of the infelicities," which demonstrates the important point that the performative is happy or unhappy as opposed to true or false.[12]

Navajos have not been silent on the occasions when ceremonials fail to cure. A systematic appraisal of the Navajo explanations given for failure would essentially amount to a Navajo "doctrine of the infelicities." If formalized, it would include these rules.

1. The diagnosis must be correct and complete. If the diagnosis discerns the wrong cause, an inadequate ceremonial process will be used and, consequently, it will be ineffective. Further, if multiple causes are only partially detected, only a partial cure will be effected.

2. The circumstances and location of the ceremonial performance must be appropriate. The ceremonial must take place in a properly

consecrated enclosure. It must take place only during the appropriate seasons of the year. The participants, particularly the singer and the one-sung-over, must have proper and serious intentions. They must demonstrate these intentions by observing specific dietary and social restrictions before, during, and after the performance of the ceremonial.

3. The elements of the ritual process must be performed exactly as required by the conventions of the religious tradition as held in the memory of the singer performing the ceremonial. This requires that (a) prayers must be uttered word perfect; (b) ritual objects must be accurately prepared and properly used; (c) songs must be sung correctly and in proper sequence; and (d) the entire ritual process must be performed completely, accurately, orderly, and timely. Errors in any of these areas may result in the failure to cure.

The character of these restrictions has commonly been observed as consistent with the nature of magical acts since exact repetition of formula and act is often considered distinctive of the character of a magical act. However, when the ritual process is seen as a sequence of performative acts, it becomes clear that the attention to accuracy is a matter of the proper execution of conventional acts. It will be recalled that in the archetypes described in mythology, the presentation of an inappropriate offering to a Holy Person effected no response and the hero continued to suffer. It is clear that careful and accurate performance of the prayer act is semantically necessary for the effect of the utterance of the prayer act to be felicitous.

Conclusion

In the above analysis I hope to have shown that the act of prayer is a religious act of curing, and that when seen in this light the very performance of the act has significant pragmatic effects. The way Navajos respond to ill health is not adequately understood when such central ritual elements as prayer are viewed as either magically compulsive acts or as pseudoscientific medical practices. For the Navajo, health is synonymous with a state of new creation and

sickness is a disruption of that state. In other words, sickness is a state of disorder. Navajo prayer acts serve to reestablish order by a process of remaking or recreating. As an especially critical part of this process, Navajo prayer acts may be seen as a language of creation with a performative force.

I must emphasize that magic and mystery have not been removed from this religious curing process. They have been placed in the more appropriate sphere of the acts of the Navajo Holy People, rather than being associated with the character of the performance of Navajo prayer acts.

The Navajo consider an act of prayer to be a person, indeed, a kind of Holy Person.[13] Upon the basis of the semantic analysis of prayer as a performative act, I believe that it is clear that this is far more than a pleasing metaphor. At the conclusion of the era of creation, the Holy People departed from the earth's surface to go to their own domain. Upon leaving they indicated that they would never again be seen as they were at that time. With this departure a great communications gap was created between the Navajo people and the Holy People. The Navajo were left on the earth with the responsibility for maintaining the world as it had been created and the kind of life that had been revealed to them. They were given prayers, songs, and ceremonial ways as the means to do so. Bridging the gap between the earth people and the Holy People is a crucial element in Navajo ceremonial practices. This is accomplished by uttering prayers who are thought of as messengers who have unique communications and travel abilities. It may be concluded that the very idea of the prayer act as a performative force is embedded in Navajo religious thought.

NOTES

1 I do not wish to encumber this paper with a summary of Austin's work (*How to Do Things with Words*, ed. J. O. Urmson and Marina Sbisa, 2d ed. [Cambridge, Mass.: Harvard University Press, 1975]). Summaries can be found in numerous works, such as Ruth Finnegan, "How to Do Things with

Words: Performative Utterances among the Limba of Sierra Leone," *Man*, n.s. 4 (1969): 537–52; S. J. Tambiah, "Form and Meaning of Magical Acts: A Point of View," in *Modes of Thought*, ed. Robin Horton and Ruth Finnegan (London: Faber & Faber, 1973), pp. 199–229; and Benjamin Ray, "'Performative Utterances' in African Ritual," *History of Religions* 13 (August 1973): 16–35.

2   In my study of Navajo prayer ("A Theory of Navajo Prayer Acts: A Study of Ritual Symbolism" [Ph.D. diss., University of Chicago, 1974]) I did not find a single challenge to Reichard's view of prayer as compulsive magic. See esp. pp. 524–38 for my critique of her approach.

3   I refrain from calling the subject of the healing ceremonials by the term "patient" and the performing specialist by "medicine man," as has often been the custom, because I feel that it indicates a predisposition toward an explanation based on medical ideology, thus precluding the perspective of religion.

4   This prayer text is taken from Leland C. Wyman, *The Windways of the Navaho* (Colorado Springs, Colo.: Taylor Museum of Colorado Springs Fine Arts Center, 1962), pp. 182–83. I have made some changes in the translation based on a careful analysis of the mode and aspect of Navajo verbs. It resembles more closely the translation of the prayer in Wyman's *Beautyway, a Navaho Ceremonial* (New York: Pantheon Books, 1957), pp. 98–102. Both are texts recorded by Father Berard Haile. I wish to thank Clark Etsitty for help in this task.

5   This is but one of eight major classes of prayer that I have identified and analyzed. See my "Theory of Navajo Prayer Acts."

6   For a definitive discussion of Austin's classifications of performatives, see especially his lectures 8–10 in Urmson and Sbisa.

7   The Navajo verb is capable of distinguishing as many as four different aspects and six different modes by alterations of the stem. The modes distinguished are: *imperfective*, indicating that the action is incomplete but is in the act of being accomplished or about to be done; *perfective*, indicating that the action is complete; *progressive*, indicating that the action is in progress; *iterative*, denoting

repetition of the act; *usitative*, denoting habituality in performing the act; and *optative*, expressing potentiality and desire. The aspects are: *momentaneous*, action beginning and ending in an instant; *repetitive*, action repeated; *semelfactive*, action which occurs once and is neither continued nor repeated; and *continuative*, action which is continued. See Robert W. Young and William Morgan, *The Navajo Language* (Salt Lake City, Utah: Deseret Book Co., 1972), p. 42.

8   For the most extensive discussion of this concept, see Father Berard Haile, "Soul Concepts of the Navaho," *Annali Lateranesi* 7 (1943): 59–94.

9   For Austin's discussion of five general classes of illocutionary forces, see lecture 12 in Urmson and Sbisa.

10   For a thorough linguistic analysis of these terms, see Gary Witherspoon, "Navajo Language: Creating, Controlling and Classifying the Universe," mimeographed (Ann Arbor: University of Michigan, n.d.).

11   An approach dubbed by William James as "medical materialism" in *The Varieties of Religious Experience* (New York: Macmillan Publishing Co., Collier Books, 1962), p. 29.

12   Austin states in lecture 2 (in Urmson and Sbisa) that the failure to satisfy any one of the following six conditions will result in the performative being infelicitious or unhappy:
(A.l) There must exist an accepted conventional procedure having a certain conventional effect, that procedure to include the uttering of certain words by certain persons in certain circumstances, and further,

(A.2) the particular persons and circumstances in a given case must be appropriate for the invocation of the particular procedure invoked.

(B.l) The procedure must be executed by all participants both correctly and

(B.2) completely.

(C.l) Where, as often, the procedure is designed for use by persons having certain thoughts or feelings, or for the inauguration of certain consequential conduct on the part of any participant, then a person participating in and so invoking the procedure must in fact have those thought or feelings, and the participants must intend so to conduct themselves, and further.

(C.2) must actually so conduct themselves subsequently.

13   The very fact that "person" for the Navajo is not restricted to human person is essential to an understanding of Navajo religion. For an especially illuminating discussion of the concept of person as it applies to the Ojibwa, see A. I. Hallowell, "Ojibwa Ontology, Behavior, and World View," in *Culture in History: Essays in Honor of Paul Radin*, ed. Stanley Diamond (New York: Columbia University Press, 1960), pp. 18–52.

9

Performance and the Cultural Construction of Reality

Edward L. Schieffelin

Introduction: Meaning-centered Analyses of Ritual

In this paper I will assess the limitations of symbolic analyses of ritual that take the form, primarily, of a meaning-centered examination of ritual text and emphasize the critical importance of the nondiscursive rhetorical and performative aspects of ritual. I will support the claim that symbols are effective less because they communicate meaning (though this is also important) than because, through performance, meanings are formulated in a social rather than cognitive space, and the participants are engaged with the symbols in the interactional creation of a performance reality, rather than merely being informed by them as knowers. I will illustrate the point by an analysis of the drama and rhetoric of curing séances among the Kaluli people of Papua New Guinea.

Limitations of the meaning-centered approach

Ever since anthropologists turned from viewing rituals in purely structural-functional terms

and began looking at them as systems of symbols, a great deal of research has focused on how rituals work: what do ritual symbols mean, how are they communicated, and how do they accomplish the social and psychological transformations that they do.[1]

The most recent anthropological studies of ritual share a similar perspective on the question of the efficacy of ritual symbols. The major premise is that symbols are effective because they somehow formulate or "make sense" of particular, often problematic, cultural, or psychological situations and then reframe, transform, or intensify this "sense," leading to a new orientation of the participants to their situation. Sherry Ortner has given perhaps the clearest characterization of this idea:

> As actors participate in or employ symbolic constructs, their attitudes and actions become oriented in the directions embodied in the form and content of the construction itself; the construct – the model if you will – makes it difficult for them to "see" and respond to the situation in a different way [Ortner 1978:8].

Edward L. Schieffelin, "Performance and the Cultural Construction of Reality," pp. 707–724 from *American Ethnologist* 12(4), 1985.

The Anthropology of Performance: A Reader, First Edition. Edited by Frank J. Korom.

A basic problem for analysis, then, is to determine what are the problematic realities in the culture to which the symbolic construction addresses itself, what strategic orientations toward those realities are embodied in the construct, and finally, how does it work? How in its peculiar construction does the symbolic construct accomplish its task in a powerful and convincing way, so that its respondents in fact accept it as an accurate rendering of "reality," and adopt its implied orientation of attitude and/or action (Ortner 1978:8)?

Most investigators have addressed this problem by focusing particularly on the symbolic meanings embodied in the structure and content of the ritual itself, viewing ritual acts and statements as a kind of coded communication, a cultural text. The analysis of ritual then takes the form of a kind of textual analysis:

[It is an] analysis of semantic structure and process that seeks to reveal how the problematic phenomena have been portrayed and interrelated, by means of various semantic devices, so as to cast the situation in the light in which it in fact emerges [Ortner 1978:8].

This basic program has been carried out in a number of different studies that, although drawn from sources as diverse as linguistics, literary criticism, and psychoanalysis, ultimately exhibit very similar analytical strategies. Whether the analysis emphasizes the multivocal, synthesizing, internal structure of the symbols themselves (as does Turner 1967), or the narrative, structural, or psychological relations between them (cf. Lévi-Strauss 1967; Devereux 1956), or integrates all of these, the main weight of the analysis rests on a demonstration of the permutations of meaning in the symbolic materials themselves.[2] The result often seems to imply that the efficacy of symbols is a rather rational, intellectual business. As Kapferer (1979a) has pointed out, it is as if the participants somehow undergo the ritual transformations automatically as they are exposed to the symbolic meanings and that an understanding of how symbols are effective is simply a matter of understanding the logic of thought that underlies them. This kind of cognitivist emphasis on the efficacy of symbols is a bit overstated here, but the emphasis is difficult to avoid when the focus of the analysis is mainly on symbolic meaning. So long as the analysis of ritual is restricted to the meaning of symbols, understanding how rituals work will appear to be largely a matter of the message they communicate.

Many anthropologists have been aware of this limitation and have tried to avoid it by calling attention to the nondiscursive dimensions of ritual, emphasizing that rituals gain their effectiveness through being enacted or performed. It is through participation in ritual singing and dancing, through viewing dramatic presentations of sacra, emblems, and masks, or through being subjected to painful ordeals that participants come to see symbolic representations as external and having a force of their own. Vivid ethnographic accounts of exotic rituals make this intuitively apparent. However, the means by which the *performance* accomplishes this, beyond providing dramatic or emphatic presentation of ritual symbols and provoking strong emotional arousal, is rarely examined. The problem is not that of recognizing the importance of nondiscursive elements for the efficacy of ritual, but rather of understanding exactly how they work.

In an important paper on ritual and political oratory, Bloch (1974) made an important step in this direction. He argued that most meaning-centered analyses of ritual assume that symbols operate primarily through their propositional force, that is, their power to convey information about, comment upon, or formulate some particular state of affairs. He maintained, to the contrary, that the significance of ritual symbols was in large part determined by the manner in which they were presented linguistically in ritual; for him this was largely a matter of the highly formalized and restricted quality of ritual language. Discussing political and ritual oratory among the Merina of Madagascar, he argued that the highly restricted code constrains ritual communication to structures of formulaic speech, singing, and dancing and renders the semantic aspect of the ritual text so predictable and redundant that far from representing an enriched and emphatic form of communication, it represents an informationally impoverished one. While the information-carrying force of the ritual language is thus reduced, its persuasive or compelling force is not. This "illocutionary" force, according to Bloch (following Searle, Austin, and others), resides, however, in aspects of language *form*, not in its semantic content. When people find themselves in situations (like ritual or political oratory) where a certain form is obligatory, there is no way the structure of role relations and authority can be challenged except by opting out of the ritual itself (and hence, out of the social group, Bloch 1974:59). In other words, ritual language and ritual modes of communication are not effective mainly because they convey information, reveal important cultural truths, or transform anything on the semantic level. Rather, they are compelling because they establish an order of actions and relationships between the participants through restricting and prescribing the forms of speaking (and, I would add, interaction) in which they can engage so that they have no alternative way to act. The situation itself is coercive.

Bloch's work can be usefully criticized on a number of grounds. The ethnographic record reveals that the rituals can by no means be universally characterized, as Bloch implies, in terms of highly formalized language and rigidly prescribed behavior. Indeed, such rituals may be characteristic mainly of hierarchical societies such as the Merina rather than egalitarian societies such as the Gnau of Papua New Guinea (Lewis 1980), where ritual language and behavior is more loosely determined and negotiable. Irvine (1979) has shown that Bloch's notion of formalization combines a number of separable aspects of speech and behavior that may vary independently of each other, do not all imply the same sorts of restrictions of role behavior, and can potentially be combined in many ways to perform different kinds of communicative functions. Finally, Bloch focuses too narrowly on formalization of speech, while leaving other aspects of the performance, situation, and context in which the speech occurs relatively unexamined (Brenneis and Myers, eds. 1984). Nevertheless, Bloch's fundamental contribution remains: the notion that the efficacy of symbols in ritual is to be sought not so much in their semantic content or propositional character (the meaning-centered approach) as in the nonsemantic,

nonpropositional aspects of performance and linguistic form that shape the content of ritual events and the relations among the participants. This opens a fruitful new direction for investigation.

Kapferer moves beyond Bloch's linguistic focus without losing sight of the importance of semantics to argue that rituals effect transformations in symbolic meaning through effecting transformations in the organization of their performance (1979a:3). In a remarkable analysis of an exorcism rite in Sri Lanka (1979b), he shows that although the movement toward cure of the patient is outlined in the logic of the symbolic enactments, it is through the performative manipulation of ritual frames, aesthetic distance, audience/participant focus, attitude, and commitment to the performance reality that the ritual actually works. Kapferer directs attention in the study of performance in ritual to (1) the arrangement of space and the organization of audience and participants in the performance setting, and (2) the media (song, dance, and so on) in which the symbolic action is carried out (1979a:7–9). It is through changes in the organization of the performance that changes in the roles and relationships of the participants (and audience) may be effected. From this perspective, while formalized speech and special modes of performance may present symbolic material in specific restrictive ways, they do not, as Bloch would have it, render that material meaningless. Instead they serve to impose that meaning upon the social event by bringing symbols and contexts into relation with one another within the order of the performance. This, however, is not merely a matter of communication of information. Performance does not construct a symbolic reality in the manner of presenting an argument, description, or commentary. Rather, it does so by socially constructing a situation in which the participants experience symbolic meanings as part of the process of what they are already doing.

The problem of what such a performative reality is, how it organizes symbolic materials, and how it is socially constructed and maintained is the subject to which I will now turn. I will explore the issue through an examination of the nondiscursive aspects of the performance of spirit séances among the Kaluli people of Papua New Guinea. For the purposes of this paper I will use the term "performance" broadly (following Kapferer 1979b) to include the action and interaction of both the medium (the central performer) and the audience (participants and onlookers) at the séance gathering.

The Kaluli Setting

The Kaluli people live in about 20 longhouse communities scattered throughout the tropical forest on the Great Papuan Plateau just north of Mt. Bosavi in the Southern Highlands Province of Papua New Guinea. Among the population of approximately 1200 people in the early 1970s there were about 15 spirit mediums. A medium is a man who has married a spirit woman in a dream or vision experience often associated with a severe illness. Thereafter he is capable of leaving his body in séance and traveling in the invisible spirit side of reality. At the same time, spirit people from the invisible may enter his body and converse with the audience gathered around.

Kaluli appeal to mediums primarily for curing illness and for help in locating lost pigs. But séances always involve much more than this, providing the setting for general conversation with the dead and with other forest spirits and serving as a kind of entertainment. The experience of séance performance for Kaluli cannot be appreciated by an outsider without some understanding of the nature of Kaluli spirit beliefs and awareness of spirit presence, nor without understanding that séances form a familiar ritual genre in which Kaluli participate and that they know how to evaluate.

Kaluli become aware of the spirit presences in the everyday world of their forest homeland. The Papuan Plateau is a vast expanse of tropical vegetation extending over several hundred square miles. The interior of the forest is bewildering to an outsider, but to a Kaluli in his home territory, the details of the tracks and watercourses, ridges and sago places, gardens and house sites are as familiar as the faces of his relatives. In the dense forest vegetation Kaluli tend to rely on sounds as much as, or more

than, on sight. A rustle in the undergrowth, the calls of the birds, the thud of a sago beater, all alert them to activities hidden from view. The calls and voices of birds are especially prominent, giving even an outsider the sense of hidden conversations: angry scoldings, raucous laughter, cooing invitations. This impression is not lost on the Kaluli. To them these sounds imply not only the presence of birds hidden in the canopy, but also the more truly hidden presence of the spirits (ane mama, Schieffelin 1976; Feld 1982). Many kinds of bird calls are also the voices of spirit people. Kaluli believe the world has a visible aspect, which is the context of everyday life, and an invisible side (largely coextensive with the everyday, but hidden from it), which is the abode of the spirits and the dead. The inhabitants of each side "show through" to some extent into the world of the other. Spirits appear to human beings as certain kinds of birds and animals (Schieffelin 1976; Feld 1982), and every human has an invisible aspect that appears to the spirits as a wild pig or a cassowary.

Where people are continually reminded of and attuned to the presence of the unseen by the calls of the birds in the forest, spirit séances can be seen as yet another way this reality manifests itself. At the same time, as we shall see later, séances themselves elaborate Kaluli awareness of the spirits as personalities and give new depth of significance to the calls of the birds.

Séances may be called for a variety of reasons, including entertainment, but most commonly are called to cure illness and to find lost pigs. One of the principle causes of illness, from the Kaluli point of view, is that a person's invisible wild pig (or cassowary) aspect may be trapped or injured by hunters of the spirit world, resulting in pain and disability for the visible person. If the animal is taken from the trap and eaten by the spirits before it can be rescued, the person will die. An even more serious cause of illness (which may or may not be involved with the trapping of the wild pig aspect) results from an invisible attack on the victim's body by a witch (sei). A sei is a living man or woman with an evil aspect in his or her heart. This evil thing creeps out of the sei's body while he or she sleeps and attacks the invisible aspect of the victim's body (not the wild pig aspect), dismembering it and hiding the pieces for later consumption. The victim suffers a severe illness, whose symptoms correspond to the parts of his or her body that have been (invisibly) injured. Thus, a person whose legs have been cut off cannot walk; a person whose head has been removed is delirious; a person whose heart has been cut out dies. It is the job of the medium and his spirit helpers to seek throughout the invisible to remove the patient's wild pig from the spirit trap, or to locate his missing body parts and restore them to his body.

The Séance Performance

If someone becomes ill, his or her relatives often seek out a medium (a:s tih'nan kalu, lit. "goes out to the spirits man") and ask him to go into the invisible to see what is the matter. A séance always takes place at night and has a characteristic form. The medium lies on his back on a sleeping platform in the men's section of the longhouse. He is surrounded by the men and youths of the community, who sit nearby on the floor. These men are called the kegel, which has the meaning more of "chorus" than of "audience." They form the core of those who actively participate in responding to the performance. The women, mainly onlookers, lean over the nearby partitions to the women's section or sit on the floor at some distance behind the men.

When all is ready, the fires of the longhouse are banked to provide almost complete darkness. After a while there is a long hissing breath from the medium, which indicates that his soul is leaving his body. This is followed by gasping sounds and bird calls as the first spirit (usually the medium's spirit child by his spirit wife) arises and softly begins to sing. The song, nostalgic and moving, is invariably about the hills and streams near where the spirit lives. The kegel, chorusing the spirit, are drawn into the same mood. When the song ends, the spirit identifies itself and people ask him to go and take a look at the invisible aspect of the sick person. The spirit child then departs and searches the spirit realm to see if the patient's wild pig aspect is caught in a trap. If it is, he will

release it, and if the pig runs away, the person will recover.

If all is well with the spirit pig, the medium and his spirit child will look at the patient's invisible body form to see if it has been injured by a sei. If it has, the medium and his child must locate the dismembered portions of the victim's body hidden by the sei and stick them back on the body. If they are successful in this, the patient will recover.

In the meantime, while the medium and his spirit child are off on their (invisible) errands of healing, other spirit people arise through the medium's body to sing and to give the people at the séance a chance to talk to their dead or to other invisible personalities of the locality, and to enjoy themselves. Séances, often quite engrossing performances, range from deeply moving as people weep while talking with their dead, to fearsome and thrilling as fierce and belligerent spirits rise up with growling voices, smacking lips and thumping and banging on the sleeping platform. The séance may also be hilariously salacious as an unmarried spirit woman and the young men of the longhouse lewdly tease and provoke each other. In this context, spirit people of the locality become well-known, even beloved, personalities as Kaluli develop a closer relationship between themselves and the invisible side of their world.

All, during the performance the kegel seated around the medium maintain active participation by serving as a chorus, asking questions and engaging in conversation with the spirits – and by making comments and speculations among themselves about the meaning and quality of the performance itself. Often this discussion is led by one or two self-appointed commentators who, while not in collusion with the medium, are familiar with his style and know how to anticipate what he is likely to do next. They often give a running commentary and interpretation of the performance as it goes along.

During the course of the night, the medium's spirit child continues his attempts to help the patient. In other publications (Schieffelin 1976, 1977) I have examined this séance healing process through a meaning-centered analysis. I have argued that in everyday life Kaluli tend to interpret and deal with many different kinds of situations as though they were situations of opposition or confrontation that could be solved by reciprocity. Illness is assimilated to this model. That is, illness is interpreted (in séance) in terms of the opposition between the patient and the *sei* (or invisible spirit hunters) who have stolen (or immobilized) part of his or her body. The opposition is mediated and resolved in a quasi-reciprocal transaction performed by the medium's spirit child when he finds and returns the patient's missing body parts. (The release of the wild pig soul from the spirit trap discontinues the opposition rather than resolving it by a reciprocal action.) The basic thrust of the argument, following Lévi-Strauss (1967) cited above, was that by assimilating the patient's suffering to a metaphoric version of a widely significant cultural scenario of resolution, the séance provided a means to make sense of, and to order and resolve his problematic bodily experience. Subsequent research in Bosavi has shown that this cannot be what happens, at least not in the way outlined by most meaning-centered arguments of this sort. I will return to this point later on. In any event, the séance usually continues well into the middle of the night, until all of the various spirit tasks have been successfully (or unsuccessfully) accomplished. The medium then returns to his body and sits up.

This brief description provides an outline of the basic events in a Kaluli curing séance. Understanding what is happening here, however, is more than a matter of showing that the séance provides a logically and symbolically plausible resolution for a problematic situation. It is also necessary to show why the Kaluli accept what they see in the séance as a convincing, even compelling, reality. That is, the question addressed here does not concern the content of Kaluli spirit beliefs, but how these beliefs are brought to life and galvanize social reality.

Playing the Urgency of the Social Situation

The compelling quality of the séance begins long before the performance itself. Although people sometimes request a séance just for the amusement of talking to the spirits, most séances are called to deal with some problematic circumstance. The people who gather about the medium in the longhouse are not excited merely by the prospect of the performance but are worried or angry about something and hope to obtain some answers. This anxiety and expectancy charges the atmosphere with a certain tension before the séance begins, and it is this tension that the séance must pick up and deal with, if it is to have an effect – and in the process become real. Some mediums have a keen sense of this preliminary urgency and play on it to create the proper opening mood. Walia of Anasi, one well-known medium, was a master at building the tension of community worry and expectation to an agonizing pitch. When asked to go out to the spirits, he would respond with diffidence, complaining that he was tired, that he didn't feel well, or that the children in the longhouse were too noisy and would disrupt the séance. The people who wanted the séance would plead with him, offer him food, promise to monitor the children, and clear their sleeping platforms for him to lie on. Walia would continue to grumble and threaten to leave right up until the moment when he lay down for the séance, by which time audience tension was high and people were eager for the performance to begin.

The séance setting

When the medium lies down on one of the sleeping platforms to begin the séance, there is an atmosphere of hushed excitement. The *kegel* and other onlookers settle themselves in the darkness, waiting for the arrival of the first spirit. Now, although this situation is reminiscent of a Western theater audience quieting down before the curtain rises, the resemblance is superficial. The cultural assumptions that shape the internal structure of the séance performance space are very different from those aroused by a proscenium stage. As a result, the implications for the relationships among the audience, actor, and characters are also very different. The stage in a proscenium theater defines a special space to house an imaginative reality. It excludes the audience; that is, the audience may accept, for the period of the performance, that they are in the presence of the court of Richard II, but not that they are part of that court. Indeed they cannot be part of it for the performance to retain its integrity. A member of the audience who mounts the stage because he believes what he sees is real finds himself among actors, not kings, disrupts the imaginative space, and spoils the show.

For the Kaluli séance, the situation is reversed. In the séance the imaginative space of the proscenium stage is exchanged for the liminal realm of the medium's trance, the actor (that is, the medium) is excluded from the performance (since his soul has left his body), and the characters (the spirits) then enter reality. This is accomplished by a double transfer across the break between the visible and invisible. The medium ascends to the invisible realm while the spirits descend to the human plane. Thus theater becomes reality, where spirits who are birds converse with men in human voices. The interactions with the characters (spirits) also have real consequences. The thrill of fear at the appearance of a fierce and belligerent spirit is not, therefore, vicarious. If the spirit becomes angry and causes the medium's body to thrash about on the sleeping platform, the audience may flee the longhouse.

This structure of the performance space – where "the characters enter reality" – is one of the shared assumptions that everyone brings to the occasion. But it must also be continually reconfirmed during the course of the performance. Kaluli nearly always approach a séance with curiosity and anticipation rather than skepticism about its reality. But if their assumptions are not sustained, they are perfectly capable of calling the medium a fraud, disrupting the performance, and leaving in anger and disgust. Sustaining the performance space means that the medium must draw the audience into the task of participating in its construction, and this is accomplished in part through the songs.

The Strategy of the Songs

Performance unity and integrity

The spirits come up one by one, and each sings a song that is chorused by the audience. Each song may be followed immediately by another song, or by a period of conversation between the spirit and the audience.

Although mediums[3] did not speak about the artistic skills required to perform a good séance (indeed, they would deny that they were even present), it was evident to an observer that certain requirements had to be fulfilled if the structure of the séance was to be sustained and if the performance was to work. One of the most important skills was the ability of the medium to control the focus of everyone's attention and maintain the right unity of mood throughout the performance. This was accomplished mainly by the medium's adept management of the songs. It is through the people's participation in chorusing the songs that their divided attention is brought together and focused, and it is through the content of the songs (as we shall see) that the mood of pathos and nostalgia appropriate to speaking with the spirits of the dead (or of the land) can be evoked and intensified.

Performance momentum

Most of the power and energy of the séance comes not from conversations with the spirits but from the songs. A successful trance medium must have the ability to compose, during performance, in trance, as many as 30 new songs, each one with a different set of underlying implications.

These songs sung by the spirits are *gisalo* songs (the same type of songs sung at *gisalo* ceremonies, Schieffelin 1976), complex and layered in meaning. For our purposes, it will be enough to summarize one or two points to provide an understanding of how they can be used as a powerful rhetorical device.

Superficially, *gisalo* songs seem simple enough. Their lines refer to various named places, hills, streams, garden spots, old longhouse sites, and the like in the local forest region. These places are framed in poetic images that evoke nostalgia, longing, and loneliness. Often the places are referred to in such a way that they mark out a definite path (*tok*) through a particular area of forest, naming landmarks and singing the calls of birds as though one were passing along there. People at the séance who are familiar with these places are led to think of people, now dead, whom they used to know and live with.

When a spirit first starts singing, the people present recognize the places referred to and eagerly try to determine who (which spirit) is singing. As the song progresses, one can hear exclamations of "There's Dogon hill! That must be my mother's brother, old so-and-so. He used to garden there." "No, no, he also sang the Galinti pool; it's somebody further down-stream." Tension mounts while people search their minds to figure out the riddle of the singer until the song ends and the spirit announces itself. If the song has built up the right mood, the spirit's living relatives break down at this point and weep. Alternatively, if the spirit that comes up is a local place spirit, not one of the dead, there will be exclamations of welcome. Often people do not know whether or not they will be weeping until the very last minute.

In a deeper strategy of the same kind, the song may not contain place names, but simply mentions trees and river pools and sago stands as though they were passed on a track without any indication of their actual location (Feld 1982:152). Those present are led to search their memories for an area that would match, and the tension and speculation mount until the mention of one or two place names near the end of the songs suddenly precipitates recognition of the locality, the identity of the spirit, and is often accompanied by a flood of weeping. These mystifications and ambiguities within the song tantalize members of the audience and force them to turn reflectively inward, invoking the places that they know and love.

The focusing of attention in nostalgia and pathos is further intensified and given momentum by the medium's strategy in performance. To some degree the strategies seem to be a matter of personal style. Two contrasting examples will serve to illustrate this point.

Aiba of Kokonesi was a socially dynamic man of considerable presence. Intense and somewhat intrusive, he had a disconcerting habit of suddenly being present when least expected.[4] He had an extraordinary knowledge of the forest geography over most of the Kaluli region and was known in nearly every village. In my experience he was an opportunistic, persistent, and manipulative individual in everyday life. In séance, Aiba projected his spirit songs in a strongly focused and carefully constructed manner. He seemed to create a style aimed at centering the séance participants' attention on himself and what he was doing, drawing them onto his ground of performance where he could control them and make them, in effect, dance to his tune. Once those at the séance were fully engaged they were driven by his energy. His carefully pointed songs were often deeply affecting, moving some people to tears. However, because the energy of his performance derived mainly from himself, there was a tendency for its intensity to collapse between songs unless the level of tension was sustained by someone weeping.

By contrast, another medium, Walia of Ana-sai, was a rather marginal character. Scruffy, wheedling, and unreliable, he was a responder rather than an initiator of any significant social action. Yet he was a powerful trance performer. In séance, Walia did not focus people's attention on himself. The opening sections of his songs were instead highly stylized and redundant, providing the opportunity to develop a cohesive group synchrony (Feld, personal communication). Walia was finely attuned to his audience's response and the predictable regularity of his songs seemed aimed at getting his chorus to sing together, to synchronize themselves to the same rhythm. Once they were unified, he did not manipulate them. He acted rather as an orchestrator and catalyst for group process. It usually took Walia longer than Aiba to build the right momentum, but once he did, he tended to sweep up the greater part of those present and carry them forward with a force that maintained its impetus through spirit conversations until the next song.

The songs, then, provide several dimensions to the performance. The singing of them, with the *kegel* chorusing the spirit, provides unity of purpose, concentration, and rhythm to those present at the séance, and builds a compelling musical momentum that supplies a sense of energy and forward motion. The mention of lands and waters, especially in an ambiguous way, provides a mounting suspense and expectancy among the listeners, who are trying to determine who they are singing with. By song's end, steeped in nostalgia for their lands and longing for their dead, they are in the right mood of emotional expectancy to converse with the spirits.

The spirits

The spirits are the central characters in the séance and provide both its edifying and its entertaining aspects. It is in the audience's engagement with the spirits that the spirits become living personalities, and at the same time the work of the séance gets done. In the darkness, the presence of a spirit is marked by a change in the medium's voice quality. In general, spirit voices sound rather pinched and smaller than the medium's normal voice, and speak in a somewhat higher register. Some mediums use the same spirit voice for most spirit manifestations, but the best, or at least the most dramatic, performers had a different voice quality for every different spirit.

Experienced mediums were able to present a cast of 20 or more spirit characters, not counting the spirits of the dead. Some spirits of a medium's locality had had traditional relationships with the local community through a series of mediums over a period of years and were well known or even beloved by the audience. (I was able to trace the history of the relationship between one such spirit and a nearby community back over 80 years to the turn of the last century [Schieffelin 1977]). Other spirits appeared only through a particular medium and might not reappear through other mediums after his death. As with the dead, these place spirits were associated with particular localities, and séance participants could often guess by the songs which one was appearing.

The Kaluli distinguish four types of spirits that can appear through a medium. First are the spirits of the dead, who can precipitate a great deal of weeping if their relatives are present. Conversations with the dead generally concern such things as where the spirit was now residing, and what had happened in the way of family news since his death. In former times there was frequently also a discussion to determine the identity of the witch responsible for the death.

Most of the spirits who arise through a medium, however, are place spirits associated with a locality. These spirits often had distinctive personalities and gained reputations among séance-goers for their different idiosyncracies and abilities. For example, one of Walia's favorite spirit personalities (inherited from his mother's brother, who was also a medium) was a spirit named Kidel, who lived at a place called Bolekini. Kidel had a deep, friendly voice and was known to be fond of tobacco. He would frequently ask someone to pass a smoking tube in his (the medium's) direction. When he came up through Walia, he projected the character of a tough, far-traveled person, who could predict when the government patrols would visit the area. Being an older spirit, he would sometimes talk about the way his children were growing or comment on recent changes in the spirit world.

Another of Walia's place spirits was a young unmarried woman named Daluami. She, like other female spirits, had a coy falsetto voice. Daluami was rather forward and provocative, and conversations with the young bachelors of the community often evoked lewd and ribald repartee, accompanied by howls of laughter throughout the longhouse.[5] By contrast, her counterpart, a spirit woman named Wabelei, was shy and demure. She would become upset by male teasing and leave if the young men at the séance became too obstreperous.

These spirits of the ground usually performed the most dramatic séance tricks. In one famous performance, for example, a spirit invited the people attending to briefly illuminate the medium. When they did so they saw a hornbill's beak (from the spirit's bird manifestation) projecting from the medium's mouth. Another spirit asked to borrow a shell necklace in order to dance in a Gisaro ceremony in the spirit world. A necklace placed on the medium's chest disappeared. Some time later, at another séance, the spirit returned the necklace stained with the fragrant vegetable resins used to anoint a ceremonial dancer.

A third type of spirit was called a Newelesu. A weedy little man with an oversized head and an enormous penis, he was said to live in the top of small wani palms (a decidedly inferior dwelling compared to the gigantic buttressed trees inhabited by most spirits). A Newelesu was a clownish, trickster-like figure always lewd and mischievous. In a squeaky voice and with a shrill high-pitched laugh, he usually demanded to be given a woman. Hilarious conversation would follow. The Newelesu was known to be a witch on the spirit side, responsible for the demise of animals occasionally found dead and decaying in the forest. Men in the audience would frequently ask him to "ripen" a wild pig or cassowary so it would fall prey to their traps or hunting arrows. Newelesu had an angry streak and would send the medium back to his body, terminating the séance if people teased him too much.

Finally there were fierce spirits known as *kalu hungo:*, or dangerous, forbidden men. These spirits were known to be rough and short tempered. They usually appeared in séance smacking their lips hungrily or uttering battle cries, and spoke in deep spooky voices. *Kalu hungo:* were known to strike people down if they became angry, and they could frighten the audience out of the longhouse. Conversations with *kalu hungo:* were generally excessively polite and conciliatory, and Kaluli appeared to enjoy the thrill of danger that these spirits provided.

In the course of a séance (and depending on the medium) a wide range of different spirit characters would arise. Some would reveal only their names before departing. Others would stay to converse, argue with, or tease people for a considerable time. The conversations with the spirits, given their lively variety, break the flow and accumulated intensity of the songs and give Kaluli séances their episodic character. From time to time during the night the medium's spirit child would return to report his progress in releasing (invisible) wild pigs or finding dismembered limbs for the patient on whose behalf the séance was called. Apart from this, there is usually little apparent continuity between one spirit conversation and another. Occasionally, however, a medium will link the succession of spirit conversations with an underlying dramaturgical strategy that leaves everyone surprised and disconcerted. In one séance, for example, Daluame, a provocative unmarried female spirit, appeared and engaged

the young men of the community in extended, racy repartee. When she departed she was followed by another female of demure and timid character. Still in a ribald mood from their conversation with Daluame, the young men teased the second spirit until she departed in embarrassment. The performance then changed again. A cooing high-pitched voice arose, heralding the appearance of a third woman. As the young men prepared to launch their usual lascivious provocations, the spirit uttered several salacious remarks so outrageous that the bachelors were taken aback. In the bewildered silence that followed, a shrill gale of familiar giggles revealed that the spirit was not a woman but a (trickster) Newelesu.

These conversations with the spirits in the darkness of the longhouse create a lively scene. The wails of grieving relatives, the matching of wits in outrageous repartee, the thrill of danger from fierce *kalu hungo:* are all engrossing and enjoyable interactions quite apart from the particular purposes for which the séance was called. If at times the conversations strike an outsider as having the quality of play, it is not like the play of make-believe; it is the play of joking relations, playing with fire, playing in an arena of forces that can have dangerous consequences. If people's attention begins to falter, new songs reestablish the mood, rebuild momentum and intensity, and maintain continuity.

The "audience"

The *kegel* gathered immediately around the medium form the principle core of séance participation. They do the chorusing of the spirit songs and generate most of the joking and banter. Other, usually older, men sit as spectators at the periphery of this group or in other parts of the men's section, talking among themselves, occasionally joining the singing, but always alert to what is going on. Women, too, mainly observe but make their presence felt through comments and exclamations or by occasionally prompting a question to the spirits.

It should be obvious by now that the people gathered to attend the séance are an integral part of the performance, and that the term "audience," with its implication of passive attention, is probably not the right word for this group. I have used it, sparingly, to refer to both active participants (*kegel*) and more passive onlookers taken together. The reality of the spirit world as it is embodied in the séance is not a result of the performance of the medium alone, but emerges in the *interaction* between all the people present and the spirits. If the people are unresponsive, or unwilling to participate, the energy of the performance drains away, and the séance collapses and comes to an end.

While the medium depends on the people's response to keep the performance going, he is also subject to their judgment. Séance audiences are sophisticated. Most of those present have seen other séances before and know how to evaluate them. People not only sing along and converse with the spirits, they also make audible comments about the spirits' character and style, comparing them to other performances, or to their appearance in another medium. Thus information about the adequacy of the performance and the characters is made available during the performance itself, where it may be considered by others present or act as feedback to the medium, if he hears them while in trance. During a performance, people exclaim in praise or approval for a particularly well-done song or enjoyable conversation. They have also been known to walk out of a séance in disgust if they believe that the spirits do not know what they are talking about or if they feel they are being tricked. The audience thus becomes the arbiter of the authenticity of the spirit séance, and, at least as much as the medium, the guardian of the rigor of its tradition.

The Ostensible Work of the Séance

Dialogic modes of constructing reality

It is in the midst of audience engagement that the work of the séance gets done. The question is: What does it actually accomplish and how? From the Kaluli point of view the two tasks most importantly accomplished in séance are the curing of illness and the recovery of runaway pigs. Despite this, the proportion of séance performance time devoted to such matters varies a great deal, sometimes being a rather insignificant and perfunctory part of the performance, and sometimes being lengthy and dramatic. In regard to curing, I have already discussed the symbolic process in the séance curing scenario where the illness is construed as a loss (on the invisible plane), resolved through a symbolic analogue of social reciprocity carried out by the medium and the spirits (see also Schieffelin 1976: Chapter 5). It would seem reasonable to argue, following the outlines of Lévi-Strauss's argument cited earlier, that the powerful symbolic process embodied in the curing scenario, delivered to and by a deeply engaged audience, might actually have the effect of transforming the experience of the patient. However, unless we postulate the operation of paranormal effects, this cannot be the case because usually the patient is not present at the séance. In addition, Kaluli believe that patients must be asleep for the medium to have proper access to them in the invisible realm. Thus, despite the powerful symbolic scenario embodied in the curing process, it cannot affect the patient in any normally understood way. Nevertheless, Kaluli laymen and mediums alike insist that the reputation of a medium rests on the success of his cures. Returning to the séance context, if the power of the curing sequence cannot affect the illness process of the patient, it can perhaps shape the expectations of the patient's community. That is, during the performance, the medium may form an assessment about the patient's condition and gear the level of success of his invisible curing efforts to correspond with his notion of the most probable outcome. In this way if he thinks the patient will not recover, he will have difficulty in locating the dismembered legs or find the patient's wild-pig soul so injured that it can barely crawl when released from the spirit trap. He thereby prepares the people of the community for what to expect – making a prediction in the guise of an attempt to cure. Be this as it may – and the evidence is not very clear on the matter – the curing scenario can be seen as a very important part of another aspect of the séance, namely, the aspect dealing with witchcraft to which we shall return a little later. In the meantime, some of what the medium is doing in the cure will be clarified by turning to a more minor matter – the finding of runaway pigs.

In listening to mediums (or rather, spirits) discuss lost pigs with the audience, it seems to an observer that they show great subtlety in negotiating information with which to construct an appropriate response. During one séance I observed, the medium's spirit child was sent to locate a missing pig described as a female with cropped ears and a white patch on the chest. Returning to the séance, the spirit later declared: "I saw the pig but I do not know the name of the ground." He went on to describe a place where a small brook ran into a larger creek with a particular kind of sago palm nearby. I recorded the discussion in my fieldnotes:

There is also a Wo:*lu* [river] banana garden nearby" he said. The [audience] said: "No, it is the Gulu you are talking about" [The particular type of sago at the confluence of two waters allowed the audience to recognize the stand of sago at the confluence of the Gulu and Gudep streams.] The audience then concluded that the banana garden referred to was the one at Mosogosaso. The spirit then described an old fish-dam diversion ditch and an abandoned garden. The audience agreed in discussion that this described the general area around the mouth of the Gudep stream. One man prematurely identified the area as a place called Gwabidano, which is nearby, but was overruled by others in favor of the Gudep again when the spirit mentioned a pandanus garden which they identified as belonging to one of themselves. By now even the writer could recognize the area from the description. That was where the pig was supposed to be. Only one man remained skeptical. He believed the spirit must have the wrong pig, because he thought the pig they were looking for should have been at a place closer to the Wolu river (author's fieldnotes).

On the following day when the pig owner visited the place designated by the spirit he did in fact find a female pig with cropped ears and a white patch on its chest. But it was the wrong pig. The pig he was looking for was much larger and he returned disgruntled to the longhouse.

Returning to the séance, the spirit's information is markedly ambiguous. There are dozens of places in the tropical forest that would fit his initial description. However, by "not knowing the name" of the ground, he avoided pinpointing a specific location.[6] This allowed the people present to specify the location by drawing implicitly on their knowledge of local lands and the behavior of pigs. The area the people actually considered was restricted to a region on the Gudep stream not too far from the lost pig's normal range. Thus, they took issue almost at once with the spirit's suggestion that the pig was somewhere near the Wolu river. From then on, the various details suggested by the spirit were sufficient for the audience to piece together a picture and reach a consensus about where the pig was located. When the location of the pig was finally determined, the séance participants doubtless felt that they had received it on spiritual authority, whereas to a Western observer, it appeared that they had constructed most of it themselves.

This event in which the spirit communicates the whereabouts of a lost pig epitomizes the process of the social construction of reality in the séance. The spirit imparts information at once clear and ambiguous and the audience is induced to determine exact locations. The effect is reminiscent of the speculative mental search people employ in pinpointing the identity of the spirit that is singing. The deciphering of the spirit's message is a cooperative construction of reality in the guise of a search for hidden meaning. That is, as the people search for clarification of the spirit's message they create the meaning they discover.

Dramaturgical means of constructing reality

Not all of the séance reality derives from the dialogic interaction between the séance-goers and the spirits. Directly dramaturgical elements incorporated and/or utilized by the performance shape the significance of the dialogue and serve as a major means by which séance and everyday realities overflow and spill into each other. This is particularly clear in the way the séances articulate the dark side of Kaluli life, witchcraft and death. Witches (*seis*) are a frequent topic of séance conversation. When there is sickness in the area, conversations in séances may be dominated by discussion of *sei*s, their habits and whereabouts. Fear and dismay over their activities are aroused through lengthy and often harrowing discussions between the audience and the spirits concerning efforts to locate the dismembered pieces of the victim's *sei*-torn body. At such times, the ambiance of anger and anxiety coupled with a jumpy alertness to small noises of the night can generate an awareness of evil presence that prickles the scalp of even an observer. In the middle of one such séance I attended, while the participants were deeply involved in chorusing the song, there was an odd noise outside the longhouse. The spirit voice suddenly fell silent and the people were left stranded at the edge of response. In the ensuing moments of consternation in the longhouse darkness everyone was poised to listen. The strange noise and the sudden disappearance of the spirit voice meant that a *sei* was creeping just outside. There could hardly be a more jarring interruption of the performance. Through the abrupt silence, the thrill of fear, and the sudden alertness of the audience, the presence of the invisible *sei* creature was rendered virtually palpable, its presence realized not by anything that was said but through the dramatic moment it evoked. The drama did not end there: the medium was paralyzed, his soul blocked from returning from the spirit world by the presence of the *sei*. In this case it took 20 minutes of concerted activity, including prayers to Jesus by Christian converts and the efforts of another medium who called down the mouth of his stricken colleague to his own helpers in the spirit world, before the spirit path was cleared of the *sei*'s presence and the séance could continue.

In this highly charged context, discussions of *sei*'s take on a disturbing immediacy. Again, the spirits rarely give the names of the *se*/*s* they see, but provide (as with songs and pigs) enough information for the members of the audience to construct their own conclusions. Once these are constructed, the audience remains committed to them. In traditional times, if the *sei* was judged responsible for someone's death, the result might have been a retaliatory murder.

The reality of *sei*s, marked by the interruption of the séance (or, at other times, by

mysterious whistles in the night) provides the context in which the instrumental activities of freeing invisible wild pigs and sticking dismembered limbs back on bodies appear as urgent, meaningful, and effective behavior. It makes sense because the séance does not simply discuss *sei*s, it presents them concretely as real. Here, theater becomes reality: the characters are not on the stage, they are out in the world.

Séance Performance and the Construction of Cosmological Context

Implications for the notion of "belief system"

While séances construct realities on the ground, they also articulate everyday and cosmological realities. Séances are, of course, understood by Kaluli in terms of cultural beliefs and assumptions about the nature of the world and the relationship between spirits and human beings. It is customary in anthropological analysis to approach the understanding of cultural performances by grasping them within such a context of the larger system of belief, and that was the apparent strategy in outlining Kaluli spirit beliefs at the beginning of this paper. However, a case could also be made for pursuing the matter the other way around. Kaluli spirit beliefs do not form a thoroughgoing and consistent system. Systematic inquiry reveals that beyond a basic set of common understandings (outlined at the beginning of our discussion of séance), there is a great deal of variation in what people know about the invisible realm and many lacunae and inconsistencies in the content of this knowledge. The piecemeal and miscellaneous nature of people's knowledge of the invisible reflects to some extent the piecemeal and miscellaneous nature of the contexts in which they acquire it. There is little formal instruction in the lore. What one learns is picked up informally in everyday context from casual remarks and conversations, from accounts told by knowledgeable people about spirit- or witch craft-related events, from alertness to sounds of the forest, and from attending and discussing séances.

Kaluli laymen are generally not aware of the variation and inconsistency in their knowledge of the invisible. When it is pointed out, they are as puzzled by it as the ethnographer. Usually they suggest he go and talk with a medium. Mediums are the final authorities on the invisible, not because they are in possession of greater traditional knowledge, but because they have been to the spirit side and seen it for themselves.

Mediums' accounts of the invisible are visually detailed and systematic, lending credence to their claim to having actually visited there during trance. However, while a common set of cultural themes seems to underly their accounts, various mediums' versions of the invisible differ considerably from each other (as well as from the laymen's). Mediums, however, do not discuss their trance experiences much among themselves and are largely unaware of the degree to which they vary. Moreover, their differences do not affect the way they perform their séances and are rarely significant in the details of performance content. The inconsistencies of the system rarely surface and thus do not pose difficulties for the Kaluli, only for the ethnographer.

One interesting consequence of this situation is the difficulty it poses for conventional ways of talking about a "belief system." A common approach would be to look for unifying themes and cultural assumptions that underlie the individual versions, but to give an account of this system by reducing it to its common denominators would clearly distort it. The best way to preserve its ethnographic integrity is to look at it in terms of the way that it is socially constructed, that is, as a system that consists in the continuing interaction between what people already know of spirits from oral tradition, everyday conversation, and remembered (or reported) past séances, and whatever new experience occurs in the present séance performance. What people know serves as a general background and constraint on what they will accept in a séance performance, but the performance confirms the presence of the spirits themselves and provides continuing information to the audience on the state of their relations with them. Any innovative information is then incorporated by those present into

their stock of knowledge. It may be communicated to others who did not attend a particular séance, held as information for future use, or conveniently forgotten. Mediums themselves sometimes contribute further by describing to others in their longhouse some of the things they have seen in trance journeys that did not emerge in séance. In this way knowledge of the spirit world is, within certain general limits, continually in flux, being constantly generated and renewed and irregularly distributed throughout the social field – where it forms part of the context for understanding new séance performances and spirit-related events. Heterogeneity is part of the system no less than its underlying shared cultural assumptions. In this sense it is more the performance of séances that accounts for the nature and content of Kaluli belief than the other way around. The accumulated knowledge of the spirit world clearly takes second place to the presence of the spirits themselves in performance, and the spirit world, however well known, like the identities of the singers of the songs, or the locations of lost pigs, seems at once familiar and just out of reach.

When Kaluli reach out to the spirits in séance, they become most clearly aware of the larger, cosmological scheme of things that the spirits represent. It is in the séance that they are most likely to experience the direct articulation of that order in their own lives. This articulation is, of course, implicit in the conversations with the spirits and the participation in chorusing the songs. But to take a more explicit example, it is in séance conversations that people enter into relationships with the spirits that individualize, consolidate, and legitimize their relationship to the land. One informant told me the story of a tabooed area near his longhouse where no one was permitted to hunt or fish. Years before, he explained, a fierce *kalu hungo*: spirit had arisen in a séance and declared that he was the owner of the area: "Don't cut the trees or the arrow-cane there," he had told them, "or I will cut off your clan." Commenting on the story, my informant remarked, "He made the arrow cane like our soul." This meant, in one sense, simply: "We die if we cut it." But, on another level what looks simply like a lethal threat is regarded by the Kaluli as a convenant.

The taboo is a mutual agreement between the community and the spirit and rather than distancing the two, it brings the people into close and familiar touch with the forces that animate their locality.

Conclusion

While some symbolic analyses might tend to look at the Kaluli séance as a text or structure of meanings, I have tried to move beyond this to see it as an emergent social construction. The reality evoked in the performance does not derive directly from its following a coherent ritual structure (though it does follow one), but from the process of dialogic interaction between the medium and the participants. What renders the performance compelling is not primarily the meanings embodied in symbolic materials themselves (the spirit characters and their pronouncements) but the way the symbolic material emerges in the interaction. Starting with the people's expectations and anxieties over problems in everyday life, the séance develops its force by weaving over and around these concerns its own theatrically generated tensions and ambiguities. The songs tease and provoke the listeners, drawing them into the performance. The séance makes sense not so much by providing information as by getting the audience into motion, bearing down on curiosity and nostalgia to force out dramatic and emotional as much as cognitive significance. It entices, arouses, and intrigues so that the participant constantly strives to get hold of something that always seems just out of his or her grasp. The performance is gripping not because of the vivid display of symbolic materials but because the symbolic material is incomplete. Reality and conviction reside not in the spirit's message but in the tension produced when some important communication seems at once clear and ambiguous. This experience of inconclusiveness and imbalance gives people little choice but to make their own moves of creative imagination if they are to make sense of the performance and arrive at a meaningful account of what is happening. In so doing, however, they complete the construction of its reality.

In this way the people reach fundamental symbolic understandings and arrive at solutions to their problems, not in a cognitive or intellectual way so much as in a participant one whose cognitive shape may not be well worked out for a given individual, but which is assumed to make sense because the realities it represents are so vivid. Once this séance reality is constructed, it may spill over into everyday life. The performance, in effect, becomes life, no less than life is reflected in the performance, and the vehicle for constructing social reality and personal conviction appears more as drama than as rational thought.

It is evident that it is impossible to separate the dramatic aspects of ritual symbols from their meanings if we want to know their significance or why they are compelling. This is not just a matter of presentation: many things are cognitively accepted in performance precisely because they are dramatic, impressive, or mysterious rather than because their rational significance is understood, provided, of course, they do not stray too far beyond the limits of cultural common sense. The presence and reality of the *sei*, for instance, was made palpable by the jarring interruption of the séance, but the interruption itself would have had no meaning if it were not for the existence, for the Kaluli, of the *sei*.

The socially emergent dimension of performance, constructed through the interaction of the performers and participants but not reducible to them, constitutes the reality in which the actual work of the séance gets done. This emergent dimension stands beyond the text or structure of the performance itself (while at the same time embodying it) so that the séance confronts the participants as an event in which they are involved and that can have consequences for them and their particular situation. This being so, the work of a performance, what it does, and how it does it, can never be discovered only by examining the text, or the script, or the symbolic meanings embodied in the ritual alone. It must be sought further in the emerging relation between the performer and the other participants (and the participants among themselves) while the performance is in progress.

Because ritual in performance is a reality apart from its participants, the participants may not all experience the same significance or efficacy. Indeed, unless there is some kind of exegetical supervision of both performance and interpretation by guardians of orthodoxy, the performance is bound to mean different things to different people. In the absence of any exegetical canon one might even argue there was no single "correct" or "right" meaning for a ritual at all. The performance is objectively (and socially) validated by the participants when they share its action and intensity no matter what each person may individually think about it. It follows that the meaning of ritual performance is only partly resident in the symbols and symbolic structures of which it is constructed. To a large degree (particularly in events like the Kaluli séance) the meanings of the symbols and of the rite itself are created during the performance, evoked in the participants' imagination in the negotiation between the principal performers and the participants.

This being the case, rituals (certainly Kaluli séances) do not exist in a vacuum of structural scripts and frames. Insofar as they are performed, they have historicity. However much a genre – a conventional, structured, symbolic enactment with a limited range of meanings – the séance is also for the participants an event that they helped construct and to which they contributed part of the ambience, action, and final significance that it evoked from them.

NOTES

1   The basic questions and general orientation to the issues of most of these studies are similar to those outlined in Clifford Geertz's influential essay "Religion as a Cultural System" (1973). Indeed, a general statement of the problem for much recent analysis of ritual might be outlined by rephrasing one of his most well-known passages:

How do rituals, as systems of symbols, operate to establish or transform powerful and pervasive understandings, moods and motivations in people through formulating conceptions of their place in a general order of existence and giving these conceptions such an aura of factuality that they seem uniquely realistic [rephrased from Geertz 1973:90]?

2   Lévi-Strauss, in a classic early paper on the shamanistic treatment of difficult childbirth among the Cuna (1967), argued that the shaman's lengthy recitation of an imaginary journey to the abode of the childbirth goddess paralleled (metaphorically) the painful experience of the woman in difficult labor:

The shaman provides the sick woman with a *language*, by means of which unexpressed and otherwise inexpressible psychic states may be immediately expressed. And it is the transition to this verbal expression – at the same time making it possible to undergo in an ordered and intelligible form a real experience that would otherwise be chaotic and inexpressible – which induces the release of the physiological process, that is, the reorganization, in a favorable direction of the process [that is, difficult childbirth] to which the sick woman is subjected [Lévi-Strauss 1967:193–194].

A similar account of shamanistic curing in the psychoanalytic tradition is utilized by George Devereux. Devereux takes the older anthropological view that shamans are psychologically troubled individuals who have gained at least partial control over their psychotic symptoms and live most of the time in remission. The shaman's psychological conflicts, however, are culturally generated and hence strike a chord with, or are shared by, a great many others in the society. During the shamanistic performance (which for Devereux is directed solely at psychological problems) the shaman releases his own psychotic symptoms in a controlled manner. The patient, recognizing his own problems in the shaman's behavior, and vicariously working them through, is provided with "a corrective emotional experience" and a "whole set of ethnopsy-chologically suitable and congenial, and culturally recognized defenses against the conflicts that torment him" which leads to a repatterning of his modes of coping (Devereux 1956:30–31).

The material the shaman presents is not regarded by Devereux as cultural symbolic material so much as controlled psychotic or neurotic symptomatology, yet, in principle, the way the symbolic process works is analogous to what Lévi-Strauss describes. In both examples the shaman's performance recapitulates and restructures the patient's experience, giving him or her a way to deal with problems and thus rendering the ritual performance effective

Victor Turner (1967) focuses not on the narrative progression of symbols in ritual so much as on the power of a few "dominant symbols" themselves that serve at once as the major vehicles for transformative meanings and as the means of grounding these cultural meanings in individual experience. The meaning of the ritual is discovered by unpacking the densely interwoven messages hidden within the dominant symbols and showing how their presentation in symbolic form obscures, combines, or mediates fundamental social and cultural issues, and thus opens the participants to new perspectives on their life situations. The symbols are compelling because they are presented in emotionally arousing imagery and contexts.

3   The Kaluli mediums that I knew did not exhibit any unusual or outstanding characteristics as individuals in ordinary life. Quite the contrary, the six mediums whom I worked with represented a wide range of personal styles, degrees of extension of social connections, and general social influence. They ranged from one man of considerable influence, who was widely traveled in the region, through less widely connected individuals of more average standing and limited range, to two socially marginal men.

4   This habit was disconcerting to the Kaluli as well as to the ethnographer and may have been part of the reason that, in addition to being respected as a medium, he was also feared as a *sei*.

5   It is worth remarking that this raucous, lascivious joking and teasing between the young men and spirit women occurred rarely between men and women in real life, and certainly never in public. Kaluli would be too embarrassed or afraid to do such a thing. The social repercussions (should relatives of the woman find out) would be serious, since it would imply the young man was taking marital/sexual liberties that were the woman's family's alone to dispose of, and hence would be acting as if he were "stealing" her (*afa di*). Because marriage-sexual activity with a spirit woman is impossible in everyday context, such sexual joking is harmless fun. It never leads to a spirit marriage which results in a man becoming a medium.

6   I should mention that the medium in this performance was not from the longhouse where the performance was being held and was not himself very familiar with the local grounds.

REFERENCES

Bloch, M. 1974. Symbols, Song, Dance, and Features of Articulation. *European Journal of Sociology* 15: 55–81.

Brenneis, D. and Fred M., eds. 1984. Introduction: *Dangerous Words: Language and Politics in the Pacific*. pp. 1–29. New York: New York University Press.

Devereux, G. 1956. *Some Uses of Anthropology Theoretical and Applied*. Washington DC: The Anthropological Society of Washington.

Feld, S. 1982. *Sound and Sentiment: Birds Weeping, Poetics and Song in Kaluli Expression*. Philadelphia University of Pennsylvania Press.

Geertz, C. 1973. *The Interpretation of Cultures*. New York: Basic Books.

Irvine J. 1979. Formality and Informality in Communicative Events. *American Anthropologist* 81: 773–790.

Kapferer, B. 1979a. Introduction: Ritual Process and the Transformation of Context. *Social Analysis* 1: 3–19.

Kapferer, B. 1979b. Entertaining Demons: Comedy, Interaction and Meaning in a Sinhalese Healing Ritual. *Social Analysis* 1: 108–152.

Lévi-Strauss, C. 1967. *Structural Anthropology*. New York: Anchor Books.

Lewis, G. 1980. *Day of Shining Red: An Essay on Understanding Ritual*. Cambridge: Cambridge University Press.

Ortner, S. 1978. *Sherpas Through Their Rituals*. Cambridge: Cambridge University Press.

Schieffelin, E. 1976. *The Sorrow of the Lonely and the Burning of the Dancers*. New York: St. Martins.

Schieffelin, E. 1977. The Unseen Influence: Tranced Mediums as Historical Innovators. *Journal de la Societe des Oceanistes* 33(56–57): 169–178.

Schieffelin, E. 1980. Reciprocity and the Construction of Reality on the Papuan Plateau. *Man* (NS) 15(3): 150–156.

Turner, V. 1967. *The Forest of Symbols*. Ithaca, NY: Cornell University Press.

10

"He Should Have Worn a Sari": A "Failed" Performance of a Central Indian Oral Epic

Joyce Burkhalter Flueckiger

On a cold autumn night of 1985, in the Chhattisgarh region of central India, I attended an unusual performance of the oral epic, *Candaini*, which resulted in what I have called a "failed performance." More than half of the audience walked away within the first hour and a half of what normally would have been a 5 to 6 hour performance; after another half an hour, only 20 out of approximately 150 audience members were still sitting in the performance clearing. Furthermore, many audience members verbalized discontent with the performance, both during and after the performance, although they did not specifically call it a "failure." While initially disconcerting, I found that the failed performance brought to light certain aspects of successful performance – for example, communication between performer and spectator and "their mutual expectations – more clearly than had it been a success. Analysis of the "failure" reveals an innovative, nontraditional performance setting that eli-

cited contradictory expectations on the part of the performers, patrons, and various groups within the audience – expectations which could not all be fulfilled.[1]

The Candaini Epic and Its Performance

Candaini is the story of the hero Lorik and heroine Candaini, both from the Raut cow-herding caste.[2] Each is married to someone else, but Candaini leaves her husband when she learns he is impotent. Back in her maternal village, she meets Lorik: they fall in love and, after some delays, elope together. In Chhattisgarh, epic performances usually center upon and elaborate various episodes leading up to and including the long, eventful elopement journey. Eventually, Lorik and Candaini return home and live with Lorik's extended family, including his first wife. But it is said that Lorik

Joyce Burkhalter Flueckiger, "'He Should Have Worn a Sari': A 'Failed' Performance of a Central Indian Oral Epic," pp. 159–169 from *Tisch Drama Review* 32(1), 1988.

was never satisfied after his return and one day wandered off into the countryside, never to be seen again.

Unlike many other South Asian oral epics, Candaini is not a religious epic, nor are its performances an integral part of a particular ritual or festival. It is sung primarily for entertainment: nonprofessional performers sing for small groups of friends and neighbors; professionals may perform for entire villages at annual village fairs (maṛhai), in conjunction with festivals such as durgā pūjā or ganeś caturthī,[3] or to provide entertainment during long winter evenings. The fact that the epic is not religious, however, does not diminish its significance for the communities in which it is performed. They identify with Candaini on several levels, often referring to it as "our story," or a "Chhattisgarhi story." The characters are not deified, nor are they held up as models to be emulated. Rather, they represent the common man and woman of the Chhattisgarh plain in larger-than-life proportions. Audiences and performers consider the epic to be unique to Chhattisgarh, and its performance helps give identity to what might be called the Chhattisgarh folklore community.

Two basic styles of performing Candaini have developed in Chhattisgarh. Both styles are most commonly called simply "Candaini," but when the styles are distinguished, the first is called "Candaini gīt," or "song," and the second nācā, or "dance-drama." Gīt may be performed both professionally and nonprofessionally, while nācā is exclusively a professional performance style. Traditionally, Candaini gīt singers were male members of the Raut cowherding caste. Although Rauts used to sing without musical accompaniment, the support of a second human voice was essential to their performance. The supporting performer, called a sangvārī (companion) or rāgī (one who keeps the tune), joined in the last words of every line and served as a respondent. It is difficult to locate Raut singers today who still sing the epic in this style. More recently, members of the untouchable Satnami caste have begun to sing Candaini.[4] The dates and circumstances under which the Satnamis began to sing the epic are vague, however it appears that when they began to sing Candaini the epic

took on a more regional rather than caste identity. The Satnamis added musical accompaniment to the gīt performance style, including harmonium and the tablá drum, and today, Candaini performers of other castes, including Rauts, also use these instruments. However, all gīt performances retain the characteristic combination of a lead singer and one or more companions who join in with and respond to the leader. The audiences of nonprofessional Candaini gīt performances are relatively small, multicaste, and male, although women are free to stand by the sidelines and listen.

The second Candaini performance style, called nācā, includes song and dance, spoken conversations between characters, and narration in the gīt style. The nācā is said to have developed between 15 and 20 years ago, and according to nācā performers themselves, emerged in response to the strong influence of the Hindi cinema, an essential element of which is also song and dance. A nācā troupe consists of up to 8 or 10 performers, some of whom are actors and others musicians. The musicians sit at the side of the stage to accompany the actors and intermittently provide gīt-style narration between conversations. An important feature of the nācā is the inclusion of costuming and minimal props. The hero Lorik wears the traditional Raut festival dress decorated with peacock feathers and cowrie shells, and male performers put on saris to act out the female roles. Candaini is only one of many narratives performed in the nācā style, but certain nācā troupes specialize in Candaini to the exclusion of other narratives. Nācā audiences, unrestricted by age, caste, or sex, are drawn from an entire village or urban neighborhood and may number several hundred people. While this style has grown in popularity, it is expensive. When sufficient funds for the nācā cannot be raised, or if singers are singing nonprofessionally, the traditional gīt style without dance is still prevalent.

The Failed Performance

The performance I saw did not clearly fall into either the gīt or nācā performance style, which may have contributed to audience dissatisfaction. The performance took place in a Gond *ādivāsī* (tribal) neighborhood at the edge of the town of Dhamtari in Madhya Pradesh.[5] The performer, Devlal, came from a small village on the outskirts of the other side of town. He is a nonliterate Satnami-caste man of about 30 whose primary occupation is rolling *bīṛī* (leaf cigarettes). However, Devlal is also well known in his village as both a professional and nonprofessional performer of several folklore genres, including Candaini. He has had no formal training in performance under a specific teacher – he learned how to sing and dance simply from watching other performers and taking a special interest in their art.

By 10 o'clock in the evening a large crowd of 150–200 people, of whom about two-thirds were women, had gathered on a clearing in the Gond neighborhood, or *pārā*. The perform-ance space was bordered on one side by a busy highway, and many audience members were passersby. There were several delays in getting the performance started; for instance, when the man who came to set up the rented mike system took time to complain about the potato curry dinner he had been served by *pārā* members. Finally, the microphone and speakers were appropriately situated in the branches of a tree at one end of the clearing, and the per-formance began.

When Devlal first walked into the center of the clearing to sing the invocation (*vandanā*) he was wearing a traditional cloth loosely wrapped as pants (*dhoṭī*), a loose shirt (*kurtā*), bells on his ankles (*ghungharu*), and a wool neck scarf. He stood under a microphone hang-ing down from a tree and sang in the *gīt* style he had used when entertaining nonprofessionally in his village. He was accompanied by a group of five musicians playing the tablā, harmonium, and what they called a *binjo*, a two-octave keyboard instrument with three strumming strings at one end. The two singers interacted with Devlal by repeating the last word or two of every line he sang, and periodically would sing a kind of chorus or refrain. While they were singing the latter, Devlal held out his arms to the side and spun around, making rhythmic movements with his feet. The total dance movement looked much like Sufi twirling.

This was the *nāc*, or dance, and was what distinguished this performance from the non-professional *gīt* performances I had seen Devlal give previously.

An hour and a half later, at least half of the audience had left. At this time, Devlal looked questioningly at several *pārā* leaders and myself, seeming to ask whether or not he should continue: the leaders indicated he should. At midnight, with only about 20 people remaining, Devlal and his accompanists stopped for a tea and *bīṛī* break. They indicated that they would like to stop the performance altogether, but the remaining *pārā* audience members insisted that they should perform until at least two o'clock, since they were being paid to do so.

During the break, the performers wanted to listen to the tape I had been making. They were dismayed at the distortion the mike and speak-ers caused. In fact, because of the placement of the speakers, the singing could be heard more clearly several hundred yards from the clearing than in the immediate vicinity of the perform-ance. However, few people complained about this since poor mike and speaker systems are common to professional public performances in rural India. The troupe decided to take the mike and speakers down, and Devlal sang directly to the remaining audience of 15 to 20 people for another hour. Most of them sat with rapt attention.

Members of an Indian audience may come and go, drink tea and talk, and even fall asleep, but I had never seen them walk away en masse before the end of a performance, even though many performances continue until the early morning hours. I was embarrassed for the performers, but neither audience members nor performers seemed particularly upset by what had happened. My dismay was heightened by the fact that I was the financial patron/sponsor of the performance; in some way I felt partially responsible for the failure.

Although I had attended several Candaini performances throughout the fall festival sea-son, I was continually asking about and look-ing for more performances. They were not easy to find out about until after the fact, since they are often not well advertised outside of the village or neighborhood of performance.

Furthermore, they usually begin at 10 or 11 o'clock in the evening, not a good time for an unaccompanied woman to ride around town on her bicycle looking for performances. I spent a lot of time in the Gond neighborhood across the street from where I lived, taping various women's song, dance, and festival traditions. The pārā residents knew of my interest in Candaini and, finally, several of them suggested I sponsor a performance in their neighborhood. It would be convenient for me and also would provide them with entertainment they could not afford to sponsor. I was hesitant to comply with their suggestion, since I had attempted in my fieldwork not to sponsor professional performances or elicit nonprofessional singing or storytelling. I knew that to sponsor a Candaini performance in a Gond neighborhood would be to create an innovative situation, a new performance setting for both performer and audience. However, I agreed to do so as thanks for the cooperation and support my friends in the pārā had given me over many months. They were delighted, and a great sense of expectation built up in the neighborhood in the days preceding the performance.

Several pārā residents suggested I call Devlal to perform. One neighborhood resident came from Devlal's village, and so there were certain informal ties and obligations between the pārā and the village. Other pārā members knew Devlal as well and thought he would give us a good performance for a good price. I was pleased with their suggestion because I had previously taped several of Devlal's performances, including Candaini gīt, in his home village and I had a good working relationship with him.

Audience Expectation and Performance Language

So, why the failure? I suggest it was not primarily caused by the quality of Devlal's performance, but by a disjuncture between audience expectations, Devlal's understanding of these expectations, and the performance itself. Audience expectations had been created, in a large part by Devlal himself, for one particular performance language – the nācā;

but Devlal spoke another language, a hybrid of nācā and gīt – what he called nāc.

All segments of the multilayered audience seemed to expect to see a nācā, but their perceptions of the performance they saw in its place were not uniform. First, there were my own expectations as the foreign patron. When I had taped Devlal singing Candaini before, he sang nonprofessionally in the gīt style; but he had mentioned several times that he also performed nācā. So, when I contacted him about performing in the pārā, I let him choose the style of the performance and the size of the troupe he would bring with him. I made it clear I would be willing to pay for either gīt or nācā. He said he would bring three or four other men, and that they would do a nāc, literally "dance." I had never heard anyone refer to Candaini as nāc and assumed he meant nācā, as did several pārā members who had gone with me to make arrangements. On our return to Dhamtari, one of my Gond companions who knew that I had been frustrated when taping other nācā performances because of the high noise level and the distortion from mike and speaker systems, said to me, "Now you'll be able to tape a nācā without so much noise." I looked forward to the relative control that I, as paying patron, might have over factors which would help the taping process.

A second segment of the audience consisted of those people who came from outside the Gond pārā; some were from elsewhere in town, others were passersby from the highway bordering the performance space. The latter were probably both town and village dwellers. While I did not speak directly with anyone from this audience, I can make generalizations from other nācā performances I attended as to why they might have expected to see a nācā.

Members of the Gond pārā comprised the majority of the audience; the performance had been sponsored for them and they might be considered its secondary patrons. Many members of this audience had strong feelings about the events of the evening, and their commentary is revealing. The comment I heard most frequently, both during the performance and the next morning when I discussed it with my friends in the Gond pārā, was "He should have worn a sari." The significance of this comment

Figure 10.1 *Male nācā actors wearing the expected saris for female roles. (Photo by Joyce B. Flueckiger)*

was explained to me when, as audience dissatisfaction was becoming evident and many people were leaving, an elderly woman told me, "It's a good story (*kissā*). But that doesn't make any difference, because these days people want nācā; they don't care about the story." The sari refers to those worn by male nācā actors who play female roles, a distinguishing characteristic of nācā (Figure 10.1). In a discussion with a group of women, one Gond woman said in Devlal's defense: "Yes, but this is Candaini; nācā is something else." However, her defense was clearly a minority opinion. The pārā members had expected a nācā production, something never seen in their own neighborhood, and were clearly disappointed by the less dramatic nāc.

I met Devlal a week after the performance and asked him why he thought so many members of the audience had left. His immediate reply was, "It was a cold night and no one is going to sit for hours in that cold." But when I

told him that several people had complained that "He should have worn a sari," he agreed that the real reason so much of the audience left was that they had wanted to see a nācā. He went on to voice his disdain for nācā. He said that nācā performers don't even have to know the story; and even if audience members are trying to listen to the story, they can't follow it: "In the nācā, Candaini is spoiled. But these days people don't care about that as long as there is song and dance. They've seen too many movies."

Expectations for a nācā performance on this particular evening had not only been created by what we may assume to be the audience's overall preference for a particular performance style, but by several specific framing devices.[6] First, Devlal insisted upon the use of a microphone and speakers, accoutrements rarely used outside the nācā for Candaini performances. Further, only large nācā performances utilize them; thus their use heightened expectations for a large, professional performance. Rental of this equipment was to cost 40 rupees (three to four dollars), and the pārā members involved in the negotiations with Devlal did not feel that they nor I should have to absorb this extra cost. They complained to Devlal that the performance was intended to be for them, not all of Dhamtari, and thus there was no need for the mike and speakers. However, when an emissary from the pārā went to make final arrangements with Devlal, he returned saying that the speakers had already been rented.

Along with the speakers, the rental company provided the service of a rickshaw which went around town announcing the upcoming event. Although the announcer called out only "Candaini," this was one more frame creating the expectation of a nācā. The rental company also played cinema music on location for three or four hours before Devlal was to begin.[7] This helped to build up a sense of expectation and festivity, and many passersby stopped to inquire about the event that was to take place. When they heard it was Candaini, several were particularly interested in who was patronizing a performance so unusual for a Gond neighborhood.

One framing device often contributes to the development of another. The rickshaw announcement implied that the performance would draw a large audience, and whenever large public performances are arranged in Dhamtari the police must be informed. If not, they are hesitant to answer calls for help with crowd control when needed. So, pārā members informed the police department, and two policemen attended the performance, incidentally collecting an evening's worth of tea and pān (betel leaf). Expectations of large crowds were growing, and the male members of the pārā thought they should organize a corps of ushers to help with seating the audience, a common custom for nācā and other large public performances. Ushers are identified by the bright pink or red ribbons pinned to their sleeves, and the young boys chosen for the role assumed an air of great importance as they donned their ribbons.

The preceding series of frames built up strong expectations for a nācā. When the invocation was over and there were still no signs of actors in saris, one of the women sitting next to me said, "Now they'll put on their saris." But the saris never materialized, and Devlal was the only troupe member to dance. I had never seen this particular performance style elsewhere, for Candaini or any other genre. It was neither gīt nor nācā; it did not fulfill expectations of either professional or nonprofessional performance. It was an unsuccessful hybrid.

Why did Devlal, a singer acquainted with a variety of professional and nonprofessional performance languages suitable for specific social and performance contexts, choose the language of nāc for this particular setting? Why did he initiate a series of nācā framing devices if he was not going to be performing a nācā? Finally, why didn't he perform nācā?

It is important to know that Devlal is basically a rural (dehātī) performer – not only does he live in a village, but he also performs almost exclusively in villages. When I asked whether or not he ever performed in towns (more specifically Dhamtari), he answered vaguely, "I sing wherever people call me." However, his acquaintances in the Gond pārā thought he was rarely called to town. During the months I spent in Dhamtari, I had asked Devlal to send word to me whenever he was going to perform. While I attended several of his village

performances, he never informed me of a town performance.

Performance standards and expectations vary between Chhattisgarhi rural and urban settings. For example, these days Candaini is rarely professionally performed in its gīt style in towns and cities. In such urban contexts, the necessary financial support for nācā performances can usually be raised through neighborhood collections (candā), which include the contributions of wealthy storekeepers. Secondly, the influence of the cinema is more strongly felt in the urban areas (although this difference between city and village is rapidly diminishing with the spread of "video halls" in the villages),[8] and audiences have come to appreciate and expect the song, dance, and drama of the cinema to be emulated in various professional folklore genres, including Candaini.

Because of the proximity of his village to Dhamtari and his frequent visits to the town, Devlal would be familiar with urban performances and audiences. He may have felt pressure to perform a nācā in the given context, but, since he does not have his own regularly performing nācā troupe, it was not possible to do so and still remain the lead performer. Thus, he may have tried to move his own performance as close to the nācā as possible without actually using its performance language. If it had been possible, I think he would have brought a nācā troupe to the pārā.

Had Devlal performed for the primary audience only – the Gond pārā and myself – in either the gīt or nāc style, without having created nācā frames, the performance may have been successful. This is suggested by the comparative success of the last hour of the performance when the mike and speakers were taken down and there were basically only Gond pārā members left in the audience. Several persons who stayed until the end commented that he sang well and that his story was good. The pārā still has strong village ties, and the neighborhood itself has retained many village qualities, including the ways in which festivals are celebrated and folk traditions are sustained. They may have been more satisfied with the gīt or nāc if initially a different context had been created.

It is also possible that Devlal has chosen not to regularly participate in or lead a Candaini nācā troupe because of some ambivalent feelings toward nācā, evidenced in his previously cited comments about the genre. He seems to have a conception of maintaining a certain degree of "purity" in the Candaini tradition by not "giving in" to the nācā and other commercializations of the epic. He calls Candaini gīt the aslī, or "real," "true," or "pure" Candaini. Devlal told me he has been called several times to perform for the local All India Radio station in Raipur, Akashvani, but has turned them down because he feels performances recorded for them have become too commercial.[9]

These are unusual attitudes for a Satnami performer of his educational and economic status. They may have been fostered in part by Devlal's contact with Chhattisgarhi director and playwright, Habib Tanvir, who maintains a high interest in Chhattisgarhi folklore. Several years ago, Tanvir sponsored a Candaini workshop in Raipur District for which he called together the best Candaini performers he had heard in his rounds of Chhattisgarhi villages and towns. Devlal was invited to this workshop. Singers from various castes, including Rauts and Satnamis, shared their stylistic and thematic repertoires. Devlal was then chosen from among the workshop participants to spend several weeks with Tanvir in Delhi to work further with him on the epic.[10] According to Devlal, Tanvir stressed the importance of keeping the tradition alive, and of singing episodes from the "entire" epic rather than focusing exclusively on the elopement. (Interestingly, the episode Devlal recounted during the performance concerned Lorik and Candaini as children, up until they met again as adults. Several audience members said they did not know this part of the story. Although this did not seem to be a major factor in their dissatisfaction, it may have contributed to it, since they have come to expect to hear episodes leading up to and relating to the elopement.)

The question of patronage – for whom and why Devlal was to sing – may also have influenced his choice of performance. I was paying for the performance, and he knew I wanted to tape it. For this reason, he told me he specifically chose an episode from the epic which he knew I had not heard before. He knew I did not care which performance language he chose, nācā or gīt, and may have guessed that the gīt style is easier to tape, but added dance to satisfy other segments of the audience.

The secondary patrons of the performance – residents of the Gond neighborhood – comprised the majority of the audience. They were responsible for the organizational details of the performance, such as setting up the performance and audience space, feeding the performers, and providing the ritual materials necessary for the invocation. Devlal may have misjudged their expertise and control as an audience, since traditionally they are not directly involved as Candaini patrons and primary audience, but only attend performances organized by other neighborhoods and caste groups. Finally, Devlal may have underestimated the numbers of people who came from outside the neighborhood and the influence their expectations for a nācā would have on the performance.

Toward New Performance Languages

A successful folklore performer both continually responds to and manipulates her/his audience and performance context. Depending upon the genre, s/he has more or less flexibility in the ways in which this can be done: through language usage, length of performance, and adaptation of thematic content. An important way in which the context is manipulated and audience expectations are built is through the frames created around the event. This must be done carefully by the Indian performer of secular genres, whose performance contexts are more flexible than those of religious genres with predetermined festival or ritual frames. Candaini is one secular genre whose performance contexts are many, a flexible genre which has adapted to the pressures of increased technology, the cinema, video hall, and radio by developing a new performance language, or style – the nācā. These multiple performance styles and settings necessitate a careful framing of the performance language the singer or troupe chooses; a performer will be judged according to the language which the audience has been led to expect by the frames drawn.

Devlal was confronted with an innovative performance setting in which there were nontraditional patrons (myself and residents of the Gond neighborhood). The situation was complicated by the fact that he was a rural performer performing in a semirural neighborhood in an urban location. He responded to this setting, with its numerous levels of expectation, by speaking an innovative performance language: a gīt singing style accompanied by dance and introduced by several nācā frames. However, the frames seemed to carry more weight than the quality of his nāc performance; when the expectations they raised were not met, the majority of the audience showed their dissatisfaction by leaving.

In everyday speech events, speakers can vary their language – through dialect, register, etc. – if they have misjudged a situation. Although there are numerous other ways in which folklore performers can respond to their audiences and performance contexts, they can rarely, halfway through, make major shifts in the performance language itself. Therefore, even after he realized the audience's dissatisfaction, Devlal could not sufficiently minimize the discrepancy between performance frames, audience expectations, and the language of nāc – his performance "failed."

With increasing literacy rates of both performers and audiences, the spread of modern communication technology, and shifting social relationships resulting in new patronage patterns, the frequency of similar innovative performance situations in India can be expected to increase. Each verbal folklore genre and its performers will adapt to new contexts in unique ways; some may not make the necessary transitions and cease to be popular, and at the same time, new genres and performance languages may emerge. The Candaini genre in Chhattisgarh has already shown its ability to make successful adaptations with the inclusion of non-Raut singers into the circles of its performers and the initiation of nācā into its singing repertoire. With more experimentation and under different circumstances, Devlal's nāc

may also emerge as a successful performance language for Candaini.

NOTES

1   The fieldwork for this paper was conducted in the fall of 1985 under a University of Wisconsin Albert Markham Postdoctoral Travel Grant.

2   For further reference to the Candaini epic in Chhattisgarh, see Flueckiger (1989); for references to its performance in the province of Uttar Pradesh in northern India, see Pandey 1979 and 1982.

3   Both of these festivals honor a deity whose clay image is prominently displayed in temporary pavilions on the sides of major thoroughfares or in neighborhood squares. In Chhattisgarh, they are primarily an urban phenomena, since they are not indigenous to the region. Neighborhoods collect offerings (candā) to cover costs of the elaborate images as well as to support the various forms of entertainment performed in front of the image, such as Candaini nācā. Durgā pūjā is a festival especially popular in eastern India and honors the goddess Durga. During ganeś caturthī the elephant deity Ganesh is worshiped.

4   The Satnamis are a sect which converted from the Chamar, or leatherworking caste, in the 1800s. However, their status has remained that of the Chamars, that is, outcaste, and they are referred to as a caste (jāti) in the local dialect.

5   The Gonds are a central Indian tribal group, many of whom have been integrated into the local caste hierarchy as a clean, but low, caste. Most residents of this neighborhood work as day laborers in agriculture or construction.

6   See Goffman 1974 for an elaboration of framing mechanisms of experience.

7   Other events at the Gond para for which the speaker system is rented and cinema music is played include the "six-day" ceremonies for newborn sons and weddings.

8   "Video halls" are rapidly spreading throughout villages in Chhattisgarh, most of which are too small to support a movie theatre and too far from towns for their residents to get to the cinema. The halls housing the VCRs

and television screens are structures made of whatever materials an entrepreneur can afford (bamboo, canvas tenting, or brick), and a small admission is charged.

9 Akashvani has regularly scheduled programs of various folk music genres for which they frequently record local artists. I was told several times by informants in Dhamtari that I should just listen to Akashvani on a particular afternoon to hear and record a certain folk song type.

10 This exposure has alienated several of Devlal's fellow villagers, who told me that since that experience Devlal has become very proud and now only wants to sing for money.

REFERENCES

Flueckiger, J.B. 1989. "Caste and Regional Variants of an Epic Tradition: The Lorik-Canda Epic." In *Oral Epics in India*, edited by Stuart Blackburn, Peter J. Claus, Joyce B. Flueckiger, and Susan S. Wadley. Berkeley: University of California Press, 33–54.

Goffman, I. 1974. *Frame Analysis: An Essay on the Organization of Experience*. Cambridge: Harvard University Press.

Pandey, S.M. 1979. *The Hindi Oral Epic Loriki*. Allahabad: Sahitya Bhawan Pvt. Ltd.

Pandey, S.M. 1982. *The Hindi Oral Epic Candaini*. Allahabad: Sahitya Bhawan Pvt. Ltd.

11
Representing History: Performing the Columbian Exposition

Rosemarie K. Bank

"The United States lies like a huge page in the history of society. Line by line as we read this continental page from, west to east we find the record of social evolution. It begins with the Indian and the hunter; it goes on to tell of the disintegration of savagery by the entrance of the trader, the pathfinder of civilization."
–"The Significance of the Frontier in American. History," Frederick Jackson Turner

"It is not a circus, nor indeed is it acting at all, in a theatrical sense, but an exact reproduction of daily scenes in frontier life as experienced and enacted by the very people who now form the 'Wild West' Company."
–Illustrated London News, 16 April 1887

"All was simulacrum: the buildings, the statues, and the bridges were not of enduring stone but lath and plaster."
–Claude Bragdon 1893[1]

Scholars have not been slow to notice the collisions and contradictions presented by and represented in the Columbian Exposition in Chicago in 1893. Alan Trachtenberg depicts it as the culminating spectacle of *The Incorporation of America* in the nineteenth century. Richard Slotkin examines the Fair as the high point in the performance history of "Buffalo Bill's Wild West" and traces the show's role in the creation of the *Gunfighter Nation: The Myth of the Frontier in Twentieth-Century America*. Richard White explores the connection between "Frederick Jackson Turner and Buffalo Bill" and representations of *The Frontier in American Culture* that offered images of peaceful or of violent conquest (Turner presented his "frontier thesis" at the American Historical Association convention during the Fair and William F. Cody's "Buffalo Bill's Wild West" performed next to the fairgrounds). Historians

Rosemarie K. Bank, "Representing History: Performing the Columbian Exposition," pp. 589–606 from *Theatre Journal* 54(4), 2002.

The Anthropology of Performance: A Reader, First Edition. Edited by Frank J. Korom.

of the Fair itself and of organizations contributing to it (such as the Smithsonian Institution and the Bureau of Indian Affairs) have produced a rich literature often critiquing the Fair's racist and sexist organization and displays, while historians of Buffalo Bill and wild west shows examine the man, the productions, their performers, their publicity, and their impact upon US, indeed international, culture in the nineteenth and twentieth centuries. A substantial scholarship has also taken up Frederick Jackson Turner and the impact of his view of American history. Many studies written recently about these subjects reflect a revised view of United States history, and specifically of "the frontier," indebted to scholarly research exposing much that is deplorable about the policies and behavior of the US government and white Americans toward Amerindians.[2]

What more needs to be said? What more can be said about these large and complex subjects, particularly in the foreshortened format of an article? Two issues seem to rise from the extensive (and increasing) scholarly literature about the Columbian Exposition, Frederick Jackson Turner's frontier thesis, and Buffalo Bill's Wild West that can, at least, be located, if hardly excavated, here. First, there is the legacy of binary thinking about history to which the late Michel Foucault alerted us. It is the legacy of seeking to drive out commanding narratives, "to pacify them by force," in order to replace them with our own. Rather, Foucault argues, the task is to map propositions "in a particular discursive practice, the point at which they are constituted, to define the form that they assume, the relations that they have with each other, and the domain that they govern." The injustices of history and of historical writing simultaneously do the work of the appeal of commanding narratives and of their undoing. Second, the binary view is particularly obstructive for what I have elsewhere called theatre culture, that is, the interconnection between performance and culture and culture and performance. Representation is not a single but a multiple and simultaneous relationship – performer to audience to role to culture to venue to cast to means of production to image, and so on – which defies the analysis it is so frequently

given in cultural histories as an ahistorical problem or 'reality.'[3]

While "unreal" cultural phenomena carry social responsibility with them because they can produce "real" effects (that is, attitudes, thoughts, emotions, and behaviors), theatre historians have been slow to formulate a way of talking about representation that considers this responsibility without recapitulating antitheatrical prejudice. This article will attempt to look at different representations of and at the Columbian Exposition – itself a simulacrum – in order to consider their interactions and constitutions as performances. What is an intellectual performance (the Anthropology Department's ethnographic exhibits on the fairground, for example, or Frederick Jackson Turner's paper)? How do the effects it produces vary from site to site and audience to audience? What characteristics do these kinds of performances share with performance more conventionally construed (Buffalo Bill's Wild West, the Indian Village on the Midway) and what truth claims did each make? My focus will be "the frontier" (or "wild west") and Amerindians, but parallels with representations of women, African Americans, and foreign nationals at the Columbian Exposition will be evident to students of these subjects. Further, since these subjects involve the theatre historian in the interrogation of a large (and growing) body of historiographical scholarship concerning cultural constructs – about fairs, museums, popular entertainments, and tourism, for example, but also the cultural constructions of anthropological and historical scholarship – it is hoped the wider application of performances at the Columbian Exposition to their subjects will not wholly be erased by the omission of material and arguments which an article of this brevity must perforce omit.[4]

It is not difficult to characterize the Columbian Exposition as a dream scenario, the "White City" (with full racial inflection) of a power elite, simulating for a mass audience its own sense of beauty, control, hierarchy, and self-secured success. Certainly, these words and their containing synonyms are those of contemporaneous participants and accounts, and have contributed to the projection of the Columbian

Exposition as a dream site in subsequent histories of it. Recent analyses of the Fair and its Columbian project, taking the dream projection literally, depict the "White City" as far from Utopian, indeed, as a dystopic, malevolent site which, by design or indifference, featured exhibits and interpretations that produced intensely racist, sexist, and ethnist effects. The demon scenario is the flip side of and depends upon the Utopian site to make its case. Rather than this binary negation and its positing of failed perfection, when the Columbian Exposition and its World Congresses are repositioned as performances of a far from ordered world, they become visible as heterogeneous spaces more nearly resembling Foucault's idea of a heterotopia, a counter-site "in which the real sites, all the other real sites that can be found within the culture, are simultaneously represented, contested, and inverted."[5]

Despite valiant efforts to promote the orderly display of goods, art, artifacts, technology, and natural products, the Columbian Exposition was a jumble of material spilling from building to building and displaced from site to site throughout the 553-acre fairgrounds and its adjoining 80-acre Midway Plaisance. Henry Adams, reflecting upon his two visits during the summer of 1893, observed:

> The Exposition itself defied philosophy. One might find fault until the last gate closed, one could still explain nothing that needed explanation . . . Since Noah's Ark, no such Babel of loose and ill-joined, such vague and ill-defined and unrelated thoughts and half-thoughts and experimental outcries as the Exposition, had ever ruffled the surface of the Lakes.[6]

The Department of Ethnology and Archaeology at the Exposition ("Department M") typified the confusion and disorder characterizing fair display. Frederic Ward Putnam, head of Harvard's Peabody Museum of American Archaeology and Ethnology, was appointed director of the Department early in 1891. Putnam's acceptance terms committed the Fair Managers to support original research. Squads of unpaid graduate students from universities around the country were put into the

field to locate and dispatch materials to Chicago. Their finds were augmented with field work gathered and sent by government employees (mostly military officers attached to US embassies in Latin America) and supported by existing collections. Though this essay features the displays of Putnam's Department M, it was not the only non-commercial exhibitor of ethnographic material. In addition to state-sponsored and foreign displays, large collections sent by the Smithsonian Institution were separately administered and displayed, chiefly in the US Government Building. In addition, the US Bureau of Indian Affairs, opposed both to ethnology and ethnologists (Indian Commissioner Thomas Morgan thought them "the most insidious and active enemies" of Indian assimilation through education), constructed its own attempt to evade the "savage" past, a schoolhouse/residence on the fairgrounds, with both mounted displays and a rotating cadre of Indian students, studying, making handicrafts, singing songs for visitors, and the like.[7]

Originally slotted for 160,000 square feet in the Liberal Arts Building and a 1,000-foot strip of land along the lagoon for outdoor exhibits, Putnam's displays found their home not there at the center of things, but at the tail end of the fairgrounds, close to the livestock exhibit and sewer works, in a building charitably described as "unpretentious and devoid of all ornamentation." Blocked off from the lake by the Forestry Building and a loop of the Intramural Railway, the Anthropological Building gave up 30,000 of the ground floor's 52,804 square feet of display space to the Bureau of Corrections and the Bureau of Sanitation and Hygiene, and surrendered still more space to large exhibits sent by foreign countries – 362 domestic but 452 foreign collections, by one count, on the ground floor and the gallery above it. One commemorative album of the Fair observed, "Only a comparative sprinkling [of visitors] invades the territory south of the Stock Pavilion. So much is to be seen in the northern part of the grounds . . . that the majority are fain to content themselves with a hasty survey of this region from the Intramural railway." The marginalization of the ethnographic exhibits affected the impact of live displays on the fairground itself.[8]

The eight rooms of laboratories in the north end of the Anthropological Building, organized by Franz Boas and staffed by professors from the University of Wisconsin and the newly-established University of Chicago, offered fair-goers comparative craniology, anthropometry, and "exhibits referring to the development of the white race in America." Significant to the cultural staging of the "native" is the Department's "introduction to America of the 'life group,'" a form of ethnographic dis-play utilized by Boas, at Putnam's instruction, which featured mannequins "'dressed in the garments of the people, and arranged in groups so as to illustrate the life history of each tribe represented.'" Descendents of the wax figures in evidence in Charles Willson Peale's museum in Philadelphia in the 1790s, "only in 1893 were groups of such costumed figures arranged in dramatic scenes from daily life and ritual" in a museum context in the United States, a con-text more Barnum than Boasian in shifting the display of ethnological artifacts from the descriptive to the performative. As Ira jacknis, the historian of this process, observes, "the life group was a presentational medium allowing these cultural connections to be *seen*," and, "not surprisingly, the life groups were enor-mously popular with visitors."[9]

The performative aspect of displays became (and remains) troubling to anthropologists, as did (and remains) the entertainment aspect of museum display. In the flush of the Columbian Exposition, however, display cases, photo-graphs, and reconstructions indoors led seam-lessly to living people in the Department's "Ethnographical Exhibit" out-of-doors. Although Robert W. Rydell locates Depart-ment M's "exhibits of Dakota Sioux, Navajos, Apaches, and various northwestern tribes on or near the Midway Plaisance," which, in his view, "immediately degraded them," there were only two outdoor displays of living native peoples on the fairground itself (there was, indeed, a commercially-operated American Indian Village on the Midway). The "Esquimaux Village," at the Fair's Northwest Pond, was a commercial exhibit owned and operated by the J. W. Skiles Company of

Spokane on a site not really "near" the Midway Plaisance, though more so than Department M's non-commercial Ethnographical Exhibit, situated near the South Pond and the Anthro-pological Building, which could not be further away from the Plaisance and still be on the fairgrounds.[10]

Putnam had instructed Boas to arrange the roughly fourteen Indian "villages" making up the outdoor Ethnographical Exhibit of his Department "with historic accuracy, in strict chronological sequence," that is, geograph-ically north to south. Contemporary accounts identify the display as including "Esquimaux" from Labrador to the north, then a Cree family and Haida/Fort Rupert peoples from Canada, Iroquois from the northeastern United States (there are also photos of a "Penobscott Vil-lage"), Chippewa, Sioux, Menominee, and Winnebago from the northeastern and mid-north states, Choctaws from Louisiana, Apaches and Navajos from New Mexico and Arizona, Coahuilas from California, and Papa-gos and Yakuis from the US-Mexico border region. (Publicity claims the Indians lived in their reconstructed dwellings, but it is not clear if they stayed there after hours.) During the day, the Ethnological Indians cooked, worked, talked with visitors (if they could), played musical instruments, sang, and danced.[11]

The conflation of real and faux continued to the south of the villages, where the Anthropo-logical Department had erected a simulation of the Ruins of Yucatan, "made of staff by means of papier-mâché." The six sections of the ruins were separated by a walkway from a commer-cial representation of the Cliff Dwellings at Battle Rock Mountain in Colorado, repro-duced by the H. J. Smith Exploring Company (at one-tenth actual size) as a series of rooms stocked with relics – including human remains – along an ascending pathway: "Admission 25 cents; catalogue 10 cents." In this hetero-topic play of imaged and real, science, culture, entertainment, and history moved freely through sites at once false and true, each offer-ing its own view of the work and culture of the "real" America and Americans.[12]

While there were only two outdoor exhibits on the fairgrounds involving what the Indian Bureau (intending disparagement) called "show Indians," Smithsonian, state, and foreign exhibits also included live displays. In addition to housing a large Smithsonian exhibit called "Women's Work in Savagery" – eighty cases of Amerindian embroidery, hide work, pottery, baskets, looms, and implements – the Women's Building, for example, featured a Navajo weaver working her loom on a staircase landing (dubbed the "Indian Alcove"), one of surely many living accompaniments to the Indian figures prominent in the Fair's art work and statuary. In addition to Amerindians working in "show" capacities producing artifacts, many Indians appeared at the Fair's special events. During the 1 May 1893 opening festivities, William F. Cody (at his own expense) invited a hundred Sioux from Pine Ridge, Standing Rock, and Rosebud to watch the ceremonies from the balcony of the Administration Building, along with his own employees – including ghost dancers, Kicking Bear, Two Strike, Jack Red Cloud, Rocky Bear, Young Man Afraid of His Horses, and Short Bull, in full regalia. On Italian Day, twelve Sioux, in full Plains dress, played the Columbus "welcoming party" of Arawaks, to shouts of "Bravo!" and "Encore!" from the audience. On Chicago Day (9 October 1893), near the close of the Fair, Chief Simon Pokagon of the Potawatomi used the occasion to speak against the treatment accorded the descendants of his father's generation, who had deeded to Chicago, in 1833, the land which became the site for the Exposition.[13]

Though Cody's guests may not have been paid performers, the Sioux far from Arawaks, and Simon Pokagon (given the occasion) both "official" and "entertainment," the distinctions designating members of the public, delegations and dignitaries, ethnographic display personnel, exhibit demonstrators, and show Indians at the Columbian Exposition were extremely fluid. Indeed, these boundaries are hardly less porous today. The interactions and interrelationships among these roles helped turn the Fair's intellectual and pedagogic intentions into a performance. Sometimes the transfer was direct. The performances the Kwakiutl gave, for example, were first shown to Franz Boas, "rituals that in some cases were no longer practiced," according to Curtis Hinsley.

Chosen for their show quality, ethnographic "classics" "blocking out the changes of time," the anthropological subject is feared frozen in the past by the progressive scenario. Performance, however, is live and critiques even the ideas it enacts. That critique is visible in Indians watching the hoopla commemorating the quadracentennial of Columbus's arrival in America at the Fair's opening, in Indians playing (other) Indians in an enactment of that event (doing it their way, the Plains way, which had become the prototypical Indian performance by 1893), and in the analysis by Simon Pokagon of what these events had wrought. Some scientists at the Exposition may have thought their intellectual order of things triumphant, but fairgoers as well as Indians would have been hard-pressed not to grasp the performative nature of the Fair exchange. The juxtaposition of equally false official and commercial exhibits stressed to fairgoers their constructed rather than "real" nature, while the difficulty of finding order as an audience, when assaulted by acres of disorderly and simulated phenomena, creates points of detachment from the intellectual performance of the "dream city."[14]

Though we may never know how many Amerindians labored in show capacities at the World's Columbian Exposition or how many appeared at the Fair's special festivities, we do know their presence helped create and define the event, and that they were vocal, as well as visible, in shaping the performances fairgoers saw. Central to issues of agency in this regard is the degree of autonomy as performers show Indians of all kinds at the Columbian Exposition enjoyed. Culture and commerce clearly went in hand at the Fair, a fact of life for theatre and shows in the United States in the nineteenth century. The reality of the Exposition as a show was emphasized when five families in the Esquimaux Village successfully sued to break their contract with their manager, the J. W. Skiles Company, and opened their own show outside the fairgrounds. In this, these performers functioned like other paid professionals at the time. The Indians in the Anthropology Department's Ethnographical Exhibit were similarly transported, housed, and paid, though the terms and conditions of work are currently unclear. The students at the BIA Indian School exhibit and those at the Carlisle Indian School exhibit of student industrial work in the Liberal Arts Building, on the other hand, appear to have been boarded rather than treated as paid employees. Theatre historians will need to compare the contracts, conditions, and compensation of Exposition Indians, show Indians on the Midway, and those at Buffalo Bill's Wild West (and compare these, in turn, to the contracts, conditions, and compensations accorded similar non-Indian acts), in order to gauge the degree of economic freedom and performative autonomy show Indians enjoyed.[15]

Opposition to show Indians and anti-theatrical prejudice deny employees (performers) are employees and that what they are doing is a performance, forestalling compensation in the first case and input into what is performed in the second. Whether the view of Amerindians performed on the fairground was that of the preservation of the customs and artifacts of "vanishing" Indians, that of the inculcation of the skills necessary to assimilate, or that of the representations of show Indian acts and artistry, however, Trennert emphasizes "the public drew little distinction between official and commercial Indian displays," either at the Columbian or at subsequent World's Fairs. Moreover, as it became clear "old" Indian culture, not new, had the public fancy, the BIA gave up education exhibits and proposed in later years to offer non-student "Indians 'dressed in native costume and carrying on native handicrafts, weaving, bead and leather-work, making jewelry and baskets, work in birch bark, etc.,' right in the school building." In time, the Bureau even constructed its own village near the conventional school exhibit where, in one case, "Geronimo and a group of Apache prisoners from Fort Sill" signed autographs and sold bows and arrows.[16]

The perils of the performative for Columbian scholars like Putnam were most sharply drawn on the Midway Plaisance, which operated under the auspices of his Department, but whose exhibits came under the management of Sol Bloom (in later years, Bloom observed that putting Putnam in charge of the Midway was "about as intelligent a decision as it would be today to make Albert Einstein manager of Ringling Brothers and Barnum and Bailey's Circus"). It is not difficult to locate the White City and, particularly, the Midway Plaisance, as sites for the expression of racism. While "visitors apparently experienced little overt discrimination in public facilities at the fair" – and all the world came to see the Columbian Exposition – access to exhibit space on the fairground was restricted (Buffalo Bill, African Americans, and Indians were among those denied it) and displays emphasized "the stages of the development of man on [at least] the American continent," which created a hierarchy of races detrimental to non-whites. Recent histories of World's Fairs view the Midway Plaisance as the malevolent topos *par excellence*. Indeed, Robert W. Rydell considers the development of Midways (ambivalent in Chicago, but endorsed by fairs thereafter) "'living proof' for the imperial calculations" of "American elites to establish their cultural hegemony," in part through the Midway's "anthropologically validated racial hierarchies." For these, Rydell concludes, "the World's Columbian Exposition became the standard with which every subsequent fair would be compared."[17]

The racism in contemporaneous material about the Columbian Exposition is wholly evident, but the binary strategies of negation, which reveal it, evade the complexities of participation by Amerindians (and other races and nationalities) in cultural performances during the Fair, and can betray a lingering anti-theatrical prejudice against performing itself. Against Rydell's charge of degradation, L. G. Moses argues, for example, that "neither the newspaper accounts nor the agency records that contain comments by and about Indians bears this [degradation] out." Performers complicate unitary readings and performance resists binary interpretations. Thomas Roddy and Henry "Buckskin Joe" De Ford, for example, managed a troupe of sixty show Indians from various tribes on the Midway which included a gash show in which Chief Twobites and Joe Strongback had four slashes cut between the shoulder blades and a rope laced through, to the horror of a *Chicago Tribune* reporter who wrote in protest against the act. The performers filed no complaints. Was this "abuse" or even "torture," as the reporter saw it, or is there a show context for even this act? Michael Chemers has suggested that critics of freak shows operate from unproblematized moral positions that are presumed to transcend the socio-historic forces shaping those positions. Characterizing such views as ahistorical and frequently influenced by "backplanted" prejudices, Chemers argues that these positions often ignore the political and economic factors that influence performers and "unduly privileges an elitist hegemony which has traditionally dominated historical research" concerning high and low art. Similar issues have been raised concerning burlesque shows and performances classified as pornographic, but also medicine shows, carnival and circus acts, magic shows, a variety of popular performers, and wild west shows (and, indeed, voices against iconographic or living representation of any kind have been raised throughout history). Autonomy weighs little if a performative choke is viewed as "so bad, I don't care if it is voluntary."[18]

Performances on the Midway Plaisance, the grittiest and most commercial part of the Fair, invite critiques of how audiences and managers behaved and of the shows performers offered. Much has been written about the first two (audiences and managers), but the third is not always transparent or even known. Were Chief Twobites and Joe Strongback really gashed, for example, or was theirs indeed a simulation for which the *Tribune* reporter was the "mark"? What was the act intended to show – bravery? savagery? – and why show it? Where on the Midway was the act done? How often could it have been done? Maps of the Midway Plaisance show (but often omit) an "Indian Village" to the west of the Ferris Wheel, yet in addition to the Roddy and De Ford show, accounts identify P. B. Wickham's exhibit of "Sitting Bull's Cabin" (rivaling the one on Buffalo Bill's campground and another in the North Dakota State exhibit) which featured nine Sioux, including Rain-in-the-Face, who had petitioned the Fair Managers for (and been denied) control over or influence in Native

American representations on the fairgrounds. Did the Wickham exhibit on the Midway offer a countersite in which the Sioux found the agency to perform their culture as they deemed appropriate? Were show Indians on the Midway the class of duped subjects their well-wishers and the Indian Bureau characterized them as being or did their view of what constituted culture or performance not conform to the senses of propriety and advantage dictated by managers (fair and commercial), anthropologists, reporters, audiences, or historians?[19]

The White City and its Midway can be seen as a heterotopia of contesting sites – the "real," the faux, and the simulated; the educational, the aesthetic, and the entertaining; the State-sponsored, Fair-sponsored, and the commercially-produced. The World Congresses reflecting the ideologies driving the White City may also profitably be viewed as heterotopic performances rather than unitary or utopic/dystopic spaces. The heavily subscribed World Congresses were held in the just completed "Permanent Memorial Art Palace" (today's Art Institute of Chicago) and organized with near military precision by an Auxiliary into twenty Departments with 224 Divisions, that ran the duration of the Exposition (15 May through 28 October 1893). The World's Historical Congress, World's Congress of Folk-Lore, and World's Congress on Philology and Literary Archaeology were in the Literature Department, while remaining branches of archaeology and ethnology were assigned to various Congress Departments. The divisions in the work of the newly founded science of anthropology, whose International Congress was also organized by the Fair, reflect what Curtis Hinsley identifies as "much confusion" at the time concerning the relationships among environment, native philosophies and religions, myths, art, practical activity, and paleontology, within larger controversies about nature versus nurture and artifacts versus contexts. Otis Mason's address on behalf of the Smithsonian exhibit, for example, counseled anthropologists to view Indians racially, on the one hand urging the distinctive features of each culture, on the other the inevitable extinguishing of cultures that failed, as Mason would later say, to "blend into 'the proper flow of true culture . . . the flow of world-embracing commerce.'"[20]

Frederick Jackson Turner's paper to the American Historical Association, "whose ninth annual meeting was held in conjunction with the World's Historical Congress, with a programme practically identical," might have passed with good, but not distinguished, notice, on a hot 12 July evening ("the afternoons being devoted to the Exposition at Jackson Park"). The up-and-coming historian and his thesis concerning "The Significance of the Frontier in American History," however, had powerful friends, and provided the unifying narrative that eluded science. As a player in the world performed by the Columbian Exposition, Turner's thesis can be seen to simultaneously affirm and negate constructs of the native and the American enacted there. To be sure, the evolution on display at the Fair and at the World's Congresses had itself shifted significantly, as Foucault observes:

> In the eighteenth century, the evolutionist idea is defined on the basis of a kinship of species forming a continuum laid down at the outset (interrupted only by natural catastrophes) or gradually built up by the passing of time. In the nineteenth century, the evolutionist theme concerns not so much the constitution of a continuous table of species, as the description of discontinuous groups and the analysis of the modes of interaction between an organism whose elements are interdependent and an environment that provides its real conditions of life. A single theme, but based on two types of discourse.[21]

The discontinuous groups evolving in Turner's view of the closed frontier conceptualized already conventional views. Richard White, in comparing Turner's and Buffalo Bill's Wild West, sees Turner's frontier as arguing the (chiefly) peaceful settlement of an (envisioned) empty space, a process Joaquin Miller poeticized as "A kingdom won without the guilt / Of studied battle." Into this Utopia, Turner inserted the frontiersman, his scholarly embodiment of James W. Steele's "sons of the border," a type of man clothed by western

life "with a new individuality" which could "make him forget the tastes and habits of early life, and transform him into one of that restless horde of cosmopolites who form the crest of the slow wave of humanity which year by year creeps toward the setting sun." More directly influential, Turner's biographer Wilbur R. Jacobs observes, were the early volumes of Theodore Roosevelt's *The Winning of the West*, positing the heroic border warrior as a "type of man [who] marked a stage in the evolutionary process of society's development," the type more significant to Turner's view of historical development than the study of individuals.[22]

Gifted with a copy of the paper, Roosevelt (the man who would subsequently claim that his use of the term "Rough Riders" had nothing to do with Buffalo Bill's Wild West) wrote Turner, "I think you have struck some first class ideas, and have put into definite shape a good deal of thought which has been floating around rather loosely." Indeed, Turner's writing depends upon accessible images:

> The wilderness masters the colonist. It finds him a European in dress, industries, tools, modes of travel, and thought. It takes him from the railroad car and puts him in the birch canoe. It strips off the garments of civilization and arrays him in the hunting shirt and moccasin. It puts him in the log cabin of the Cherokee and Iroquois and runs an Indian palisade around him. Before long he has gone to planting Indian corn and plowing with a sharp stick; he shouts the war cry and takes the scalp in orthodox Indian fashion.

"At the frontier," Turner thought, "the environment is at first too strong for the man." Perceived as a boundary line, or grid of lines that had marched from east to west, from frontier to ranches, to farms, to manufacturing, and to cities, Turner's frontier marches in file to fill in the image of an empty space. The 1890 census had declared this frontier line dissolved and Turner's thesis offered a closed (and nostalgic) explanation of its significance and a history of its passing. Though himself a son of the (mid)west, of the open prairies and plains, Turner's thesis is an urbanist view of the glory (and cost) of progress: the White City rising where log cabins and the homes of the Potawatomi once stood.[23]

Historians have not failed to note the many aspects of American history Turner's thesis omits – economic explanations, class antagonisms, imperialism, the development of American capitalism and its connections to world economies, among them – and the many sins of interpretation it commits (emptying the land, tying the development of national democracy to the pioneer, separating American history from political history elsewhere in the world, sectionalizing diversity, nativism, and the positing of a unique American spirit name some of the transgressions cited). So initially successful was the thesis among historians, however, that, by the 1930s, "the American Historical Association was branded one great Turner-verein." Poised historiographically somewhere between racial and geographic determinism, Turner's frontier mapped a terrain simultaneously closed and opened, a history written yet just beginning to write itself, in the discontinuous discursive mode of nineteenth-century American evolutionism described by Foucault and evident at the Columbian Exposition and its Congresses. Elevated to a position of influence by Herbert Baxter Adams (the Secretary of the AHA and Turner's doctoral advisor at Johns Hopkins), who referred to the paper several times in his report of the proceedings. Turner's frontier is irrevocably the environment of the Indian, but it is a frontier of change. In it, the frontiersman "must accept the conditions which it furnishes or perish, and so he fits himself into the Indian clearings and follows the Indian trails. Little by little he transforms the wilderness."[24]

It is curious to find this frontier described as a line, "the meeting point between savagery and civilization," bounded and filled in edge to edge, when Turner's thesis simultaneously creates a frontier which is a space, "not the old Europe" bordered anew, but a space shaped and inhabited by those "who grew up under these conditions . . . the really American part of our history." Turner segments the space, envisioning it in developmental stages – "line by line we read this continental page from west to east" – from frontier to city, but his is actually a history of simultaneous spaces, even in the moment Turner wrote of these spaces as past. Those present spaces were very much on view at the Columbian Exposition in Buffalo Bill's Wild West, to which Cody had specially invited the historians on the afternoon of Turner's presentation, an invitation which the procrastinating young scholar had to decline.[25]

What, then, is the intellectual performance of Frederick Jackson Turner's frontier thesis? In bringing Turner's frontier and Buffalo Bill's Wild West into the same display space, Richard White's essay for the Newberry Library's 1994–95 exhibit rightly underscores the absent Amerindian players who suffer equally in peaceful and in violent stories of the American frontier. Both scenarios argue, however (as does the Columbian Exposition site), the presence rather than the absence of those key players.) To be sure, Frederick Jackson Turner had neither artifacts, art technology, nor Indians to assist him. Like any dramatist, Turner had only the word to offer, but it was not the detached word of the novelist (still less the objective, scientized language of the ideal historian of the 1890s), rather the representative, imaged language of the playwright in which actors perform history. So effective was Turner's staging that it came to enjoy the same representative afterlife of performance material. Other Columbian scholars used even more elements of performance. Washington Matthews, for example, illustrated his lecture about "Sacred Objects of the Navajo" during the Folk-lore Congress both with specimens (baskets, painted sticks) and phonograph records of Navajo music. Confronting "the limitations of verbal description by offering to play Indian," as Barbara Kirschenblatt-Gimblett observes, Matthews and other Congress speakers who offered enactments sought to make "the apparently trivial interesting by performing ethnography." Captain H. L. Scott, of the Seventh US Cavalry, went further still toward the performative by using show Indians from Buffalo Bill's Wild West to illustrate his lecture for the Folk-lore Congress, "The Sign Language of the Plains Indians" (the folklorists were invited to be Cody's guests the same afternoon as the historians, 12 July 1893).[26]

Buffalo Bill's Wild West represented still another history, one which served both as site and counter-site for the histories offered by the Columbian Exposition and its Congresses. The show brought these sites together in one performative display, one simultaneous showing of the simulation that had, by 1893, become the history of the "native" and the "American." Cody's "campground, arena, and grandstand" next to the fairground offered foot-weary fairgoers both a chance to sit down and to enjoy the entertainment they sought at the Exhibition (and perhaps at its Congresses). A specific construction of history and the authentic came with a seat at Buffalo Bill's Wild West. "It is not a 'show' in any sense of the word, but it is a series of original, genuine, and instructive OBJECT LESSONS," a broadside promised patrons, "in which the participants repeat the heroic parts they have played in actual life." William F. Cody and his show Indians had lived the frontier they invoked and their acts in the Wild West program for Chicago reflected that. International contingents of cavalry and show riders had been added to the Wild West during the European tour which preceded the Exposition, and Cody's General Manager, Nate Salsbury, opened the Wild West for business in April of 1893, before the Fair itself commenced, to assure high quality for the Exposition's international audience.[27]

From the Grand Review introducing "Buffalo Bill's Wild West and Congress of Rough Riders of the World," through its seventeen acts, to the farewell salute by the entire company, the show underscored the presence, rather than absence, of Indians and the frontier. Present as evidence were people and things to materially attest to the reality of Indians and frontiers: performers who had been frontier scouts, wagons that had carried emigrants across the prairies, an "authentic" Deadwood Mail Coach, Indians who were not only truly Indians, but Indians who had (like William F. Cody) lived the history of bison hunts, skilled riding, battles with US Cavalry, and ghost dancing (if not of attacking wagon trains or

stage coaches), and bison who nearly were (as the program declared) "the last of the known Native Herd." That these persuasive presences told audiences a tale they wanted to hear made the Columbian Exposition the show's most successful season (186 days of continuous performance in one location, from 26 April to 31 October 1893, before six million people, clearing an estimated million dollars).[28]

At the time of the Columbian Exposition in Chicago, Buffalo Bill's Wild West had just completed two triumphal tours abroad before the crowned heads and millions of Europeans. The show trumpeted this achievement as a "wondrous voyage." Like Columbus, the publicity none-too-subtly implied, the Wild West (as America) had completed a journey which paralleled the trajectory of W. F. Cody's (and American) life, "from prairie to palace." Now one with the great nations of the world, the Wild West wrote a history in which the Indian Wars were a thing of the past and "the Former Foe-Present Friend, the American" (as a poster captioned an Indian portrait) one among the many who now took the name "American" as their own. The warrior life celebrated in the Wild West had vanished, but the Indians themselves remained. In Buffalo Bill's Wild West, the "dead" rose up from the dust of the arena, rode on as well as off, were there for the opening act at the start and for the salute that ended the show. Historian L. G. Moses has recently observed, "Indians survived [the] 'Winning of the West,' both in reality and then as portrayed in the shows." Furthermore, he argues, "Show Indians had won the battle of images," for, although Buffalo Bill's Wild West portrayed Indians "heroically and sympathetically as a vanishing American" way of life, it did not portray them – as did the Indian Bureau, the ethnologists, or Turner's frontier thesis – as savages without history or culture.[29]

Of the visions of history, ethnology, and performance escaping the "New World" of the Columbian Exposition and Buffalo Bill's Wild West in 1893, the closed and the open, the positive and the negative, the publication of more show-tolerant histories in recent years offers ground for recovering subjects erased by racism. In Vine Deloria's view, for example, "Unlike the government programs, the Wild

West treated Indians as mature adults capable of making intelligent decisions and of contributing to an important enterprise." Nate Salsbury, the Wild West's general manager, refused to control how show Indians spent their salaries or, beyond exercising "a constant vigilance that they do not fall into the hands of tradesmen who are sharpers," to assume a patronizing posture toward an Indian performer who, in Salsbury's words, both "knows the value of a dollar quite as well as a white man," and who "is quite capable of choosing his occupation and profiting by it."[30]

Show-tolerant history does not deny the presence of the racism that histories like Rydell's, Slotkin's, and White's have been at pains to reveal, but it does suggest both that the performative is ubiquitous and that it resists too narrow a reading. Examining issues of authenticity, for example, at the heart of much of performance analysis, widens the analytical field for viewing the Columbian Exposition, its Congresses, and Buffalo Bill's Wild West. Vine Deloria suggests how and why show Indians were able to put themselves into the authentic world of Buffalo Bill's Wild West:

Intead of degrading the Indians and classifying them as primitive savages, Cody elevated them to a status of equality with conti[n]gents from other nations. In so doing, he recognized and emphasized their ability as horsemen and warriors and stressed their patriotism in defending their home lands. This type of recognition meant a great deal to the Indians who were keenly aware that American public opinion often refused to admit the justice of their claims and motivations. Inclusions of Indians in the Congress of Rough Riders provided a platform for displaying natural ability that transcended racial and political antagonisms and, when, contrasted with other contemporary attitudes toward Indians, represented one that was amazingly sophisticated and liberal.

In this world, attack acts are a demonstration of skills valued by performers as well as by audiences. As Deloria concludes, "the Wild West served to give them confidence in themselves by emphasizing the nobility of their most cherished exploits and memories." This Wild West was a shared history and memory, a jointly occupied arena in which competing claims for authenticity could be presented and evaluated.[31]

Viewing the New World of the Columbian Exposition as a heterotopia permits historians to see "simultaneously represented, contested, and inverted" counter-sites. Some of those contests are evident in the experiences of show Indians at the Fair, in their contracts and living conditions no less than in what they performed and how audiences received them. Today, more than a century after the Columbian Exposition, "Buffalo Bill's Wild West" is a featured part of Euro-Disney, by 1997 the most popular of its performing attractions, drawing over three million people to a two-a-day, ninety-minute performance (with barbecue), for which the 1,058-capacity house is consistently sold out. According to R. L. Wilson, nearly all the enactors are from the United States, and several of the native American performers claim descent from show Indians who worked with William F. Cody. That there is pride among Amerindian performers in being performers and a willingness to be part of the Wild West tradition should not be surprising. "Spirit Capture," an exhibition mounted and catalogue published by the National Museum of the American Indian, records a long history of show Indians and Indian shows, including performers with Buffalo Bill, the Seneca Edward Cornplanter's Indian and Minstrel Show (active in 1899), a performance of Hiawatha given by the Iroquois of the Cattaraugus Reservation in New York in 1906 (it toured the United States and Europe), the participation of Porcupine (a Cheyenne) in the 45th anniversary re-creation of the Battle of Little Big Horn in 1921, Navajo dancers entertaining a tourist train in 1963, and most Americans have seen native performers, "show Indians" and amateurs, in some capacity, recently as part of the Indian-centered opening ceremonies of the 2002 Winter Olympics in Salt Lake City.[32]

Is it the case that audiences don't know the difference between the actual and the assumed, the real and the simulated, or is performance the canny creation of a self-conscious perception of the simultaneous presence of actual and assumed, real and simulated, and of the cultural assumption of the other as self? If, in addition, elements of stagings of this kind can be located in anthropology, history, folklore, and disciplines not conventionally considered performance or performative, theatre historians can increasingly locate elements of those disciplines in their own. This essay has that wider world of the Columbian Exposition in view and a heterotopic historiographical strategy for what it perceives as a heterotopic historical site. What more can be said about the theatre culture of a Columbian Exposition that takes in Frederick Jackson Turner's frontier thesis and Buffalo Bill's Wild West as well as the Fair may be their very insistence upon their authenticity: that the Exposition showed what the 'real' America (US) had accomplished in a hundred years, that Turner's thesis showed the "true" history of that America, and that Buffalo Bill's Wild West showed an "exact" reproduction of the frontier life lived by those who enacted it. The form these discourses assumed, the domain they sought to govern, the internal relationships among their constituent parts, and their relationships with other discourses help theatre historians consider authenticity within representation, where Rydell's, Slotkin's, and White's histories assume it does not reside.[33]

It seems to me likely that fairgoers in 1893 moved among the real and the simulated, the actual and the assumed, and were able to understand contradictions offered by the site. Moreover, it is significant that, at the putative end of America's Columbian period, the end of its frontier, and at the supposed vanishing point for Amerindians, there is a contest concerning what and who constitutes the native and the American. Histories tell us this contest reflects power's insecurity – company owners over workers, nativists over immigrants, men over women, racist whites over non-whites, and so on – and all these contests are evident in the wider performances of the Columbian Exposition in 1893. My on-going work with stagings of "the native," however, suggests as well the emergence of a new world at the time of the Fair, constructing the Indian as the American and insisting upon the authenticity of its version of that story. At the same time, the native is enacted in ways that underscored the real-life distance between and within competing representations in, for example, the three performance spaces considered here.[34]

NOTES

1 Frederick Jackson Turner, *The Significance of the Frontier in American History*, facsimile of the 1894 *Annual Report of the American Historical Association* (Ann Arbor: University Microfilms, 1966). *Illustrated London News*, 16 April 1887. Architectural critic Claude Bragdon is quoted (without attribution) by Russell Lewis, "Everything Under One Roof: World's Fairs and Department Stores in Paris and Chicago," *Chicago History* 12.3 (1983): 44.

2 Alan Trachtenberg, *The Incorporation of America: Culture and Society in the Gilded Age* (New York: Hill and Wang, 1982). Richard Slotkin, *Gunfighter Nation: The Myth of the Frontier in Twentieth-Century America* (New York: Athenaeum, 1992), and see his "Buffalo Bill's 'Wild West' and the Mythologization of the American Empire," in Amy Kaplan and Donald E. Pease (eds.), *Cultures of United States Imperialism* (Durham, NC Duke University Press, 1993), 164–81. Richard White, "Frederick Jackson Turner and Buffalo Bill," in James R. Grossman (ed.), *The Frontier in American Culture, An Exhibition at the Newberry Library, August 26, 1994–January 7, 1995* (Berkeley: University of California Press, 1994), 7–65.

3 Michel Foucault, *The Archaeology of Knowledge and the Discourse on Language*, trans. A. M. Sheridan Smith (New York: Pantheon Books, 1972), 155–56. For theatre culture, see *Theatre Culture in America, IS2S–1860* (New York: Cambridge University Press, 1997).

4 In addition to Philip J. Deloria's *Playing Indian* (New Haven: Yale University Press, 1998), Barbara Kirshenblatt-Gimblett explores ethnographic objects and agencies of display in her *Destination Culture: Tourism, Museums, and Heritage* (Berkeley: University of California Press, 1998). These boundaries are also explored by performance and theatre historians. See, for example,

Christopher R. Balme, "Cultural Anthropology and Theatre Historiography: Notes on a Methodological Rapprochement," *Theatre Survey* 35.1 (May 1994): 33–52 and his "Staging the Pacific: Framing Authenticity in Performances for Tourists at the Polynesian Cultural Center," *Theatre Journal* 50.1 (March 1998): 53–70, Dennis Kennedy, "Shakespeare and Cultural Tourism," *Theatre Journal* 50.2 (May 1998): 175–88, and Bank.

5   Robert W. Rydell, *All the World's a Fair: Visions of Empire at American International Expositions, 1876–1916* (Chicago: University of Chicago Press, 1984), is exemplary among recent scholarly studies characterizing the Columbian Exposition (and other fairs) as a demon scenario, but see also the early chapters of his *World of Fairs: The Century of Progress Expositions* (Chicago: University of Chicago Press, 1993), Rydell, John E. Findling, and Kimberly D. Pelle, *Fair America* (Washington, D.C.: Smithsonian Institution Press, 2000), Neil Harris, Wim de Wit, James Gilbert, and Robert W. Rydell, *Grand Illusions: Chicago's World's Fair of 1893* (Chicago: Chicago Historical Society, 1993), Slotkin, Robert Muccigrosso, *Celebrating the New World: Chicago's Columbian Exposition of 1893* (Chicago: Ivan R. Dee, Inc., 1993), and Curtis M. Hinsley, *The Smithsonian and the American Indian: Making a Moral Anthropology in America* (Washington: Smithsonian Institution Press, 1981). Michel Foucault, "Of Other Spaces," *Diacritics* 16.1 (Spring 1986): 24.

6   For acreage, see *The Best Things to be Seen at the World's Fair*, John J. Flinn, comp. (Chicago: Columbian Guide Co., 1893), 12. Henry Adams, *The Education of Henry Adams*, ed. Ernest Samuels (Boston: Houghton Mifflin and Co., 1974), 339–40. Adams's assessment of this disorder was grim. "For a hundred years, between 1793 and 1893," he reflected, "the American people had hesitated, vacillated, swayed forward and back, between two forces, one simply industrial, the other capitalistic, centralizing, and mechanical." The Fair, Adams concluded, made clear America had "slipped across the chasm" (see Hinsley, 231).

7   Putnam was in charge of the exhibits on the Midway as well as those of Department M.

The racist aspects of this relationship have often been noted by scholars (see particularly Rydell, *All the World's a Fair*, chapter 2). For the Bureau of Indian Affairs, see particularly Robert A. Trennert, Jr., "Selling Indian Education at World's Fairs and Expositions, 1893–1904," *American Indian Quarterly* 11.3 (Summer 1987): 210–11, but also his "A Grand Failure: The Centennial Indian Exhibition of 1876," *Prologue* 6.2 (Summer 1974): 118–29. Located near Putnam's Anthropological Building and its outdoor Ethnographical Village, the BIA's Indian School was described by the Secretary of the Board of Indian Commissioners as "a little, mean-looking building in the midst of those grand and imposing structures" (L.G Moses, "Indians on the Midway: Wild West Shows and the Indian Bureau at World's Fairs, 1893–1904," *South Dakota History* 21 (Fall 1991): note 11, p. 214, and see Muccigrosso, 151). Encircled by the southeast loop of the fair's Intramural Elevated Electric Railway, the School operated 15 May through October, 1893.

8   Rossiter Johnson, *A History of the World's Columbian Exposition Held in Chicago in 1893*, Vol. II (New York. D. Appleton and Co., 1898), 316. According to Rand McNally's *Handbook of the World's Columbian Exposition* [vol. 1, no. 180 (2 May 1893) of the Globe Library] (Chicago: Rand McNally and Co., 1893), 90, the Anthropological Building measured 415 feet long and 225 feet wide. For the assessment of the area's appeal, see *The Columbian Gallery: A Portfolio of Photographs from the World's Pair* (Chicago: Werner Co., 1894), pages in the volume are unnumbered. The quoted matter is from a caption to "Down in the Windmill Section," as the area was called.

9   Johnson, 329–31, and 356 for the "white race" quote. The academics in the laboratories included Joseph Jastrow from the University of Wisconsin, who ran the Psychology Section, and H. H. Donnaldson of the University of Chicago, who ran the Neurology Section. Ira Jacknis, "Franz Boas and Exhibits: On the Limitations of the Museum Method of Anthropology," In George W. Stocking, Jr. (ed.), *Objects and Others: Essays on Museums and Material Culture*

(Madison, WI: University of Wisconsin Press, 1985), 81 and 76. The "life group" is not unrelated to the "habitat group" for animals, said to have been introduced by the Biologiska Muséet in Stockholm when it opened in 1893 (see A. E. Parr, "The Habitat Group," *Curator* 2 [1959]: 119). Jacknis notes (99) that Boas's model maker at the American Museum of Natural History in New York, Casper Mayer, took plaster casts of faces and body parts from the life: "These casts came from diverse sources: some were collected along with the artefacts in the field . . . , some from the visiting circus or Carlisle Indian School, and some from occasional visits of natives to New York." Such figures, Jacknis observes, deserved a performance setting, thus the museum introduced "the staged, theatrically lit diorama, popularized after 1910" (102). Hinsley (112) cites an unpublished paper by facknis adding to this discussion that, "without the proper control of scholarly texts subject to 'professional' standards, an exhibit could in fact feed the taste for racist exoticism that it was meant to curb." For Rydell's discussion of the Anthropological Building's laboratories, see *All the World's A Fair*, 57.

For Peale's use of wax figures to contrast the "races of mankind" in 1797, see Charles Coleman Sellers, *Mr. Peak's Museum: Charles Willson Peale and the First Popular Museum of Natural Science and Art* (New York: W. W. Norton, 1980), 92, and my "Archiving Culture: Performance and American Museums in the Earlier Nineteenth Century," in Jeffrey D. Mason and J. Ellen Gainor (eds.), *Performing America: Cultural Nationalism in American Theater* (Ann Arbor: University of Michigan Press, 1999), 37–51.

10   For Rydell's certainty that the Native Americans who participated in all these exhibits were "degraded" and "the victims of a torrent of abuse and ridicule," see *All the World's A Fair*, 63. Concern that peoples from the Arctic have time to acclimatize to Chicago, and their show's need for a water feature, brought the performers to their priviledged location in the autumn, near the "official opening" of the Exposition (12 October 1892), well before the "Grand Opening" (1 May 1893) that admitted the public to the fairgrounds. Rydell identifies the performers in the Esquimaux Village as Inuit.

11   *The Best Things to be Seen at the World's Fair*, 63. *The Columbian Gallery*, n.p. *Handbook*, 89–91. Johnson, 331–32. The Ethnographical Exhibits were located between the Anthropological and Dairy Buildings and the elevated tracks on the east. South Pond on the west (where the Viking ship from Norway and Indian canoes and kayaks were moored), and, on the north, the Indian School (situated near the mock-ups of the Niña, Pinta, and Santa Maria). Guidebooks also feature a photograph of a "Mayan Woman and Child" and identify an exhibit of a group of Arawaks from British Guiana. Presumably they were not Putnam's "wards" (as one source calls the inhabitants of these "villages"). There was also a "pioneer" log cabin on the grounds.

12   The moulds for the Ruins of Yucatan were "taken from the original ruins by Edward H. Thompson, the United States consul to Yucatan, under Professor Putnam's instructions." They included a simulation of a figure of Kukulkan ("the great feathered god"). *Handbook*, 86–90.

13   Jeanne Madeline Weiman, *The Fair Women* (Chicago: Academy Chicago, 1981), 402–04, and see Rydell, *All the World's A Fair*. Amy Leslie depicted Cody's guests and performers as the "vanishing Indians," whom she saw picturesquely retreating in the face of Columbian culture ("Amy Leslie at the Fair," *Chicago News*, 1 May 1893), and see Moses, "Indians on the Midway," 214–15. See also Muccigrosso, 151, L. G. Moses, *Wild West Shows and the Images of American Indians, 1883–1933* (Albuquerque: University of New Mexico Press, 1996), 134–35, and Joy S. Kasson, *Buffalo Bill's Wild West: Celebrity, Memory, and Popular History* (New York: Hill and Wang, 2000), 192–93. Twenty-three of the thirty Ghost Dancers imprisoned at Fort Sheridan were paroled to Cody and toured Europe with him prior to the Fair. At least same were still with him in Chicago in 1893.

14   Curtis M. Hinsley, "The World as Marketplace: Commodification of the Exotic at the World's Columbian Exposition, Chicago, 1893," in Ivan Karp and Steven D. Lavine (eds.), *The Poetics and Politics of Museum*

Display (Washington, D.C.: Smithsonian Institution Press, 1991), 350. John C. Ewers, *Indian Life on the Upper Missouri* (Norman: University of Oklahoma Press, 1968), see chapter 15, "The Emergence of the Plains Indian as the Symbol of the North American Indian" (187–203). A cartoon depicting "a major event! Indian woman throws out dishwater," burlesqued both the performative and quotidian character of ethnographic displays.

15 Hinsley reports the fourteen Kwakiutl from Fort Rupert in British Columbia "slept on the floor of the Stock Pavillion" ("World as Marketplace," 349). What this means and whether the Kwakiutl used it before or while their own and the livestock exhibits were installed – sleeping with the livestock seems unlikely for a variety of reasons – is currently unclear to me. Putnam had control of a Dairy Barn next to the Anthropological Building, which he used as an annex until he lost the barn to a cheese exhibit. For the Carlisle exhibit, see Trennert, "Selling Indian Education," 209–11. Emma Sickles wrote to the *New York Times*, after her discharge from Putnam's staff, that Amerindian exhibits at the fair showed Indians as savages in need of government education, while "every means was used to keep self-civilized Indians out of the Fair" (Rydell, *All the World's A Fair*, 63). I take Sickles to mean the Indians were civilized, but in ways other than those dictated by the BIA and Department M.

16 Trennert, "Selling Indian Education," 213–18.

17 Sol Bloom, *The Autobiography of Sol Bloom* (New York: G. P. Putnam and Sons, 1948), 119, and see R. Reid Badger, *The Great American Fair: The World's Columbian Exposition and American Culture* (Chicago: Nelson-Hall, Inc., 1979), 81, Rydell, *All the World's A Fair*, 61–62, and Hinsley, "The World As Marketplace," 348. See Rydell, *All the World's A Fair*, 53, 57, 236, and 71, for the quotes. Rydell charts the migration of some Columbian personnel or their views to the Pan-American Exposition at Buffalo in 1901 (see *All the World's A Fair*, 130 and 137).

18 Moses, "Indians on the Midway," 217 For the Midway show, see Harris, de Wit, *et al.*, 160–61. Michael Chemers, "On the Boards

in Brobdignag: Performing Tom Thumb," *New England Theatre journal* 12 (2001): 81–82, and 86 and 81 for the quotes, respectively. For an Indian defense of working as show Indians for Buffalo Bill's Wild West, see Moses, *Wild West Shows*, 101–02.

19 Omission of the Indian Village from maps suggests a late opening, after guides to the fair were printed. For an indication of some of the Indian acts there, see Moses, *Wild West Shows*, 139. He observes, "none [of the Midway Indians] apparently possessed a contract, which violated Bureau [of Indian Affairs] procedures." For Rain-in-the-Face and petitions by Indians to have exhibits at the fair, see Harris, de Wit, *et al.*, 160. In addition to Indian defenses of their show Indian work, see also Ewers, 201–203.

20 Rossiter Johnson, *A History of the World's Columbian Exposition Held in Chicago*, Vol. IV (New York: D. Appleton and Co., 1898), 501 and 412. Hinsley, *The Smithsonian and the American Indian*, 110. Jacknis, 108. The "confusion of views" among the fair's anthropologists deserves detailed study it cannot be given here. For Otis Mason, Smithsonian Curator of Ethnology, see Rydell, *All the World's A Fair*, 58–59, and Hinsley, *The Smithsonian and the American Indian*, 110–12.

The Congresses published their proceedings. Particularly germane to this essay are: C. Staniland Wake (ed.), *Memoirs of the International Congress of Anthropology* (Chicago: Schulte Publishing Co., 1894); Helen Wheeler Bassett and Frederick Starr (eds.), *The International Folk-Lore Congress of the World's Columbian Exposition, Chicago, July 1893, Vol. I: Archives of the International Folk-Lore Association* (Chicago: Charles H. Sergel, Co., 1898); and Herbert Baxter Adams (ed.). *Annual Report of the American Historical Association for the Year 1893* (Washington: Government Printing Office, 1894).

21 Johnson, IV, 169. Foucault, 36.

22 White, 7–65. White argues Turner reflects the peaceful conquest side and Buffalo Bill's Wild West the violent conquest side of the same frontier, stories that contradict each other. The verse is from "Westward Ho" (see Joaquin Miller, *The Complete Poetical Works of Joaquin Miller* [San Francisco:

Whitaker and Ray, 1897], 187–88). White cites it on 18, and see 26 for his quoting from Steele's popular 1873 history. Wilber R. Jacobs, *The Historical World of Frederick Jackson Turner* (New Haven: Yale University Press, 1968), 4. Ray A. Billington's biography, *Frederick Jackson Turner: Historian, Scholar, Teacher* (New York: Oxford University Press, 1973), also explores Turner's historiography, as does Billington's *The Genesis of the Frontier Thesis: A Study in Historical Creativity* (San Marino, CA: Huntington Library, 1971). Critiques of Turner's view of American history can be found in George R. Taylor (ed.). *The Turner Thesis: Concerning the Role of the Frontier in American History* (Boston: D. C. Heath, 1949).

23 For Roosevelt's less than paean to Turner's originality, see Jacobs, 4, and White, 10. Thomas Jefferson made observations in 1824 similar to Turner's:

"Let a philosophic observer commence a journey from the savages of the Rocky Mountains, eastwardly toward our seacoast. These [the Indians] he would observe in the earliest stage of association living under no law but that of nature, subsisting and covering themselves with the flesh and skins of wild beasts. He would next find these on our frontiers in the pastoral state, raising domestic animals to supply the defects of hunting. Then succeed to our own semibarbarous citizens, the pioneers of the advancing civilization, and so in his progress he would meet the gradual shades of an improving man until he would reach his, as yet, most improved state in our seaport towns. This, in fact, is equivalent to a survey, in time, of the progress of man from the infancy of creation, to the present day."

See Avery Craven, "Frederick Jackson Turner," 102–03, in Taylor. For the Turner quotes, see Turner, 201 and 207.

24 For opposition to the thesis, see Taylor, Jacobs, Billington's biography, and *Genesis,* 172–76 (for the Turner-verein, 3–4). Turner, 201.

25 Turner, 200, 207. For Buffalo Bill's invitation, see Billington, *Genesis,* 166. Turner did tour the fair, evidently after his presentation (171).

26 Bassett and Starr, 227–47, for Matthews, 206–20 for Scott, and 14 for Cody's invitation. See also Kirshenblatt-Gimblett, 33–34, for the Folk-Lore Congress, 34 for the quoted matter. Kirshenblatt-Gimblett observes (note 37, page 288), "Anthropologists frequently 'played Indian' as a way of demonstrating what was difficult to describe verbally."

27 Jack Rennert, *100 Posters of Buffalo Bill's Wild West* (London: Hart-Davis, MacGibbon, 1976), back cover for the broadside. Slotkin (*Gunfighter Nation,* 67) states the Salutatory notice "was added to the program of the 1886 Wild West and . . . appeared in every program thereafter." (There is a clear similarity of language between it and the 16 April 1887 excerpt from the *Illustrated London News* fronting this essay.) Of the joining of the Wild West and the Congress of Rough Riders of the World, Slotkin asserts, "Beside each American or European unit rode representatives of horsemen of the non-white tribesmen recently conquered by the imperial powers" ("Buffalo Bill's Wild West," 173).

28 The acts are listed in "Buffalo Bill's Wild West and Congress of Rough Riders of the World, Historical Sketches and Programme" (Chicago: Blakely Printing Co, 1893), in the collection of the Newberry Library, Chicago. R. L. Wilson (with Greg Martin), *Buffalo Bill's Wild West: An American Legend* (New York: Random House, 1998), 159, gives the opening date as 26 April 1893, but his closing date of 31 October adds up to 189 days, not 186. Annie Fern Swartwout's *Missie: An Historical Biography of Annie Oakley* (Blanchester, OH: Brown Pub. Co., 1947), 204, says the show was open a month before the Fair itself. The most quoted attendance figure for the fair is 27,539,041.

29 The "wondrous voyage" and "from prairie to palace" themes appeared in posters for Buffalo Bill's Wild West. See Rennert, 27 and 110, and Don Russell, *The Wild West* (Fort Worth, TX: Amon Carter Museum of Western Art, 1970). For the Indian as definition of the American, see Rennert, 52. Moses, *Wild West Shows,* 194 and 149. For William F. Cody's view of Indians, also see his *Life and Adventures of Buffalo Bill* (Chicago: Stanton and Van Vliet Co., 1917), and Don Russell, *The Lives and Legends of Buffalo Bill* (Norman: University of Oklahoma Press, 1960).

30 Vine Deloria, Jr., "The Indians," in *Buffalo Bill and the Wild West*, an exhibition of the Brooklyn Museum of Art, Carnegie Institute, and Buffalo Bill Historical Center (New York: Brooklyn Museum of Art, 1991), 53–55. Moses (*Wild West Shows*, 116) locates Salsbury's letter among records at the Pine Ridge Reservation and compares Salsbury's figures to those stated in Wild West contracts in the Federal Archives and Record Center (see note 24, page 305). See also Luther Standing Bear, *My People the Siaux* (Boston: Houghton Mifflin Co., 1928), 260–61, who traveled with Buffalo Bill's Wild West and reports Cody's defense of equal, indeed preferential, treatment of the show Indians in his company.

31 Vine Deloria, 53–54.

32 See Wilson, 254–55 for photos from Euro-Disney and 256 for details about the show. Cowboy hats are issued to all who will wear them. Reproduction Wild West posters are available in the gift shop and a western bar (with dance hall girls) awaits thirsty patrons nearby. Tim Johnson (ed.), *Spirit Capture: Photographs from the National Museum of the American Indian* (Washington: Smithsonian Institution Press, 1998), see pages 32, 140, 150, and 152. The people and buildings of the fair also had a history. Frederick Ward Putnam and Franz Boas went to work for the Field Columbian Museum, housed in the Fine Arts Building after the Fair closed, opening as the Field Museum on 2 June 1894. A new building was completed after World War I, which is today the Field Museum of Natural History in Chicago. The Fine Arts Building cum original Field Museum was renovated (under the sponsorship of Julius Rosenwald of Sears, Roebuck) and is today's Museum of Science and Industry in Chicago.

33 I emphasize that Rydell, Slotkin, and White are not wrong about the racism in the three sites and that a show-tolerant perspective of them could not erase race because race defines these scenes.

34 Alan Trachtenberg notes, apropos power's insecurity, the Dawes Severalty Act of 1887 concerning immigrants, the corporate image offered by the "white city," and the Pullman strike of 1894. Joy Kasson's final take on Buffalo Bill resonates in the context of the Columbian "world": "an apt hero for the modern era, an age when images have become indistinguishable from what they purport to represent and the content of national identity seems identical to its performance" (273).

12

The Palio of Siena:
Performance and Process

Alice Pomponio Logan

The *palio* is a unique horse race. Twice a summer, 10 jockeys, representing 10 of Siena's 17 *contrade*, or districts, race bareback three times clockwise around the main square of the city. The winning horse gains for the *contrada* a silk banner, which bears the image of the Virgin Mary and is also called a *palio*. Although horse races and tournaments with *palios* as prizes were common in the 13th century in such cities as Florence, Verona, and Ferrara, *the palio* of Siena has endured with as much, if not more, excitement and vigor. It is by far the most popular of contemporary races and tournaments in Italy.

Most accounts of the *palio* have described it in terms of its history, artistic splendor, emotional excitement, or attraction to tourists. The notable exception is the recent ethnography written by Dundes and Falassi,[1] who offer an interpretation from a Freudian psychoanalytic perspective. My own approach is to consider the *palio* as a "cultural performance," i.e., a ritualized, coordinated, public activity in which participants view their culture as "encapsulated in . . . discrete performances which they could exhibit to visitors

and to themselves" (Singer 1955:27). It is, moreover, a cohesive system of communicated symbols, values, and norms of behavior which plays an important role in what Hallowell (1954) has termed the "culturally-constituted behavioral environment" of the "self." My analysis demonstrates that this urban ritual delineates and dramatizes the structural aspects of the city and contributes to individual Sienese identity by providing membership and participation in one of 17 geographically determined corporate groups. The competition between these urban districts provides a dramatic assertion of each group's uniqueness over the other 16, as well as a kaleidoscopic portrait of the unity of these groups into a single city whose cultural heritage is molded by the pervasive themes of history, religion, and warfare. The *palio* thus provides present-day competition between the city's independent districts, which symbolically recreates the cultural history of the city as a whole. As we shall see, membership in a *contrada* is a lifelong enterprise that dictates the patterns of social interaction within the walls of the city.

Alice Pomponio Logan, "The *Palio* of Siena: Performance and Process," pp. 45–65 from *Urban Anthropology* 7(1), 1978.

Siena

Siena is a small nonindustrial city of about 60,000 inhabitants, located in the heart of Tuscany about 35 miles southwest of Florence. Though devoid of large industries, it is surrounded by industrial towns.

Most of the city is contained within its ancient walls. It is divided into 17 districts, or wards, called *contrade*.[2] These are named, corporate, and ideally endogamous groups. Each group has definite geographical boundaries, self-government, and a Catholic church. The *contrade* also function as mutual aid societies and social clubs. Each *contrade* has its own patron saint, who is honored annually in the form of masses, street festivals and a parade of its young boys and men.

Siena is prominent in Italian religious culture for several reasons, most notable of which is its identity as the "city of the Virgin." Throughout history, the city offered itself to the Virgin Mary in time of war or other crises. The first occasion was the battle of Montaperti in 1260, in which the Sienese were outnumbered and under heavy siege from the Florentines (documented in Heywood 1899: 11–44). The Sienese petitioned the Virgin for protection, their cause was successful, and this date has remained prominent for the Sienese as a major milestone in their history.

The *palio* is, in some respects, a race in honor of the Madonna. Each race, however, is dedicated to a "different" Madonna and each commemorates a different holy day in her honor. The July *palio* celebrates the Visitation, in honor of the "Madonna of Provenzano"[3]; the August *palio* is dedicated to the "Madonna of the Offering" and is run the day after the Feast of the Assumption.

Before each race, the *palio* banner is hung in the church of the respective Virgin (the church at Provenzano for the July race, the Duomo for the August race), where the Sienese people may see it and pray to the Virgin for a victory. Thus, the custom of making an offering to the Virgin in time of crisis continues in the symbolic crisis caused by the *palio*. After the race, the winners return to the church with the banner, in order to give thanks and to receive blessing for the coming year.

Tradition looms large in the running of the race and the life-style of the Sienese people in relation to it. Three elements are ever-present in the *palio*: history, religion, and warfare. These three themes mold the Sienese behavioral environment of beliefs, goals, behavioral models, and expectations vis-à-vis the *palio*, and are incorporated in the value system that has its locus in the life of the *contrada*.

The *Contrada*

As mentioned above, each *contrada* is a corporate group, with geographical boundaries and its own governmental structure, finances, and church. Each group also has a museum in which are displayed the *palii* it has previously won. The name of each group is based on its emblem, which usually is either a mythical or a real animal. These names stand in either metaphoric or metonymic relation to the emblems. Some emblems appear with a crown, which depicts the *contrada*'s status as *nobil* (noble) (e.g., Aquila, Bruco, Nicchio, Oca).[4] Giraffa claims the title *Imperiale* (Imperial), because it won the July *palio* of 1936, which was dedicated to the Italian "Empire" of the fascist era. Onda claims the title *Capitana* (Captain), referring to the fact that it is predominantly Onda men who serve as guards at the *Palazzo del Commune*, the City Hall. Finally Civetta claims the title *Priora*, intending to say it is Number One, or the best *contrada*. There are also special colors associated with each *contrada*, in which the emblems are depicted. The important point is that each *contrada* strives to claim its uniqueness with respect to the other 16. The various titles and idiosyncracies claimed by each help support this claim (see also Dundes and Falassi, 1975:22).

Contrada Structure

The internal organization of the *contrada* is very complex. There are four major divisions of administrative authority: the general administration, which I shall call "peacetime" administration; the leaders during the *palio*, which is analogous to "wartime"; religious administration; and the recreational or social administration.

The peacetime administration is set up like a parliamentary government. The operational heart of the *contrada* is the *Consiglio Generate* (General Council), of which all contrada members are technically members. The leader of the council is the *priore* (president), who is assisted by the *vicario* (vice-president). Advising the *priore* is the *Collegio di Maggiorenti*, made up of past *priori* of the *contrada*. There are several other administrative positions, which are unimportant for my purposes. The important point is that the position of *priore* is one of the most powerful and hence the most prestigious positions, and that the *priore* represents the *contrada* both in internal affairs and in dealings with other *contrade*.

The *capitano* (captain) of the *contrada*, the "wartime" leader, is elected by the *Consiglio Generale*, which takes into consideration the suggestion of the priore.[5] He is assisted by two or three *tenenti* (lieutenants) who are commonly referred to as *mangini*. The *Consiglio Generate* informs the captain how much money is available for *partiti*, agreements between *contrade* or between *contrade* and jockeys, which are attempts to ensure victory in the *palio*. There is no betting on the race itself. There are, however, a number of steps that can be taken to influence the outcome. These "agreements," analogous to clandestine wartime maneuvers, can be of various sorts, ranging from the mere exchange of jockeys to the actual bribing of a jockey. The responsibility for cementing *partiti* falls squarely on the shoulders of the captain, who has but one duty: to win the *palio*.

The captain and his *tenenti* are modern-day replicas, in Sienese terms, of mercenary soldiers and their leader, the *capitano di ventura* (soldier of fortune), familiar from Italian Renaissance history. Since this soldier usually was in command both of the city's army and his own, there is an analogy between his position and the veritable carte blanche given to the *contrada* captain and his *tenenti* during the days of *the palio* (see Dundes and Falassi 1975:34–35).

Each *contrada* has its own priest, called the *correttore*, who leads the *contrada* in religious worship. Special functions of the *correttore* include baptism, weddings, funerals, and blessing the horse in church on the day of the *palio*, right before the race.

The "recreational" or social division of the *contrada* organization is partially subsumed under the general administration. The locus of *contrada* social life and activity is geographically centered around the *società*, which is the bar, social club, and general gathering place of *contradaioli*. Though they are open to the general public, these cafes are recognized as *contrada* property and are frequented predominantly by *contrada* members. During the *palio* season, which runs from April to September, the *società* serves as an information center where *contradaioli* discuss the upcoming *palio*. In short, the *società* provides members of the *contrada* with an opportunity for reinforcing *contrada* unity as well as fostering a sense of excitement over the *palio*.

Besides the parliamentary structure of the *contrada*, there is a division into three "age sets." Children belong at birth to the Little Ones' Group (*Gruppo Piccoli*) until the age of about 12. Christmas, Easter, and various other holidays (especially *contrada* titulary festivals) are celebrated at parties at the *contrada società*.[6] Adolescents belong to the Young People's Group (*Gruppo Giovani*), which has its own slate of officers and organizes its own group social activities (dances, parties, fundraising drives, etc.). At the adult level there is usually a women's group, but no "men's group" as such, since the men *are* the *contrada*, in the sense of being the locus of its power and authority.

Participation in these groups affirms one's identity within the *contrada* and promotes solidarity and familiarity. The division into age sets guarantees a place for all, regardless of age or sex. In this sense, the *contrada* is like a second family. It is also a moral community in Durkheim's sense, since its members are united toward a common goal and share the same ideals. Included in this sense of moral community and "family" atmosphere is the awareness on the part of *contrada* members that they are responsible for one another's behavior in public. This is especially true during the days of *the palio*, when it is not uncommon to see older *contradaioli* reprimanding younger ones for inappropriate or un- (whatever the *contrada*)-like behavior that could detract from the *contrada*'s public image or, in more volatile instances, lead to a fight.

Each *contrada* considers itself an independent republic or state, reminiscent of the free Sienese Republic of the 13th–16th centuries. Like a republic or state, *each contrada* belongs to an intricate network of relationships with other *contrade*, such as alliances, treaties, and enmities. Enmities are dyadic[7] and normally constant, but degrees of friendship seem to fluctuate according to the outcome of each race. As Dundes and Falassi (1975:40) note, "it is in the running of the race that these relationships are either confirmed or broken."

The solidarity of the *contrada* is also reinforced by a democratic ideology with respect to *contrada* operations.

Rich and poor, left wing and right wing, nobleman and plebian, all are bound up in the commonality of contrada spirit. The democracy of the contrada is stressed by nearly everyone. Working men are proud to use the familiar "tu" form instead of the more formal "Lei" to the patrician members of the contrada (and vice versa). And yet the very fact that so many individuals commented on the "classlessness" of the contrada suggests that *although the barriers of social class tend to fall within the contrada, they are never completely absent.* The same people who boast of the democracy of their contrada also say how proud they are to have a count or a nobleman as a "protector" or elected officer of the contrada. Also, in published lists of contrada office holders, any and every title possible is mentioned. (Dundes and Falassi, 1975:21, emphasis added)

This contradiction between democratic ideals and other attitudes expressed about the "classless" nature of the *contrada* is manifested in several spheres of social interaction in Siena. Careful analysis reveals that, despite its "official" democratic ideology, bureaucracy and socioeconomic class divisions contribute to an unofficial attitude that influences the actual operation of the *contrada* and the election of its leaders in much the same way as they influence the operation of any political democracy.

An understanding of *contrada* "life-cycle dynamics" shows that the privilege of extending the "tu" form of pronominal address, when viewed in cultural-historical perspective, results largely from the long-standing relationships among grown-up children of the same neighborhood. Secondly, given the traditional geographic distribution of *contrada* members, it results from interrelated consanguineal and affinal kinship ties.[8]

Contrada Members

The members of a *contrada*, the *contradaioli*, have a name that is derived from the name of the *contrada* itself. The 17 contrade and the respective designations of their members are:

Aquila	Aquilini	Nicchio	Nicchiaioli
Bruco	Brucaioli	Oca	Ocaioli
Chiocciola	Chiocciolini	Onda	Ondaioli
Civetta	Civettini	Pantera	Panterini
Drago	Dragaioli	Selva	Selvaioli
Giraffa	Giraffini	Tartuca	Tartuchini
Istrice	Istriciaioli	Torre	Torraioli
Leocorno	Lecaioli	(Val di)	
Lupa	Lupaioli	Montone	Montonaioli

The suffixes *-ini* and *-aioli* connote "little ones" and "born of," respectively. *Contradaioli* identify themselves strongly with their *contrada* emblem. The emblems depicted are "living symbols" (Dundes and Falassi 1975:18) of each *contrada*.

The Individual and Contrada Life

Defining the *contrada* and explicating its significance for an individual is a complicated matter. Each group is a more or less self-contained and autonomous structural unit, yet an intricate network system of alliances, enmities, and other forms of interrelationships unite these 17 "states" or "republics" into a single city. Kinship, social, and professional ties increase the complexities of *contrada* interaction by virtue of the "double" aspect of each person's identity. Each is an individual, yet, like the *contrada* emblem, each is a "living symbol" of a particular group from which he or she derives identity and projects this to others. This identity is grounded in the cultural history and traditions of the city as a whole, as well as of the *contrada*, one of its integral parts.

In the most frequent case in which both parents belong to the same *contrada*, the standard means by which a Sienese child attains membership into the appropriate group is by birth.[9] When a child is born, a *contrada* flag with an appropriately colored ribbon (pink for a girl, blue for a boy) is placed outside the window, indicating that the *contrada* has a new member.

Along with his name, a child learns immediately to say, for example, "*Sono dall' Oca*," or "*Son' Ocaiolo*" ("I'm from the Goose"; "I'm a member of the Goose *contrada*"). He also learns to associate goodness, beauty, and valor with his *contrada* and its members; badness, filth, and cowardice with his archenemy and its members. This association is immediate, and encouraged. Children learn these values and associations even before they can talk, supplying horrible faces and associated noises at the mere mention of the enemy *contrada* or sight of its emblem.

There are numerous toys for children which signify *contrada* membership. Boys practice waving the flag and playing the drum so they can qualify one day for the *comparsa*, the group that represents the *contrada* in the piazza during the "historical parade" before the *palio*. Girls play with these and other toys when they are very young, but because these toys are considered to be "boy's things," they are gradually discouraged from playing *palio* too much as they reach adolescence. Girls generally have ceramic bells and little dolls of *contrada* pages in costume. Though only males participate in the actual *palio* parade and its related activities, women are just as involved in *contrada* life as men – it is a matter of traditional division of labor according to sex roles and of keeping with the general theme of *the palio*, which will be discussed later.

The *contrada* is present at every major *rite de passage* of its members (see also Dundes and Falassi 1975:35). Following the regular church

baptism, on the appropriate saint's day celebration (*festa titolare*), the child is officially baptized into *contrada* membership in a secular ritual performed by the *priore* (president), at the *contrada* fountain. The *contrada* is also represented formally at communion,[10] graduation, wedding, and funeral ceremonies. After death, departed members are remembered in a solemn mass in the *contrada* church on November 4, the Day of the Dead, and on the *contrada* saint's day they are commemorated with a mass and a procession to the cemetery where flowers are placed on their graves.

The pride in *contrada* membership is continually manifested in a variety of anecdotes (Tailetti 1967), mottoes, epithets, and songs having to do with the *contrada*. There are some mottoes that are associated with particular contrade. A Torraiolo who says, "*O rosso o rosso*" ("It's either red [Torre's identifying color] or else it's red"), is asserting that the Tower way is the only way and that whatever happens, if the Tower is involved, the outcome will be advantageous to the Tower *contrada* (Dundes and Falassi 1975:20). Another instance typical of *contrada* braggadocio concerning colors is the description of Ondaioli of their colors, white and pale blue, in relation to the power of their *contrada*:

I colori del cielo
la forza del mare.

(The colors of the sky the power of the sea.)

Giraffa offers a motto involving its physical characteristics:

Più alta la testa
Più grande la gloria.

(The higher the head the greater the glory.)

These two examples indicate well enough how proud of their identities in their respective contrade the Sienese really are. Each *contradaiolo* takes part in these verbal duels both within the *contrada*, to strengthen and perpetuate the unity of the group, and with other *contrade*, to demonstrate the strength of this unity and the power of his or her *contrada*.

Each *contrada* is keenly aware of its own history, triumphs, and peculiarities as well as those of other *contrade*. Each has its own cheers, shouted after each song, which reinforce group identity (see also Dundes and Falassi 1975:25–26). Children are taught to recite the *contrada* cheer and use it in the company of relatives and friends to demonstrate their loyalty, or in the company of enemies to reinforce their identity and insult the opposition. *Contrade* are also identified by special sobriquets, some of which are positive, some negative, depending on who is talking.

The songs sung by each *contrada* express publicly both their self-image and their image of others, especially of their enemy. For example, Oca sing,[11]

S'è sempre commandata	We have always commanded
E sempre si commanda	And we always [will] command
Siamo di Fontebranda	We are of Fontebranda
Siamo di Fontebranda	We are of Fontebranda
S'è sempre commandata	We have always commanded
E sempre si commanda	And we always [will] command
Siamo di Fontebranda	We are of Fontebrand
E paura non se n'ha.	And we don't have [know] fear.

Torre counters this with the following:

Dicevi commandavi	You said that you command
Invece si commanda	Instead [we are] commanding
Abasso Fontebranda	Down with Fontebranda
Abasso Fontebranda	Down with Fontebranda

Dicevi commandavi	You said that you command
Invece si commanda	Instead [we are] commanding
Abasso Fontebranda	Down with Fontebranda
E nel culo vi si va!	And up your ass we will go!

Insulting songs are not limited to the enemy *contrada*. Since Oca is the most powerful *contrada* (i.e., it wins the most, it is one of the largest, and its members are among the most aggressive), it is also among the least popular. It therefore falls prey to indirect insults in songs sung by other contrade to their archenemies.

Each *contrada* has its own renditions of this song, sung as if no other *contrada* were singing it. The verses adopted by each *contrada* are primarily concerned with identity, in a variety of ways:

1. They state who the *contrada* is.
2. They describe where it is located in local geographical terms.
3. They assert that the *contrada* is the best of all and demands the respect of all others.
4. They praise the *contrada* that is singing, and taunt the enemy.
5. Finally, the verses express that each *contrada* and its members are, by their participation and beliefs in the *palio*, distinctly Sienese.

Contrada enmities have replaced the traditional family feuds of medieval and Renaissance times (Dundes and Falassi 1975:41–42). Although they may seem comparable to old family feuds, or to college rivalries in America (p. 41), *contrada* feuds are more intense and may last for centuries. Children learn immediately who their enemies are, how to regard them, and how to behave toward them. Expressions of this ritualized mutual hatred are found in the popular songs and epithets that are sung by *contrada* members of all ages.

Role Reversals

The enmities between *contrade* are strong hatreds in some cases, but whatever the degree, it should be noted that it is "hate without guilt, but *not* without rules" (Falassi 1975). In the normal course of events and aggressive displays, the rules are clearly specified. Every one has an identity and a social position vis-à-vis everyone else, and knows how to behave accordingly. Thus the question "which *contrada* are you from?" (*Di que contrada sei?*) defines the situation from the start. The rest of the interaction proceeds according to the unofficial rules of the "game" just defined. In terms of overflow into other aspects of Sienese life, the important point is that one must take the grief as well as give it, or the game ends (Falassi 1975).

It is interesting to note at this point that during the *palio*, or in social situations where one's *contrada* identity is at stake, certain role reversals take place. These are about the only times when, for example, mothers will *encourage* their children to be offensive and to use *parolacce* (bad, or ugly, words). They will even teach the children which ones to use.

Mothers and fathers (and other *contrada* members, for that matter) have also been known to encourage young men to go out and fight against the enemy, saying, "*Spaccategli il capo!*" (Split their heads open!) Although head splitting is a less commendable activity today than in previous generations, *contrada* youths will express the fact that they are always ready. During the *palio* season, groups of teens and young men (ages about 16–25) walk around the city as a sort of street gang boldly singing their *contrada* songs. On particularly spirited occasions they may venture into or near their enemy's territory, under peril of vile insults, potential fistfights, or of being hit with buckets of water flung from upper-story windows. These are usually avoided, however, except during the days of the *palio* when tensions are exceptionally high and patience thin.

Women also reverse traditionally expected role behavior. It is not uncommon for women married to men of their enemy *contrada* to leave their husbands and return to their natal homes to be with fellow *contradaioli* for the days immediately preceding the *palio*. During the race, almost anything goes. Besides encouraging offensive behavior in their children,

women have been known to scare horses or use their handbags to knock jockeys off their horses during the race. The women will also return insults to their *contrada* with a solid punch, smack, or kick. They are as adamant as the men when it comes to asserting the nobility and force of their *contrada* and the inferiority and lowliness of their enemy *contrada*.

Even religious figures are involved in reversals and potential abuse during the *palio*. The saints are regarded as obligated, in a sense, to live up to their supportive roles as *contrada* patrons. Chiocciola, after losing a *palio*, threw their statue of St. Anthony (their patron) down a well in anger. Twenty years passed and the *contrada* still did not win. Some women of the *contrada* decided that the saint was offended by this rash act so they retrieved it. The *contrada* won the next *palio*.[12] Consequently, Chiocciola members are called *affogasanti* (drowners of saints). They identify themselves as such, as a proud twist on the events, and have since taken the name as the title for their *contrada* newspaper (for more examples, see Heywood 1899:217; Tailetti 1967).

We can see, then, that even religious figures are expected, as *contrada* members, to be faithful and supportive of the *contrada*. In other cities in Italy, as in other Catholic countries, such a desecration of sacred objects and manipulation of religious beliefs are totally abhorrent. The Sienese value system, on the other hand, includes such acts as permissible and even desirable at times. Thus the relationship with saints and other deities is viewed as reciprocal: worship for *palio* victory. This does not imply that the Sienese are not religious. It simply points out the way in which certain values common to Italian culture as a whole are permuted in the behavioral environment of Siena through its participation in the *palio*.

Space and Time

Through *palio* songs, stories, and epithets children associate their *contrada* with a place. They also learn the geography of the city, with particular importance ascribed to certain places – e.g., where *not* to go, and why (see also Falassi

1974). For example. Oca sings of its arch-enemy, Torre, and Torre's territory:

Abasso Salicotto	Down with Salicotto Street [main street of Torre]
Mercato e pescheria	Market and fish market
Tutta una porcheria	The whole [area] is pig filth
Tutta una porcheria	The whole [area] is pig filth
Che fa schifo alia città	That disgusts the [entire] city

Each *contrada* has its own versions of these negative territory-debasing songs, sung about the appropriate enemy's territory. (Note that the *contrada* is not always referred to by name, either in song or social interaction. It is alluded to by its place name, which may be a street, fountain, or other local landmark. These place names are applied both to *contrada* members and *by* them, to express their location and identity.)

Time in Siena, in addition to hours, days, months, years, etc., is marked off by *palio* events. The year is punctuated by saint's day celebrations, *contrada* titulary feasts, and the events of the race itself.

On a broader scale, a person's lifetime is often referred to by the number of *palii* the *contrada* has won. To be born in a victory year is a sign of blessing, so ages are often calculated by reference to the last *palio* won in a given person's lifetime.

On the grandest scale, the *palio* is a historical flashback to the golden age of Siena, between 1260, when Siena first dedicated itself to the Madonna and won the battle of Montaperti, and 1555, when it fell as a republic. This flashback is performed in the *corteo storico* (historical parade) for the whole of Siena, before the actual horse race. For each *contrada*, the center of attention is the *comparsa*.

The *comparsa* is a group of young men of the *contrada* dressed as medieval soldiers going to war. The costumes are in the colors of the *contrada* going to the "ritual war" (the *palio*) in a historical reenactment of the past.[13]

The *comparsa* is the symbolic embodiment of the *contrada* in the image of medieval pageantry. There is a definite order of positions within the formation and explicit motives involved in choosing its personnel: physical appearance, for standard-bearers, and talent, in the case of the drummer and the flag handlers (but see Gelli, 1905, for the physical attributes required of flag handlers). Since each young man is representing what for him is the most beautiful and most powerful group, he endeavors to appear suitably convincing for the occasion.

During the historical parade, Siena's history is recreated, thus reminding each participant of Siena's glorious years as an independent republic (see also Dundes and Falassi 1975:100–109). Past and present are constantly merged in the reenactment of medieval pageantry and warfare, complemented by the present-day alliances and enmities between *contrade*, for in Siena "the *patria* is . . . the *Contrada*" (Heywood 1899:197).

For a Sienese participating in the *palio*, as either actor or spectator, the most explicit illustration of the time element and the locus of allegiance is the *comparsa*. During this dramatic recreation of the past, the following must be noted among the messages being communicated symbolically by the Sienese: (1) The days when Siena was a powerful, independent republic are recreated and transmitted to children and visitors to the *palio*, thereby (2) creating the illusion of its continued prosperity and independence, and causing the feelings of solidarity and pride in being a Sienese to continue and (3) make Siena, symbolically and conceptually, at least, endure as the great, independent entity it once was, by (4) associating the winning *contrada* with the free, powerful, ruling Sienese Republic of the past. (One could speculate that the winner relives the victory of Montaperti of 1260, the loser the defeat of the Sienese Republic of 1555.)

In contrast, then, to what Peacock has termed a "rite of modernization" (Peacock 1968), the *palio* may be called a "rite of traditionalization." The *palio* is system in flux and the *contrada* is constantly changing. There are, however, basic themes and purposes that are always maintained. For example, the aim of the *comparsa*'s performance in the *palio* activities is to reinforce to the world and to themselves that their *contrada* is the best look-ing, most dignified, most powerful in the city, as if it had always been so. In other words, *they are acting out behaviorally what they have been boasting about in song.* Lyrics and costuming may change in minor detail, but the overall message – that the *contrada* is unique, power-ful, beautiful, the best – remains the same.

In this "cultural performance" the Sienese people as a body are expressing that *they* are unique, powerful, the best, in their own right. They are saying, moreover, that they have always been and will continue to be so. In sum, the *palio* is, to borrow a phrase from Clifford Geertz (1972:26), a story the Sienese like to tell themselves about themselves.

After the *Palio*

There is implicit in all *palio* motivation, behav-ior, and symbolism the notion of "limited good" (Foster 1965). There is only one winner, one *contrada* that is the strongest and best and demands the most respect. The motivational orientation of each group is clear: to win the *palio*. Each individual seeks to perpetuate *con-trada* power and unity by his or her member-ship, friendships, and involvement in *contrada* life throughout the year, for it is believed that only through unity and strength will the *con-trada* win the *palio*. The goal of victory pro-vides the motivation for obtaining the spoils, ritual and otherwise, that such a victory prom-ises the winner. Regardless of the degree of active participation in the activities of the *con-trada*, one never entirely sheds one's identity as a member of Oca, Istrice, Onda, etc., as the case may be. No Sienese, therefore, can ever be entirely aloof to the consequences of each *palio*.

For the days immediately following the *palio* the winning *contrada* "owns" the city. There are daily parades, complete with drum-mers, flag handlers, *contrada* members, and the winning horse.[14] All join in singing *contrada* songs, adding the new ones generated by the race, some in praise of the jockey and horse, others mocking the enemy (the losers, whether or not they have actually raced).

Palio songs thus provide an oral history of the jockeys, the horses, the events surrounding

the *palio*, and the race itself (see Falassi 1974). They may be positive, lauding both the jockey and the horse, or negative, alluding to sellouts, briberies, and other "cheats." The songs describe the *contrada*'s positive image of itself (especially in the case of a *contrada* singing its own victory praises) or the negative reputation of its enemy. It is also conceivable that one song contain both images, juxtaposed in such a way that the *contrada* that is singing always asserts its own superiority over the other 16 *contrade*, particularly its archrival.

The *contrada* that wins is said to be "reborn." This idea is expressed in a number of ways. Linguistically, the notion of rebirth is marked by the expression È *nato un cittino* (A little one is born). This expression is acted out in the post-*palio* parade of the victor. In addi-tion to symbolic paraphernalia of *contrada* membership (flags, drums, costumes, scarves, etc.), the *comparsa* for this parade also adopts baby bottles and large pacifiers, declaring to the city and to themselves that the *contrada* is "reborn."

The notion of rebirth is contrasted with that of aging and death. The *contrada* that has not won in the longest time is said to be the *nonna*, the grandmother, as opposed to the *cittino*, little one, or newborn victor. The object of a winning *contrada* is to see to it that its arch-enemy becomes the *nonna*. Likewise, when a *contrada* that has not won in many years finally wins, the victory is that much greater, thereby symbolically defying death by reversing the aging process. Hence, to win is to live; to lose brings the *contrada* closer to death.

Discussion

Dundes and Falassi analyze the *palio* by com-bining a classic Freudian model of virility, aggression, and Oedipal elements with a Levi-Straussian series of oppositions. They list a series of opposing pairs (e.g., sacred/profane, life/death, sexuality/nonsexuality, newborn baby/aging *nonna*, wedding/funeral, in/out, buying/selling, good fortune/ill fortune, etc.) and postulate that the *palio* serves to mediate these oppositions by merging them all simultaneously (1975:234–240).

The *palio*, in Freudian terms, is interpreted as "a male initiation ritual . . . which demands that . . . boys prove their phallic prowess" (Dundes and Falassi 1975:188). What I have called the religious element, the Virgin on the *palio* banner, represents for them a complex of several nurturant female roles simultaneously (e.g., mother, bride, daughter), so that winning the *palio* represents gaining "both a virgin bride and a nursing mother" (p. 204). Dundes and Falassi maintain, moreover, that such a metaphoric condensation of roles constitutes "a dramatic enactment of the traditional courtship and marriage patterns in Sienese (and Mediterranean) culture" (p. 199). Finally, they see in the paraphernalia associated with *palio* victory (baby bottles, pacifiers, etc.) the notion that the *palio* represents "a form of socially sanctioned regression such that the winner is once again the secure, happy infant being nursed by a loving mother" (p. 203). Hence, Dundes and Falassi conclude that the *palio* is a "metaphor" for Sienese "world view" – i.e., a metaphor of male sexual prowess, female nurturance and submission, and a generalized symbolic regression to the womb.

Although I subscribe to an interpretation of culture as a coherent "system" of symbols and meanings (Geertz 1966), such an interpretation makes sense only in terms of the relation it bears to the behavior or behavior patterns it helps to explain (see Geertz 1972; Schneider 1968, 1972). My major objection to a psychoanalytic explanation of the *palio* is that it presupposes a psychoanalytic interpretation of the behavioral data. That is, in order for a psychoanalytic explanation to make any sense, one must already accept a description of the data in psychoanalytic terms. Thus there is no independent criterion for the validity of a psychoanalytic explanation and such an explanation must therefore beg the question.

To insist on a psychoanalytic interpretation of collective behavior based, for the most part, on an analysis of linguistic data and folklore contradicts the fundamental assumption of Freudian psychoanalytic theory – namely, that individual behavior is motivated and patterned by inherent, *unconscious* psychological drives that are in conflict within the *individual* psyche, and thus inaccessible to the individuals

themselves. Most *palio* symbolism, as I hope to have demonstrated, is quite consciously executed and explicit in meaning. It is, moreover, *deliberate*, especially in the case of song dueling, cheers, jeers, epithets, and anecdotes. Most of the behavior relating to *palio* activities is explicitly directed, on an individual level, toward demonstration of group membership and, on a collective level toward maintenance of the group as a viable structural unit within the boundaries of Sienese sociopolitical life.

A good example of the inappropriateness of a psychoanalytic analysis of cultural phenomena is Dundes and Falassi's notion of rebirth in *palio* victory as "symbolic *male* rebirth" (emphasis added). I suggest that it is the rebirth of the *contrada* as a whole, which includes females and children. The interpretation of the *palio* as *male* rebirth and a *male* "initiation ritual" does not explain why *women* are as emotionally involved as men when *c'è la terra in piazza* (there is dirt in the square – i.e., when the *palio* is near or about to be run) and their *contrada* is competing. Nor does it account for why women reverse traditionally prescribed role behavior during this time.

Throughout the Dundes and Falassi analysis, the image of women's roles in *palio* activities is reduced to psychoanalytic "types," so that women's behind-the-scenes maintenance activities become the nurturant activities of a loving mother to her infant (1975:203). If the *palio* is, as I suggest, a reenactment of medieval warfare and pageantry, then the role women have today in the *palio*, as symbolic warfare, is behaviorally congruent with that of women of medieval and Renaissance times. Just as the men in the *comparsa* act out the part of Renaissance soldiers going to war, so the women act out their historically supportive role of cooking, mending uniforms, and other maintenance activities that prepare the men for battle.

Winning the *palio* results in a rebirth or, if you will, a *regeneration* of interest in the *contrada* on the part of its members, and a *reclassification* of the winner's image on the part of the other *contrade*. In fact, the entire hierarchy of *contrada* status is reshuffled with every race. This does not deny the apparent significance of the symbols of nurturance, virility, aggression, or sexual prowess; it gives them new focus, and suggests that they may be more *expressions of* "the spoils of victory" and the "weapons of war" rather than the objects of the battle. Much of the physical aggression of medieval and Renaissance sports and battles has been replaced by verbal dueling in song and ritualized insults. The aggression and hostility have not necessarily dissipated; they are just channeled differently. It seems, therefore, that an interpretation focusing on historical reenactment and sociocultural preservation is more appropriate than the Freudian model of virility and aggression.

The *palio*, as symbolic warfare, is a more or less "male" domain, if we wish to use such terminology. The religious significance of it would suggest "female" elements, in the form of the image of the Virgin Mary. This does not, however, erase the centrality of the religious and medieval-warfare-cum-joust elements. Hence, instead of gaining "both a virgin bride and a nursing mother," it seems reasonable to suggest that the winner of the *palio* is by historical reenactment reliving the victories of the once free Sienese Republic, thereby reasserting the independence and superiority of the *contrada* as expressed in song, proverb, epithet, etc. The winner is also, it must be noted, claiming the *right to life itself* as the victor; and *this* is what is being demonstrated by the baby bottles, pacifiers, and all the other paraphernalia associated with victory.

After a victory the *contrada* is reborn in a concrete behavioral, as well as metaphorical, sense. Interest in the *contrada* is renewed and there is a resurgence of *contrada* spirit among its members. This is especially true of a *contrada* that has not won in many years, e.g., the *nonna* (grandmother). With renewed spirit comes an increase in participation on the part of *contradaioli* and consequently more money into the *contrada* treasury from pledges, contributions, and profits from the *società*, the *contrada* nightclub (if it has one), etc. These, in turn, allow for more dinners, trips, plays, and other activities to be sponsored by the *contrada* for its members (and sometimes for the city as a whole), which keep the *contrada* functioning as a strong social and cultural institution. The notion of rebirth, then, is more than a

metaphor. It is grounded in concrete, observable behavior on the part of *contradaioli*, who are revitalized and themselves "reborn" through victory and continue to live *the palio*.

Dundes and Falassi do acknowledge the historical importance of the *palio* and the cyclicity of the status shuffles after each race (1975:187), but these cultural-historical elements are overshadowed by their extension of this reversal to psychoanalytic processes. Instead of interpreting this cyclicity in psychologically regressive terms (i.e., symbolic return to the womb), it seems more appropriate to view the *palio* as a dynamic self-regenerative sociocultural "system." Victory in the *palio* involves a progressive recreation and *continuation* of that system, which, though minor details in expression change with time and new ideas, keeps the *palio* intact as a public performance of Sienese cultural identity – an identity that merges past and present continually in the *palio*. Continuation of the system means continuation of the city as a structured whole of 17 independent but interrelated parts and, a fortiori, maintenance of the *contrada* as an important social institution in city life.

Although it is beyond the scope of this paper to give a full analysis of the meanings and uses of *palio* symbols, let us note the following when analyzing the *palio*:

1. The *palio* is a "rite of traditionalization" and as such maintains its connection with the past, i.e., the free Republic of Siena from the 13th to the mid-16th century. Hence, many symbols still in use today have either changed in their original significance or have, through the years, acquired new significance in this dynamic cultural system of symbols and meanings.
2. This rite of traditionalization involves ritual warfare. In depicting Renaissance "soldiers of fortune," the image projected by the *comparsa* will therefore be congruent with that of warriors going to battle – i.e., one of virility, strength, and invincibility. It is, moreover, as much in keeping with the ideology of "warfare" that women occupy the place they do (behind-the-scenes maintenance and support) as it is with male superiority in Mediterranean culture.

3. The *palio* is a synthesis of several other ritual games acted out in Siena during the Middle Ages, not unlike other games popular in other cities, except for the explicitly *religious* significance (e.g., the image of the Virgin Mary, the dedication of the city to her in times of trouble) that is one reason for its preservation through time. The combination of the religious observance with the sportive elements of "the joust" sets the scene for other such blends of "sacred" and "profane" elements in its execution.

4. The metaphor of "rebirth" in *palio* symbolism is supported in concrete behavior. This behavior manifests itself (a) in the daily lives of the Sienese and (b) on a symbolic level in which the history of the city as a separate sociocultural entity is recreated and thus the city as a whole is "reborn." Through the running of the *palio* and the whole gamut of rituals that surrounds it, from the intra-*contrada* activities to the *palio* itself, contemporary Sienese social life is justified and made meaningful in terms of culturally significant past events. Thus the performance aspects of the *palio* help create certain social realities, through which the cultural identity of the Sienese people is sustained.

Conclusion

Since the works of Durkheim, anthropologists have analyzed ritual symbolism and behavior in order to elucidate aspects of social structure and human social interaction. Though we have learned much from "primitive" rituals and societies through this approach, we seem to abandon the notion of culture in cities. Rituals in Western urban settings, unless viewed as explicitly "religious rituals," have become "folk festivals." Their relation to the patterning of daily social behavior is underemphasized or ignored in favor of other types of analysis on the level of folklore or, in this case, psychoanalytic interpretation of symbols. If anthropology is to maintain its ideal as a "holistic" discipline, our theoretical schemes must explain cross-cultural variations in human behavior, ritual and otherwise, in the same terms, regardless of where it occurs (i.e., in the bush or on city streets.)

In Siena, and unlike the case in many American cities, what is worthy of explanation is not why cultural identity diversifies, but why cultural identity remains constant and retains a certain continuity with the past. I have tried to analyze the *palio*, an urban "ritual," in terms of its own social organization and cultural history, and in terms of its effects on everyday social interaction within the city of Siena. Though other cities in the world may celebrate past events or enduring beliefs in "folk" and "religious" festivals, Siena is a unique city because it has not only retained its cultural heritage, i.e., that of a free republic, but it also symbolically *reproduces it* twice annually. Furthermore, during the year, the structural units that participate in this recreation of past events continue this heritage on a daily basis via the ritualized rules for social interaction of the individual Sienese who are its members.

I have combined the approaches of Hallowell, Peacock, and Geertz in the hopes of elucidating some of the cultural (as opposed to psychological) aspects of individual identity in Sienese terms, and the role of the *palio* in molding and maintaining this identity and the social interaction it entails. It is important to note that such an approach does not run counter to the views that the Sienese have of themselves. Hence there is no need to distort the data to fit a predisposed interpretation. This interpretation, moreover, enables us to see how the Sienese have been able to retain a cultural identity continuous with the history of their city and apart from the history of the rest of Italy.

In Siena each individual's identity is bound up with that of the *contrada*. This social identity provides the individual with a perceptual lens through which to interpret and interact with others, both within and outside of his or her own *contrada*. On the one hand, the hierarchy is always in flux, each *contrada*'s image changing vis-à-vis other contrade with each running of the *palio* (Falassi 1975). On the other hand, the *palio* can be compared to what Geertz calls "deep play," where the change is one of *attitude* and no one's status really changes (Geertz 1972). There are, however, certain elements that remain constant, though their expression in behavior may change in minor details. Hence, my use of the term *rite of traditionalization*. The important point is that each individual's conceptions of self and of others are patterned by *contrada* membership and participation, and this conception patterns Sienese social interacton.

NOTES

1   For the most up-to-date, complete bibliography on all aspects of the *palio*, the reader is referred to Dundes and Falassi (1975), the major ethnographic reference used here.
2   I have retained in most instances the Italian words, even in plural forms.
3   Trie "Madonna of Provenzano" refers to a terra cotta image of the Madonna, located in Provenzano, the section of the city notorious in the 16th century as the center of prostitution, and for miracle regarding the curing of "occupational diseases" of prostitutes (Dundes and Falassi 1975:7–8, 200). (Note that Siena has also been called *Civitas Veneris*, City of of Carnal Love. See pp. 200–201 for a discussion and further references.) The Madonna of Provenzano was petitioned during the famine and pestilence of 1594; later a church was built and a *palio* run in her honor.
4   These honorifics were usually conferred upon the *contrada* by royal visitors to Siena in honor of *palii* won during their visits. For a more detailed discussion of *contrada* honorific titles, see Dundes and Falassi (1975:21–22).
5   This suggestion formerly carried more weight than it does now and virtually amounted to an outright appointment. Though it remains true that his recommendation is influential, and that the *Consiglio Generate* normally adopts it, cases in which the council elects someone else are nowadays more frequent.
6   The most important events celebrated at the *societa* include the saint's day feast, during which everyone "plays *palio*" either in board games, raffles, or the *palio dei ragazzi* (children's *palio*), in which the boys of the *contrada* participate as both horse and jockey. For more detailed discussion, see Dundes and Falassi (1975:148–151).
7   The exception to this is Selva, who, in 1975, claimed no enemies.
8   Young people and children *do* use the respectful *Lei* form when addressing *contrada* elders. It remains unclear when, if ever, the verbal transition occurs in cross-generational interaction.

9   There are actually four ways to attain *contrada* membership: birth on *contrada* soil (the hospital is today considered "neutral" territory, so this means that one's parents reside within *contrada* territory); taking the *contrada* of one's parents (in the case of residence outside *contrada* territory); "adoption" into the *contrada* by living in its territory and participating in its activities (particularly in the cases of non-Sienese who move to Siena or in-marrying spouses, provided they do not belong to the archenemy *contrada*); and by choice, according to the *contrada* of one's friends. Birth within *contrada* territory remains the most prestigious claim to *contrada* identity, and many anecdotes and stories are still told of the pains taken by parents and other relatives to ensure it (see Tailetti 1967:94–95; Dundes and Falassi 1975:56).
10 Dundes and Fallassi (1975:39). This was not confirmed by my informants and was thought to be an exception, performed for the children of the upper classes, particularly children of prominent Sienese families.
11 This is a shortened version of the most popular *contrada* song used by the Sienese to sing about *contrada* life and the *palio*. A fuller treatment of *contrada* songs may be found in Falassi (1974); Dundes and Falassi (1975:162–184). The Italian texts are not underscored, for convenience and easy reading. All original texts are on the left and the English translations on the right.
12 Also documented in Tailetti (1967:75–76).
13 A *comparsa*, made up of more members (usually the younger and less skilled at flag waving and drum playing), also marches in a parade to honor *contrada* "protectors" and friendly *contrade* as part of the saint's day festivities.
14 The horse is usually paraded only for a day or two after the race and then is returned to its owner. It is present again at the victory dinner, some time in September. Interestingly enough, it is the horse, not the jockey, who wins the *palio*. As long as the *spennacchiera*, the plumed headpiece, remains intact, the *contrada* can win the *palio* even if the jockey falls off. A horse who wins without a rider wins the race *scosso*. At the victory dinner in such a case, the seat of honoris left vacant, as it belongs to the horse.

REFERENCES

Dundes, A. and Alessandro, F. 1975. *La Terra In Piazza: An Interpretation of the Palio of Siena*. Berkeley: University of California Press.

Falassi, A. 1974. Per Forza e Per Amore. *Nuovo Corriere Senese* 7(32): 3.

Falassi, A. 1975 personal communication.

Foster, G. 1965. Peasant Society and the Image of Limited Good. *American Anthropologist* 67: 293–315.

Geertz, C. 1966. Religion as a Cultural System. In *Anthropological Approaches to the Study of Religion*, Michael Banton (ed.). London: Tavistock, pp. 1–46.

Geertz, C. 1972. Deep Play: Notes on the Balinese Cock Fight. *Daedalus* 101 (Winter): 1–37.

Gelli, J. 1905. I Giuochi di Bandiera nel Seicento. *Emporium* 21. 237–244.

Hallowell, A.I. 1954. The Self and its Behavioral Environment. *Explorations* 2 (April): 106–165.

Heywood, W. 1899. *Our Lady of August and the Palio of Siena*. Siena: Enrico Torrini.

Peacock, J.L. 1968. *Rites of Modernization: Symbolic and Social Aspects of Indonesian Proletarian Drama*. Chicago: University of Chicago Press.

Pomponio, A. 1976. 17 Truths: The Palio of Siena as a Life Process. Unpublished MA thesis, Bryn Mawr College.

Schneider, D.M. 1968. *American Kinship: A Cultural Account*. Englewood Cliffs, New Jersey: Prentice-Hall.

Schneider, D.M. 1972. What is Kinship All About? In *Kinship Studies in the Morgan Centennial Year*, Priscilla Reining (ed.). The Anthropological Society of Washington, D.C., pp. 32–63.

Singer, M. 1955. The Cultural Pattern of Indian Civilization. *Far Eastern Quarterly* 15: 23–36.

Tailetti, A. 1967. *Aneddoti Contradaioli*. Roma: Olimpia.

Part IV

Performance and Politics in the Making of Communities

13
Poetry and Politics in a Transylvanian Village

Gail Kligman

Hey, boyar, you dog
Let me see you my servant
I'd send you here and there
But food I would not give you
   (pro-Party song, 1952).

What a life it used to be
It was good but it passed
This life of today
Be it or not
Let it burn in hell!
Since the Russians came
much has happened
bad, not good
They took all our land
and we remained with trouble only
and we must go into the world at large
to earn our food
   (former *chiabur* [landed peasant],
   Maramureş, 1979).

It has been noted by E. P. Thompson that "what changes, as the mode of production and productive relations change, is the *experience* of living men and women" (1979:21). In Romania, poetry constitutes the "privileged" language that makes sense of experience. Poetry, folk and literary, is considered to be the

"chosen music" of words. As a traditional couplet explains: "he who experiences much, he is the one who makes songs." Or as a seventh grader of the same village offered: "poetry is a good comrade in joy and in sorrow." Poetry is the child of experience. And experience during the last thirty some years in Romania has been confronted with rapid socio-economic transformation.

In this paper, I will examine the symbolic manipulation of poetic content for purposes of both pro- and anti-communist commentary.[1] While rhymed couplets, traditional or improvised, generally constitute the primary mode of communication during ritual occasions, they are also utilized effectively during informal social interactions as well as in written form for general correspondence or for educational, ideological purposes.

Fieldwork was done in 1978–79 in Ieud, Maramureş. "Old" Maramureş is surrounded by mountains to the west, south and east. The Tiza River forms the northern border along the Russian Ukraine. Ieud is one of the oldest and largest villages in Maramureş (population approximately 5,500). Religion has had profound influence in Maramureş and in Ieud

Gail Kligman, "Poetry and Politics in a Transylvanian Village," pp. 83–89 from *Anthropological Quarterly* 56(2), 1983.

particularly. Ieud used to be one of the wealth-iest villages in Maramureş; it is now one of the poorest. Forced semi-cooperativization (1950, 1962) has transformed the economic organiza-tion of the village. This necessarily resulted in the diversification of the family, one or more persons being compelled to enter the wage-labor force to supplement income. Over the intervening years, agriculture has been steadily feminized or left to the aged (Chirot 1978; Moskoff 1978). The results of socio-economic change imposed by the goals of communist state planning have often been contradictory and even confounding (Jowitt 1974; Chirot 1978; Moskoff 1978). Most strikingly, in Ieud, it is the ritual system that has emerged as the stable organizational factor in a much-altered village life.

Ritual occasions feature a particularly rich oral tradition characterized by *strigături* (shouted couplets), laments, and songs, all in the form of rhymed couplets. Content ranges from the expression of fundamental attitudes about life, norms, and values, to direct confessions revealing the most personal sentiments of an individual. Thus, these rhymed couplets include literal and metaphor-ical commentary on general matters such as morality, drinking, kinship and aging as well as upon more specific problems of socializa-tion, dispute, change and personal trauma. Though their content is seemingly determined by the event, it also points to loci of transcen-dent social concern, thereby providing a forum for the expression of ideological trans-formation. While the use of formalized speech as culturally salient media of social manipu-lation is not unique to Romanian poetic forms, repression of individual opinion is cur-rently at a premium there. Because strigături and songs are implicitly understood to be objectified forms,[2] no one can be held respon-sible for incriminating remarks. Conse-quently, these poetic forms make possible the expression, oral or written, of that which is normally suppressed; individuals do not express opinions, strigături do. And so the traditional reminder:

He whose mouth it is is not guilty
That's how the strigătură (saying) goes!

Thus, "poetic license" (broadly taken) permits social and political commentary to enter into the realm of discourse.[3] Poetry serves as a vehicle to help constitute and define the nature of social relations, most importantly in the contemporary context, the relations of the individual to the State.

Cultural ideologues use poetic forms to inculcate progressive values by manipulating the symbolic content. What Clark has recently written about to the Soviet novel per-tains to the RCP's (Romanian Communist Party's) explicitly didactic use of poetry "to popularize ideology, to disseminate it in a form both attractive and accessible to the masses" (Clark 1981:44; see also Meiţoiu 1965:12). As the Romanian scholars Pop and Ruxandoiu have written:

In addition to the traditional themes which have been preserved, there have appeared new themes which mirror the multi-lateral reality of the State: concepts about work, about familial life, about the cultural and political life . . . .
(Pop and Ruxăndoiu, 1976:351)[4]

One's relations to the State are presented in terms of social ideals. New meanings are incor-porated into action. Whereas *patria* used to condense a set of meanings within a circum-scribed spatio-temporal locale, i.e., patria Maramureşenesc, now it is meant to reify a complex set of concepts that comprise a national ideology.

Through the symbolic construction of a national ideology, the RCP legitimates itself, and, in the process, encourages the transforma-tion of peasants into Romanians. National ideology attempts to articulate various levels of identity (individual to regional to national). Part of the RCP's claim to legitimacy is seen to stem historically from the heroic tradition of the Romanian people themselves. Ceauşescu has noted:

If in the past, anonymous creators expressed their revolt against social injustices, today, people just as passionately express in their songs the joys of free labor, the fulfillment of humanistic potential, in one phrase, the joy of a new life.

Pro-communist poetry underlines the socio-culturally transformative merits of socialist work, education, commitment to progress through scientific rationalism, technological advance and the Party.

Loyalty to and respect for the Party are based upon construing the Party as the symbolic family of the people, therein reflecting the transposition of the traditional hierarchical ordering of relations within the family, especially with regard to authority. The Party becomes a symbolic equivalent of *patria, România*, in short, the family and home:

Romania, how dear you are to me
for in you I was born
and in you I grew up.

(This is a variant of a traditional verse about mother-child relationships.)

And however long I'll live
in you I'll work
in good and bad
I'll support you with my soul.

The nature of the bond between the individual and the State is considered to be as sacred as the vows that bind a couple in marriage.

In the Marxist-Leninist tradition, it is the Party that must guide the masses to consciousness, the "new life." Therefore, it is the Party that is:

. . . the most beautiful word
from the Romanian land
land where people work
from dawn until sunset
in factories and smoking plants
for the color
of these times of fulfillment.

Work leads to progress, and the commitment of the people to this goal has changed the tenor of life from insufficiency to relative sufficiency. The emphasis upon industrialization as the means to modernization is evident.

However, modernization through technological advancement requires basic skills and knowledge. The Party, like any good parent, provides the chance for its "children" to better their living conditions through educational opportunity and development. Education is now compulsory through the tenth grade. The benefits of the three R's have long been recognized:

The Party has raised us
to school they've sent us
girls and boys
to learn to write letters
to write letters to comrade Stalin
and to my sweetheart.

Today, Stalin is replaced by the Party or Ceaușescu. The text acknowledges the Party's ideological support for the equality of women.

Through cooperativization, in conjunction with general education, the Party asserts it has freed peasants from the oppressive mode and relations of production that characterized their harsh existence prior to 1949:

We didn't have bread
nor clothes
how my hair grayed
working for the chiabur.

But now:

Who works in the cooperative
doesn't lack anything
he has grain and rye
he has what to take to the mill
(Amzulescu 1962:13).

However, the establishment of the cooperative's legitimacy in Ieud was not easily accomplished. The "conditions of constructing socialism" betrayed the system of social relations and values that organized village life. For many villagers, centuries of experience working the land lent empty tones to the pro-cooperative songs' messages. History as lived seemed to contradict history as posited from center to periphery. In Ieud, the chiaburi were not perceived by the majority of peasants to be overtly exploitative; hence, many supported the wealthier peasants in their attempts

to maintain their private property.[5] While the
soil in this isolated region is generally poor, it
was nonetheless theirs. Also at this time, the
village en masse resisted the State's repression
of their Greek-Catholic priests, but to no
avail.[6] Eventually, Orthodox priests arrived
and a cooperative was formed.

Resistance and/or criticism were punished.
In the beginning, humiliation, jail and even
death were common sentences. During this
period, poetry took on new meanings, acquiring a poignant salience as the means to express
one's suffering and recount the detailed unfolding of events that constitute history, personal
and social. This is not a period that is discussed
openly either among themselves, or, needless to
say, in front of foreigners. When discussed, it is
often managed through the veiled speech of
poetry. My introduction to the experience of
this period occured at a wedding in another
valley of Maramureş when a woman who had
married out of Ieud shouted a strigătură:

Oh poor Ieud
How it was and how it is now
It was a wealthy village
And in one moment, it was done in
They fought until they
stuck it in the colhoz.

"They" refers to the Party and their local supporters, many of whom delighted in carrying
out their role to excess. *Colhoz* is the borrowed
term used in the vernacular when talking about
the cooperative.

Not surprisingly, class is a distinctive
feature determining the content of pro- and
anti-cooperative songs. The latter, of course,
are little known, the experience having been
masked by the mythologization of history that
ignores the means to the end. History according
to ideology is readily obtainable; history according to experience, less so. A glimpse into the
transformation of Ieud is provided in the following excerpts:

They made the collective
and I managed how I could
because they took my land
and put me in jail.
Green flowers with thick leaves

I was beautiful and lovely
and they all wanted me
Because I had land and a mill
and they called me
to ask at the village council
my quotas. . . . . when will I give them?
if I enter the colhoz
then they won't do anything to me
they took my cow
then, I had milk
only as I managed to get it
The cow was taken to the colhoz
and I got nothing in exchange
not even a nettle
just wait – everyone will pay
for how they've made everyone suffer
and flour they took from us
and cornmeal they stole
then they celebrate
and divide everything between them
let them divide what's theirs
and not that of others
    (a 77-year-old woman).

The interweaving of personal and sociological
narrative is compelling. This woman resisted
"signing" into the cooperative as long as she
was able. The exacting of exorbitant quotas
was a standard tactic employed to ruin the
wealthy (see Cernea 1974:98). Moreover, people were called to the village council at all hours
of the night. The sexual innuendo implied by
the summons to the council in conjunction with
the statement about her beauty and wealth is
intentional. She was a desirable woman; these
qualities were those that normally attracted
suitors for dowry and marriage. However, in
this instance, the State wanted her wealth and
local officials wanted to shame her dignity as a
woman. (Many women acquiesced to "save"
their property; this one was not among them.)
It is important to note that the class struggle
engendered by collectivization in this area
transformed the nature of social relations in
the village. Long-established networks of
patron–client relations, ritual kin relations,
neighbors – all were affected by deepening
alienation among themselves. The text points
to the cruel and unjust methods resorted to;
again, at the local level, central authorities
lacked the means to control the excesses of
those tasting power.[7] What was happening to

the system of values and norms governing social behavior?

My Stalin, what have you done?
From horses you've made sausages
From gypsies, deputies!

Order was inverted.

To be sure, the experience of changing structure and values disrupts that which is familiar. However, it cannot be denied that life *is* easier. Conspicuous consumption is evident and within the reach of many. A song of today summarizes the ambivalence felt about the changing times:

The State has done much
it's done something good
all fools have wristwatches
When I was young
Life was very hard
There wasn't nice work
and we went only on foot
over mountains, over springs
with axes on our backs
for a crust of corn
until we found work
it was hard to earn a little
to pay a Jew
for a meter of flour
you gave him a guarantee slip
if you didn't pay on time
he took your cow to the market
and sold it for a profit
to make up for your debt
Now how good it is
I owe nothing to the Jews
nor to the wealthy in the village
Until I got smart
I worked for others
For the rich in the village
. . . .
The Party did good
for that landowner is now like me
He doesn't have wagons nor oxen
nor large herds of sheep
nor cheese to sell
nor milk to exchange
now everyone sees
that even he wears a work coat.

The State is ideologically committed to the elimination of social-class disparities and to the equal distribution of material goods. As the song attests, the State has done much to alter basic inequities. However, generalized well-being has been at the expense of what are seen to be the merits of differential opportunity according to status and worth. Standards are no longer critically evaluated. Meanwhile, work conditions have improved in that one works for the State and not at the behest of privileged individuals (the Jews are practically non-existent in Transylvania). Now those individuals are no different than anyone else; they too must sport the worker's blue coat, symbol of the industrializing worker state.

Despite the advantages resulting from the profound changes in the conditions of daily life, people worry about the demise of the basic values that have ordered their world. Promiscuity, increased crime, violence, divorce . . . , the propaganda against Western excesses has been influential in creating despair about the rise of similar phenomena in their very own midst. "Things are easier now, one doesn't have to toil so much, but is it worth it?" Religion, the opiate of the masses; communism, the saviour of social action; the RCP, contemporary gods of consciousness:

The brilliant Party guides us
toward a beautiful garden
a garden as in stories
it is named communism
tomorrow we'll make our country
finer than spring
with many factories
rivers of milk, plentiful bread
all years to blossom
long live the Party
    (Robea 1962:19).

The Party is leading the masses to the promised land, for communism brings heaven to earth. Men make their own destiny. Hence, the holy trinity of today's secular religion consists of:

Parental home
the village
and homeland
we, lovers of poetry
bless them that are everything.

Language use is contextualized social action: poetry is indeed a good comrade in joy and sorrow. Through it, one makes sense of life's happenings. By objectifying experience, poetry personalizes general cultural meanings. It mobilizes perceptions and values that are often not consciously recognized, thereby offering a means to come to terms with the ambiguities of what one thinks and feels about the unfolding of experience. In this respect, poetry is a powerful medium through which the living experience of change at personal, local and national levels may be articulated and understood. As has been seen in this paper, the process of socio-economic, political and/or cultural change is not a clear cut one; the experience of it is frought with ambiguity, contradiction, and ambivalence. Hence, the content of recent critical poetic commentary is, in actuality, more ambivalent than it is ardently negative. Such is the result of the ongoing dialectical relationship that exists between thought and action, ideology and praxis.

NOTES

1 I am not herein concerned with the formal features that distinguish a poem as a poem (Jakobson 1960; 1980) or that distinguish a Romanian poem from similar poetic forms found in eastern Europe and Russia.

2 Jakobson (1960:371) notes that an effective and inherent property of poetry is its ability to convert a message into an enduring entity.

3 This is eloquently elaborated by Lampland (1981).

Note that the verses cited in this paper are translations from the original Romanian texts. Those that are not followed by citations indicating source were collected by me in the village.

4 See also Amzulescu (1962:7–18; 1975:19–28); Robea (1962:7–21); Meiţoiu (1965); Firescu (1975:17–22).

5 The chiaburi were considered to be hard-working peasants like everyone else. Moreover, they were descendents of nemeşi, an important factor in status-conscious Maramureş. Because of their resources and position, chiaburi often served as godparents for many other families.

They were key figures in village social organization. See also Chirot (1978); Kideckel (1981:4–5); Verdery (in press).

6 The Greek-Catholic or Uniate Church was introduced into this area in the 1700s. For a cursory overview of religion in eastern Europe, see Sanders (1982).

7 In 1951, the Central Committee of the RCP publicly denounced these local abuses and threatened their continuation with stringent measures:

any infraction of the principle of liberal consent, any economic or administrative pressure placed upon the peasant workers to convince them to enter the cooperative will be severely punished, including expulsion from the Party and legal trial of those guilty of excess.

See Cernea (1974:98) for further discussion of the abuses and infractions that occurred during the initial period of socialist transformation.

While deep bitterness lingers on with regard to these events, those affected most dramatically by them acknowledge that life today is much easier.

REFERENCES

Amzulescu, A. 1962. Perspective folclorice ale satului colectivizat. *Revista de folclor* 7: 3–4: 718.

Amzulescu, A. 1975. Evoluţia actuală a culturii populare şi unele consideraţii de prognoză folcloristică. *Cîntecul popular românesc* III: 19–28.

Cernea, M. 1974. *Sociologia cooperativei agricole*. Bucureşti: editură academiei R. S. R.

Chirot, D. 1978. Social change in Communist Romania. *Social Forces* 57: 2: 457–88.

Clark, K. 1981. *The Soviet novel: history as ritual.* Chicago: Chicago University Press.

Firescu, A. 1975. Folclorul contemporan – object de cercetare sociologică. *Cîntecul popular românesc* III.

Jakobson, R. 1960. Linguistics and Poetics. In *Style in Language*. J. Sebeok, ed. Cambridge: MIT Press, pp. 350–377.

Jakobson, R. 1980. On poetic intentions and linguistic devices in poetry. *Poetics Today* 2: 1 A: 87–96.

Jowitt, K. 1974. An organizational approach to the study of political culture in Marxist-

Leninist systems. *American Political Science Review* LXVIII: 3: 1171–1191.

Kideckel, D. 1981. Socialism, prestige and alcohol use in rural Romania. Paper presented at Northeastern Anthropological Association meeting.

Lampland, M. 1981. *Paint our flags red and black: the Hungarian revolt of 1956.* MA thesis, University of Chicago.

Meitoiu, I. 1965. *Folclor poetic nou.* Bucureşti: Comitetul de stat pentru cultură şi artă.

Moskoff, W. 1978. Sex discrimination, commuting and the role of women in Romanian development. *Slavic Review* 37(3): 440–56.

Pop, M., and P. Ruxandoiu 1976. *Folclor literar românesc.* Bucureşti: editură didactică şi pedagogică.

Robea, M. 1962. Imaginea partidului în creatia populară contemporană. *Revista de folclor* VII: 1-27-21.

Sanders, I. 1982. Church-state relationships in southeastern Europe. *East European Quarterly* XVI: 1: 59–71.

Thompson, E. P. 1979. *Folklore, anthropology and social history.* Studies in Labor History, pamphlet. Sussex: John L. Noyce.

Verdery, K. 1983. *Transylvanian villagers: three centuries of political, economic, and ethnic change.* Berkeley: University of California Press.

14

The Matter of Talk: Political Performances in Bhatgaon

Donald Brenneis

When I had recently returned from my doctoral field research, a study of conflict-related discourse in a Fiji Indian community, one of my professors remarked, 'Fascinating, but does talk really matter?' He argued that, as interesting as speeches, for example, might be in themselves, such performances would only reflect the political structure and distribution of power in a society and would rarely be consequential. While an analysis of the content and style of dispute discourse might be valuable in demonstrating the constraints and privileges associated with various offices and fora, he felt that such linguistic features were epiphenomena of the underlying political process.

This paper argues that talk indeed matters. One base for this argument is the cross-cultural salience of language as a medium for political activity. As Bloch (1975:4) suggests, 'If political language and procedure are of little importance politically, it would be surprising to see how strongly they are valued and insisted upon by

participants in many societies.' Other anthropologists have shown the prominence of verbal ability as a criterion for leadership (see, for example, Frake 1963; Albert 1972); Irvine's (1975) discussion of the studied incompetence of Wolof nobles supports the importance of performance, albeit in an inverted form. Such organizational features of discourse as precedence and turn-taking (Albert 1972; Sacks, Schegloff & Jefferson (1974) have significant political implications.

This paper presents a detailed analysis of two performance genres in Bhatgaon, a village of Hindi-speaking Fiji Indians. These genres - parbachan ('religious speeches') and 'song challenges'[1] (villagers use the English phrase) – are quite dissimilar in 'texture, text and context' (Dundes 1964). They often serve similar pragmatic ends, however, as opportunities for political performance. This contrastive analysis provides the core of an ethnography of political speaking in Bhatgaon. Through the consideration

Donald Brenneis, "The Matter of Talk: Political Performances in Bhatgaon," pp. 159–170 from *Language in Society* 7(2), 1978.

of the settings, styles and content characteristic of the two genres, such features as the interaction of performer and audience and community standards for evaluation and interpretation are highlighted. One can also see these features affect individual performers; their strategies within the constraints of the genres are crucial components of political behavior and figure strongly in the course which a community conflict takes.

Bloch's analysis of Merina oratory points to the focal role of formalization as a constraint on both rhetorical performance and subsequent action; successful speechmaking 'moves the communication to a level where disagreement is ruled out since one cannot disagree with the right order' (1975:16). The opportunity to speak is a limited political resource; having the right to speak is in itself an accomplishment. The oratorical franchise is more extensive in Bhatgaon as all males may participate. The chance to perform is not as important as the persuasiveness of individual performers. Such rhetorical force lies not so much in logical argument as in skillful attention to and manipulation of stylistic, contextual and content features. In arguing for the effectiveness of talk, I will delineate some of the most salient of these features and suggest the ways in which their successful use compels audience involvement and support.

Bhatgaon: A Fiji Indian Community

Bhatgaon is a rural village of 671 Hindi-speaking Fiji Indians located on the northern side of Vanua Levu, the second-largest island in the Dominion of Fiji.[2] The villagers are the descendants of north Indians who came to Fiji between 1879 and 1919 as indentured plantation workers. Bhatgaon was established in the early 1900s and now includes 90 households; there has been little migration to or from the village for the past 20 years. Most families lease rice land from the Government of Fiji, and, although they may work as seasonal cane cutters or in other outside jobs, most men consider themselves rice farmers. Rice and dry-season vegetables are raised primarily for family use, although surplus produce may be sold to middlemen. Leaseholds are generally small, and rice farming does not offer Bhatgaon villagers the same opportunities for wealth available in sugar-cane raising areas.

The political activities of men and women are often directed to the same ends but usually take place in different fora. Both *parbachan* and challenge singing are public and male genres; this paper is concerned with men's politics. Women's political participation occurs in less public settings,[3] as does much male politicking through such genres as *talanoa* ('gossip', from Fijian).

Among males an overt egalitarian ideology prevails. Although ancestral caste appears to influence marriage choice (Brenneis 1974:25), it has few daily consequences in Bhatgaon. As one villager said, *gaon me sab bar abba hei* ('In the village all are equal'); this overt equality is symbolically expressed by such practices as sitting together on the floor during religious events and equal opportunity to speak. The roots of this egalitarian outlook lie in the conditions of immigration and indenture;[4] the belief is reinforced by the relative similarity in wealth throughout Bhatgaon.

As in *Animal Farm*, however, some are more equal than others. Adolescents are treated with considerably less respect than older, married men. A number of men are recognized as *bada admi* ('big men') because of their past participation in village affairs, religious leadership, education or other personal success. Individual reputation (*nam* = 'name') is central to one's actual social position. A man's *nam* is subject to constant renegotiation through his own words and deeds, and through those of others. Villagers are quite sensitive to perceived attempts by others to lower their reputations. They are also attuned to the successes of others; too much success is seen by many as both a personal affront and a violation of egalitarian sentiment. In disputes reputation management is a constant concern, for conflict often arises from apparent insult, and the remedy lies in the public rebalancing of one's reputation with his opponent's.

There is a police station three miles away, but there are no formal social control agencies in Bhatgaon itself. The village has a representative to the district advisory council, but he is not empowered to regulate affairs within the village. With the decline of caste as an organizational feature of Fiji Indian life, such bodies as caste councils are no longer available for conflict management. Conflict in Bhatgaon remains largely dyadic, the concern of the contending parties alone, yet as long as disputes are dyadic, the chances of settlement are slim. A major goal of dispute discourse, therefore, is to attract and maintain the interest and involvement of third parties.

The most salient organizations in Bhatgaon are religious associations. Two Hindu sects are represented, the orthodox *Sanatan Dharam* and the reformist *Arya Samaj*; their local-level organizations are called *mandalis*, a term referring both to the groups and to the weekly prayer and fellowship meetings which they hold. There is one *mandali* for the 29 reform households, and there are three for the 50 orthodox families. The seven Muslim households belong to a mosque association, but they gather only for special events such as festivals and weddings.

Contexts

The nature of the audiences for the two types of performances is the critical contextual difference between them. To show this, a distinction between primary and secondary audience is needed.[5] The primary audience is composed of the individuals or group at whom the performance is chiefly aimed, i.e., those whom the performer hopes to influence directly. The secondary audience includes others who are present. It is not merely a residual category, however, as the secondary audience provides both evaluation and an element of control. The spectators limit and shape the performance; this constraint makes the event possible, as will be shown below.

Song challenges. These are competitions between different religious groups; while they are cast as interreligious contests, they are often motivated by personal conflict. Men in competition or conflict with members of other sects may organize song challenges as opportunities to attack and shame their opponents; such events afford a chance for individual as well as group political performances. Challenges take place at neutral households, usually by formal invitation by one group or the other.

The performers are groups of coreligionists, with a lead singer and a chorus accompanied by drums and harmonium. The parties alternate turns, beginning with moderate songs about their own religion and escalating to increasingly abusive and personal attacks upon members of the other group.

The primary audience for song challenges is the opposing group; the goal is 'to make them so mad they cry. The secondary audience consists of the general audience. Spectators usually sit between the dueling parties; they respond eagerly to skillful insults and jeer when a performer displays embarrassment. They are crucial to the performance as they limit the responses of the groups to each other's outrages; the insults exchanged in challenges would in ordinary circumstances lead to violence or other types of revenge. The conventions of the genre prohibit such reactions, and the secondary audience, by both its physical presence and performers' fear of gossip should they break the rules, enforces the conventions. Challenges end when one group feels it cannot restrain itself much longer and sends for outsiders to end the competition. Villagers expect that enmity should end with the conclusion of the contest; any subsequent mischief directed against the victors would be interpreted as bad sportsmanship and lower the reputations of the losers.

Parbachan. These are speeches with ostensibly religious content given at weekly *mandali* meetings. Although members of other religions are welcome, the participants in a *mandali* are almost all members of the same Hindu sects. The *mandali*s take place in the *belo*s ('sitting-houses') of members' homesteads. *Parbachan* are part of the program which follows a ritual butter sacrifice or readings from the Ramayana; programs also include religious songs. The program is set by the chairman of the *mandali*; anyone may be called upon for a speech, but those who want to speak may ask beforehand to be included. Not all *parbachan* have a political intent; many are spontaneous speeches on purely religious subjects. *Parbachan* do, however, offer an important medium for political performance, and I will focus on those speeches which are designed for such purposes.

The primary audience for *parbachan*, when they are being used politically, comprises those members of the *mandali* not directly involved in the conflict. Spectators sit quietly on the floor while the orator speaks from a standing position. Unless the speaker makes a deliberately humorous remark, audience demeanor is serious; they do not laugh at grammatical mistakes. The speaker's goal is to provoke their interest and to gain their support for the future; *parbachan* can serve to attract third-party involvement, either as partisans or as mediators. The secondary audience is one's opponent or his supporters; if the enemy is not present, one can be sure that word of what is said will reach him rapidly. This secondary audience constrains by intimidation. If a speaker makes an overt attack upon someone, the offended party may wreak revenge through such actions as cutting down the speaker's banana trees. While such a response is not necessarily considered virtuous, villagers hold that it is an understandable reaction and that the speaker brought it upon himself. Speakers, therefore, are very wary; *parbachan* are allusive rather than direct. *Parbachan* are more open ended than song challenges. They are designed to have implications for future behavior. A successful speech may influence the course of a dispute in one's favor, while an overly direct attack may lead to justifiable revenge.

Textures

Each genre implies a constellation of paralinguistic, proxemic, gestural and other stylistic features. In this comparison, however, I will focus on two linguistic variables, the choice of code and patterns of pronoun use.

Bhatgaon villagers recognize two general varieties of Hindi. One, *shudh* ('sweet') or 'radio' Hindi, is a formal code characterized by such features as gender, carefully inflected verbs and a heavily Sanskritic vocabulary. The other code is the local dialect, referred to *jangli bat* ('jungly talk'); *jangli* vocabulary includes many English and Fijian items, and it is much less complexly inflected. *Jangli bat* is the mother tongue for villagers; sweet Hindi is learned through school, reading, and listening to the radio and formal speeches.

In a song challenge, the initial texts are frequently performed from books published in India; they are therefore in sweet Hindi. Most challenge songs, however, are in *jangli bat*, especially those composed spontaneously.

Singers use both singular and plural first person pronouns (*mai* (s) and *ham* (pl) in *shudh* Hindi; *ham* (s) and *hamlog* (pl) in *jangli bat*). For the singular second person pronoun, demeaning forms which are the same in both codes are employed – either *tum*, the familiar address term which is demeaning to strangers, or *tu*, which is usually limited to wives, children and animals. A variety of reference terms are used, including the third person pronouns *u* and *waha*. Singers also refer to their targets by name, using both proper names and nicknames such as *langru* ('gimp') which are usually spoken only behind an individual's back. Challenge songs are characterized by demeaning address and direct and often insulting reference.

Parbachan are given in *shudh* Hindi, or at least in as formal a code as the speaker can muster. Villagers' competence in sweet Hindi is quite variable. Illiterate older men know little formal Hindi, while educated and younger men are relatively fluent. Limited knowledge of the formal code does not limit the speaker's effectiveness; audiences consider the attempt to speak properly to be more important than the results.

Parbachan have a more complex structure than challenge songs. They follow a tripartite structure. The introduction consists of thanks to the host and apologies for any mistakes which the speaker might make. In this section speakers attempt to anticipate and defuse any criticisms which might be made of them; introductions are largely formulaic. The second section, the message, concentrates ostensibly on some aspect of the moral character of a good member of the *mandali*. Messages are expected to be didactic; in *parbachan* one should give *shikcha* ('instruction'). Finally there is a coda in which the thanks and apologies of the introduction are repeated.

The choice of pronouns varies from section to section. In the introduction and coda, speakers use the first person singular pronoun *mai*. In the message the singular first person rarely occurs; instead speakers employ the plural *ham*. This has a dual effect. First, it identifies the speaker directly with the group's moral ideal, as in 'We believe this'. It also distances the speaker from his text and implies that the group shares responsibility for his sentiments. The only speeches in which *mai*, the first person singular, was used were those catalyzed by the misdeeds of adolescents; *ham* is always used in *parbachan* engendered by conflicts between adults. I have argued elsewhere (Brenneis 1977a) that the relative equality or inequality of disputants is a crucial feature in the community interpretation and evaluation of conflicts; this linguistic distinction further supports the qualitative difference between the two types of conflicts. One does not need to worry as much about offending youths as with fellow adults, at least in the eyes of the audience. The second person pronoun is either *aap* (singular) or *aaplog* (plural), the honorific forms.

Styles of reference are the most interesting aspect of pronoun choice in *parbachan*. In the introduction and coda, references are direct; names and third person pronouns are used, as reference there is invariably flattering. Complimentary reference remains direct in the message, but a number of strategies are available to deal with more derogatory topics. No proper names are used in negative contexts. Although *u* and *waha* may appear, their antecedents are implied rather than present in the text.

Speakers do often rely upon a type of construction I have labelled the 'coy reference'.[6] Coy references employ the indefinite pronouns *koi* ('some(one)') and *kya* ('some(thing)') and, occasionally, relative pronouns such as *jo* ('who'). The following examples suggest the use of these constructions:

Koi admilog hei, jo mandali me nahi jata hei. ('There are some people who do not go to *mandalis*.') *Kya karn se koi laḍkalog badmash karta hei.* ('For some reason some boys are making mischief.')

Coy references are often used to provide vague antecedents for later uses of *u* and *waha*; one can be as derogatory as desired about an unidentified malefactor. The rhetorical effect of coy references lies in their implied contrast between 'some people' and their indecipherable motives and 'us', i.e., *mandali* members, with 'our' understanding of how people should behave. The coy reference serves as a 'membership categorization device' (Sacks 1972:326), delineating those who fulfill the moral criteria for *mandali* membership from those who do not. These constructions also enable the speaker to shield himself from retribution, as he does not make direct accusations. Their ambiguous reference piques audience interest as well.

Texts

The central issue in contrasting the characteristic contents of the two genres is Kenneth Burke's (1950) idea of identification. As Rosaldo suggests, it is necessary to examine the ways in which a 'speaker will identify the objects, persons or events of his descriptions with examples, categories or concepts whose typical fates and motives have the sorts of moral implications which are relevant to his interest and intent' (1973:206). In challenge songs the identification is quite direct, focussing on unambiguous 'objects, persons or events' and leaving moral implications to the audience to unravel. As the following text demonstrates, the objects of one's derision and the consequences of their opposition are made quite clear.

You're going to come and beat me? You and who else?
Who will dare to boast in front of me?

We will beat you and break off your head; streams of blood will flow. Who will come to your aid?

Your mother and sisters will mourn after your death; your wife will become a widow, and who will care for her?

Your sister has become a prostitute, and she roams from village to village. She has become a prostitute, and who will pay for her?
(Brenneis & Padarath 1975:288)

Constrained as he is by fear of his opponent's revenge and by the expectations of this audience, the *parbachan* speaker employs a considerably different strategy for identification. It is in fact the reverse of that found in the songs. Instead of providing 'objects, persons or events', speakers refer to general concepts and categories, e.g., to moral notions such as 'generosity' and 'devotion' and to categorizations such as 'true *samaji* or 'false *sanatani*'.[7] Speakers leave it to their audiences to relate these generalities to the specific circumstances engendering their invocation.

This reliance on the audience suggests a second crucial facet of identification. While the strategies used by speakers within their texts are important, they would be ineffective without the audience's interest in and identification of their meanings and motives. The persuasiveness of performances depends upon listeners' understandings of both what is said and what is intended in saying it. If through identification the performer is linking the specific with the general, the audience is also trying to link the specific performance with what they know generally about the speaker, his relationships with other members of the community, and his 'interest and intent'.

Now, in the genre of challenge songs the overt content of songs and performers' purposes in singing them are ostensibly congruent. Singers make it very clear what they intend. Erickson & Schultz (1973:2) have suggested that a direct explanation of 'what we are doing now' be called 'explicit formulation'. Song texts contain many examples of explicit formulation, such as 'About those scoundrels I'll let everyone know'.[8]

There is a great disparity between content and intention in *parbachan*. Although I understood Hindi well and was on the lookout for manifestations of conflict, during my first few months of fieldwork I saw no reason not to interpret *parbachan* as purely religious discourse. A friend's comment on the successful political attack a speaker had made in an apparent homily on the virtues of *mandali* attendance suggested that I was missing the point. The contents of *parbachan* are not in themselves ambiguous, apart from such constructions as coy references. It is easy for the Hindi-speaking outsider to follow an analysis of, for example, the fidelity of Sita, the wife of the epic hero Ram. The relationship between text and intended function, however, remains quite opaque; the audience knows that some speakers have no hidden agenda while others are using *parbachan* as a political performance. In the latter case there is no explicit formulation, e.g., 'I'm going to talk about my enemies', but speakers provide cues that, in Albert's phrase, 'something is in the wind' (1972).

Chief among these cues are coy references. Other cues include references to such topics as anger, jealousy and contention. These themes do not necessarily signal political intent, but they usually pique the audience's suspicions. A speaker's skill in introducing such cues depends upon two factors. First, speakers should be able to develop their topics; a repertoire of relevant proverbs, scriptural quotations and legendary examples is an important asset for such amplification. Second, skillful orators provide a verbal context in which such topics fit naturally. The entire text should make internal sense without reference to an outside context. Good speakers are both knowledgeable and unobtrusive; an overly brief and apparently irrelevant reference to animosity or moral failings would not be effective.

The lack of explicit formulation in politically motivated *parbachan* is linked to speakers' fears of retribution and public censure for overstepping the limits of the genre. It also reflects the greater familiarity of coreligionists with each others' affairs. Even so, members of the audience will have differential access to the social knowledge necessary to interpret the speeches; some will be fully aware of what is going on while others may be in the dark.

This differential knowledge is an important resource for the effectiveness of allusion as a rhetorical device. *Parbachan* play constantly upon the theme of membership criteria – what one must do to be a 'real' member of the *mandali*. Members are concerned about their acceptance as *samajis* or *sanatanis*; the *mandali* is an important reference group in the fluid social structure of

Bhatgaon. The audience feels that it should be able to uncover speakers' motives, to unravel their allusions and to interpret the social as well as the literal meanings of their performances. Audience members have an investment in the interpretation of intra*mandali* events; the failure to understand suggests less than full participation. Skillful speakers imply that explicit formulation is unnecessary, as members should comprehend their purposes. If a listener is uninformed, he is sure to try to gain the necessary knowledge as rapidly as possible. Speakers can thus, through allusion, compel the audience's interest and involvement. In Bhatgaon, where the recruitment of third-party participation is an important political goal, successful allusion is indeed consequential.

Unconventional Performances

The preceding sections have outlined some of the salient characteristics of the two genres. These features provide limits and guidelines for performers, and they enable the audience to anticipate the course of a performance. A good performer fulfills the conventional expectations of his audience with perhaps a novel image or clever allusion thrown in. The two most memorable and effective speeches during my fieldwork, however, did not follow the canonic specifications of *parbachan*.

The first speech violated the content conventions. Usually the message section of a *parbachan* presents, in Bailey's term, an 'ideology' (1969). The speaker began with an appropriately ideological theme but shifted to a 'plan' (Bailey 1969), a straightforward series of suggestions for accomplishing a cooperative *mandali* project. Plans are out of place in *parbachan*, but the speaker introduced his suggestions so effectively that *mandali* members carried them out during the following weeks. Villagers also asked to listen to my recording of the speech, as they felt it was a particularly fine example of oratory, even though it broke the rules.

The other performance was unconventional in both style and format. The speaker used *jangli bat* rather than formal Hindi. More strikingly, he assumed the roles of both speaker and audience. Audience appreciation of performances other than speeches is often shown by shouts of *wavai* or *wa*; the speaker consciously interspersed *wavais* throughout his performance, in effect congratulating himself, a gross departure from conventional behavior. Instead of taking offense, however, the audience enjoyed it greatly and acted upon the ideas suggested in his speech.

The successful and unconventional performances suggest a more radical strategy for speechmaking. Rather than staying within the limits of appropriate performance, one can break the rules, carefully gauging the audience and how much they will tolerate.[9] This is obviously a high-risk strategy as a miscalculated attempt may lead to ridicule. Both speakers were *baḍa admi* ('big men') with considerable social credit; I do not think, however, that such status is a necessary prerequisite for rule-breaking, although it may diminish the risks. More important are the internal coherence and consistency of the performance. Violations must not appear to be mistakes. They should be considered deliberate features of the speech and must be carried out with aplomb and without embarrassment. Although violating the conventions of *parbachan*, the first speaker's plan was topically congruent with his earlier ideological theme, which focussed on the need for *mandali* participation; coherence was maintained. In the latter example, the use of *jangli bat* and self-congratulation was maintained throughout the performance. Such consistent and painstaking rule-breaking focussed audience attention upon the message itself and upon the speaker's artistry.[10]

Havranek has defined foregrounding as the 'use of the devices of the language in such a way that this use itself attracts attention and is perceived as uncommon' (1964:10). Mukarovsky further argued that 'foregrounding means the violation of the scheme' (1964:19). These speakers foregrounded their performances; they flaunted their skill in the genre by flouting its conventions. Through their creative rule-breaking, they also marked their speeches as special; such salience compelled audience interest in their messages and attention to their underlying goals.

NOTES

1 Different aspects of challenge songs are analyzed in Brenneis and Padarath (1975).

2 These data represent the situation in early 1972.

3 Wynne Furth, who also conducted research in Bhatgaon, has noted that women carry out considerable public politicking through discussions with other women at weddings and similar events; men are not privy to such performances, as they sit separately.

4 A fuller discussion of the development of egalitarianism in Bhatgaon may be found in Brenneis (1977b).

5 I am indebted to Ray Petersen for suggesting the relevance of this distinction.

6 I am thankful to Ronald Macaulay for coining the phrase. Coy references appear to be socially if not linguistically analogous to 'whimperatives' (Sadock 1969) in English, as both are usually employed in ambiguous situations in which personal offense is undesirable.

7 *Samaji*s are members of the *Arya Samaj; sanatani*s belong to the orthodox *Sanatan Dharam*.

8 In their study of junior college counselors, Erickson & Schultz (1973) found that counselors used explicit formulation far more frequently with students with whom they felt they had little in common – the more apparent shared experience, the less frequently 'what we are doing' was explained. In Bhatgaon explicit formulation is usual in challenge songs, where personnel are by definition members of different religious associations.

9 An analogous instance of successful rule-breaking is discussed by Salmond (1974).

10 Message is used here in the sense suggested by Jakobson (1960), who argues that a focus on message is linked to the poetic functions of language; in this instance, the performance has both poetic and conative implications.

REFERENCES

Albert, E.M. (1972). Cultural patterning of speech behavior in Burundi. In J. J. Gumperz & D. Hymes (eds.), *Directions in sociolinguistics: the ethnography of communication*. New York: Holt, Rinehart & Winston. 72–105.

Bailey, F.G. (1969). Political statements. *Contributions to Indian Sociology*. (New Series) 3. 1–16.

Bloch, M. (1975). Introduction. In M. Bloch (ed.), *Political language and oratory in traditional society*. New York: Academic Press. 1–28.

Brenneis, D. (1974). Conflict and communication in a Fiji Indian community. (Unpublished PhD dissertation, Harvard).

Brenneis, D. (1977a). Strategies of offense choice: malice and mischief in Bhatgaon. MSS.

Brenneis, D. (1977b). Conflict in Bhatgaon: the search for a third party. MSS.

Brenneis, D. & Padarath, R. (1975). 'About those scoundrels I'll let everyone know': challenge singing in a Fiji Indian community, *JAF* 88 (349). 283–91.

Burke, K. (1950). *A rhetoric of motives*. Berkeley: University of California Press.

Dundes, A. (1964). Texture, text and context, *SFQ* 28(4). 251–65.

Erickson, F. & Schultz, J. (1973). Talking to an 'us' or a 'them': differences in performing the speech function 'formulation' in school counseling interviews. Paper presented at the Annual Meeting of the American Anthropological Association, New Orleans.

Frake, C. O. (1963). Litigation in Lipay: a study in Subanun law. In *Proceedings of the Ninth Pacific Science Congress. Bangkok*. Vol. 3. 217–22.

Havranek, B. (1964). The functional differentiation of the standard language. In P. L. Garvin (ed. and trans.), *A Prague school reader on esthetics, literary structure, and style*. Washington: Georgetown University Press. 3–16.

Irvine, J.T. (1975). Wolof speech styles and social status. Austin: *Working papers in sociolinguistics No. 23*.

Jakobson, R. (1960) Linguistics and poetics. In T. Sebeok (ed.), *Style in language*. Cambridge: MIT Press. 350–77.

Mukarovsky, J. (1964). Standard language and poetic language. In P.L. Garvin (ed. and trans.), *A Prague school reader on esthetics, literary structure, and style*. Washington: Georgetown University Press. 17–30.

Rosaldo, M.Z. (1973). I have nothing to hide: the language of Ilongot oratory, *LinS* 2 193–223.

Sacks, H. (1972). An initial investigation of the usability of conversational data for doing sociology. In D. Sudnow (ed.), *Studies in social interaction*. New York: Free Press. 31–74.

Sacks, H., Schegloff, E. & Jefferson, G. (1974). A simplest systematics for the organization of turn-taking for conversation, *Lg*. 50(4). 696–735.

Sadock, J. (1969). Whimperatives. In J. Sadock & A. Vanek (eds.), *Studies presented to Robert B. Lees by his students*. Edmonton: Linguistic Research Inc. 223–38.

Salmond, A. (1974). Rituals of encounter among the Maori: sociolinguistic study of a scene. In R. Bauman & J. Sherzer (ed.), *Explorations in the ethnography of speaking*. Cambridge: Cambridge University Press. 192–212.

15

Celebrating Cricket:
The Symbolic Construction of
Caribbean Politics

Frank E. Manning

Cricket has suffered, but not only cricket. The aestheticians have scorned to take notice of popular sports and games – to their own detriment. The aridity and confusion of which they so mournfully complain will continue until they include organized games and the people who watch them as an integral part of their data.

(C. L. R. James 1963:191–192; emphasis in original)

The failure of art critics to appreciate the aesthetics of popular sport has been no less myopic than the failure of anthropologists to grasp its social importance. Although folklorists and protoethnologists of the previous century showed an interest in games – much of it inspired by E. B. Tylor's evolutionary and diffusionist speculations – the anthropology of play did not advance appreciably until the late 1950s (Schwartzman 1978:5). A great deal of the recent attention, however, has been directed at either children's play or at relatively small-scale games – a corpus pioneered by the early collaborative studies of Roberts and Sutton-Smith (1962, 1966). A significant literature on mass ludic spectacles such as popular sports events and public celebrations is only now emerging, much of it inspired by the interest of Gluckman and Turner in "secular ritual" (Moore and Myerhoff 1977) and by Geertz's (1972) paper on the Balinese cockfight.

The seminal work of these latter figures converges on a conceptual approach to the relationship between symbolic and social phenomena. For Turner (1977), "liminoid" performative genres such as festivals and carnivals are "proto-" or "metastructural," generating cultural comprehension by abstracting and recombining – often in novel, metaphorical ways – a social structure's basic principles. For Gluckman (see Gluckman and Gluckman 1977),

Frank E. Manning, "Celebrating Cricket: The Symbolic Construction of Caribbean Politics," pp. 616–632 from *American Ethnologist* 8(3), 1981.

whose views were articulated in the last article published before his death, symbolic events such as sports attractions and theatrical productions differ from traditional religious rites in being an imaginative "presentation" of society rather than a "re-presentation" or copy of it. For Geertz (1972), the cockfight is a fictive story about its social context, a "metasocial commentary" on it that is analogous to a literary text in using the devices of aesthetic license to disarrange conventional semantic contexts and rearrange them in unconventional ways. Geertz also underscores a point that is less forcefully made by Gluckman and Turner: that symbolic forms are not only a reflexive interpretation of social life, but also a means through which people discover and learn their culture. The lesson for anthropology is that symbolic inquiry, besides laying bare a social system, can also tell us a great deal about the epistemological processes whereby that system is revealed to those whose lives it shapes.

Drawing from these positions, as well as other perspectives that have thrown light on public play and mass performance, this paper examines Bermudian cricket festivals. I focus on the social history of these festivals, on the manner in which they are celebrated, and on a highly significant side activity, gambling. My contention is that the total genre dramatizes a fundamental, racially oriented conflict between cultural identity and economic interest – a conflict that is generalizable to the Caribbean (and perhaps other decolonizing areas) and that underlies the region's political situation. Consistent with Cohen's (1979:87) observation that anthropology's chief contribution to the study of politics has been the analysis of nonpolitical symbols that have political implications and functions, I propose that celebration can provide a unique understanding of the conceptual parameters in which political awareness is developed and expressed.

Blacks in Whites

In the West Indies the game of cricket is played with elegant skill, studied with scholarly intensity, argued with passionate conviction, and revered with patriotic pride. Young boys with makeshift bats and balls play spiritedly in yards, fields, and beaches, learning the skills that in the past century have made West Indians among the world's outstanding cricketers. Organized competition begins in school and continues – often through middle age – in amateur sports clubs. Island-wide teams drawn from the clubs provide the Caribbean's premier sports attraction when they play annually in a touring series known as the Shell Shield. There is also a pan-West Indian team that represents the region in "test" (international) matches and that has been the outstanding exception to a catalog of failed attempts at West Indian unification.

One gleans the historical significance of the game in *Beyond a Boundary*, C. L. R. James's (1963) autobiography cum cricket analysis. A Trinidadian journalist, teacher, historian, political critic, and, above all, cricket devotee, James contends that in the West Indies cricket was traditionally seen as embodying the qualities of the classic British character ideal: fair play, restraint, perseverance, responsibility, and the moral inflections of Victorian Puritanism. Paradoxically, Afro-West Indians were taught to esteem those standards but were denied the means of achieving and demonstrating them. Cricket organizations – clubs, leagues, selection committees, governing bodies – conformed to the wider system of color-class stratification, and when the races occasionally played together, it was customary for whites to bat and blacks to bowl (St. Pierre 1973:7–12).

The phrase "put on your whites" is instructive. Literally, it means to don the several items – white or cream-colored – that make up a cricket uniform: shoes, pants, shirt, sweater, protective gloves, knee pads. Figuratively, it is a metonym of the black struggle in cricket, itself a metonym as well as an instrument of the more general black struggle under British colonialism. In cricket there were a succession of black goals: to get to bat, to gain places on island-wide teams and regional tours, and, as recently as the 1960s, to be named vice-captains and captains of test teams, positions reserved for whites even after racial criteria had been virtually eliminated from selection procedures. Cricket successes brought recognition to Afro-West Indians both internationally and, more begrudgingly, in the upper strata of local society, gradually transforming the sport into a powerful symbol of black ability, achievement, and aspiration.

Bermudian cricket is a variation on these themes, but one that, like Bermuda itself, caricatures and often strikingly illuminates the Caribbean pattern. Lying a thousand miles and a climatic zone north of the West Indies, Bermuda has a five-month summer cricket season and therefore does not participate in most major West Indian tournaments, which are held during the winter. Nor do Bermudians take the game as seriously or as professionally as West Indians do. In the Caribbean, for example, festival games – occasions when a cricket match takes place in a setting of festive sociability – are relatively informal, localized, and of little general interest (James 1963:20–21).[1] In Bermuda, however, festival games are both the highlights of the cricket season and, aside from Christmas, the calendar's most significant holidays. Bermudian festival cricket is the counterpart of Caribbean carnivals, but it enriches the spirit of celebration with the drama of a popular sporting classic.

The racial division of Bermudian cricket was shaped by an apartheid-like form of segregation, rather than by the West Indian system of color-class stratification. Introduced by British military personnel in the 19th century, the game was originally played in white sporting clubs. Blacks responded by forming neighborhood cricket clubs that have since evolved into the country's major centers of sport, entertainment, and sociability (Manning 1973). Through the clubs, blacks gained unquestioned superiority in cricket; when racial integration was nominally introduced in the 1960s, whites virtually withdrew from the game.

Two of the oldest black clubs, Somerset and St. George's, were begun primarily to promote an informal cricket contest held each August 1st in commemoration of the 1834 emancipation of slaves in British territories – an occasion marked by varied festivities throughout the Commonwealth Caribbean. Under club sponsorship the event developed into Cup Match, the oldest and most prominent cricket festival. Now held on the Thursday and Friday closest to August 1st, the game's historical identification with blacks is maintained by the white practice of observing the first day of Cup Match as Somers's Day, named after the British Admiral Sir George Somers who discovered Bermuda in 1609.

Besides Cup Match there are the Eastern, Western, and Central County Games, each involving four clubs in a series of three matches staggered between June and September. As these series progress there is a buildup of festivity and sporting interest, so that the final games – in effect, sequels to Cup Match – are like Cup Match as occasions of mass celebration. In white society the County Games are paralleled by summer yachting competitions, notably the renowned Newport-Bermuda race. Nowhere in the Caribbean is there a more striking example of the pluralistic segmentation that Smith (1965) attributed to British West Indian societies.

While Cup Match commemorates emancipation from slavery, the County Games celebrate diffuse aspects of the black tradition and life-style. The Eastern and Western series, the two most popular, reflect variants in the black situation that figure in the deeper-level meaning of festival cricket. Begun in 1904, the Eastern Games involve clubs that draw from old, demographically stable neighborhoods. In each neighborhood there is a core of black extended families, typically small property owners deriving modest incomes from family stores, trades, service jobs, and, in earlier generations more than now, part-time farming and fishing. The principle of family-neighborhood integrity is the basis of Eastern County selection rules. Eligibility is based on having been born in the club's neighborhood – the usual and preferred criterion – or having been a resident of it for at least two years. Although in a number of cases current players have moved away from their ancestral neighborhoods and play for other clubs in league games, their return for the County Games makes each club roster a roll call of familiar surnames, re-creating the networks and reviving the sentiments of traditional social organization.

The Western County Games, begun in 1962, are a product of newer social influences. The Western parishes have grown appreciably since the time when the series started, as new luxury hotels have created employment and as the demand for housing among blacks short of middle age has been met by the conversion of large estates into fashionable residential subdivisions (Newman 1972:3). Reflecting these trends, the Western Games are touted not as neighborhood rivalries, but as slick, highly competitive all-star games. Clubs vie intensely for Bermuda's best cricketers, offering lucrative incentives that lure players from outside the Western parishes and that encourage opportunistic switching between clubs from one year to the next. The clubs have even extended recruitment into the Caribbean, scouting the region for prospects and arranging their immigration. In the mid-1970s, the final game of the Western series was extended from one day to two, a move aimed at raising the caliber of play, generating wider public interest, and boosting gate receipts. The emphasis on aggressive commercialism is also seen in other areas of club activity, notably entertainment. Two of the clubs involved in the series (as well as other clubs in the Western parishes) have built elegant lounges which remain open as late as 5 a.m., offering formidable competition to the area's hotels.

Underlying the varying inflections of the Eastern and Western County Games are changes in the terms of clientage, the basis of the black Bermudian socioeconomic condition. Traditionally, Bermuda was run by a white aristocracy whose relations to blacks were paternal in both a biological and social sense. Descendants of the original 17th-century British settlers, the aristocracy were seafarers until the 1870s, agricultural exporters from then until the 1920s, and more recently an interlocking establishment of merchants, bankers, and corporate lawyers. Functioning as a ruling class in an almost feudal sense (Lewis 1968:323), they used the instruments of patronage – jobs, loans, credit, mortgages, charity – to maintain the allegiance and even the endearment of blacks, who make up three-fifths of the population, as well as a white underclass consisting of old "poor cousin" families, newer immigrants from Commonwealth countries, and Azorean Portuguese imported as indentured agricultural laborers. Patron-client relations were typically transacted within neighborhoods and parishes and between extended families, reinforcing residential identity and producing alliances between black and white kin groups that cross-cut the system of institutionalized racial segregation. The common Caribbean metaphor of island society as a single large family (Wilson 1973:47) was powerfully resonant in Bermuda, yielding a meaningful context in which patronage took the social form of a relationship between benevolent, although demanding, white patriarchs and filial black dependents.

Since the early 1960s, however, the power and prestige of the aristocracy have been substantially eroded. The tourist boom has made foreign-owned hotels the major employers and, along with the development of an offshore corporate business sector, brought to Bermuda a class of expatriate managers who wield an appreciable influence in local affairs. In addition, the buoyancy and expansion of the economy has allowed the aggressive rise of underclass whites, notably Bermuda-born Portuguese, and a handful of black professionals and entrepreneurs. Tellingly, many of the aristocracy's merchant houses on Front Street, the commercial frontispiece of Hamilton, are now dominated by whites whose rise to economic prominence has come about within the past two decades.

What these changes have done to the patronage system is alter its character and style while maintaining, and perhaps strengthening, its grip on the overwhelming majority of blacks. The benevolent paternalism of the aristocracy has been replaced by the bureaucratic orientation of the new elite, and largess has been escalated to include company directorships, investment opportunities, business partnerships, and well-paid managerial positions. Blacks enjoy the life-style provided by an affluent economy, but at the cost of remaining in a position of clientage and subordination.

"We black Bermudians," an old man cautioned, "can easily fool you. We're laughing on the outside, but crying on the inside." This commonplace statement derives its impact from oxymoron, the figure of speech that combines conceptual and emotional antitheses. Viewed as a collectively enacted "text," festival cricket is also built on oxymoron. Overtly and purposefully, these games articulate the meaning of freedom, family, community, club, and, above all, cricket itself – symbols that manifest to blacks their identity, their solidarity, their survival. But the games also reflect, implicitly but no less significantly, the field of socioeconomic relations in which blacks are dependent on a white power structure that has lost its traditional character but preserved its oppressive force. In this juxtaposition – this dramatic oxymoron – lies the basis of both the political system and the political imagination.

Food, liquor, clothing, and money

Soliciting a description of festival cricket early in my first Bermudian fieldwork, I was told it was the time "when we eat everything in Bermuda, drink everything in Bermuda, wear everything in Bermuda, and spend everything in Bermuda." Although popular interest in the game runs unusually high, festival cricket is an occasion of participation, not spectatorship. The festival ethos is one of hedonistic indulgence, gregarious sociability, histrionic exhibitionism, lavish hospitality, conspicuous consumption – behaviors that epitomize and celebrate the black Bermudian self-image. In Singer's (1955) terms, festival cricket is a cultural performance, a dramatic spectacle in which a people proclaim and demonstrate their sense of who they are.

Like Carnival, festival cricket involves a period of preparation that is considered nearly as much fun as the event itself. For weeks before Cup Match there is intense speculation about the selection of teams. Pundits offer their personal choices in letters to the editor, and the subject is heatedly discussed in bars, in buses, and on street corners. The principal centers of activity are the black clubs, where people go, in the words of one informant, "just to hear the arguments." The arguments peak a week before the game, when the club selection committees announce their picks to the membership at a meeting in which dramatic suspense, flamboyant and often fiery oratory, and uproarious entertainment combine ritualistically to induct chosen players into the club tradition. In the final days before the game there is a general buildup of festive sociability,

a flurry of shopping activity for food, liquor, and clothing, and extended expressions of team loyalty through the display of club colors on cars and items of apparel. For County Games the scenario is similar, but on a smaller scale.

Game days begin early, as fans laden with coolers, umbrellas, collapsible chairs, and briefcase-sized portable radios arrive at the grounds several hours before the first ball is bowled at 10 a.m. Locations around the periphery of the field are carefully staked out, mostly by groups of friends who have made arrangements to contribute to a common supply of food and liquor. A more enviable location is in makeshift pavilions erected at the edge of the field or on surrounding hillsides. Wooden frames covered with canvas or thatch, the pavilions bear colorful names such as "Honey Bee Lounge" and often fly flags made of liquor banners or team insignia. Organized by club-based peer groups, the pavilions accommodate 10–20 couples who pay a set fee – as much as $100[2] for the two days of Cup Match – for food, liquor, and other amenities. Most pavilions are wired to the clubhouse, enabling the use of lights, appliances, and stereos that typically have auditorium-sized electronic speakers.

In all groups there is emphasis on extravagance, sophistication, ostentation. Bottles of brand-name liquor ranging from the 40-ounce to the 1-gallon size are set out on coolers and tables, flanked by cherries, lemons, limes, angostura bitters, and more specialized garnishes and liqueurs for concoctions that gain popularity during a particular festival season (Scotch, milk, and grenadine was the favorite one year). Food is plentiful and of two kinds: the cherished "soul" dishes built around chicken, fish, and "hoppin' john" (black-eyed peas and rice); and festive specialties, notably cassava pie and a chicken and pork filling baked pastry made from shredded cassava). At the Eastern County Games one is also likely to see a number of festive seafood dishes, including mussel pie, conch stew, and hash shark. For those without enough food or liquor, there are at least 2 bars in the clubhouse and 2 or more bar concessions, along with 20 or more food concessions, on the grounds.

Liquor is a basis of hospitality patterns that link individuals and groups with the larger audience. People generously offer drinks to passing friends, whose visit is enlivened by joking, teasing, insult swapping, and other forms of verbal performance characteristic of Afro-Caribbean and Afro-American culture (Abrahams 1970; Kochman 1970). The visitor invariably extends an offer of reciprocal hospitality, creating an opportunity, and something of a social obligation, for the hosts to return the visit later in the day. In the pavilions persons are allowed to entertain two guests at a time, an informal rule that balances the importance of hospitality with a check against overcrowding.

The continuous traffic around the field is known as the "fashion show." Celebrants sport outfits acquired for the festival cricket season, occasionally handmade but more often purchased during the advertising campaigns that retail merchants mount in the weeks before Cup Match. Drawn from black American and West Indian trends, styles are valued for combining smartness with sexuality. A decade ago, for example, the style known in Bermuda as "black mod" was dominant. Women paraded in arousing "hot pants" outfits, suggestive two-piece ensembles, bell-bottom and two-tone slacks, close-fitting pants suits, wool knit skirts and jerseys, low-slung chain belts, bubble blouses, leather collars, suede fringed handbags, large round earrings, ostentatious bracelets and necklaces, pink and yellow tinted sunglasses, and "natural" coiffures. In the same period, men wore jump suits, silk shirts slit open to expose the chest, two-tone and wide-cuffed flair pants, bolero and ruffled shirts with dog-ear collars, and suede vests over the bare skin. More recent styles have been varied, ranging from "black disco" to "unisex chic." Women have adopted pleated balloon pants, terry cloth outfits, and "cornrow" coiffures elaborated with beads and braids – a style that can cost upwards of $100 in Bermudian hairdressing salons. Men have taken to West Indian styles, notably shirt-jacs, kareba suits, and among youth, Rastafarian dreadlocks. The jewelry portfolios of both sexes center on a half-dozen necklaces of various sizes and designs. Designer jean outfits are in vogue, as

are athletic shorts that are worn by women with halter tops, by men with athletic shirts, and by both sexes with inscribed T-shirts.

The popularity of T-shirts warrants special comment. The leading black dealer in the field estimates selling 1,000 to 1,500 shirts for Cup Match alone, many of them at the cricket grounds in a concession stand that he equips with his printing and dyeing machines. His most popular line is what he calls his "black" shirts – motifs about festival cricket, pan! African identity, racial solidarity, and black entertainment genres. Next in popularity, and sometimes combined with racial motifs, are sexual themes, most of them using slang double entendres for genitalia and copulation in conjunction with humorous inscriptions of invitation, challenge, and braggadocio. The manufacture of T-shirts at the game epitomizes the rapid popularization of new styles and the ready satisfaction of customer demand for them, central values in black Bermudian fashion culture.

Performative and provocative, the fashion show is closely observed by radio commentators, who mix accounts of the cricket game with animated descriptions of fashion plates. Indeed, one of the major reasons fans bring radios to the game is to hear these accounts of themselves and their fellow celebrants. Like liquor, fashion is a medium of exchange that integrates an aggregate audience into a cultural community. It is also, again like liquor, what Sapir (1934) termed a symbol of condensation: it exemplifies what it signifies, namely an ethos of affluence, hedonism, sophistication, and display. An observable result of this symbolism is that fashion evokes the black conversational mode known as "rapping," a lewd and lively exchange between men and women aimed both at entertainment and at the initiation or enhancement of sexual partnerships. Like Carnival, festival cricket has a rich lore as a period of license and sexual hyperactivity.

Other modes of performance compete with fashion for public attention. Steel, brass, and rock bands play on the sidelines, stimulating impromptu dancing. Also present are Gombey Dancers, masked mummers who render a Bermudian version of the John Canoe dance to the rhythm of drums, fifes, snares, and whistles.

High on surrounding hillsides are groups of Rastafarians, who smoke *ganja*, translate the festival ambience into poetry, and orate philosophically about a black millenium. A profane version of that millenium is enacted on adjacent waterways, where "boojee" (black bourgeois) yachtsmen display their boats and hold swank deck parties.

The cricket match concludes at 6:30 p.m., but festivities continue well into the night. The clubhouse is jammed with revellers who fraternize with the cricketers, replay and comically argue every detail of the game, and get very drunk as the evening wears on. Other fans extend their merriment onto the field and may remain there all night. Several clubs run evening events ranging from dances and parties to outdoor concerts featuring black American and Caribbean performers.

A final ancillary activity warrants separate discussion for both ethnographic and analytic purposes. That activity is gambling, which takes place during the cricket game on the periphery of the field in a large tent known as the "stock market." As festival cricket amplifies a mode of behavior that is manifest in less spectacular ways on a day-to-day basis, stock market gambling caricatures a general style of acquisition premised on calculated opportunism (Manning 1973:87–114), as well as a particular fondness for gambling that has put soccer pool agencies and off-track betting parlors among Bermuda's lucrative businesses and has, within the club milieu, given rise to regular bingo nights, organized card games, raffles, lotteries, and so on. The significance of gambling here is twofold: first, it explicitly symbolizes a relationship between culture and money that is represented more implicitly in other phases and spheres of festival cricket; second, at a deeper level, it dramatizes the culture-money relationship in a manner that qualifies and questions the meaningful thrust of the total festival. Juxtaposed to its own context, gambling illustrates the tension that pervades black political life.

The stock market

Framed with wood or tubular steel and covered with canvas or sheet plastic, the stock market is a makeshift casino for a dice game known as "crown and anchor." Played on boards set atop wooden horses, the game involves betting on one or more of six choices: the four suits of cards, a red crown, or a black anchor. Three dice are rolled, their sides corresponding to the choices on the board. Winners are paid the amount of their bet times the number of dice on which it is shown, while losers have their money taken by the board. If a croupier rolls a crown and two spades, for example, he collects the money on the four losing choices, pays those who bet on the crown, and pays double those who bet on the spade

Like cricket, crown and anchor is a game of British origin that has gained immense popularity in the Caribbean, particularly at festivals. I have personally watched it being played by Antiguans at Carnival and by Jamaican Maroons at the celebration of Captain Cudjoe's birthday in the remote moutain village of Accompong.[3] In Bermuda the game is distinguished by the amount of money that is displayed and bet. Croupiers hold thousands of dollars in their hands, and players are likely to hold several hundred. The minimum bet is one dollar, but only novices and casual players, mostly women, bet that little. Regular players tend to bet between $10 and $50 each time, although much higher bets are common. Some boards place a ceiling of $100 on bets, but the larger boards – i.e., those with bigger cash floats – generally have no ceiling. An informant lighted on the ostentatious display of cash as the chief difference between festival cricket and Christmas, the calendar's two major holidays. At Christmas, he observed, money is spent; at festival cricket, it is both spent and shown.

Crown and anchor is marked by a peculiar paradox. Although the odds marginally favor the board, regular players say that an effective strategy is to bet on choices that have not come up for two or three rolls of the dice and are therefore "due" simply by the laws of probability. A more defensive tactic, and one that is easily combined with the above, is simply to double bets on the same item until it eventually comes up and all losses, as well as the initial bet, are recouped. The only limitation is lack of ready cash, but this is minimized by the substantial sums that players carry and by the ready willingness of the boards to accept personal checks and even to loan money.

In practice, however, players tend to bet erratically and lose, often substantially. In the parlance of the stock market, they succumb to "greed" and "lose their heads" in a futile attempt to "break the board." What is potentially a game of strategy – the type associated with mastering the environment – is in effect a game of chance – the type associated with divining an uncontrollable environment (Roberts, Arth, and Bush 1959). The following example from my field notes is representative of a pattern evidenced by the stock market's "high rollers":

Placing $10 and $20 bets unsystemmatically, a man lost his own money – about $60 – as well as $50 that he borrowed from the board. He then borrowed another $50 and increased it to about $85 by winning a few small bets. He next bet $70 on the club, which came up on three dice to add $210 to his money. But although he owed the board $100, he kept playing rather than pay back the debt and quit with a net winning. Within a half hour he had lost all his money, as well as a third loan of $50. As he left the board he quietly told the croupier: "I owe you $150. I'll see you Monday morning."

The familiar experience of losing is offset by the claim that gambling money is expendable. As one man put it after losing $100, "If I have money to spend, I spend it. If I lose it, I don't give a fuck. I'll go back to work next week and get some more."

Although the overwhelming majority of bettors are black, the running of boards – the profitable side of the stock market – has been dominated by the Portuguese. In the 1930s, Manuel de Souza (a pseudonym), the teenage son of an Azorean-born farm laborer, watched crown and anchor being played in the segregated white section of the racetrack. Surmising the game's appeal to blacks, he started going to festival cricket matches with a dice cup, a small table, and a tarpaulin that he stretched between some trees to make a crude tent. De Souza's winnings put him on the road to acquiring a modest complex of businesses: a fleet of taxi cabs, several small farms, and a restaurant.

"You can say that I owe what I have to crown and anchor," he acknowledged. "It gave me my start in life."

As de Souza's business and gambling profits grew, he began running more boards in partnership with other Portuguese. In the 1960s he was challenged by the clubs, which successfully pressed the claim that the stock market should be under their control. De Souza countered with patronage, supporting club building projects and occasionally contributing a share of his winnings. In return he was given first option on buying the entire gambling concession, an arrangement that gave the clubs a substantial cash flow to stock their bars for festivals and that made de Souza something of a "czar" or, better perhaps, "godfather," of the stock market. With his partners he ran a half-dozen tables and reports that his share of their net profits averaged $30,000 per season. He made a further profit by selling the remainder of the space in the stock market, chiefly to a growing group of Portuguese who had acquired gambling reputations in private house parties.

Although de Souza and other Portuguese board operators were generally astute enough to hire black assistants, black gamblers gradually pushed the clubs for a bigger stake in the stock market, and ultimately for control of it. Their efforts have been partially successful; for several years the concession of Cup Match and the Western County Games has been sold to a syndicate of black businessmen, while in the Eastern County series one club continues to favor de Souza and the others run the stock market themselves. The change has resulted in more blacks and fewer Portuguese, although the new concession holders sell choice space (near the outside and sheltered from the afternoon sun) to the remaining Portuguese, including de Souza, who are respected in gambling circles and known to attract heavy bettors.

Yet the racial change in the stock market is less radical than it may appear. Many of the black-run boards, and a clear majority of those which have no ceiling on bets, are backed financially by whites, including Portuguese, or by racially mixed investment syndicates. The backers provide the cash float – as much as $15,000 at some boards – in return for a 40 to 60 percent share of the winnings. The parallel between the stock market and the wider economic system is frequently observed: blacks are in visible positions and appear to be making money, but whites are behind them and in control. Reflecting on the situation, one black gambler observed: "You know, come to think of it, I don't know a single black person in this country who has made money without having a white sponsor."

Another parallel between the stock market and the broader Bermudian situation is observed in connection with mid-1970s legislation requiring the host club to pay $500 for a one-day gambling permit and preventing the boards from taking bets later than one hour after the scheduled end of the cricket game. The cost of the permit has been passed on to the concession holders and, in turn, to individual board operators, while the time regulation has stopped boards from staying open to increase winnings, recoup earlier losses, or simply capitalize on late betting action – a restriction that has hurt mainly the smaller, black-run boards, which are on the inside and therefore wait longer for bettors. For blacks, these new statutes typify a pattern of reaction against black economic gain. As one black board operator put it, "When the stock market was run by the Portuguese, it was wide open. As soon as we boys started to get a little piece of the action, Government stepped in. That's the general trend in Bermuda."

Whatever the economic position of blacks in the stock market, their cultural presence there is highly visible and clearly dominant over whites – another correspondence, of course, to the larger society. The Portuguese play quietly and dress plainly, almost dourly. Their boards are about six feet long and staffed by two, or at most three, croupiers. They keep a supply of cold beer but do not offer it until a player has begun betting. They rarely socialize with bettors or other operators, viewing the gambling relationship as an exclusively economic transaction. As de Souza explained, "People don't play at my board because they like me. They play because they want to break me." The Portuguese leave unobtrusively after the game and abstain from the evening festivities. I once went looking for de Souza after an Eastern County Game and found him working

soberly in his restaurant. He said that he cleared $1,800 from his three tables – "a day's pay" – but volunteered that his lack of emotion made it impossible for most people to tell whether he had won or lost.

The image of black gamblers, by contrast, is an ideal type of the highly performative, black-oriented expressive style that Wilson (1973:227–228) terms "reputation – the ethos that pervades the entire festival. Croupiers dress and behave flamboyantly, standing on platforms to increase their visibility, spreading their bills like a fan, throwing their dice cups high in the air, handing out one dollar bills to passersby to engage them in the game, and barking stock invitations to bet: "Get some money for your honey. . . . Come in here on a bike, go home in a Rolls Royce. . . . Take your hands out of your pocket and put your money on the table. . . . Wall Street slumps, but this stock market pays double. . . ." The black tables average eight to ten feet, with sets of betting squares on each end and often with added decorations such as the signs of the zodiac. At the larger tables there may be a staff of six, typically a "house man" who shakes the dice and holds the $50 bills, two or three assistants who collect and pay the bets, and one or two others who serve as bartenders and greeters. Both liquor and beer are freely offered to onlookers as well as bettors, and when a person's drink is half empty it will be wantonly thrown on the ground and replaced with a fresh drink.

Black gamblers extend and exploit the festival's sexual license. At least two black operators have reportedly imported prostitutes, a commodity virtually absent from Bermuda, from the United States. The more common practice is to give gambling money to well-endowed women in return for their appearing at the board in plunging necklines, loosely crocheted blouses, diaphanous T-shirts, tight shorts, and similar fashions aimed at attracting – and distracting – male gamblers. As a sequel to this gimmick, a few black operators have begun hiring female croupiers and even forming gambling partnerships with women. Conversely, women have increasingly become regular and sometimes heavy bettors, a trend that is particularly noticeable in the western parishes where a good number of well-paid hotel positions are held by women. The effort to attract – and hold – women bettors enlivens the barking calls with colorful exchanges.

A middle aged woman was about to bet on heart, but withdrew the money. The operator countered: "Don't blame me if three hearts come up, lady. 'Cause you and I – I've been looking at you for a long time – I figure our hearts could get together. We don't need no crown and anchor, honey. Our hearts could really do something."

A woman was betting, and winning, on the black choices (spades, clubs, the anchor), which are all on the bottom of the board. The operator tried to persuade her to diversify her betting: "You gottago topside. No woman in the world is satisfied on the bottom side."

A woman in her early thirties had been breaking even on small bets and drinking heavily. Towards the end of the day she put a double entendre to the operator. "All I want is a piece of you." He took up the challenge and carried on a series of lewd but playful insults that drew raucous laughter from those at the table. But she got the last word: "Knobby, you wouldn't know what to do if you tripped and fell on top of me."

Black operators indicate that their gambling success depends on establishing their reputations within a broader context of public sociability. One prominent operator spends several hours per day outside the bar that he owns in partnership with another black and two whites, engaging passersby in brief conversation, waving at pedestrians on the other side of the street, and shouting at passing cars. This strategy, he explains, provides the exposure that is needed to attract people to his crown and anchor board (as well as to his bar and to a nightclub that he owns with his partners).

A modern Bermudian proverb is at this point appropriate: "Black is black and white is white, but money is green." Culturally different and socially divided, the races nonetheless come togther for a common goal: the acquisition of money. There is no better illustration of this proverb than stock market gambling, which magnifies the unique black cultural identity that is celebrated in festival cricket at the same time that it brings the races together in a staged encounter aimed at fast and easy wealth. That scenario is a dramatic rendition of what Bermudian politics, at bottom, is all about.

Festival and politics

Racial inversion underlies the dramatic form of festival cricket. Blacks dress up in "whites" to play a white game that they have transformed into a celebration of black culture. Blacks take a white gambling game and make it the setting for a hyperbolic performance of their social personality. Whites enter a black milieu and baldly demonstrate their superordinate position Such inversion exemplifies the carnivalesque, a genre in which the characteristic multiplexity of symbolic expression is extended by the tendency for symbols to be used playfully and for primarily aesthetic effect. This tendency creates what Babcock (1973) calls a "surplus of signifiers," a Rabelaisian profusion of images and condensed metaphors framed in a mode of liminality.

While the range of significance is vast, fragmented, and often highly individualized, the exegete can take clues from recurrent and centrally placed symbols. A major, meaningful thrust of festival cricket, manifest in the tradition and style of celebration, is the relation of a reflexive version of black identity to hedonism, high style, and money. Turner's (1964:29–31) contention, that dominant clusters of symbols interchange social and sensory-material themes, is appropriate. Like similar symbolic formulations in the club milieu, festival cricket contributes to the multifaceted process whereby black Bermudians are rejecting a stance of social inferiority in favor of a positive and assertive sense of self-awareness (Manning 1973:149–183).

There is also an antithetical thrust of meaning, reminding blacks of their economic subordination and dependency on whites. The reminder is implicit in the overall emphasis on fashion and indulgence, for Bermudian blacks are acutely aware, even in festival, that consumerism keeps them in clientage. In the stock market, however, the message is explicit: big money and effective power are still in white hands. Blacks can commemorate their traditions and exhibit their ethos, but they must also deal with whites, who have the odds – mathematical and psychological – in their favor. If festival cricket is viewed as a dramatic form, the black gamblers are both heroes and clowns. In the former role they glamorize a social vision of black culture, while in the latter they enact an economic relationship in which the vision is transparently irrelevant. Like the ludic inversion of racial categories, this sense of juxtaposition and self-parody is characteristic of the carnivalesque.

As a formative feature of the black Bermudian experience, the culture-economics interplay has a variety of demonstrable references. The most clear and currently paramount, however, is the system of party politics. An arena of intense interest and extraordinarily high participation, Bermudian politics bears both a striking conceptual similarity and an uncanny ethnographic correspondence to festival cricket. Let us briefly consider this double relationship.

Party politics came to Bermuda in 1963 with the formation of the Progressive Labour Party (PLP) by black groups who had previously been active in the successful universal suffrage movement.[4] In the election of that year, the party contested 9 of 36 parliamentary seats, winning 6 of them and clearly demonstrating the practical benefits of party organization. The aristocracy responded to the challenge a year later by forming the United Bermuda Party (UBP), which was initially joined by 24 of the 30 independents in the House of Assembly, all but 1 of them white. For the remainder of the decade the UBP sought to co-opt the issues pressed by the PLP, espousing, at least nominally, constitutional reform and the bread-and-butter issues of universal free education, health and welfare benefits, and the Bermudianization of the labor force. The UBP's trump card, however, was the promise of a thoroughgoing "partnership" – the term used in campaign slogans – between blacks and whites in the running of Bermuda. The partnership was demonstrated politically by strenuous efforts to recruit black candidates in the 1968 and subsequent elections, a general tactic of putting blacks in highly visible positions in both the party organization and the Cabinet; the naming of a black premier between 1971 and 1975; the appeasement of a black-dominated parliamentary "reform" group which forced the resignation of that premier's white successor in 1977; and, from the late 1970s onward, the gradual implementation of demands put forth by an internal black caucus seeking greater leverage in both the party and the national economy.

Rhetorically, the UBP presents the partnership as a guarantee of security as well as an opportunity for gain. Only through the visible demonstration of racial integration, it is claimed, can Bermuda continue to attract tourists and international companies, the sources of prosperity. The UBP couples this appeal with an emphasis on its traditional role as manager of the economy. In the 1980 election campaign, for example, Premier David Gibbons, a white who also holds the finance portfolio and whose family controls Bermuda's largest conglomerate, told an audience:

This election is not about personalities. It is about the conditions of people's lives. Day in and day out. People's jobs, income, housing. And, above all, the strength and stability of our economy, upon which all else depends.

Look to the United Bermuda Party's management of our economy. At a time when so many nations in the West are struggling and losing ground, Bermuda maintains one of the highest rates of per capita income in the world. . . . Stability, security. These are facts. And they've come to pass because of experience and prudent, efficient management.

The UBP gave its economic theme a dimension of grave urgency in a full-page newspaper advertisement published on polling day:

Today is the day when you vote . . . either to maintain Bermuda's economic growth and your own financial security and stability or . . . take a chance on the PLP. Think carefully and vote UBP.

The UBP's accommodations to black interests and its emphasis on economic security have given it an unbroken winning record at the polls, albeit by successively reduced majorities. The PLP's reaction, moderated in tone as its political position has improved, has been to emphasize its "true" blackness and therefore its legitimate and logical claim to black voter support. For the first decade of its existence, the PLP projected a posture of militant racial chauvinism, articulated through American and Caribbean "Black Power" rhetoric. In the middle 1970s, the PLP embraced the idiom of revivalist religion, a move aimed at making inroads among black church groups and, more generally, at appealing to racial consciousness implicitly rather than explicitly by stirring the powerful and pregnant association between revivalism and black culture. In the 1980 campaign, the PLP balanced the emphasis on religion with a more secular appeal to racial identity. The campaign slogan was "Xpress yourself," a black Bermudian colloquialism borrowed jointly from American soul music and Jamaican reggae lyrics and combining an allusion to the marking of a ballot paper with a slang encouragement for self-assertion. One television commercial showed a group of blacks, dancing funky style, while a singer chanted "express yourself" and an announcer extolled the merits of the PLP.

Whatever their stated differences on issues – and these have converged considerably in recent years as both parties have sought a center ground – the essential partisan distinction is racial. Recent surveys indicate that whites vote almost unanimously for the UBP, and that four-fifths of the black votes go to the PLP – a division that crosscuts and overrides class, age, sex, ideological disposition, and other pertinent social factors (Manning 1978a:199–209). The choice for blacks remains what it has always been: cultural attachment or economic security, loyalty and commitment to blacks, or strategic alignment with whites.

The distinction between the parties is manifest ethnographically in the festival setting. Hodgson (1967:311), a black Bermudian historian and PLP polemicist, describes Cup Match as "the one and only true symbol and celebration of the black man's emancipation." Her enthusiasm, however, is offset by a

skepticism that blacks will forsake such symbols in order to participate in white festivities that have now dropped the color barrier. This concern, while lacking empirical foundation, has prompted PLP politicians to present a high profile at cricket festivals, making the general environment one in which PLP supporters are familiar and welcome and UBP supporters are somewhat isolated and uncomfortable. The festival's partisan association is extended by the PLP's considerable efforts to court the club constituency (Manning 1973:210–249), a tactic exemplified by party leader Lois Browne-Evans's speech at a club dinner in 1978.

Your long and illustrious history . . . needs to be told. Essays ought to be held for your children to write what they think Daddy's club is all about . . . .

Let not economic strangulation be the cause of your enslavement. For I am convinced that you have a part to play in the Bermuda of the future, just as your forbears played a vital role in the Bermuda of the past.

You must continue working until your country is free from paternalism and patronage, free from all the shackles that we know. Do not remove one form of chains for another. You must avoid the tendency to be dependent . . . .

The stock market, however, presents a striking contrast to the overall festival milieu. The black table operators, like their Portuguese counterparts and white backers, are primarily UBP supporters. The coterie is informally led by a black UBP member of the House of Assembly, who is also renowned, on a few occasions scandalously, for the organization of invitational crown and anchor parties in private homes. At least two prominent backers also hold UBP seats in Parliament, and it is widely known that several black board operators are being groomed as future UBP candidates. Talking to me on the street, one of the blacks who operates a table on which there is no betting limit explained his support for the UBP as follows: "There is not one black person in Bermuda with any money who is PLP. Not one . . . . If the [white] man looks after you, then you've got to protect him . . . ." When a

PLP member within earshot began to challenge him, the gambler yelled: "Shut the fuck up. It's niggers like you that are holding back mother-fuckers like me."

PLP activists, on the other hand, tend to eschew the stock market, or at most to congregate outside or walk through without betting. Observing the action at a crown and anchor board, one PLP politician told me with a wink: "I only watch the stock market. I never invest." This avoidance is encouraged by the PLP's oft-stated position that gambling is functionally supportive of the status quo and by its general desire to adhere, publicly at least, to the strong moral condemnation of gambling made by the black churches.

Festival cricket, then, is a metapolitical commentary. It is a carnivalesque rendition of the semantic context in which Bermudian politics is conceived, institutionalized, and transacted. Through celebration, black Bermudians dramatize – and, indeed, define and discover – a fundamental aspect of their social position and its relationship, conceptual and ethnographic, to their political options. (Logically, of course, the argument is reversible; politics could be construed as a concordance for festival cricket. From a Bermudian standpoint, however, it is politics, not festival, that requires comprehension, choice, and commitment. Festival is merely for enjoyment, and perhaps profit.)

It is here that the relationship of symbolic to social phenomena, of festival to politics, is crucial, and that the convergent positions of Turner (1977), Gluckman and Gluckman (1977), and Geertz (1972), attributing creative autonomy to ludic symbolic forms, are useful. Although festival cricket evidences myriad correspondences to the political system, it is no more a mere reflection of politics than it is a functional appendage of it. The festival version of black culture is not the ideological and instrumental type of racial awareness propounded by the PLP, but a comical caricature of the black life-style and a joyous fantasy that links racial identity to the material wealth and glamor promised by a white-dominated, consumer-oriented economy. Likewise, the festival version of biracial partnership is not the liberal and pragmatic plea for partnership advanced by the UBP, but a naked dramatization

of white control that lays bare both the crass acquisitiveness of blacks and their continuing subordination to whites, and that further plays on these meanings in a burlesque of the whole patronage system that transforms money from an object of need to one of show.

In Durkheimian terms – which are the ancestry of much symbolic theory – festival cricket is a "transfiguration" of Bermudian political society (cf. Nisbet 1965:74). The semantic essence of festival cricket is that it throws the realm of politics into relief by disassembling its parts and reordering them in patterns consistent with the aesthetics of celebration, fun, and performance. Festival cricket *reveals* politics in the way that only an extended metaphor can – by creatively connecting disparate realms of experience in a manner that highlights the definitive features (in this case, the interplay of cultural identity and economic interest) on which the connection is predicated. To borrow Bateson's (1972:177–193) classic model of cognition, festival cricket is a map for the territory of politics – not a literal, drawn-to-scale map that merely replicates its referent, but a metaphorical map, an interpretive guide, that figuratively situates its referent and conveys social knowledge about it. It is this knowledge that makes Bermudian politics a comprehensible phenomenon.

Conclusion

Like any venture into the analysis of symbolic forms as texts, the interpretation offered here rests ultimately on the anthropologist, who "strains to read over the shoulders of those to whom they [the texts] properly belong" (Geertz 1972:29). In part, the validity and value of such an interpretation depends on whether it can be generalized, as a theoretical construct and heuristic device, to other cultures. Limitations of space and scope make it impractical to address that consideration here, but a few condensed examples from the West Indies may suggest the basis of a comparative approach.

The major festival genre of the eastern Caribbean is Carnival, which evolved in Trinidad but has diffused throughout the Windward and Leeward islands with minor changes in format.[5] Like Bermuda's Cup Match, the historical referent of Carnival, for blacks, is emancipation from slavery. The festival's major performative symbols – from the canboulay parade, ritualized stickfighting, and gang warfare in earlier times, to calypso and steel bands in recent generations – make it unequivocally black. Naipaul (1973:364), one of the Caribbean's leading literary figures, describes Carnival as "a version of the lunacy that kept the slave alive . . . the original dream of black power, style, and prettiness . . . a vision of the black millenium." Calypsonians put it more simply, toasting Carnival as the "Creole bacchanal."

But the blackness of the Carnival ethos is confronted by a strong nonblack influence in the festival's economic organization. East Indian, Chinese, and Lebanese bandleaders predominate, as do white and mulatto choreographers, and, of course, the government-controlled Carnival Development Committee – all of these groups striving, rather successfully in recent years, to make the event an international tourist attraction. Celebrants are exposed to the poignant contrast between the revelry of "jump-up" on the streets and the ribaldry of the calypso tent, on the one hand, and a variety of scenarios that demonstrate the racially based socioeconomic class system, on the other hand: the judges' stand, the paid grandstand, the commercial nightclub scene, the maze of bureaucratic rules imposed by organizers and censors, and the presence of local elites, and even metropolitan tourists, in the privileged sections of masquerade bands.

Jamaica lacks a Carnival tradition but has the entertainment idiom of reggae music, a symbol system replete with religious and political significance (Barrett 1977; de Albuquerque 1979). One of the best indigenous artistic commentaries on the reggae milieu is Perry Henzell's (1973) film *The Harder They Come*. Its protagonist is a country boy who comes to Kingston to learn the fast side of Jamaican life. The voyage of discovery is twofold. He becomes a reggae star and a "rudie" (rude boy), mastering expressive styles that are quintessentially black, often in a militant, even revolutionary sense. But he also learns that the

music industry is controlled by Chinese, mulattoes, and other groups deemed white from the black cultural viewpoint, and that the authorities – police, government, and international economic interests – are geared to crushing the challenge that he represents. Ultimately, he is shot down by their guns.

Are such symbolic forms a metacommentary on West Indian politics? Correspondences are harder to draw than in the Bermudian case, partly because, in the Caribbean, race is a figurative more than a phenotypical category. Virtually all local political actors are generically black, and whiteness is associated less with a visible local elite than with the abstractions of foreign ownership and imperial influence. In short, a racial analysis is a more complex and problematic task in the West Indies than it is in Bermuda.

Still, it is notable that, ever since the "Black Power" wave of the early 1970s, the most dynamic and ideologically intense political conflict in most of the West Indies has come from the challenge made to established political parties by radical movements, most of them extraparliamentary. These radical movements revive indigenous linguistic terms (Morris 1973), stress cultural affinity and social solidarity with Africa, and associate themselves with Afro-Caribbean religions, notably Rastafarianism, which has spread from Jamaica throughout the Caribbean and has become a cultural rallying ground and pervasive symbol for revolutionary politics (de Albuquerque 1980). Contrastingly, established politicians are villified as "Afro-Saxons" (Lowenthal 1972:278), imitators of white values who court foreign investment, sell out to multinational corporations, embrace the image promoted by mass tourism, and compact unholy alliances with metropolitan countries.

A litany of citations from academic, popular, and polemical literature could be introduced here, most of them familiar (and indeed, redundant), to scholars of the Caribbean. For present purposes, however, it is better to make two broad and general assertions. First, economic interest and cultural identity are often perceived in the West Indies as conflicting concerns. Second, the conflict is focused in racial symbolism, dramatized in festivity and other artistic productions, and current to political discourse. If these assertions are granted, they suggest an agenda aimed at integrating symbolic and political analyses of Caribbean societies, and perhaps of other areas that have undergone comparable historical experiences. The discussion of Bermudian cricket festivals offered here shows one direction in which such an agenda can proceed.

NOTES

1 I know of no other written sources on West Indian festival cricket, but am informed by a Jamaican student that "bush cricket" in Jamaica has the same general characteristics as James's example from Trinidad.
2 The Bermuda dollar is at parity with the US dollar [as at 1981].
3 I am told by Jeanne Cannizzo (1979: personal communication) that a version of crown and anchor is played at festivals in Sierra Leone. I have also seen it played at a number of fairs and amusement exhibitions in Canada, usually in booths where a wheel is spun, rather than dice thrown, to determine winning bets.
4 For a fuller discussion of Bermuda's recent political history, see Hodgson (1967), Manning (1973, 1978a), and Ryan (1973).
5 The most accessible general overviews of the Trinidad Carnival are those of Hill (1972) and Pearse (1956). Literature on other Caribbean Carnivals includes Abrahams (1970) on Tobago, Abrahams and Bauman (1978) on St. Vincent, Crowley (1956) on St. Lucia, and Manning (1978b) on Antigua.

REFERENCES

Abrahams, Roger. 1970. Patterns of Performance in the British West Indies. In *Afro-American Anthropology: Contemporary Perspectives.* Norman E. Whitten, Jr. and John Szwed, eds. pp 163–179. New York: Free Press.

Abrahams, Roger, and Richard Bauman. 1978. Ranges of Festival Behavior. In *The Reversible World: Symbolic Inversion in Art and Society.* Barbara Babcock, ed. pp. 193–208. Ithaca: Cornell University Press.

Babcock, Barbara. 1973. The Carnivalization of the Novel and the High Spirituality of Dressing Up. Paper presented at Burg Wartenstein Symposium No. 59, Ritual: Reconciliation in Change. Gloggnitz, Austria.

Barrett, Leonard. 1977. *The Rastafarians. Sounds of Cultural Dissonance.* Boston: Beacon Press

Bateson, Gregory. 1972. *Steps to an Ecology of Mind.* New York: Ballantine

Cohen, Abner. 1979. Political Symbolism. *Annual Review of Anthropology* 8: 87–113

Crowley, Daniel. 1956. Festivals of the Calendar in St. Lucia. *Caribbean Quarterly* 4: 99–121.

de Albuquerque, Klaus. 1979. The Future of the Rastafarian Movement. *Caribbean Review* 8 (4): 22–25, 44–46.

de Albuquerque, Klaus. 1980. Rastafarianism and Cultural Identity in the Caribbean. Paper presented at the Caribbean Studies Association meeting, Willemstad, Curacao.

Geertz, Clifford. 1972. Deep Play: Notes on the Balinese Cockfight. *Daedalus* 101(1): 1–38.

Gluckman, Max, and Mary Gluckman. 1977. On Drama, and Games, and Athletic Contests. In *Secular Ritual.* Sally F. Moore and Barbara Myerhoff, eds. pp. 227–243. Assen/Amsterdam: Van Gorcum.

Henzell, Perry. 1973. *The Harder They Come.* Kingston, Jamaica: New World Films.

Hill, Errol. 1972. *The Trinidad Carnival: Mandate for a National Theatre.* Austin: University of Texas Press.

Hodgson, Eva. 1967. *Second-Class Citizens, First-Class Men.* Hamilton, Bermuda: Published by the author.

James, C.L.R. 1963. *Beyond a Boundary.* London: Hutchinson

Kochman, Thomas. 1970. Toward an Ethnography of Black American Speech Behavior. In *Afro-American Anthropology: Contemporary Perspectives.* Norman E. Whitten, Jr. and John Szwed, eds. pp. 145–162. New York: Free Press.

Lewis, Gordon. 1968. *The Growth of the Modern West Indies.* New York: Monthly Review Press.

Lowenthal, David. 1972. *West Indian Societies.* New York: Oxford University Press.

Manning, Frank. 1973. *Black Clubs in Bermuda: Ethnography of a Play World.* Ithaca: Cornell University Press.

Manning, Frank. 1978a. *Bermudian Politics in Transition: Race, Voting, and Public Opinion.* Hamilton, Bermuda: Island Press.

Manning, Frank. 1978b. Carnival in Antigua: An Indigenous Festival in a Tourist Economy. *Anthropos* 73: 191–204.

Moore, Sally F., and Barbara Myerhoff. 1977. *Secular Ritual*. Assen/Amsterdam: Van Gorcum.

Morris, Desmond. 1973. On Afro-West Indian Thinking. In *The Aftermath of Sovereignty: West Indian Perspectives*. David Lowenthal and Lambros Comitas, eds. pp. 277–282 Garden City, NY: Doubleday Anchor.

Naipaul, V. S.. 1973. Power to the Caribbean People. In *The Aftermath of Sovereignty: West Indian Perspectives*. David Lowenthal and Lambros Comitas, eds. pp. 363–371. Garden City, NY: Doubleday Anchor.

Newman, Dorothy. 1972. *The Population Dynamics of Bermuda*. Hamilton, Bermuda: Bermuda Government, Depart- ment of Statistics.

Nisbet, Robert. 1965. *Emile Durkheim*. Englewood Cliffs, NJ: Prentice-Hall.

Pearse, Andrew. 1956. Carnival in Nineteenth Century Trinidad. *Caribbean Quarterly* 4: 176–193.

Roberts, John, Malcolm Arth, and Robert Bush. 1959. Games in Culture. *American Anthropologist* 61: 597–605.

Roberts, John, and Brian Sutton-Smith. 1962. Child Training and Game Involvement. *Ethnology* 2: 166–185.

Roberts, John, and Brian Sutton-Smith. 1966. Cross-Cultural Correlates of Games of Chance. *Behavior Science Notes* 1: 131–144.

Ryan, Selwyn. 1973. Politics in an Artificial Society: The Case of Bermuda. In *Ethnicity in the Americas*. Frances Henry, ed. pp. 159–192. The Hague: Mouton.

St. Pierre, Maurice. 1973. West Indian Cricket. A Sociohistorical Appraisal. *Caribbean Quarterly* 19: 7–27.

Sapir, Edward. 1934. Symbolism. *Encyclopaedia of the Social Sciences* 14: 492–495.

Schwartzman, Helen. 1978. *Transformations: The Anthropology of Children's Play*. New York: Plenum Press.

Singer, Milton. 1955. The Cultural Pattern of Indian Civilization. *Far Eastern Quarterly* 15: 23–36.

Smith, Michael G.. 1965. *The Plural Society in the British West Indies*. Berkeley: University of California Press.

Turner, Victor. 1964. Symbols in Ndembu Ritual. In *Closed Systems and Open Minds. The Limits of Naivety in Social Anthropology*. Max Gluckman, ed. pp. 20–51. Chicago: Aldine.

Turner, Victor. 1977. Variations on a Theme of Liminality. In *Secular Ritual*. Sally F. Moore and Barbara Myerhoff, eds. pp. 36–52. Assen/Amsterdam: Van Gorcum.

Wilson, Peter. 1973. *Crab Antics: The Social Anthropology of English-Speaking Negro Societies of the Caribbean*. New Haven: Yale University Press.

16

Performing the Nation: China's Children as Little Red Pioneers

T.E. Woronov

As the International Children's Day holiday approached at the end of May in 2001, excitement was building at the Pine Street Elementary School, a small, working-class school of around 350 students in northwestern Beijing.[1] That year, the sixty first-graders at Pine Street had been selected to participate in a ceremony at Tiananmen Square, where, along with several thousand other children, their induction into the Little Red Pioneers – the Chinese Communist Party's formal organization for children aged 7 to 13 – would be broadcast to the entire nation via the national state-owned television network.

Since the 1950s, China has celebrated International Children's Day on June 1st as a day of games, songs, and presentations at school, and special treats at home. And since the beginning of the reform era, roughly the early 1980s, June 1st has also been designated for holding the ceremonies to induct the nation's first-graders into the Little Red Pioneers. Because 2001

marked the 50th anniversary of the Pioneer organization, Ministry of Education officials decided to note the occasion by televising a mass induction of first-graders at Tiananmen Square, something that had never been attempted before. Being chosen to participate in the celebrations was considered quite an honor by the Pine Street School teachers and their students, and with much excitement plans were made to have the children dressed in their school uniforms and on buses before dawn, so that they would be lined up on Tiananmen in time for the early morning ceremony.

On the evening of June 1st, International Children's Day, I rushed home to watch the broadcast of that morning's ceremonies. But neither the national nor local news had coverage of the Tiananmen ceremonies, nor did the special children's variety shows later in the evening. Frantically flipping stations, I found some coverage of Children's Day festivities elsewhere in China, but nothing from Beijing.

T.E. Woronov, "Performing the Nation: China's Children as Little Red Pioneers," pp. 647–672 from *Anthropological Quarterly* 80(3) 2007.

Astonished that the children's induction, which they had been looking forward to for weeks, did not make it on to television, the following Monday morning I went looking for Teacher Li, one of Pine Street School's first-grade teachers, to find out what happened.

"Oh, what a mess," she sighed. "I was so exhausted it took me all weekend to recover." According to her description, it took several hours to get the thousands of first-graders[2] lined up across Tiananmen Square; by then it was mid-morning and the temperature was already above 90 degrees Farenheit.

Teacher Li said:

"The television producers wanted all the children to look and act alike, but the kids weren't disciplined enough. They were supposed to all be standing, but one would get tired and sit down and then everyone around them would sit down too. And they weren't supposed to wear their school hats, but it was so hot that some did to protect their heads from the sun, but then they didn't all look alike."

"So the TV cameras didn't film anything at all?" I asked.

"Oh, they tried. But Communist Party officials made speeches for hours. The children were really bored, and the cameras couldn't get reaction shots when the kids weren't either yawning or talking or crying. So the television people ended up not using anything they filmed. They were pretty pissed off (*fannao le*)."

She then added: "After the speeches the people in charge decided to take all the children through Chairman Mao Memorial Hall.[3] Can you imagine how long it took to line up 10,000 seven-year-old kids to go through one building?"

Teacher Li then took me to her classroom so that I could talk with her first-graders directly about their experience. When I asked how they felt about entering the Pioneers, one said:

"I was so excited about entering the Pioneers and going to Tiananmen, I woke my parents that morning at 4:00 a.m."

Others reminded me that although they were happy and excited, once they were lined up on Tiananmen Square, it was all very difficult (*tebie nanshou*). None of the children were allowed to drink any water (because there are no bathrooms available on the Square); as a result, they were hot, thirsty, and even a little dizzy.

"I wanted to cry," said one child, "but I tried not to."

"Well," another admitted, "I did cry. I was really hot and thirsty."

"So," Teacher Li asked, "did any of you regret going?"

"NO!" was the resounding response. They clamored to tell me: "Entering the Pioneers is an honor! Once we took the pledge to enter the Pioneers I forgot about how hot and thirsty I was!"

"What did you think of Chairman Mao's Memorial?" Li then asked.

Most of the children agreed: "It was great." Why? "Because it was out of the sun." Teacher Li had to think about that for a minute; it was not the answer she was looking for, but she obviously silently agreed with them.

"But how did you feel about seeing Chairman Mao?" I asked.

"It was a little scary," one child said.

"Why?" I asked, wondering what she might have learned about Mao to make him a frightening figure. In response, she gave me an exasperated, "adults-ask-such-stupid-questions" look.

"Because," she said, rolling her eyes, "he's *dead*."

Yet others were particularly honored by the opportunity, because, they told me, Chairman Mao had "kicked the butts" of the Japanese devils (*ta da le Riben guizi*) during the anti-Japanese war; to demonstrate, several children jumped out of their seats and gleefully showed me moves copied from Hong Kong kungfu movies. Here Teacher Li rolled her eyes, sighed deeply, and intervened:

"Boys and girls, Chairman Mao founded the New China. He led our Liberation Army to defeat the Japanese and the imperialists. Your grandparents will never forget this and will always love him."

The children, somewhat chastised, agreed.

"It was a great honor to see him," one child responded. "And my parents said they were very proud of me, even if they couldn't see me on TV."

This story seems to describe an anomaly wrapped in an anachronism: a state spectacle never seen by the public, conducted by children living in a capitalist economy who vow loyalty to communism and to the Chinese

Communist Party. This paper looks at the Little Red Pioneer system in urban China today, to argue both that the organization is *not* an anachronistic holdover from the socialist era, and that a close study of children's daily activities as Pioneers provides privileged insight into the nature of contemporary Chinese nationalism. This article argues for a performative approach to nationalism, which, I suggest, augments our understanding of the ways that children are produced as nationalist subjects, and which outlines the changing contexts for participation in the contemporary Chinese nation.

An approach based in performativity helps us understand both the presumed contradiction in this story – capitalist children vowing loyalty to the Communist Party – and the supposed "failure" of the children to perform appropriately for the television cameras. There are, of course, apparently simple answers to both of these issues: loyalty vows are required by the totalitarian state, while these children, only 7 years old, are simply too young to perform the bodily disciplines appropriately. Yet I argue that there is more to this "failed" performance than a poor match between assigned tasks and children's capabilities or that it is merely an example of the state's power to muster demonstrations in its honor; instead, this example indicates how nationalism is not (only) something that children acquire through the state-based institution of Chinese public schools (cf. Althusser 1971), but is something that they *do* through repetitive daily activities (Butler 1990; 1993). As I will discuss below, children's nationalism requires repeated performances, reiterations of an ideal that can never be entirely achieved (Butler 1993). At the same time, the norms for performances of nationalism are constantly changing in the context of China's rapid social and economic changes, rendering them impossible to achieve fully. Every reiteration of nationalism has the potential to "fail" in some way, which requires further reiterations. A close study of how children in particular are being prepared as national subjects through performativity elucidates the unattainability of the ideal, as well as the compulsion to continue reiterating the norms of nationalism during transformation.

Accounting for Natio....

Many different theories have been proposed to explain how national subjects and subjectivities are formed, including through sharing print media and the development of print capitalism (Anderson 1983), shared language (Handler 1988; Golden 2001), state-sponsored clubs and other institutions (Bowie 1997), and commemorative activities (Connerton 1989). Others have also looked more broadly at the daily life of the nation (Navaro-Yashin 2002), including the "banal nationalism" of daily practice (Billig 1995), and the politics and poetics of collective identity (Herzfeld 1997).

These works have two broad features in common. First, in spite of predictions of the end of the nation in today's globalizing world, these works agree that "rumors of the death of the nation have been greatly exaggerated" (Aretxaga 2003:393; Chalfin 2006). While some scholars have argued that the nation-state form is weakening, as borders are challenged by transnational corporations, NGOs and other transnational organizations, as well as cross-border flows of people, material, and global consumer society, the nation and nationalism are "still alive and kicking" at the turn of the 21st century (Weiss 2002:37). The point, then, is to account for continuing – and growing – nationalism in this increasingly global age.

Accounting for contemporary nationalism is a particular challenge in China today, where nationalism is an extremely potent force. Observers[4] generally agree that the ruling Chinese Communist Party (CCP) has deployed nationalism strategically, as a way to retain legitimacy after abandoning socialist ideology and embracing capitalism. As one scholar notes, "Chinese communism is turning to nationalism to legitimate one-party rule" (Chang 1998:83). Today the Communist Party posits itself as the vanguard of the Chinese *nation* – not the proletariat – and as the privileged agent to carry forward the Chinese nation's long-deferred dream of wealth, power, and international respect (see Zhao 1998). This has led many western analysts to assume that Chinese nationalism is therefore a top-down phenomenon: because the CCP uses nationalism as the grounds of its political legitimacy, the Party imposes nationalist sentiment on the Chinese people.

More recent research, however, acknowledges that this analysis is simplistic, and notes instead that "popular nationalism" in China cannot be explained as solely the effect of top-down Party ideology. By the late 1990s, most scholars agreed that Chinese nationalism was not "the sole province of state propaganda and intellectual discourse" (Zhao 2004:11), but is instead a potent combination of popular sentiment, state authority, and intellectual approval (Guo 2004).

The question remains, however, as to precisely how nationalism is understood, experienced, and generated by people in their everyday lives. There is extensive and fascinating historical work on how the Chinese nation was socially and discursively produced in the early 20th century (Duara 1995; Fitzgerald 1996), and on the ways that nationalism was generated through a range of practices during the Republican Era (1911–1949) including consumption (Gerth 2003) and physical activity (Morris 2004). Much less of this kind of work, however, has been done in reform-era China.[5] This article is intended to contribute to this line of inquiry, arguing that the daily practices of the Little Red Pioneers provide a particularly powerful site from which to view the complex links between the CCP and the nation's children, thus illuminating a central question in China today: how Chinese nationalism is lived and experienced within the context of the many contradictions of the reform era.

The second broad theme that anthropological theories of nationalism have in common is the they are predicated on the theory that nations are imagined communities (Anderson 1983) rather than contemporary reflections of primordial allegiances (e.g., Huntington 1996). The study of children and children's nationalism is, from this perspective, particularly important, because all nations must in some way teach children how to imagine themselves as members of a national community.

Most scholars who address these questions start with inquiries into formal education, which is "ubiquitously cited as the main motor of nationalism and the source of patriotic allegiance" (Bryant 2001:583). Bryant notes that this tendency "goes back at least to Durkheim's later works on the nation-state, which had heralded formal education as the ritual *par excellence* for the socialization of the youth in what he called 'moral culture'" (ibid; Durkheim 1956; 1973). Anderson's (1983) work on the nation as imagined community continued in this vein, positing classrooms as a privileged site for developing the social bonds among classmates that transcended parochial village loyalties and made national collectivities possible.

From this position have come studies of classrooms as incubators of nationalist sentiment, and of textbooks as materializations of state ideology. Studies of textbooks that are produced by national educational ministries can indeed be mined to understand how states (or agents of the state) understand their own histories, how some events are remembered or forgotten, and how changing curricular material reflects changing politics (e.g., Grinker 1998, Culp 2001, Hein and Selden 2000). If states exist only as reifications (Abrams 1988, Aretxaga 2003), then textbooks and other school materials can provide particularly good evidence to show how the state is reifying itself.

One example of how seriously states take textbooks and classrooms as incubators of nationalist sentiment is China's ongoing scrutiny of the ways that Japanese textbooks portray the Japanese invasion of China (see e.g. Reilly 2004). This concern – and the political controversies that arise from it – is based on the assumption that what is taught in schools structures what children – and, later, adults – can understand about their nations and histories. At the same time, the CCP has employed its own attempts to raise patriotism through educational interventions, such as the patriotic education campaign launched after the 1989 Tiananmen Massacre, which was designed to teach Chinese children that Western objections to China's crackdown on protesters were anti-Chinese, not anti-Communist (Zhao 2004).

This classroom- and textbook-based approach is extremely useful, and sheds light on the ways that schools as state apparatuses (cf. Althusser 1971) attempt to produce children as national subjects. But as the many studies of nationalism have shown, the nation is also lived and experienced as part of everyday life. How can we understand the ways that children become nationalist subjects through practices beyond reading textbooks? If we accept Connerton's (1989) claim that national identity is embodied, and that the nation is incorporated in its members, what kind of embodied practices are producing children as national subjects? It is in this context that I suggest that the concept of performativity offers new insight into nationalism and national subjects.

Performing the Nation

Strongly influenced by Judith Butler's work (1990, 1993), performativity theory has developed to describe the processes by which gender identities are constructed in and through discourses of sexuality (Morris 1995:569). For Butler, gender is neither an essence nor a biological given, but is instead a "consequence of the enactment of social norms" (Schein 1999:369). Building on Austin's (1975) linguistic theories that some utterances are performative in that they *do* something rather than describe or express something, Butler argues that gender is something that is *enacted*, rather than being a culturally and historically specific expression of a pre-existing biological state. Gender is thus not something one *has*, but rather is something one *does*, through "the stylized repetition of acts through time." (Butler 1990:141).

Repetition is central to performativity, for gendered subjects are brought into being not through single acts, but only through reiterations of social norms. In this way, performativity is linked to the disciplinary and normalizing strategies described by Foucault (1977) that establish and respond to categories of the normal and the pathological (Lloyd

1999:196), for Butler proposes that gender is an effect of power secured through the repeated performance of norms that produce the effect of coherent substance (Butler 1990:145; Feldman 2005). In this way, "gender is not an inner core or static essence, but a reiterated enactment of norms, ones that produce, retroactively, the appearance of gender as an abiding interior depth" (Butler 1997:14, cited in Mahmood 2001).

Thus, according to Butler, gender performances do three things. First, they construct the gendered subject, who has "no ontological status apart from those acts that constitute its reality" (Butler 1993:173). Because there is no essence or origin outside the enactment of multiple performances, the gendered subject is brought into being through these performances. Butler thus rejects the idea that an autonomous agent authors performative utterances, and disavows a voluntarist subject who chooses his or her gender (Lloyd 1995:199). Second, repeated performances of the normative conceal gender's lack of a stable essence or foundation, by "sustaining the idea that biological sex preceeds gender." (Feldman 2005:221). Butler asserts that "bodily gestures, movements and styles constitute the illusion of an abiding gendered self" (1990:139). There is thus no *a priori* sexed subject who learns gender roles; instead, the subject him/herself is constituted through performances. Third, gendered performances are compelled to be repeated, because performances can never fully approximate the socially and historically generated norms of gender (Butler 1993).

Anthropologists have extended this theoretical perspective beyond gender, to look at other aspects of performativity. Feldman (2005) argues that state power can be seen as performative: the state, rather than being an enduring and pre-constituted entity, is instead produced through the performance of difference. Schein (1999; 2000) argues that modernity is at least partly constituted as a performance, through negotiations of cultural politics by members of the Miao minority group in China. Mahmood (2001) uses performativity to investigate the agency of Egyptian women and their veiling practices today.

The concept of performativity can also be usefully extended to help us think about the construction of children as national subjects, and the ways that nationalism is *performed* in some of the same ways that gender is. From this perspective, nationalism is understood as something children *do*, not something they *acquire*. It thus takes us beyond state-sponsored textbooks and propaganda, and focuses instead on children's daily lives to inquire how and where the nation is performed. These performances may include reading textbooks, but also a range of other daily activities.

Performativity also helps us rethink the agency of the child as national subject. Rather than being an *a priori* subject onto which the nation is either forced (through propaganda) or chosen (by children who elect to become patriotic), an approach based in performativity argues that the child is instead constituted as a national subject through repetitive performances of the nation. In other words, a cognitive theory of nationalism presupposes an *a priori* child who is then imbued with nationalist sentiment through the institutional vehicle of schools. Yet rather than positing the child as a pre-national subject who learns what it means to be part of a nation through cognitively-based material and then chooses his or her national identity, a performative analysis argues that part of the maturation process for contemporary children entails repeated performances of the nation, which then, over time, constitute the child as a national subject. Thus in looking at children's performances, we can more clearly see nationalism as a convention, a set of norms about being Chinese that both precede and constrain children.

This then raises an ethnographic question: what kinds of performances are normative in different societies today? Following Connerton (1989), what are the embodied forms of collective memory and social practice? How might these differ from or extend "inscribed" practices based in text? My argument is that the *Chinese* child is produced through performances of the nation, which are embodied and habituated through repetition in daily life. Since performativity is "rooted within a matrix of discursive norms" (Diamond 1996:5), the following sections explore the Little Red

Pioneers as the matrix of nationalism for Chinese children, and looks at the ways that Pioneer activities are performative acts, which "are part of regulatory practices that produce social categories and the norms of membership within them. They are sites where hegemonic definitions of the collective body relate to multiple injunctions of individual bodies" (Fortier 1999:43). Focusing on the daily practices of young children (ages 7–10) in Beijing, the following sections look at the Pioneers as a performance, where the social category of the Chinese nation is (re)produced through daily practices.

The Little Red Pioneers

Although children are annually inducted into the Little Red Pioneers on or around International Children's Day on June 1st, the nationally-broadcast public performance in 2001 was highly unusual. The Pine Street School teachers explained that special ceremonies were called for that year, because 2001 marked the 50th anniversary of the formal Little Red Pioneer organization.[6] Modeled on a similar institution in the Soviet Union (Lane 1981), the Pioneers serve as the first Communist Party affiliation for Chinese children aged seven to thirteen; after that, qualified teenagers can apply for membership in the Communist Youth League (*Qingnian tuan*).

The goal of the Pioneers has long been to inculcate in children organizational and leadership skills, discipline, collectivism, obedience to Party directives, and patriotism.[7] Through the 1970s Pioneer membership was highly competitive: in order to enter the organization, children had to prove their moral and political worthiness, as well as demonstrate that they came from an appropriate class background.[8] In fact, during the Cultural Revolution era (1966–1976), a primary goal of the Pioneers was to teach children how to recognize and reject class enemies (Unger 1982).

By the time I arrived in China in the late 1990s, however, membership in the Pioneers was largely *pro forma*, and in Beijing virtually all children were automatically inducted into the organization upon finishing first grade. The only exceptions were those very few who either had not yet passed their seventh birthday by the end of the school year, or those for whom membership was postponed for a year as punishment for had behavior in first grade. The teachers explained that the Pioneers' admission standards had been changed in order to avoid the bad feelings and rivalry among the children that competitive membership had sparked. In my experience, every first grader in the two elementary schools in which I conducted research in 1999–2001 entered the Pioneers on June 1st.

While the switch to automatic Pioneer induction meant that members no longer focus on identifying and excluding class enemies,[9] at the institutional level the Little Red Pioneer organization still has strong formal ties with the Chinese Communist Party. In Beijing, every elementary school's Pioneer cell is linked to the Communist Youth Organization in their local school district, and each school assigns at least one teacher to supervise Pioneer activities and report regularly to district-level Party authorities. Every semester, these authorities then specify curricular themes for home-room teachers to address each month with their students; in 2000, for example, these included activities to celebrate Macao's return to the Chinese Motherland at the end of the year, and to mark anniversaries of events in Communist Party history.

Using these assigned themes, Pioneers in the older grades (the fifth and sixth graders) are also responsible for designing and drawing murals on the large chalkboards on the back wall of every classroom. Between 1999–2001, when I conducted field work in two elementary schools in Beijing, themes for back-of-the-classroom blackboards included pictures of rocket ships with descriptions of China's space program, exhortations condemning Falun Gong,[10] essays and drawings about Macao and Hong Kong returning to the Motherland, and suggestions for how students could best emulate the selfless spirit of Lei Feng.[11] At one of my research field sites, an elite elementary school called University School that served children of faculty and staff at one of China's most prestigious universities, the school's Little Red Pioneer cell was also responsible for

decorating the school's hallways. Every few months the elected Pioneer leaders in each classroom would collect essays by their classmates on these same themes, then select the best ones to display prominently on bulletin boards lining the school's hallways. One example that I found particularly striking was posted in the hallways in late October, 2000. The children had been assigned to write about their reactions to the annual National Day Parade in Tiananmen Square, held a few weeks earlier on October 1st. According to their posted essays, many of the University School children had attended the parade in person. In the essays, more than one child expressed: "I saw our Liberation Army march along Tiananmen Square while our leader Jiang Zemin watched. I especially liked seeing the weapons displayed. Seeing this makes me want to grow up to be a scientist, so that I can build better weapons to defend the Motherland." This is an excellent example of the ongoing production of social memory, in Connerton's (1989) sense: Children attend national commemorations, where, proudly sporting their red scarves, they stand at attention to recognize the nation's achievements, then inscribe their patriotic fervor in publicly-displayed essays. At the same time, these assigned essay themes also crossed content areas, as Party officials used the Pioneer system to build children's love of the nation, respect for Party history and ideological conformity with Party policies, as well as inculcating high modernist yearnings towards national development through science and technology.

Ideologically, the strong links between the Pioneers and the Communist Party are most clearly evinced during the annual International Children's Day celebrations, which, unlike the spectacle described at the beginning of this paper, usually take place within the confines of each elementary school. During these celebrations, Pioneer members carry and salute the national flag, take loyalty oaths to the Chinese Communist Party, and perform patriotic plays or soliloquies that they write themselves as paeans to the Party and the Chinese motherland. The climax of these performances is always the ritual tying of a red scarf around the neck of each of the first graders, to mark their entry into the Pioneers. This red scarf is a sacred symbol (Chan 1985; Unger 1982) that represents a corner of the national flag stained by the blood of the revolutionary martyrs; wearing it daily around their necks is supposed to symbolize a child's ties to the Party and the nation, and their remembrance of those who died for the revolution. And, lest the younger children not fully understand this point, in the weeks leading up to Children's Day, the older children formally instruct the first graders in how to tie, wear, and appropriately respect the scarves they will soon receive (cf. Bowie 1997).

During initiation, children chant the Little Red Pioneer pledge:

I am a Little Red Pioneer! Beneath the Pioneer flag I swear that I am determined to obey the teachings of the Chinese Communist Party, that I will study, work and labor diligently, and that I am prepared to dedicate all my efforts to the cause of communism.

The pledge is performative in Austin's (1975) sense: "an act of enunciation that brings into being the object it names" (Morris 1995:572). Children become Pioneers by declaring themselves so, and then repeat the pledge at regular Pioneer events during the school year, including celebrations for National Day and other major state holidays. Each child also wears a red scarf to school every day, thus reiterating their link to the nation through the Pioneers, and thereby performing the norms of national membership on a daily basis.

But these performances extend beyond the pledge and the red scarves, for children's subjectivity as Pioneers is also reiterated in the context of extensive structural links between schools and the CCP. Structurally, the Pioneer system in each school mirrors the hierarchical organization of the Party. Starting in second grade, the Pioneers in each homeroom class elect ranked leaders; in the older grades, teachers also elevate some children to school-wide Pioneer leadership positions. The rights and responsibilities of these various leadership positions vary in different schools. For example, University School had a special conference room dedicated to the Pioneer organization; it featured a huge mural of Chinese scientists

planting the national flag in Antarctica, as well as posters with the text of the Pioneer anthem and pledge (see Figure 16.1). In the corner stood a large bust of Lei Feng. And, as I discovered one day when a teacher and I tried to use the room for a short meeting during the lunch hour, a cabinet in another corner of the room held a large color television. That day, we found the room full of the school's fifth- and sixth-grade Pioneer leaders, eating lunch and happily watching Japanese cartoons (dubbed into Chinese) via cable on the TV. The teacher in charge of University School's Pioneer activities later explained that this was one of the privileges of being chosen as a high-ranked cadre at their school: having a special room and access to cartoons was one way to make these positions highly coveted among all the children. Not to mention, of course, that this was also an important lesson in the special privileges of Party-based power in China, and what children can expect when they become adults.

Pioneers and the Nation

This reproduction of Party hierarchy and privilege, the ritual of bestowing of the red scarf, the performativity of the loyalty oaths and the children's swearing to dedicate themselves to the cause of communism all make it seem that membership in the Little Red Pioneers produces a direct and unmediated relationship between children and the Chinese Party-State. On the level of daily practice, however, the Little Red Pioneers operate much more like a school-based youth group focused on Chinese patriotism, school spirit, and social service, than a system for turning young children into communist ideologues. In the daily life of elementary schools, the Pioneer system is a way to organize and discipline children, and a means of teaching them skills in both leadership and obedience. Most importantly, though, the Pioneer system manages and disciplines children's time and space (cf. Foucault 1977).

Decorating classrooms, washing the blackboard between classes, and sweeping and mopping the floors were all tasks assigned to the Little Red Pioneers, and which the children

Figure 16.1 *Little Red Pioneer meeting room at University School, showing a mural of Chinese scientists in Antarctica, and a bust of Lei Feng (back right corner). The slogan above the mural reads: "Be Prepared to Struggle to Achieve Communism!" (Photo by T.E. Woronov)*

organized and completed daily, largely without adult intervention or supervision. Pioneers at University and Pine Street schools ran recycling drives, participated in tree-planting activities on the outskirts of the city, and organized visits to elderly shut-ins. The students at both schools spent long hours preparing for Pioneer-sponsored weekend competitions in chorus, band, exercise, track and field, calligraphy and other extra-curricular activities. Today, the Little Red Pioneers organization is the site of the inculcation of collectivist morality – no longer a collectivism that identifies and excludes class enemies, but a nationalist, social-service based collectivity. Thus, while at the level of slogans and organization the Pioneers are very explicitly part of the Communist party, in practice the system is largely de-politicized, or, perhaps more accurately, "de-socialist-ized."

My fieldwork generated many examples of how this took place. During the International Children's Day and Pioneer induction celebrations at both Pine Street and University Schools, children's declarations of love for the Party and dedication to the goals of communism were mixed with other kinds of entertainment prepared by the same students. During ceremonies at both schools, I observed children performing choreographed disco dancing, displays of kungfu prowess, a fashion show, recitations of Tang Dynasty poetry, and arias from Chinese operas. The students themselves generally arranged the agendas (although the teachers were more involved in the more professionalized performances at the University School). They did not in any way mark the different performance registers, as they easily mixed styles, genres, and metaphors. International Children's Day is thus a kind of global *bricolage* by Beijing children, as they pick and choose elements from traditional high Chinese culture (Tang poetry), low culture (Peking opera and martial arts), global youth culture (albeit a few years out of date, judging by the

American disco music chosen), and Communist ideology. It is a fairly accurate representation, in fact, of their lives in contemporary Beijing, and of the constitution of contemporary Chinese nationalism: an ever-changing *bricolage* of communist ideology, pride in Chinese history and culture, and links to global modernity. The fact that the Children's Day celebrations now accommodate these different kinds of performances indicates the continuously changing norms for participation in the Chinese nation, as well as how children's performances constitute them as modern national subjects.

Another example of how Pioneer activities combined a range of practices was found on the blackboard-lined walls along the entranceway at Pine Street School. Every few weeks the Little Red Pioneer leaders of the school (in 5th and 6th grades), in consultation with the school's art teacher, designed and drew elaborate messages to the student body on these blackboards. One posted near the end of the semester taught students the appropriate bodily diciplines necessary to perform well on the up coming end-of-term exams (see Figure 16.2). Titled "The end of the semester is here!" the picture showed children washing their hands before meals (to prevent sickness which would influence ability to study); children going to bed and getting up

early; and illustrated the proper sitting position at a desk and the right position for a lamp so as to maximize studying effort and minimize eye strain. Two negative examples were also included: one, a child watching television until late at night; another of children eating unclean food from an itinerant sidewalk snack seller, which makes them too sick to study.[12] This Pioneer-sponsored didactic material shows the ways that the Pioneers are naturalized as part of daily bodily disciplines which produce the right kinds of bodies, which then produce morality via good study habits and good grades.

In fact, the Pioneer system is so deeply naturalized as the only possible means to inculcate appropriate behavior and to keep schools running by organizing children's time, that every teacher I met in Beijing at some point asked me to describe to them the workings of the Little Red Pioneer system in the United States. This question flustered me, but once I realized that they were not teasing me, I was at a loss of where to begin to explain the decentralized American educational system. More as a joke than an explanation, I finally resorted to reminding them that there is no Communist Party in the US empowered to run such a system. Their response, however, was more puzzlement: even if a different political party

Figure 16.2 *Blackboard at entrance to Pine Street School. The caption reads: "The end of the semester is here!" (Photo by T.E. Woronov)*

ran the organization, surely some kind of equivalent system must exist. Otherwise, how were American children organized? How did they spend their free time? How were classrooms kept clean?

Pioneer activities are thus naturalized and repeated every day: children live the Pioneers and the Chinese nation through a series of embodied activities that they perform as national subjects. Their nationalism is inscribed not only through formal rituals, but through repeated daily practices that include wearing red scarves and swearing fealty to the Communist Party, and also recycling, cleaning classrooms, and learning disco dancing. Their induction, loyalty oaths, and red scarves are not an anachronism, but are the ways that children are performing and embodying nationalism, one inflected by Party history. At the same time, these practices are part of the contemporary moment, inscribing children into the capitalist moral economy. Party membership is directly linked to capitalist-style benefits (watching cartoons), while the Party organization for children has also become a place to teach the role of adults in the new, neoliberal moral order. Now that the Chinese State has withdrawn from the social service sector and smashed the "iron rice bowl" that marked the Mao era, individuals must learn how to donate time, money and energy to society. Rather than building collectivism, as in the past, now the Party guides individualist interventions in the social field through social service.[13]

At the same time, children and teachers assume that just as their lives reflect increasing global influences, these practices must be just as naturalized globally as they are in China. Since their performances of nationalism now incorporate elements from global youth culture, it makes sense for them to assume that other children's performances are similar to theirs.

Western observers are deeply vexed by the apparent contradiction of a Communist Party leading a capitalist economy. The ethnographic data above shows how this is not necessarily experienced as a contradiction in children's daily practices – not because they are subjected to tyrannical power which dictates what they must think and feel, but because they perform their membership in the Pioneers through activities that reflect the continuously changing norms for moral participation in the nation. Lauding the Communist Party is mixed with disco dancing; displays of rocket ships and Party heroes mix with adumbrations to eat right and get enough sleep. All are part of the daily performances under the purview of the Pioneers. The repetitions of Pioneer life are multiple, linked to the ways that the Party, via the Pioneers, is producing the nation and its future.

Fear of Water: Performance, Reiteration, and "Getting It Wrong"

On International Children's Day in 2000, in a ceremony with the University School firstgraders and children from a dozen other schools in Haidian District in northwestern Beijing, I was inducted as an honorary member of the Little Red Pioneers. At the end of the ceremony a reporter from the local Haidian cable TV station interviewed some of the participants. Several teachers and I watched as the reporter held a microphone up to one of the seven-year-olds who was wearing his new red scarf, and asked him: "How do you feel?" The child stood up very straight, took a deep breath, and responded: "This is the happiest day of my life. Because. Because. Because. . . ." He then turned to the reporter, shrugged his shoulders, and cheerfully admitted: "I forgot." The reporter, teachers, and I all roared with laughter.

A similar story occurred one afternoon near the end of the school year in Spring, 2000. I was drawn to the fourth grade teachers' room[14] at Pine Street School one afternoon by the sound of a sudden howl of laughter. When I entered, one of the teachers, still chuckling, handed me a student's homework paper. The homework assignment was a worksheet that had been written by the Haidian District education authorities, that students were to complete as part of the preparations for their upcoming end-of-semester exams, which were standardized across the district. The worksheet read:

I am sitting on a plane next to Grandma. I look out the window and watch the clouds and ocean below me. My heart races and my blood pounds. Soon I will be back in the Motherland. I enjoyed my time in the US with Grandma and Grandpa. My classmates in America were kind to me, and before I left they even offered me to give me a new little red scarf. I declined, though, because I wanted to keep wearing the scarf that my classmates in Beijing had given me before I left. Oh – how exciting! The plane is touching down in Beijing I stride down the gangway towards my waiting mother, "Mama!" I announce proudly, "I'm back!"[15]

The first question on the homework work-sheet read: "Why, when 'you' look out the window of the airplane, is 'your' heart racing and your blood pounding?" Virtually all of the fourth-grade students had responded correctly, "because I'm so excited about returning to the Motherland!" Yet two of the Pine Street fourth-grade students had instead answered: "Because I'm afraid of water!" For several weeks afterwards, this line could bring the teachers room to tears of laughter.

I recount these stories in order to return to the question raised at the beginning of this paper: how to understand the ways that children continue to "get it wrong," the many ways that they "fail" to perform the nation appro-priately. Thousands of children on Tiananmen Square do not perform appropriately for the television cameras; some may forget why join-ing the Little Red Pioneers is "the most impor-tant day" of their short lives, while others confuse the nationalist lesson in a text with the problem of grammatical deixis.

There are two possible explanations for these mistakes: first, that they are developmental, that the children are simply too young to understand what is expected of them or to carry out the bodily or intellectual disciplines required. Their tender age might also explain the teachers' and parents' reactions, the adults' tendency to laugh and see these failures as examples of kids "saying the darndest things." A second possi-bility is to see these "mistakes" as a form of children's resistance, a choice on their part to resist adults' disciplines, regulations, and imposed meanings of nationalism, and an effort to generate their own meaning of the nation.

I suggest, however, an alternative explana-tion, based in performativity. These "failures" in performances of nationalism occur because in China today, the nationalist ideal is always in some way unattainable. As Butler notes in her discussion of gender performances:

To the extent that the naming of the "girl" is transitive, that is, initiates the process by which a certain "girling" is compelled, the term or, rather, its symbolic power, governs the formation of a corporeally enacted femininity that never fully approximates the norm. This is a "girl," however, who is compelled to "cite" the norm in order to qualify and remain a viable subject. Femininity is thus not the product of a choice, but the forcible citation of a norm, one whose complex historicity is indissociable from relations of discipline, regulation, punishment (Butler 1993:232).

In other words, gender performances never fully approximate the norm; therefore, addi-tional reiterative performances are always compelled in order to continuously produce the gendered subject. If, as Lloyd claims, "gender performativity may be inevitable, but it is always open and incomplete" (Lloyd 1999:200), then the same may be true of child-ren's performances of nationalism. These "failures," then, are an example of the ways that regimes of nationalism in China today do not "fully legislate or contain their own ideals" (ibid.), making the ideal unattainable. Nation-alism ts an ever-changing mix of the socialist past, the glories of "traditional" Chinese cul-ture, and global consumerism; therefore, no performance can ever contain or embrace all aspects. Further performances of the nation are always necessary.

In this respect, the fact that the ideal is unattainable – and the ways that children strive, but sometimes fail, to perform the nation appropriately – tells us something important about nationalism in contemporary China. The many elements in the *bricolage* of contempo-rary children's lives, including the socialist, capitalist, consumerist, and global, are not experienced as contradictory or mutually exclusive; instead, they come together to produce children as Chinese subjects, embedded in the complexity of the contemporary world. Thus the puzzle that vexes many Western observers of China – how a capitalist economy can be run by a communist party – is no puzzle at all to the children inducted into the Little Red Pioneers. Their practices of nationalism include paeans of loyalty to the Communist Party, consumption of Japanese cartoons as a "privilege" of Party rank, and disco dancing. They are caught in a regime of childhood that is both so highly naturalized and so linked to the global consumer market, that education officials can write homework essays about *American* children's wearing of red Pioneer scarves. These come together in a not-quite-seamless whole, reiterated every day.

At the same time, it is important to note that adults' reaction to these "failed" performances is laughter. Not all "mistakes" by children are treated so lightly by adults; even errors that can clearly be attributed to their youth, such as math or grammar mistakes on school assignments, or incorrect moral stances in their interactions with others, are vigorously corrected by adults (Woronov, n.d.). Yet I suggest that there are so few repercussions for these "failed" performances of nationalism because in the many other reiterations of nationalism, children's performances are so successful. Even at age 7, the children I knew were deeply patriotic. They may not always get the details correctly, and the regulation and discipline are still being worked out, but by age 7 these children had already been produced as Chinese subjects through their repeated performances. This is not surprising: in Butler's scheme, 7-year-old children are fully aware if they are boys or girls, and understand the norms of gendered performances, even as their daily lives require on-going reiterations of gender. In China, children know that they are subjects of the Chinese nation, which they love dearly.

This leads to the second possible explanation for their "failed" performances, that of resistance. I have argued above against relying solely on a cognitive approach to nationalism, and suggest that like gender, nationalism is not a choice that children make, but instead performed as the citation of a norm (Butler

1993). Like all subjects, children perform within the parameters that are open to them, which, I argue, are the ever-changing contexts of Chinese nationalism. Their personal views are rarely solicited or expressed in these contexts. During the Children's Day celebrations they perform in spectacles that are highly scripted; contents of essays and themes for blackboards and coloring projects that line the halls of schools are not spaces for children to develop their individuality or learn how to work out the "meaning" of the nation. In this respect, areas where they "fail" are not sites of resistance to the norms of the nation, but instead are sign posts pointing to the wide range of practices that are possible as performances of the contemporary nation. In fact, asking the children directly about their patriotism leads to the same kind of incredulous eye-rolling I described at the beginning of the paper. "Of course we love the Motherland!" was the response I would invariably get to any question I was able to frame about their patriotism, a response usually accompanied by a snort of exasperation at the dumb questions foreigners ask. Or, as one child advised me: "You should come to the Children's Day celebration at school. There you can see what we think." Children's mistakes in these performances – forgetting why entering the Pioneers is an honor, not performing for television cameras – does not challenge their fundamental patriotism, and does not express resistance on their part to the disciplines of the nation-state.

I therefore argue against a solely cognitive approach to children's nationalism. Textbooks are important, and reading and memorizing the content of state-sponsored textbooks is one of the many ways that the nation is repeatedly performed in daily life. But the state is reified in many ways in their lives; in China, children's connection with the nation-state extends to the Party-sponsored Little Red Pioneers. Children wear red scarves while disco dancing, recycling batteries, and imitating Hong Kong kungfu movies.

And, since children perform the nation in different ways than adults, they provide privileged insight into the performativity of the nation. Apart from the military, most adults are not required to wear a token of their patriotism everyday – such as a red scarf – nor do adults celebrate national holidays today by writing and performing skits, poems and dances of love for the Motherland. Children, however, still do, and expand our theories of nationalism in the process.

NOTES

1   The names of all the schools and individuals have been changed. Unless otherwise noted, all translations from Chinese are my own.
2   Teacher Li said that there were "*yiwan*" children on the Square that day, which literally means "ten thousand," but is often used colloquially in China to mean "an extremely large but unspecified number." From her description, I assume that between 8 and 12 thousand children participated in this performance.
3   Chairman Mao's Memorial Hall is located near the south end of Tiananmen Square. Visitors to the Hall are required to enter and traverse the displays in single file (Wakeman 1988; Wagner 1992).
4   There is a tremendous literature on the multiplicities of Chinese nationalism in the post-Mao era (roughly late 1970s-today). See e.g. Unger 1996; Pan et. al. 2005; Dittmer and Kim 1993; Wei and Liu 2002; Zhao 2004; Gries 2005.
5   Exceptions include Brownell 1995; Lozada 2006, and several studies on ethnicity and nationalism in China, e.g., Schein 2000; Gladney 2004.
6   Little Red Pioneer groups do participate in other state "parades," particularly on National Day on October 1st, but filming a mass induction into the Pioneers on International Children's Day was unique (Wu 2005).
7   The Pioneers came out of CCP experiments with children's groups in the 1930s, when these qualities were first identified and various institutional forms for inculcating them were first developed (Unger 1982; Woronov n.d.).
8   See Unger 1982 for a discussion of the changing constitution of "appropriate class background" for Pioneer – and, later, Red Guard – membership.

9   In 1978, the Chinese leadership officially declared that class struggle in China had come to an end.
10 Falun Gong is a quasi-religious group established in the early 1990s by charismatic leader Li Hongzhi that espouses a set of meditation practices. The PRC government banned the group in 1999, labeling it an "evil cult."
11 Lei Feng was an extremely important Cultural Revolution-era model for selfless socialist morality, love of the Party and the nation, and devotion to the Party. His image and example are still used in China today (see Farquhar 2002; Landsberger 2001).
12 This drawing of "unclean" food sold to unsuspecting children by "dirty" migrant workers indexes the complex relationships between local Beijingers and the growing migrant population. See Woronov 2004.
13 I thank Char Mackley for her help with this argument.
14 In Beijing public schools, each grade's teachers share an office space, where they prepare classes and correct homework.
15 The expression "I'm back!" (*Wo huilai le!*) had been widely used in public service announcements that year to celebrate the return of Macao to the Chinese motherland.

REFERENCES

Abrams, P. 1988. "Notes on the Difficulty of Studying the State." *Journal of Historical Sociology* 1: 58–89.
Althusser, L. 1971. "Ideology and Ideological State Apparatuses." In *Lenin and Philosophy and Other Essays*. New York: Monthly Review Press.
Anagnost, A. 1994. "The Politicized Body." In *Body, Subject and Power in China*. Angela Zito and Tani Barlow, eds., pp. 131–156. Chicago: University of Chicago Press.
Anderson, B. 1983. *Imagined Communities*. NY: Verso.
Aretxaga, B. 2003. "Maddening States." *Annual Review of Anthropology* 32: 393–410.
Austin, J. L. 1975. *How to Do Things with Words*. 2nd edition. Cambridge. MA: Harvard University Press.
Billig, M. 1995. *Banal Nationalism*. Thousand Oaks, CA: Sage.

Bowie, K. 1997. *Rituals of National Loyalty: An Anthropology of the State and the Village Scout Movement in Thailand.* New York: Columbia University Press.

Brownell S. 1995. *Training the Body for China: Sports in the Moral Order of the People's Republic.* Chicago: University of Chicago Press.

Bryant, R. 2001. "An Aesthetics of Self: Moral Remaking and Cypriot Education. *Comparative Studies in Society and History,* 43(3): 583–614.

Butler, J. 1990. *Gender Trouble: feminism and the Subversion of Identity.* London: Routledge.

Butler, J. 1993. *Bodies That Matter: On the Discursive Limits of "Sex."* London: Routledge.

Butler, J. 1997. "Further Reflections on Conversations of our Time." *Diacritics* 27(1): 13–15.

Chalfin, B. 2006. "Global Customs Regimes and the Traffic in Sovereignty." *Current Anthropology* 47(2): 243–276.

Chan, A. 1985. *Children of Mao: Personality Development and Political Activism in the Red Guard Generation.* London: Macmillan.

Chang, M.H. 1998. "Chinese Irredentist Nationalism: The Magician's Last Trick." *Comparative Strategy* 17(1): 83–100.

Connerton, P. 1989. *How Societies Remember.* Cambridge: Cambridge University Press.

Culp, R. 2001. "China – The Land and its People': Fashioning Identity in Secondary School History Textbooks, 1911–37." *Twentieth-Century China* 26(2): 17–62.

Diamond, E. 1996. "Introduction." In *Performance and Cultural Politics*, Elin Diamond, ed., pp. 1–12. London: Routledge.

Dittmer, L. and S. S. Kim, eds. 1993. *China's Quest for National Identity.* Ithaca, NY: Cornell University Press.

Duara, P. 1995. *Rescuing History from the Nation.* Chicago: University of Chicago Press.

Durkheim, E. 1956. *Education and Sociology.* Glencoe, IL: Free Press.

Durkheim, E. 1973. *Moral Education: A Study in the Theory and Application of the Sociology of Education.* New York: Free Press.

Farquhar, J. 2002. *Appetites: Food and Sex in Post-Socialist China.* Durham, NC: Ouke University Press.

Feldman, G. 2005. "Essential Crises: A Performative Approach to Migrants, Minorities, and the European Nation-State." *Anthropological Quarterly* 78(1): 213–246.

Fitzgerald, J. 1996. *Awakening Chino: Politics, Culture and Class in the Nationalist Revolution.* Stanford, CA: Stanford University Press.

Fortier, A-M. 1999. "Re-Membering Places and the Performance of Belonging(s)." *Theory, Culture and Society* 16(2): 41–64.

Foucault, M. 1977. *Discipline and Punish and the Birth of the Prison.* New York: Vintage Books.

Gerth, K. 2003. *China Mode: Consumer Culture and the Creation of the Nation.* Cambridge, MA: Harvard University Press.

Gladney, D. 2004. *Dislocating China: Reflections on Muslims, Minorities and Other Subaltern Subjects.* London: C. Hurst.

Golden, D. 2001. "Now, like Real Israelis, Let's Stand Up and Sing': Teaching the National Language to Russian Newcomers in Israel." *Anthropology and Education Quarterly* 32(1): 52–79.

Gries, P. H. 2005. "Chinese Nationalism: Challenging the State?" *Current History* 104(683): 251–256.

Grinker, R. 1998. *Korea and its Futures: Unification and the Unfinished War.* New York: St. Martin's Press.

Guo Yingjie. 2004. *Cultural Nationalism in Contemporary China: The Search for National Identity.* London: RoutledgeCurzon.

Handler R. 1988. *Nationalism and the Politics of Culture in Quebec.* Madison: University of Wisconsin Press.

Hein, L. and M. Selden. eds. 2000. *Censoring History: Citizenship and Memory in Japan, Germany, and the United-States.* Armonk, NY: M.E. Sharpe.

Herzfeld, M. 1997. *Cultural Intimacy: Social Poetics in the Nation-State.* New York: Routledge.

Huntington, S. 1996. *The Clash of Civilizations and the Remaking of World Order.* New York: Simon & Schuster.

Landsberger, S. 2001. "Learning by What Example?: Educational Propaganda in Twenty-first Century China." *Critical Asian Studies* 33(4): 541–571.

Lane, C. 1981. *The Rites of Rulers: Ritual in Industrial Society: The Soviet Case.* Cambridge: Cambridge University Press.

Lloyd, M. 1999. "Performativity, Parody, Politics." *Theory, Culture and Society* 16(2): 195–213.

Lozada, E. 2006. Cosmopolitanism and Nationalism in Shanghai Sports. *City and Society* 18(2): 207–231.

Mahmood, S. 2001. "Feminist Theory, Embodiment, and the Docile Agent: Some Reflections on the Egyptian Islamic Revival." *Cultural Anthropology* 16(2): 202–236.

Morris, A. 2004. *Marrow of the Nation: A History of Sport and Physical Culture in Republican China*. Berkeley: University of California Press.

Morris, R.C. 1995. "All Made Up: Performance Theory and the New Anthropology of Sex and Gender." *Annual Review of Anthropology* 24: 567–592.

Navaro-Yashin, Y. 2002. *Faces of the State: Secularism and Public Life in Turkey*. Princeton: Princeton University Press.

Pan, Z., and Lee Chin-Chuan, Joseph Man Chan, and Clement K.Y. So. 2005. "To Cheer for the Family-Nation: The Construction of Chinese Nationalism during the Hong Kong Handover." In *Cultural Studies in China*. Tao Dongfeng and Jin Yuanpu, eds. Singapore: Marshall Cavendish International.

Reilly, J. 2004. "China's History Activists and the War of Resistance against Japan: History in the Making." *Asian Survey* 44(2): 276–294.

Schein, L. 1999. "Performing Modernity." *Cultural Anthropology* 14(3): 361–395.

Schein, L. 2000. *Minority Rules: The Miao and the Feminine in China's Cultural Politics*. Durham, NC: Duke University Press.

Unger, J. 1982. *Education Under Mao: Class and Competition in Canton Schools, 1960–1980*. New York: Columbia University Press.

Unger, J., ed. 1996. *Chinese Nationalism*. Armonk, NY: ME. Sharpe.

Wagner, R. 1992. "Reading the Chairman Mao Memorial Hall in Peking: The Tribulations of the Implied Pilgrim." In *Pilgrims and Sacred Sites in China*. Susan Naquin and Chun-Fang Yu, eds. Berkeley: University of California Press.

Wakeman, F. 1988. "Mao's Remains." In *Death Ritual in Late Imperial and Modern China*. James L. Wason and Evelyn S. Rawski, eds. Berkeley: University of California Press.

Wei, George C.X. and Xiaoyuan Liu, eds. 2002. *Exploring Nationalisms of China: Themes and Conflicts*. Westport, CT: Greenwood Press.

Weiss, M. 2002. The Body of the Nation: Terrorism and the Embodiment of Nationalism in Contemporary Israel. *Anthropological Quarterly* 75(1): 37–62.

Woronov, T.E. 2004. "In the Eye of the Chicken: Hierarchy and Marginality among Beijing's Migrant Schoolchildren." *Ethnography* 5(3): 289–313.

Woronov, T.E. n.d. "Governing China's Children: Governmentality and 'Education for Quality." Unpublished manuscript.

Wu, Hung. 2005. *Remaking Beijing: Tiananmen Square and the Creation of a Political Space*. London: Reaktion Books.

Zhao, B. 1998. "Popular Family Television and Party Ideology: the Spring Festival Eve Happy Gathering." *Media, Culture and Society* 20: 43–58.

Zhao, S. 2004. *A Nation-State by Construction: Dynamics of Modern Chinese Nationalism*. Stanford, CA: Stanford University Press.

Part V
Tourist Performances and the Global Ecumene

17

The Promise of Sonic Translation: Performing the Festive Sacred in Morocco

Deborah A. Kapchan

IT WAS AN UNUSUALLY cold May night in Fes, Morocco. The locals were wrapped in their woolen burnouses and jellabas, whereas many of the tourists had borrowed blankets from their hotel rooms. The concert venue was outside, the stage set up in front of a large 19th-century portal called Bab Makina and the chairs extending for hundreds of rows. I had managed to get a press pass that year and so proceeded to the reserved section. There was a buzz of excitement – television cameras from Morocco and France, dignitaries arriving, and Arabic, French, and English conversations swirling in the air. But then Faouzi Skali, the founder of the Fes Festival of World Sacred Music, stepped onto the stage. He announced the evening's concert in Arabic, and his words

were then loosely translated into French by artistic director Girard Kurdjian and then into English by Zeyba Rahman. The audience broke into loud applause, but a hush quickly fell over them as the Whirling Dervishes from Turkey took the stage and the ritual of *sama'*, or attentive listening, became a shared ritual for thousands.

How do international music festivals like this one perform sacred imaginaries for multi-faith audiences? What is their part in creating transnational communities of affect?[1] And what role does the sonic play in "sacred tourism?"[2] Although religious festivals and pilgrimages to them are certainly not new, I assert that international festivals that are marked for the sacred do create something

Deborah A. Kapchan, "The Promise of Sonic Translation: Performing the Festive Sacred in Morocco," pp. 467–483 from *American Anthropologist* 110(4), 2008.

different at the level of the transnational. Drawing together heterodox (that is multifaith) audiences from all over the globe, these festivals create public sentiment through the reappropriation and fetishization of the category of "the sacred," creating in the process a new form of pilgrimage in sacred tourism and a new kind of liturgy in world sacred music.

If the predominant narrative of both European and US secularisms has been a promise of freedom and peace through a universalizing and redemptive rationality – Max Weber's forecasted "disenchantment of the world" (Weber 1930) – then the promise of the festive sacred shifts that balance, locating those promises in the sacred and sonic traditions of the religious.[3] This promise literally reenchants the world (from the Latin, *incantere* – meaning to work magic, often through the incantation of spoken or chanted words, tones, or formulae). It does this, however, without erasing the particularities of discrete religious traditions – being inclusive without threatening dissolution. This is possible because the meeting of these traditions is not found in orthodoxy but in aesthetic praxis, and particularly in sacred sound.

Taking place in a Muslim country, what has come to be known as the "Fes Festival" sculpts a public face for Islam both nationally and internationally while also creating a forum for a nonsectarian experience of the sacred. On the basis of more than a decade of research with Sufi practitioners in the Boutshishiyya *tariqa* (a Sufi path in the Qadiri lineage, whose members have until recently been prominent at the festival), I demonstrate that the complicities of religion and tourism produce more than just commercial effects (Meyer and Moors 2006:3). Although not representing a resurgence of religious interest per se, I argue that the phenomenon of the sacred music festival draws on the religious sentiment evoked by sacred music to create a transnational (thus mobile) notion of "the sacred" that is in many ways a counterpoint to the specificity and ideology of more orthodox forms of religious practice. It does so by enacting a promise – what I refer to as the "promise of sonic translation" – premised on the belief that music can translate affect across cultural and linguistic divides. What part of this promise is fulfilled?

The Festive Sacred and the Promise of Sonic Translation

Sacred music festivals are proliferating worldwide. Not only does the Fes Festival attracts thousands of sacred tourists each year but also it has spawned sister festivals: the Festival of World Religious Music in Gérona, Spain; the Festival of World Sacred Music in Dijon, France; and others in Perpignan, France, Sintra, Portugal, and Florence, Italy. These festivals are linked to the festival in Fes, in that they often have the same musicians, the same theme, and many of the same sponsors. What is more, the Fes Festival and what is called "the Fes message" has recently toured 18 cities in the United States.

The Fes Festival is an international affair, and its influence is expanding. I was at the home of festival founder, Faouzi Skali, the day the fax came from the Dalai Lama, announcing his plans to also create a series of sacred music festivals in Geneva, Los Angeles, and elsewhere. Skali – a charismatic Sufi who also has a doctorate in anthropology from the Sorbonne and is the author of several books on Sufism (see Skali 1989, 1993, 1996, 2000) – had recently attended an interfaith meeting with the Dalai Lama and others at which the Fes Festival had been a topic of discussion. Not long afterward, the Dalai Lama gave his sponsorship to a sacred music festival in Geneva and in Los Angeles that brought international artists to local stages. The World Festival of Sacred Music in Los Angeles was born. This festival now takes place every three years. The website for 2005 exhorts potential audience members to "open your hearts and listen" (World Festival of Sacred Music n.d.).

The promise of sonic translation is ubiquitous around the world. Indeed, audiences at the Fes Festival come from Morocco, France, and the United States year after year to listen to the sacred sounds of many religious traditions. They are the festive faithful. How then do heterodox audiences become perennial coauditors of sacred and affecting sounds?

I assert that these listeners find common ground not through their religious beliefs per se but, rather, through participation in a common promise: that of translation, which holds that all languages, although different, are allied through kinship and thus may be known (Benjamin 1969). This promise does not have to be fulfilled to be effective; indeed, translation contains the seeds of its own failure. As Jacques Derrida notes in his study of Walter Benjamin, a "translation never succeeds in the pure and absolute sense of the term. Rather, a translation succeeds in promising success, in promising reconciliation. . . . a good translation is one that enacts the performative called the promise with the result that through the translation one sees the coming shape of a possible reconciliation among languages" (Derrida 1985:123). For Derrida, this reconciliation is ultimately impossible. Nonetheless, the discourse that posits the belief in and hope for a kind of utopian "transparency of codes" does important social work (Crapanzano 2004; Miyazaki 2004).[4] It is the work of the promise that moves mountains, so to speak, at sacred music festivals around the world.

A promise is a "performative": it enacts rather than refers and by its very action accomplishes its goal, which is to create an inter-subjective contract that is often affective and implicit rather than acknowledged and juridical (Austin 1962). But the verb *to promise* is also a transitive construction: I promise to meet a deadline, to arrive on time, to be faithful, and so forth. A promise engages the promiser and promisee in an affective exchange that extends beyond the moment of utterance. Indeed, a promise and a translation are akin in their assumption of an unstated trust:

All understanding, and the demonstrative statement of understanding which is translation, starts with an act of trust. This confiding will, ordinarily, be instantaneous and unexamined, but it has a complex base. It is an operative convention which derives from a sequence of phenomenological assumptions about the coherence of the world, about the presence of meaning in very different, perhaps formally antithetical semantic systems, about the validity of analogy and parallel.

(Steiner 1998:193)

As an "operative convention," translation – and its promise – takes us into the heart of what it means to be human together, cocreating "the presence of meaning" in embodied and semantic domains. This is not just a cognitive endeavor. As Benjamin reminds us, "translation is a mode" (Benjamin 1969:70). Like music, translation is emotionally inflected, carrying mood and character, whether translating from language to language (interlingual translation) or across semiotic systems such as from music to words, for example, and back again (Jakobson 2000:139). Translation is an act that requires the translator to imagine "reconciliation" and to embody that imagination.

Audiences in Fes inhabit the promise of this reconciliation, but the language of promise is musical: that is, what festival organizers promise – in brochures, travel literature, and conference discourse – is sonic translation, the "trust" in the ultimate translatability of aural (as opposed to textual) codes. In the Fes Festival, the promise of translation is cultivated first in publicly circulating discourse and subsequently created somatically in sonic experience.

Learning to Listen

This promise falls on well-tilled ground and on educated ears. Indeed, the phenomenon of world beat music has been instrumental in creating new auditory practices that prepare audiences to embrace and enact this promise. Although music is often held up as the "universal language," in fact aesthetic attunement is always learned (albeit often early and unconsciously). World beat has tuned the ear to difference by developing new ways of listening and new things to listen to and for (see Erlmann 2003; Feld 1994; Taylor 1997). These "literacies of listening" (Kapchan n.d.) create an audience defined by diverse tastes but a common desire: namely, to consume and sonically inhabit a multiplicity of (in this case, sacred) cultures. When US auditors listen to qawwali music at the Fes Festival, for example, they can identify the Pakistani origins of the music, but they also hear the resonances of world music radio programs, of concerts in university auditoriums, and perhaps even of interviews on National Public Radio.

"Qawwali" indexes "Pakistani music" and "Sufi Music" but also the ubiquity of global trance and new-age mysticism – at least for those in the United States and Europe. Not surprisingly, Moroccan audiences are smallest at qawwali concerts. Unlike gospel or jazz music, qawwali is rarely heard on the Moroccan airwaves. World beat, although pervasive, is not even in its influence.

Nonetheless, the self-selecting festival audience embraces the promise. Whether meditatively listening to gamelan music, bobbing the head up and down in trance to the Moroccan Gnawa, or rocking out to the gospel music of Doctor Bobby Jones, auditors open their ears to new sounds and their minds to new understandings of what "sacred" might mean in different traditions. These include Hasidic songs from Eastern Europe, Gregorian chants from England, Mudéjar music from Spain, religious gypsy songs from France, qawwali music from Pakistan, and Sufi music from Morocco, Turkey, and Egypt. Couple these traditions with "dancing monks" from Tibet and South African choral music and a large section of the sacred globe is represented. By employing sounds iconically linked to particular sacred traditions and recontextualizing them in contexts of heterodoxy, festival organizers self-consciously create a sort of doxa of their own, one that downplays national and religious differences to emphasize "spiritual" or "sacred" homogeneity (Bourdieu 1977). The sacred is extracted from these traditions like essence is extracted from flowers.

The Festive Sacred: Beyond the Nation

"We must learn to judge a society more by its sounds, by its art, and by its festivals, than by its statistics."

— Jacques Attali, *Noise: The Political Economy of Music*

Historically, festivals in Morocco brought people together around the celebration of a saint or religious holy day (Eickelman 1976). Festivals were set apart from quotidian time, creating a "time out of time" – and space (Caillois 1960; Falassi 1987:4).[5] Of course, large gatherings of pilgrims provided an ideal opportunity for commercial exchange, and saints' festivals (or *moussem*s) and markets were often held at the same time and in the same place. This practice continues today in such celebrations as the moussem of Moulay Brahim in the High Atlas mountains (Hell 2001). After independence in 1956, however, nonreligious festivals like the Marrakech Folklore Festival became increasingly popular. This festival and others that followed displayed the cultural diversity of Moroccan music and dance traditions to both European and Moroccan tourists. In the 20th century, international festivals – in Morocco and elsewhere – continue to display national diversity to local audiences but increasingly attract diverse audiences to exotic and often "sacred" locales (cf. Bauman et al. 1992; Brandes 1988; Guss 2000; Noyes 2003; see also Abrahams 1987; Turner 1982). Moreover, it is now necessary to demarcate festivals that self-consciously construct "the sacred" from those that enact it under other guises; some festivals, that is, are specifically marked for "the sacred" with strategic intent.

In postindependence Morocco, festivals became both more international and more secular. Indeed, Morocco is now a country of festivals. Although there are still religious festivals associated with a local saint, each year the Ministry of Culture sponsors more than a dozen nonreligious festivals that celebrate local traditions as much as they fete the diversity of national culture. The Festival of Andalusian Music is held in Chef Chaouen, for example, the oldest Andalusian city in Morocco. Likewise the 'Aita Festival is held in Sai, the city most known for this genre of music (often called shikhat music). Several of these festivals celebrate the cultural and linguistic diversity of Morocco (particularly the Festival de Poésie et Chant Amazigh in Midelt and the Festival Poésie et Chant Hassani in Dakhla), thereby giving value to populations and races that have been marginalized, if not oppressed and discriminated against, in the past (Guss 2000). There are also celebrations of *zajal*, spoken poetry in dialect, as well as symposia on Moroccan literature and visual arts. In addition to these national festivals, there are several international festivals in Morocco patronized by the King and sponsored by the private sector: these include the Mouazzine ("Rhythms") Festival in Rabat, the Tangier Jazz Festival, the Essaouira Gnawa Festival of World Music (Kapchan 2008), and the Fes Festival of World Sacred Music.

The Moroccan monarchy has many stakes in the spate of yearly festivals. They construct a public discourse of neoliberalism and engage the producers (usually artists and academicians nominated to political positions in the Ministry of Culture) in the active creation of Moroccan culture as a product for national and international consumption (the tourist industry being one of the most lucrative sources of income for the Moroccan state). In short, the nation has much to hope for in festival production, both materially and otherwise.

These festivals, however, are not without their public opponents. On June 25, 2004, for example, the imam of the Hassan II mosque in Casablanca delivered a sermon (khutba) in which he condemned several practices in the Moroccan public sphere, among them, women's access to public beaches, mixed-sex working conditions, and music festivals. This sermon, broadcast on Moroccan radio and television, exemplified a conservative backlash provoked by both the newly instituted family code laws (giving women more rights) and the fear unleashed by the Casablanca bombings a year earlier. Coming at the height of the festival season in Morocco, journalists as well as festival promoters did not fail to counter this attack in their own media coverage, writing passionately about the sociopolitical benefits of festivals and touting the ability of religiously diverse crowds to live and celebrate together. Such public debates place festivals in the center of moral, political, and religious scrutiny.

As sacred festivals take on lives of their own, they become a testing ground for free speech, free-market capitalism, and civil liberties – the hopes, it may be said, of a modernizing nation. Yet, the hand of the state is not the only agent in the production of these festivals. Despite the fact that they take place in very historic cities like Fes, the festivals are in no way local in their effects. Religious and cultural identities are also constructed and contested in these forums. Indeed, the festive sacred participates in a new order that is, in part, a response to the proliferation of sectarian and mobile movements that characterize the postmodern moment (Appadurai 2006). These movements – exemplified in Morocco by Islamists but also by the so-called "good Muslims" (Mamdani 2002), in this case Sufi groups with local roots but international followings – thrive in the tension between the centripetal forces of nationalism and the centrifugal forces of transnationalism.

Sacred music festivals represent the antithesis of religious conservatism not only because they are explicitly denounced by people like the imam of the Hassan II mosque but also because the festival organizers as well as the participants self-consciously construct an alternative notion of "the sacred" for public and popular consumption. It is not just "the secular" that threatens the imam, at least in the case of the festival, but another way to define the religious.

Defining the Sacred

Since the Enlightenment, "the sacred" has often been understood as a transhistorical and universal category (Asad 2003). Yet as Anna Tsing has shown, the construction of the "universal" is often deliberate and strategic (Tsing 2004). Just as scholars of religion like Émile Durkheim created the very concept of "the sacred" in analyses of world religions (Asad 2003), what we witness almost two centuries later in the age of the international festival is a similar re-creation of the sacred as universal category – now defined not in terms of abstract concepts and theologies but in terms of lived aesthetics. Festival creators are unaware that their use of this category actually redefines the sacred as a mode of multifaith "worship." Yet it is clear that the festive sacred is sedimenting new aesthetic practices in a community whose beliefs are diverse but who are united by a promise: not the secularist promise of peace through the (disenchanting) human capacity for universal rationality (Weber 1930; cf. Jakobson and Pellegrini 2008) but, rather, the promise of reenchantment through belief in the universality (translatability) of sonic devotion.

An example will illustrate this: there is a French journalist who comes to the Fes Festival every year. Having spent time in conflict areas in the Middle East, she understands how difficult it is to get Jews and Muslims to listen to and really "hear" one another. Yet at the Fes Festival, she attends a concert where Jewish performer Françoise Atlan sings with Muslim Aisha Redouane and Christian Monser-rat Figueras. "It is quite remarkable," the journalist tells me later. "Here in Fes there is a part of magic. We have an example of what the world could be if we listened to each other (*si on était à l'écoute l'un de l'autre*). It's only then that we know how to get along. I think it has something to do with the music" (conversation with author, June 2, 2003). The journalist's use of an idiom that has to do with hearing is not spurious: to be *à l'écoute* is to be tuned into (as the radio), to listen or be attentive to. This idiom inundates the festival literature as well, where audition, not textual literacy, becomes a means of accessing the universal, and music, not negotiation, is the means to social change. Defining "the sacred" through sound and developing new literacies of listening are foundational strategies in the festival agenda.

The Fes Festival of Sacred Music In Situ

The Fes Festival was initially a local response to a global crisis – the (mis)representation of Islam to the West during the first Gulf War. Since then, the festival has attracted thousands of spectators each year who, during ten days, listen to music from different religious traditions, watch films, and attend panels that bring together religious, political, and cultural leaders (including scholars, artists, and "secularists") to discuss the role of religion and religious expression in contemporary societies (see Curtis 2007). People such as Jacques Attali (France), Benjamin R. Barber (United States), Leïla Chahid (Palestine), Rabbi Bradley Hirschield (United States), Mireille Mendes-France (France), Siddhartha (India), and Wim Wenders (Germany), among many others, come to lend their ears and ideas to a dialogue for peace. Although it is billed as a "festival"

(and thus partakes in the politicoeconomic history of other large-scale display events in late capitalism), it has an explicit political agenda, embodied most clearly in the permanent theme of the yearly colloquium: "giving a soul to globalization." The interlocutors at the Fes Festival, in other words, attempt to wed religion to politics via music. Furthermore, religions are represented by and consequently redefined through their musical traditions. Although the colloquium that accompanies the festival involves (sometimes heated) debate, the constant reference point for the speakers – their counterpoint so to speak – is the sacred music that brings them together.

The Fes Festival has kept in step with current political crises and is now deeply implicated in creating counternarratives to that of the Muslim as fundamentalist and terrorist. What is unique about this effort is the use of aesthetics as a primary tool of encounter. As Sufis, Faouzi Skali and his associates believe that actively listening to the sacred sounds of another tradition creates a mode of reception and communication not usually accessible in rational thought. "All cultures and religions have sacred musical traditions," Skali told me, "whether chanted prayers or calls to prayer" (conversation with author, June 25, 2003). Indeed, the participants at the festival and its yearly colloquium share this interest in comparativism. Commenting on the relation between the Fes Festival and the sacred arts, the late dancer and choreographer Maurice Béjart noted that "chant is the origin of all spiritual traditions. The Qur'ran in Islam or the Upanishads in Hinduism are sacred texts that are chanted, like psalms. Behind this chant, the primordial sound links us to the creation of the world" (2004:108). For Béjart, Skali, and others, there is a universality to these expressions of praise, although the aesthetic systems differ from place to place. Indeed, tuning the ear of diverse audiences to different aesthetic systems to create attunement across religions is one of the challenges of the festival.

This aesthetic enterprise is of necessity implicated in an economic one as well, involving the creation of sacred tourism – in this instance, "Sufi tourism." Although pilgrimages often exist hand-in-hand with a tourist economy (Badone and Roseman 2004; Delaney 1990; Kirshenblatt-Gimblett 1998), the sophisticated markets created in the production of an international festival of this dimension and in its wake mean that the pilgrimages taken to destinations like Fes are highly orchestrated capitalist events. They have included post-festival tours to the Sahara Desert to participate in Sufi *dhikr* ceremonies and specialized tours for groups of new-age adherents from the United States and France. In Barbara Kirshen-blatt-Gimblett's words, "destination culture" becomes here "destination religion" (1998).

These groups are not visible at the concerts so much as in the hotel lobbies and restaurants, sometimes wearing Moroccan robes and scarves and often carrying prayer beads or other religious insignia. Indeed, it is at the hotels (two through five star) that the different interest groups meet and often politely avoid each other, usually mingling only with their language group.

"The Spirit of Fes" and and the Reification of Place

"Fes doesn't reveal itself easily. To have access to it, it is necessary to go in through the big door, both visible and invisible, of the sacred. Because Fes is a shrine. It is thus that the Soufis, the initiates of Islam, have always called it: the *zawiya*."

(Skali 2004, translation by author)

The Fes Festival builds much of its promotional materials around the "shrine" of Fes. Fes is the home of al-Qarawiyyen, a theological university, or *madrasa*, built in the ninth century (CE 857) that is one of the largest centers for Islamic learning in North Africa. The famous Sufi saint Ibn al-'Arabi had a vision in Fes, and it is the spiritual home to numerous Sufi *turuq*, or paths. Indeed, the 2001 brochure describes Fes as what Pierre Nora would call a "lieu de memoire" (Nora 1989), a site of memory for the "Sacred," with a capital "S":

This festival was created from the meeting of people of diverse interests and itineraries with Fez [sic], a city that holds the memory of what

once was the culture and tradition of the Sacred. Tied to this past, the medina (medieval city) of Fez still continues to live by the rhythm of the call to prayer and religious celebrations . . . . Founded by Moulay Idriss in 809, Fez is the oldest of the imperial cities, and the religious and intellectual metropolis of Morocco. The city has opened its doors to many populations: the Berbers, Arabs, Andalousians, Jews.

(Association Fes-Saiss 2001)

Like the music it hosts, the city becomes an actor in this narrative, offering the rhythms of the "Sacred" and opening its doors to heterogeneous populations, including Jews who comprised a significant part of the Fes population until a mass migration to Israel after Moroccan independence in 1956. (The Jewish cemetery is a popular tourist destination.) But this attitude toward Fes as a place of diversity and power is not restricted to festival brochures. As political scientist Roland Cayrol noted, "I believe in the necessity of making tradition live. I think that Fes, where in only turning a corner one meets Ibn Khaldoun, [and] Ibn al-Banna or Maimonides, is marvelously placed to do this, since as a [former] capital, it knows how to make intellectual and religious contributions live together" (2004:96, translation by author). Stressing its history as a crossroads of multiple ethnicities and faiths, Fes – like Andalousia in much contemporary scholarship (Shannon 2007; see also Menocal 2003) – comes to represent a place of tolerance and multiculturalism in a world torn by intolerance and religious strife.

A considerable amount of Morocco's revenues come from tourism, and the Fes Festival attracts the largest amount of international tourists to this destination. Nonetheless, it is difficult for the Fes business people to sustain themselves on tourism alone, especially after the attacks of September 11, 2001, in the United States and the subsequent war with Iraq. Tourism to Arab countries (on the part of citizens of the United States and United Kingdom, in any case) is down. As one bed-and-breakfast owner put it: "Fes comes alive for the ten days of the festival and then goes back to sleep for the rest of the year" (conversation with author, May 20,

2003). Nonetheless, Fes continues to perform its role as a site of pilgrimage, the *zawiya*, the city as sacred shrine. Indeed, for the ten days of the festival, Fes becomes a "living museum in situ" where tourists can visit the tanneries, the spice markets, some old *madrasa*s, and the public ovens and baths (Kirshenblatt-Gimblett 1998:54). Only Muslims, however, can visit the mosques. In Morocco, this sacred space is off-limits to non-Muslim tourists.

Among Moroccans, Fes has the reputation of being a conservative Muslim city where religious activity is particularly fervent. State elections were postponed in 2003, for example, as it was estimated that the religious right would have won the city of Fes as well as a few other major areas. It is considered the spiritual capital of Morocco because of the religious conservatism present but also because of the presence of many (not necessarily conservative) Sufi groups.

Attending to Audition

Ambivalence about what qualifies as sacred music, however, haunt the Fes Festival. In the early years, the musicians were drawn from the three monotheistic religions "of the book" – Judaism, Christianity, and Islam (particularly Sufism) – but more recently the festival has featured Tibetan Buddhist "dancing monks" as well as Balinese gamelan music. When I expressed a bit of dismay to and asked Skali how he defined "sacred" music, he replied, "All music that praises God qualifies as sacred" (conversation with author, June 25, 2003). Indeed, the musical director has taken pains to be inclusive of as many traditions as possible. As the festival has grown in popularity, however, the program has featured more music that is indisputably secular, artists like the Israeli singer Noa and the late South African Miriam Makeba. Again, when I pressed Skali to respond, he said that "some music is also included for its political presence – an Israeli singer whose repertoire includes songs in Hebrew, Arabic, Ladino, and English, for example, sends a message of tolerance. Makeba's songs against racism contain messages important to the festival's ideology" (conversation with author, June 25,

2003). He went on to say that his aspirations for the festival exceeded sacred aesthetics: "My hope for the festival," Skali told me, "is that it be a model for inter-cultural civil society" (conversation with author, June 25, 2003).

However, there are some musicians who seem to be there just to attract a crowd. The Moroccan performer Rouisha has rarely, if ever, performed a sacred repertoire, but he is a performer whose fame as an Amazighi (Berber) artist in the 1960s has entered him into the Moroccan canon of popular music. (The Amazighi population in Morocco are considered the autochthonous peoples of North Africa; they converted to Islam in the sixth century after the Arab invasion.) His 2004 performance, with female singing and dance accompaniment, took place in the ancient Roman ruins of Volubulis, in implicit deference, it may be said, to the antiquity of the Berbers on Moroccan soil but more because of their value as emblems of national folklore and heritage (Boum 2007). Likewise the songs of Syrian singer Sabah Fakhri are mostly nonreligious, although he begins his sets at the Fes Festival with songs of the *muwashshahat* (an Arab-Andalusian genre) that exist in both sacred and secular repertoires, with only the lyrics changing in each case. Given his status as an internationally renowned musician, Fakhri draws a large and very enthusiastic crowd. It is clear that the "sacred" music festival has loosened its criteria a bit with the passing years to please audiences and to bring in larger revenues. However, there are sacred standards that are consistent: every year the whirling dervishes are on the bill, as are musicians from the three religions of the book such as Sister Marie Keyrouz, for example, who sings Christian song in Arabic, and Rabbi Louk, who sings song from the Jewish diaspora. Indeed, the festival always begins with a concert of voices: Muslim, Jewish, and Christian singer collaborating together.

It is the activity of listening, however, that festival organizer deem even more sacred than the music itself. *Sama'* – attentive and active listening, called "deep listening" by Western scholars and composers (Becker 2004; Oliveros 2005) – is a method of spiritual discipline in Sufi doctrine that leads to the development of what may be called the "higher senses and emotions."[6] The doctrine of sama' imbues much of the discourse in festival brochures. "In the musician-auditor couple," notes artistic director Girard Kurdjian, "it is the latter who is really able . . . to allow him- or herself to focus on the extremes of intensity and celestial delight that obtains from this 'spiritual audition' (Sama')" (2004:10). In discourses like this one, the Sufi practice of sama' becomes the modus operandus for the festival itself. Kurdjian goes on to say,

> sacred musics are . . . works of reason and lucidity, in which art, technical mastery and knowledge are linked to the potential for exaltation and trance-states at the heart of all sacred music. The intense concentration borne over the moment connects to outpourings of enthusiasm (in the proper sense of the original Greek Enthousiasmos, 'carried away by God') that flows from the heart.
>
> (Kurdjian 2004:10)

Here Kurdjian writes a kind of manual for the concert-goer that links the "enthusiasm" inspired by the music with spiritual states in the listener. Indeed, like the city of Fes, "musics and songs of the sacred" are given their own agency, functioning as "a sort of direct illumination that, partly without our being aware of it, and beyond the limitations of words, languages and distinct customs, touch our bodies, our souls and Spirit, and awaken them to vast and profound orders of higher reality" (Kurdjian 2004:10). In this brochure and other promotional materials, the technique of deep listening (what Kurdjian calls "spiritual audition") carries the promise of a "trans-temporal Knowledge" or spiritual gnosis that auditors learn together.

Deep listening is a pedagogy at the festival, and auditors become apprentices of this method. Insofar as they learn an auditory discipline, they become symbolic disciples of sacred sound, sharing in the communion that such colearning constitutes. The audience is encouraged to become a coauthor, or in this case a coperformer, in the musical event (Brenneis 1987; Duranti and Brenneis 1986). This is not a mundane event but a "sacred" one. Audiences come to the festival predisposed to have transcendent experiences and, listening together, they often have them. The music at the Fes Festival is, to borrow the words of Attali, "more than an object of study: it is a way of perceiving the world" (1985:4). It is the goal of the Fes Festival to create a new perception.

Not unlike the Egyptians in the piety movement that Charles Hirschkind studies, many of the audience members with whom I spoke "listen with their heart" (Hirschkind 2006; Shannon 2006) to cultivate a spiritual self and community with others. Unlike those in the piety movement, however, the audiences in Fes do not delimit themselves doctrinally but are encouraged to listen as a way to bridge and even transcend ideologies. Seated under a huge magnolia tree at the afternoon concerts, French and US tourists in jellabas, turbans, and scarves sway with eyes closed to the music of Egyptian Sufi, Shaykh Yassin al-Tuhami. But Moroccans are also swaying with eyes closed. This is not to say that listening practices are uniform among heterogeneous audiences. To the contrary, the participatory nature of Arab music and the ecstasy (tarab) it produces are very different than Western practices of audition, particularly in regard to sacred and classical music (Shannon 2003; see also Racy 2003). Although Moroccan audiences often chat, socialize, and express their appreciation with verbal exclamations at the festival performances, Western audiences are offended by such behaviors, turning around to "shush" their Moroccan neighbors. In 1999, when the opera diva Montserrat Caballe and her daughter Montserrat Marti were on the bill, my Moroccan neighbors were having an animated conversation during the performance. The French couple next to me were appalled and made their feelings evident: "Taissez-vous" [be quiet], they said, turning with annoyance to the Moroccans, who rolled their eyes at the reprimand. But even these intercultural enactments are instructive. As the years have passed, Moroccan audiences have become quieter during operatic performances, for example, and Western audiences have become more expressive, especially during performances of more popular Arab music where they witness the rapture of Moroccan audience members surrounding them. During one Sabah Fakhri concert, the Moroccans were the first to stand up and dance, but the French and US tourists did not tarry in following their lead. Pointing to the Westerners doing their renditions of belly dance, one rather formal Moroccan gentleman near me laughed in amusement and then got up to join the fun. Tarab may be said to be contagious in this regard.

In the 11th century, al-Ghazzali presciently noted that "whenever the soul of the music and singing reaches the heart, then there stirs in the heart that which it preponderates" (1901). In the context of the sacred music festival, what the heart preponderates is often its own opening and transformation: so promised, so experienced.

Sufi Nights, Sacred Tourism

Experience is, in fact, key. The Fes Festival now sponsors what are called "Sufi Nights" after every major concert. These "nights" are held in the open air in the courtyard of the Fes-Saiss headquarters. Beginning after ten each evening and sometimes lasting until three or four in the morning, the Sufi Nights are intended to give audiences a taste of authentic Sufi ritual, including music, al-hadra (a form of Sufi movement that leads to ecstasy and transcendence), and chanted prayer. On the bill in 2004 were the 'Aissawa brotherhood, the Hamdouchia, the Sqalliya, and others.

These rituals are free and open to the public. They therefore attract a large crowd, including a large number of Moroccan youth. There are also food tents set up in the area where attendees may refresh themselves with soft drinks, soup, dates, and sweet mint tea. ("Taste" is the sense most utilized in Sufi metaphor: it is necessary to actually incorporate the transcendent, to taste and become one with the divine.) These "nights" are particularly important because they extend the reach of the sacred music festival to people who may not be able to afford to attend the main events or to those whose enthusiasm for sacred music reaches beyond the mere pleasure of audition to the enactment of ritual.[7] Although the ritual practitioners are clearly set apart in their dress, the demarcation between performer and audience is much more porous at the Sufi Nights, with audience

members in trancelike states in close proximity to the performers. These ceremonies display a formerly private event for initiates to an eager and often naïve public. In so doing, they gain publicity for the Sufi tariqa and its particular musical styles (all without exception made a compact disc recording that was on sale at the event), while adding an element of mysticism and excess to the festival program, as festival goers stay up until the small hours of the morning to have an "authentic" experience.

Although music has always been a part of Sufi ritual, the category of "Sufi music" was essentially born with the world beat phenomenon, as Sufi musicians from Morocco to Pakistan toured the world, entrancing Western audiences with hypnotic and holy beats (Bohlman 1997; Keil and Feld 1994; Shannon 2003; Taylor 1997). Perhaps the most well-known (commodified) example is that of the Whirling Dervishes who spin on the balls of their feet with one arm extended up toward God and the other down towards the earth, seeking axis with and access to divinity. Just as the dervishes have become the emblem of Turkey for the tourist industry despite their repression in the sociopolitical sphere for so many years, so Sufism writ large has become the banner of Muslim tolerance in the face of more orthodox forms of Islam represented in the press (Bohlman 1997:66–67). Moreover, in the transnational era of sacred tourism where pilgrimages involve air travel, hotels, and often new disciplines of the body at holy sites (yoga, chanting, and forms of dress), sacred tourism – which in Morocco becomes "Sufi tourism" – finds its own special niche (see Cornell 1998; Eickelman 1976). Sufism comes to signify an ancient and mystical knowledge that tourists can nonetheless experience through music, movement, and the senses.

The Sufi Nights provide the most intimate listening experience at the festival. People walk around, talk, and eat. They also push against each other while straining to see the musicians, sway in trance, sit knee to knee, and strike up conversations. But the performance of Sufi ritual has more than just aesthetic import. Now, as in Moroccan history, Sufism plays a strategic political role (Cornell 1998). Although the forms of Islam practiced in

Morocco are influenced by many kinds of Sufism, one path is particularly prominent: the *tariqa qadiriyya boutshishiyya*, a Sufi path in the Qadiri lineage (named after shaykh Sidi Boumadyane Ben al-Mnawwaral Qâdiri al-Butchîchi) whose living leader is Shaykh Hamza in northeastern Morocco.[8] Since the death of King Hassan II in 1999 and the ascension to the throne of his son, Mohammed VI, several high government positions have been filled by Sufi practitioners in this path, including the Minister of Religious Affairs, Ahmed Toufiq. The founder of the Fes Festival, Faouzi Skali, is also an adherent to this path. The close alliance of the Monarchy and this branch of Sufism is strategic. Although politics and religion are of necessity intertwined in an Islamic society, the new prominence of Sufis in the political leadership provides an ambiance that is recognized as tolerant (a counterinfluence to the growing Islamist movements in Morocco and abroad) and that accepts musical traditions as expressions of faith.

"Giving Soul to Globalization"

Since 2002, a conference has been taking place during the festival that explores the difficult issues and intersections of religion and globalization. Like the festival, this conference is the brain child of Faouzi Skali and proceeds on the premise that deep, attentive listening, even in the intellectual domain, may be transformative. Katherine Marshall, the former director of "Ethics and Values" at the World Bank, has been instrumental in garnering the funds and the speakers for this conference, which has included scholars, activists, diplomats, and artists from all continents of the globe. The 2002 "Giving Soul to Globalization" conference had such politically divergent speakers as Thai public intellectual and social activist Sulak Sivaraksa and World Trade Organization director Mike Moore. Putting spiritualists and materialists together was a challenge to everyone's capacity to listen to one another and was sometimes frustrating, verging on argumentative. I remember one prominent French participant turning to me, shaking his head and mumbling, "*on ne fait rien ici*" ([we're not doing anything here]; conversation with author, June 2, 2002). In 2004 the conference participants were more united, whether by design or because the Iraq War garnered the criticism of most all the participants. Palestinian activist Leila Chahid and Moroccan-born Israeli filmmaker Simone Bitton brought the audience to tears with their testimonies concerning the war in the Middle East. Economist and former advisor to former French president Mitterand, Jaques Attali, argued with Buddhist monk and activist-author Mathieu Ricard about the agency of compassion. Hans-Peter Duerr, nuclear physicist, philosopher, and former director of the Max Planck Institute, advocated a cosmic approach: "Reality is made of matter," he said, "but matter disappears in nuclear physics and only the connection remains. It is necessary to focus not on unity, but [on] the connectedness of everything" (field notes, May 29, 2004). These scholars rarely stress religion; rather, the "sacred" in all traditions becomes the universal currency.

Internationally recognized intellectuals have given their stamp to the Fes Festival as a forum where not only music moves audiences but also audiences, in turn, move out into the world with what has come to be called "the Fes message." What's more, the participants are now referred to as "le club de Fes"; they are the musicians, intellectuals, and perennial attendees who, despite differences in religion, ideology, nation, race, or gender, believe that the "spirit of Fes" is an affective force generated at the festival by the collective efforts of the participants and then transported outside its context of origin to spiral into the world. The people who come to the Fes festival are elites: artists, intellectuals, filmmakers, and scientists. They (like I) can carry the "Fes message" beyond the borders of Fes.

Conclusion: Sacred Aesthetics and the Festive Sacred

"Imagination understands in modes foreign to reason."

– Ibn Al-'Arabi, *The Sufi Path of Knowledge: Ibn Al-'Arabi's Metaphysics of Imagination*

What is the difference between "world music" and "world sacred music" as represented in Fes? Much like the Moroccan multilingual who is able to understand elaborate code switching from Arabic to French to Berber to English and back, the auditor for world music has a trained ear that is able both to identify the different stylistic components of the music and to locate their own identity as global citizens in its iconic resonances. The world beat phenomenon, in other words, has produced a "literacy of listening," an ability to hear the components in the mix (Kapchan n.d.). Indeed, it is this literacy that allows the festive faithful to inhabit a promise, without which these festivals could not exist. World beat has gone out into the world like a prophet preparing the way (Attali 1985).

World sacred music, however, is usually not a hybrid fusion of traditions and styles. In the case of the primarily monotheistic religions of the Book presented at the Fes Festival, it is the voice that carries power and purity (not hybridity) that is celebrated (however invented, reconstructed, or revived). The majority of the acts are vocal and represent a singular religious tradition (however hybrid the tradition has been in the making). The voice – which carries the connotation of the unmediated in all the "religions of the book" – becomes iconic of the authentic and the true.

The discrete traditions presented at the Fes Festival have a long history of decontextualization from their ritual contexts, yet the festival commodifies the aesthetic elements of religious traditions to the exclusion of their concomitant beliefs. This is not a simple process of secularization, however. To the contrary, the recontextualization of these "sacred" musical traditions in a festive environment is accompanied by a promise of affective reenchantment. Although the organizers of the Fes Festival invite people of different religions (but often the same class) to experience the transcendent aspects of discrete traditions, promising to translate what is recognized as religious sentiment across cultural and aesthetic divides, they are also invested in creating something that can be formalized and repeated. To this end, compact discs are made every year, and the festival-goers return to their place of origin with sounds

that link them to Fes as well as to each other. Audiences are brought back to the "sanctuary" and their pilgrimage through sonic memory and an auditory token.

The Fes Festival reifies existing sacred aesthetic traditions, drawing on concepts like "heritage" (*turath*) and "tradition" (*taqalid*) in their literature, while spinning these concepts in the direction of the universal. "To enrich the cultural memory of *humanity*," noted Turkish musician Kudsi Erguner in the 2001 colloquium, "it is indispensable that each person be able to access their *own* cultural heritage" (Erguner 2003:203, emphasis added and translation by author). Being grounded in one's "home" tradition is a necessary prerequisite to contributing to the more "universal" heritage of world sacred music (Tsing 2004).

Victor Turner's insights into the "communitas" created in festive environments delimits the way embodied ritual performances create common feeling for social actors who usually share a common history (Turner 1974). In the age of the global festival, however, neither history nor religion are held in common. Indeed, it is the work of the international festival, especially those whose express theme is the "sacred," to create common cause and common affect across lines of religion, ethnicity, nation, and – to the extent that women perform sacred Islamic repertoire – gender. Feeling together, however, is not the same as feeling the same thing. By making deep or attentive listening (sama') the designated sacred practice of the festival, organizers draw on the literacies fostered by the world music market to cultivate auditory practices that themselves perform promise, engaging audiences in a work in common – a kind of listening for peace at a moment in history when tensions between religious groups are high.

It is no accident that the Fes Festival takes place in a Muslim country at a time when all Muslim productions are being heavily scrutinized and analyzed by "the West." Nor is it accidental that the "moderate" and tolerant face of Sufism is being used by the Moroccan government for political ends. The Fes Festival creates both a national profile internationally and a transnational community in a Muslim locale. It also produces revenues for the state and for the city residents. There are times when the hopes of artists, intellectuals, NGOs, the state, and international banks coincide.

Ultimately, however, interests of national and global corporations fit uneasily with artistic and, in this case, sacred visions. To wit, in 2007 the Fes Festival changed directors. The budget of the festival was curtailed and its ownership put into question, despite the fact that Skali claimed the copyright for the festival and its name (Alami 2006). In short, Skali's power and autonomy were challenged, so he left the festival and began another – "The World Festival of Sufi Music and Culture" – the goals of which are more specific: to promote Sufi culture to non-Sufis, whether Moroccan or US and European.

The (re)turn to Sufism is significant. As a Sufi, it is what Skali knows best. But the implications are broader than that. Sufism does important political work both nationally and internationally, challenging the conflation of Islam with orthodoxy and conservatism. (Indeed, Skali is currently involved in the opening of a Sufi university in Morocco.)

"Sufi music" is also more "authentic" to Morocco, appealing to the adept in sacred festivity who wants to deepen knowledge of a particular strand of mystical tradition. The promise of sonic translation is still extant but the comparative base is smaller. The festive sacred as a configuration of aesthetic and embodied practices is also present, although with a twist: that is, people of different religions and nations create and cohabit an experience of the sacred through heightened attention to auditory, sense-based, and Sufi modes of devotion. There is precedent for this more specialized enactment in festivals like the Estonian International Festival of Orthodox Sacred Music (CREDO) or even the Alwan Sacred Music Festival in New York, billed as "Arab Sufi Music with Tarab" (ecstasy). The interdependence between particular ritual and universal sacredness is itself a credo.

Although Skali's relations with the organizers of the Fes Festival of World Sacred Music are now amicable, he nonetheless has decided to consecrate himself entirely to what he most recently has called the Fes Festival of Sufi

Culture, having incorporated a forum called "a soul for globalization" into the mix (conversation with the author, September 26, 2008). These recent events signify Skali's refusal to be co-opted as well as the power of capitalist interests to produce (or at least fund) the festive sacred on a large scale. Indeed, sacred tourists continue to attend the Fes Festival of World Sacred Music. Broken promises at the local level do not necessarily abrogate the need for the promise of sonic translation on the international level. As long as the circumstances that necessitate such promises continue to exist (war, terrorism, xenophobia, racism, religious fanaticism, etc.), sacred tourist markets that produce the festive sacred will proliferate, catering to people of different religions and nations who hope to learn and embrace a new sonic imaginary defined as "universal."

This is not to wax cynical about the effects of such promises, however. Market economies can also be spiritual ones. Pilgrims are, and have always been, tourists of a certain ilk. The sacred is, in part, a commodity with use and exchange value, both circulated as a kind of spiritual capital and causing the circulation of people, things, and affect. This is evident in the profusion of sacred music festivals internationally: the World Sacred Music Festival of Hiroshima, the Michigan Festival of Sacred Music, The Festival of Universal Sacred Music in Manhattan, the Brighton Festival of World Sacred Music, the Festival of Sacred Music and Art in Rome, the Fireflies Festival of Sacred Music in Bangalore, India, and the list goes on. There is even a Foundation for Universal Sacred Music, whose mission is to "gather written and recorded examples of works that exemplify the spirit of universal sacred music" (Foundation for Universal Sacred Music n.d.).

The festive sacred not only produces a Turnerian communitas but also creates new transnational imaginaries that mediate religious sentiment and reenchant the world (although the world has never, in fact, been "disenchanted"). It is this enchantment, this magical engagement, that is promised and delivered. Translations fail. Not all sacred music moves the auditor toward universal transcendence. But the promise of translation cannot fail. The promise performs its own fulfillment: it mobilizes and it generates hope, capital, affect, and community. Most importantly, it creates an intersubjective and affective contract. Attending to the sacred through sound, audiences learn to listen – and sometimes to hear – difference, while labeling it "universal." Holding the categories of "cultural alterity" and "heritage of humanity" together may generate paradox and perhaps spiritual bewilderment (*hayra* in Arabic). In Sufi thought, however, it is precisely the ability to embrace paradox that opens the heart and soul (Chittick 1989:4). Although this does not guarantee social transformation, it does hold out some promise.

NOTES

1   On community and affect, see Munoz 2000.
2   On the history of secularisms and the creation of the modern subject, see Asad 2003; Jakobson and Pellegrini 2008; Mahmood 2005.
3   I have attended nine festivals as a participant-observer, a speaker at multiple colloquia, and an interviewer. I have talked at length with the founders of these festivals over the years as well as with the musicians, audience members, and local residents. Although I do not explore the "reception" of sacred music at these festivals, I do examine the intentional production of a promise that shapes audience expectations and that posits a community of sacred affect that tourist-pilgrims then inhabit.
4   Hope is an emotion imputed with intention, a driver of religious fervor and activity, integral to notions of temporality and to conceptions of utopia (Crapanzano 2004:97–123).
5   According to Caillois, they offered an agonistic and ludic alternative to war. Indeed, for Caillois, festivals were all about the transformation of sacred – and often savage – affect into social performance.
6   See Becker 2004; Oliveros 2005. Becker equates deep listening with trance:
Both trancing and deep listening are physical, bodily processes, involving neural stimulation of specific brain areas that result in outward, visible physical reactions such as crying, or rhythmical swaying or

horripilation. . . . Both, I suspect, are initially aroused at a level of precognition that quickly expands in the brain to involve memory, feeling, and imagination. Deep listening and trancing, as processes, are simultaneously physical *and* psychological, somatic *and* cognitive. [2004:29]
7   The Fes Festival has recently diversified its class base as well. Although the majority of the festival concerts during the first eight years were for paying customers, limited to an elite Moroccan minority and foreign tourists (Belghazi 2006), its audience quickly expanded as demand for public access grew. In response, there are now outdoor and free concerts for the local residents who cannot afford the expensive prices of the festival program as well as food stands that give an impression of general celebration. The festival is also televised live. Nonetheless, the perception by Moroccans that the Fes Festival caters to the elite of Morocco and other nations is pervasive.
8   It is noteworthy that the Sufi poet of the 11th century, Abdeljalal Rumi, is the best-selling poet in the United States (rendered into very contemporary language by Coleman Barks).

REFERENCES

Abrahams, Roger D. 1987. An American Vocabulary of Celebration. In *Time Out of Time: Essays on the Festival*. A. Falassi, ed. Pp. 173–183. Albuquerque: University of New Mexico Press.

Alami, Saad. 2006. A Qui Appartient le Festival des Musiques Sacrees (To whom does the Fes Festival of Sacred belong?) *L'Economiste* (The Economist), October 26: Culture Section.

Appadurai, Arjun. 2006. *Fear of Small Numbers: An Essay on the Geography of Anger*. Durham, NC: Duke University Press.

Asad, Talal. 2003. *Formations of the Secular: Christianity, Islam, Modernity. Cultural Memory in the Present*. Series. Stanford: Stanford University Press.

Association Fes-Saiss. 2001. *Fes Festival of World Sacred Music: Giving Soul to Globalization*. Festival Brochure. Fes: Association Fes-Saiss.

Attali, Jacques. 1985. *Noise: The Political Economy of Music*. Brian Massumi, trans. Minneapolis: University of Minnesota Press.

Austin, J.L.. 1962. *How To Do Things with Words: William James Lectures, vol. 1955.* Cambridge, MA: Harvard University Press.

Badone, Ellen, and Sharon R. Roseman, eds. 2004. *Intersecting Journeys: The Anthropology of Pilgrimage and Tourism.* Urbana: University of Illinois Press.

Bauman, Richard, Inta Gale Carpenter, and Patricia Sawin, 1992. *Reflections on the Folklife Festival: An Ethnography of Participant Experience.* Special Publications of the Folklore Institute, vol. 2. Bloomington, IN: Folklore Institute, Indiana University.

Becker, Judith. 2004. *Deep Listeners: Emotion, Music, and Trancing.* Bloomington: Indiana University Press.

Béjart, Maurice. 2004. Depouillement et Unique Verite (Stark essence and unique truth). In *L'Esprit de Fes: En Quete de Sens et de Beauté* (The spirit of Fes: In search of meaning and beauty). Nathalie Calme, ed. pp. 108–111. Mesnil-sur-L'Estree: Editions du Rocher.

Belghazi, Taieb. 2006. Festivalization of Urban Space in Morocco. *Critical Middle Eastern Studies* 15(1): 97–107.

Benjamin, Walter. 1969. The Task of the Translator: An Introduction to the Translation of Baudelaire's Tableaux Parisiens. In *Illuminations.* Hannah Arendt, ed. Harry Zohn, trans. pp. 69–82. New York: Schocken.

Bohlman, Philip V. 1997. World Musics and World Religions: Whose World? In *Enchanting Powers: Music in the World's Religions.* Lawrence E. Sullivan, ed. pp. 219–235. Cambridge, MA: Harvard University Press.

Boum, Aomar. 2007. Dancing for the Moroccan State: Ethnic Folk Dances and the Production of National Hybridity. In *North African Mosaic: A Cultural Reappraisal of Ethnic and Religious Minorities.* Nabil Boudra and Joseph Krause, eds. pp. 214–237. Cambridge: Cambridge University Press.

Bourdieu, Pierre. 1977. *Outline of a Theory of Practice.* Cambridge: Cambridge University Press.

Brandes, Stanley H. 1988. *Power and Persuasion: Fiestas and Social Control in Rural Mexico.* Philadelphia: University of Pennsylvania Press.

Brenneis, Donald. 1987. Performing Passions: Aesthetics and Politics in an Occasionally Egalitarian Community. *American Ethnologist* 14(2): 236–250.

Caillois, Roger. 1960. *Man and the Sacred [Homme et le Sacré].* Glencoe, IL: Free Press of Glencoe.

Cayrol, Roland. 2004. Un Festival Unique, Dans Une Ville Unique (A unique festival in a unique city). In *L'Esprit de Fees: En Quete de Sens et de Beauté* (The spirit of Fes: In search of meaning and beauty). Nathalie Calme, ed. pp. 94–97. Mesnil-sur-L'Estree: Editions du Rocher.

Chittick, William C. 1989. *The Sufi Path of Knowledge: Inb al-'Arabi's Metaphysics of Imagination.* Albany: State University of New York Press.

Cornell, Vincent J. 1998. *Realm of the Saint.* Austin: University of Texas Press.

Crapanzano, Vincent. 2004. *Imaginative Horizons: An Essay in Literary-Philosophical Anthropology.* Chicago: University of Chicago Press.

Curtis, Maria. 2007. *Sound Faith: Nostalgia, Global Spirituality, and the Making of the Fes Festival of World Sacred Music.* Ph.D. dissertation, Department of Anthropology, University of Texas at Austin.

Delaney, Carol. 1990. The "Hajj": Sacred and Secular. *American Ethnologist* 17(3): 513–530.

Derrida, Jacques. 1985. Des Tours de Babel. (The Towers of Babel) And Appendix to Des Tours de Babel. In *Difference in Translation.* Joseph F. Graham, ed. pp. 165–248. Ithaca: Cornell University Press.

Duranti, Alessandro, and Donald Brenneis, eds. 1986. The Audience as Co-Author. Special issue, *Text* 6(3).

Eickelman, Dale F. 1976. *Moroccan Islam: Tradition and Society in a Pilgrimage Center.* Austin: University of Texas Press.

Erguner, Kudsi. 2003. De la Place du Musicien Traditionnel Aujourd'hui (The place of the traditional musician today). In *Donner Une Ame à la Mondialisation: Une Anthologie des Rencontres de Fès* (Giving a soul to globalization: An anthology of the Fes meetings). Patricevan Eersel, ed. pp. 199–204. Paris: Albin Michel.

Erlmann, Veit. 2003. Communities of Style: Musical Figures of Black Diasporic Identity. In *The Black Diaspora: A Musical Perspective.* Ingrid Monson, ed. pp. 83–102. New York: Routledge.

Falassi, Alessandro, ed. 1987. *Time Out of Time: Essays on the Festival.* Albuquerque: University of New Mexico Press.

Feld, Steven. 1994. From Schizophonia to Schismogenesis: Notes on the Discourses of World Music and World Beat. In *Music Grooves*. Charles Keil and Steven Feld, eds. pp. 257–289. Chicago: University of Chicago Press.

Foundation for Universal Sacred Music N.d. Foundation for Universal Sacred Music. Electronic document, http://www.universalsacredmusic.org/, accessed March 20, 2008.

al-Ghazzali. 1901. *Emotional Religion in Islam as Affected by Music and Singing: Being a Translation of a Book of the Ihya 'Ulum ad-Din of al-Ghazzali with Analysis, Annotation, and Appendices*. Duncan B. MacDonald, trans. pp. 730–732. Hartford, CT: Journal of the Royal Asiatic Society.

Guss, David M. 2000. *The Festive State: Race, Ethnicity, and Nationalism as Cultural Performance*. Los Angeles: University of California Press.

Hell, Bertrand. 2001. L'Esclave et le Saint. Les Gnawa et la baraka de Moulay Abdallah Ben Hsein (Maroc) (The slave and the saint: The Gnawa and the Baraka of Moulay Abdallah Ben Hsein [Morocco]). In *Saints, Saintete et Martyre. La Fabrication de l'Exemplarite* (Saints, saintliness, and martyrs: The production of exemplarity). P. Centlivres, ed. pp. 149–174. Paris: Editions de la Maison des Sciences de l'Homme.

Hirschkind, Charles. 2006. *The Ethical Soundscape: Cassette Sermons and Counter-publics*. New York: Columbia University Press.

Jakobsen, Janet R., and Ann Pellegrini. 2008. Introduction: Times Like These. In *Secularisms*. Janet Jakobsen and Ann Pellegrini, eds. pp. 1–35. Durham, NC: Duke University Press.

Jakobson, Roman. 2000. On Linguistic Aspects of Translation. In *The Translation Studies Reader*. Lawrence Venuti, ed. pp. 138–143. New York: Routledge.

Kapchan, Deborah. 2008. The Festive Sacred and the Fetish of Trance: Performing the Sacred at the Essaouira Gnawa Festival of World Music. *Gradhiva: Revue d'Anthropologie et de Museologie* 7: 53–67.

N.d. Literacies of Listening: World Music and the Essaouira Gnawa Festival. Unpublished MS, Department of Performance Studies, New York University.

Keil, Charles, and Steven Feld. 1994. *Music Grooves*. Chicago: University of Chicago Press

Kirshenblatt-Gimblett, Barbara. 1998. *Destination Culture: Tourism, Museums, and Heritage*. Berkeley: University of California Press.

Kurdjian, Gerard. 2004. L'Esprit des Musiques Sacrées du Monde: Festivals de Fes 1994–2004 (The spirit of sacred world musics). In *L'Esprit de Fees: En Quete de Sens et de Beauté* (The spirit of Fes: in search of meaning and beauty festivals of Fes 1994–2004. Nathalie Calmé, ed. pp. 29–38. Mesnil-sur-L'Estrée: Éditions du Rocher.

Mahmood, Saba. 2005. *The Politics of Piety: The Islamic Revival and the Feminist Subject*. Princeton: Princeton University Press.

Mamdani, Mahmoud. 2002. Good Muslim, Bad Muslim: An African Perspective. *American Anthropologist* 194(3): 766–775.

Menocal, Maria Rosa. 2003. *The Ornament of the World: How Muslims, Jews, and Christians Created a Culture of Tolerance in Medieval Spain*. Forward by Harold Bloom. New York: Little, Brown.

Meyer, Birgit, and Annelies Moors, eds. 2006. *Religion, Media, and the Public Sphere*. Bloomington: Indiana University Press.

Miyazaki, Hirokazu. 2004. *The Method of Hope: Anthropology, Philosophy, and Fijian Knowledge*. Stanford: Stanford University Press.

Munoz, Jose Esteban. 2000. Feeling Brown: Ethnicity and Affect in Ricardo Bracho's The Sweetest Hangover (and Other STDs). *Theatre Journal* 52(1): 67–79.

Nora, Pierre. 1989. *Between Memory and History: Lieux de Memoire*. Marc Roudebush, trans. Representations 26:12.

Noyes, Dorothy. 2003. *Fire in the Placa: Catalan Festival Politics after Franco*. Philadelphia: University of Pennsylvania Press.

Oliveros, Pauline. 2005. *Deep Listening: A Composer's Sound Practice*. New York: iUniverse.

Racy, Ali Jihad. 2003. *Making Music in the Arab World: The Culture and Artistry of Tarab*. Cambridge: Cambridge University Press.

Shannon, Jonathan. 2003. Sultans of Spin: Syrian Sacred Music on the World Stage. *American Anthropologist* 105(2): 1–12.

Shannon, Jonathan. 2006. *Among the Jasmine Trees: Music and Modernity in Contemporary Syria. Music/Culture Series*. Middletown, CT: Wesleyan University Press.

Shannon, Jonathan. 2007. Performing al-Andalus, Remembering al-Andalus: Mediterranean Soundings from the Mashriq to the Maghrib.

Journal of American Folklore 120(477): 308–334.

Skali, Faouzi. 1989. *Futuwah: Traite de la chevalerie Soufie de Muhammad ibn al-Husayn Sulami* (Futuwah: Mumhammad Ibn al-Hussein Sulami's treatise of Sufi chivalry). Paris: Albin Michel.

Skali, Faouzi. 1993. *La Voie Souie* (The Sufi path). Paris: Albin Michel.

Skali, Faouzi. 1996. *Traces de Lumieere: Paroles Initiatiques Soufies* (Traces of light: Words of Sufi initiation). Paris: Albin Michel.

Skali, Faouzi. 2000. *Le Face-a-Face des Coeurs: Le Soufisme Aujourd'hui* (The face-to-face of hearts: Sufism today). Paris: Editions du Relie.

Skali, Faouzi. 2004. La Cite de Moulay Idris (The city of Moulay Idriss). In *L'Esprit de Fes: En Quete de Sens et de Beaute* (The spirit of Fes: In search of meaning and beauty). Nathalie Calme, ed. p. 49. Mesnil-sur-L'Estree: Editions de Rocher.

Steiner, George. 1998. *After Babel: Aspects of Language and Translation.* 3rd edition. Oxford: Oxford University Press.

Taylor, Timothy Dean. 1997. *Global Pop: World Music, World Markets.* New York: Routledge.

Tsing, Anna. 2004. *Friction: An Ethnography of Global Connection.* Princeton: Princeton University Press.

Turner, Victor, ed. 1974. Liminal to Liminoid, in Play, Flow, and Ritual: An Essay in Comparative Symbiology. *Rice University Studies: The Anthropological Study of Human Play, vol. 60, no 3.* Edward Norbeck, ed. pp. 53–92. Houston: Rice University Press.

Turner, Victor, ed. 1982. *Celebration: Studies in Festivity and Ritual.* Washington, DC: Smithsonian Institution Press.

Weber, Max. 1930. *The Protestant Ethic and the Spirit of Capitalism.* Talcott Parsons, trans. London: G. Allen and Unwin.

World Festival of Sacred Music N.d. Open Your Heart and Listen. Electronic document, http://www.festivalofsacredmusic.org/festival_2005/home.html, accessed October 10, 2008.

18

Ethnic Tourism in Hokkaidô and the Shaping of Ainu Identity

Lisa Hiwasaki

Introduction

On 8 May 1997, with the enactment of the Ainu Culture Promotion Law, the Japanese government took a significant step towards officially acknowledging the existence of the Ainu as an ethnic minority.[1] The law is Japan's first legislation to acknowledge the existence of an ethnic minority in the country and, unlike the Hokkaidô Former Aborigines Protection Act which the new law replaces, the Ainu were involved in the process of its enactment. This preliminary move, however, stopped short of recognising the Ainu as an indigenous people as defined by the United Nations. The Hokkaidô Ainu thus remain virtually invisible in a country they have inhabited for hundreds, if not thousands, of years. One venue that plays a vital role in the representation of the Ainu in Japan today is ethnic tourism, which centres on tourist villages scattered across Hokkaidô.[2]

The existence of the Ainu is virtually ignored elsewhere in the society, most conspicuously in the classroom. A report conducted in 1993 showed that only ten out of twenty high school

Japanese history textbooks mentioned the background of contact between the Ainu and mainstream Japanese (*Wajin*)[3] and the assimilation policies forced upon the Ainu since the nineteenth century; only four mentioned the Hokkaidô Former Aborigines Protection Act.[4] Although many, if not most, Wajin consider Japan a monoethnic country and take pride in the belief, they go on tours to Hokkaidô and are comfortable seeing, as a travel guide book put it, "pseudo 'Ainu' villages with Disneyland surroundings and souvenir shops selling tacky carvings."[5]

Using data gathered during fieldwork in Hokkaidô in 1995, this paper will explore Ainu cultural and identity expressions as they manifest themselves through ethnic tourism. At the present time when Ainu visibility is increasing, especially in the political realm, it is integral to examine tourist centres where Ainu identity expressions are overt. The purpose of this paper is to emphasise the importance of ethnic tourism both in Ainu contemporary culture and in representations of the Ainu in Japanese society today, as well as to explore

Lisa Hiwasaki, "Ethnic Tourism in Hokkaidô and the Shaping of Ainu Identity," pp. 393–412 from *Pacific Affairs* 73(3), 2000.

Ainu identity negotiations occuring through ethnic tourism. I first situate the Ainu in Hokkaidô tourism, then lay out the various ways in which the Ainu have been influenced through their participation in tourism. Next I will examine the importance of tourism as an arena where Ainu ethnic identities have been formulated, consolidated and reinforced. I discuss ways in which Ainu identities are negotiated through tourism and, in doing so, show the multifarious nature of the identities that are established.

My objective in conducting this study was to examine the relations between the Wajin and Ainu in Japanese society today. Tourist villages are at the crux of Ainu-Wajin relations.[6] The first part of the fieldwork was spent travelling around Hokkaidô, visiting and observing museum exhibits, tourist villages and souvenir shops. The second part consisted of interviews with people involved in the Ainu tourist industry, which included shop owners, Ainu activists and members of Ainu tourism associations. Interviews were also conducted with museum curators, researchers and others, both Ainu and Wajin, who are involved with the representation of the Ainu to the public. Because tourism is not an aspect of Ainu contemporary culture that is commonly studied, and much of the discussion of the topic has been negative, this paper attempts to fill a gap in the literature on the Ainu.[7] This study will call for further research on the topic of Ainu ethnic tourism, especially as it opens the way for insight into Ainu ethnic identities and the representation of the Ainu in Japanese society today.

Ethnic Tourism and the Commoditisation of Cultures

According to van den Berghe and Keyes, tourism is a "mass recreational nomadism undertaken in foreign parts in quest for the other."[8] The study of tourism is meaningful because tourism is "the largest scale movement of goods, services and people that humanity has perhaps ever seen" and tourism is of fundamental importance to an increasing number of people.[9] Ethnic tourism is a form of tourism in which the cultural exoticism of the host population and its "products," such as clothing, music and dance, are the main attractions for the tourist. Ethnic tourism leads to the formation of three main roles: (1) the *tourist*, who travels to seek an experience that cannot be duplicated in ordinary life; (2) the *touree*, the performer who modifies his or her behaviour to suit the tastes of the tourists for gain; and (3) the *middleman*, who mediates the two groups and profits by their interaction. Ethnic tourism constitutes a complex kind of ethnic relations among the three roles, and is an integral feature of the economic infrastructure of ethnic relations.

A culture is commoditised for tourism when the customs, rituals and arts are performed or produced for touristic consumption. Examining tourism and the commoditisation of culture which can accompany it is necessarily a broad topic because it raises issues of political, economic and social relations between the producer and purchaser of the commodity. Commoditisation of a culture can change not only the meaning of cultural products, but also the human relations between the producer and the purchaser, the history of these relations, and their ethnic identities.[10] In the literature on the anthropology and sociology of tourism, tourism has been, at best, blamed for the invention of cultural traditions and, at worst, accused of staging inauthentic events without any historical antecedents. Moreover, tourism is also looked upon as a possible agent for facilitating economic, political and cultural dependency and thus a comprehensive dependency on another society.[11]

At the same time, scholars have noted the beneficial aspects of tourism, economically, culturally and politically, and these are the aspects I focus on in this paper. Tourism can stimulate national and local economic growth and enhance the quality of life of those involved by creating employment from tourist-related services. Tourism can enlighten the tourists as well as the natives themselves about the native culture, and it can serve as a means of cultural conservation. Moreover, ethnic tourism can bring international attention to the political claims of oppressed minorities.[12]

An aspect of ethnic tourism that has received much attention in recent years is its generative power. Instead of viewing touristic events as "inauthentic" or "invented," tourism can be seen as culturally generative in that it can stimulate the creation of new meanings for traditional rituals and objects and revitalise older ones. As Simpson put it: "tourism is creative of culture."[13] In this perspective, it is possible to consider the notion of "emergent authenticity":

> Since authenticity is . . . negotiable . . . a cultural product, or a trait thereof, which is at one point generally judged as contrived or inauthentic may, in the course of time, become generally recognized as authentic . . . Similarly, craft products initially produced merely for sale to visitors and tourists, may eventually become "authentic" products of an ethnic group or region.[14]

Here, "authenticity" is viewed as a socially constructed concept whose connotation is not given but "negotiable." Just as an "invented tradition"[15] can become authentic, it is also possible that rituals, dances and other cultural traditions can acquire new meaning through commoditisation. Although the original meaning may have been lost, these "may become a culturally significant self-representation before an external public." This can give the producers of commoditised cultures an opportunity to incorporate messages in them, which become new cultural expressions.[16]

Thus it is possible to view tourees not just as passive entities existing simply to serve the interests of the tourists. They are on show, playing at being themselves, making it their business to "preserve a credible illusion of authenticity," and create their art, dress, music and dances to "satisfy the ethnic tourist's thirst for authenticity."[17]

Ainu Ethnic Tourism in Hokkaidô

Tourism is an important aspect of leisure for Japanese people. According to a government survey, in 1997, approximately 205 million people travelled for pleasure within Japan; the average individual spent approximately ¥67,100 (US$610) on domestic overnight travels for tourism/recreational purposes, which amounted to a total of approximately ¥8.45 trillion (US$77 billion) spent on domestic tourism alone. Over half of those surveyed said the primary object of travel is to relax at a hot-spring bath and nearly half the respondents wished to view the beauty of natural landscapes.[18] Moreover, Hokkaidô is one prefecture which has invested much money and effort into the promotion of tourism. According to a survey, Hokkaidô ranked first among the forty prefectures in Japan in the prefectural tourism association's total revenues as well as in the amount of prefectural subsidies going into tourism.[19]

Going to Hokkaidô is, for those Japanese living in Honshu – the main island of the Japanese archipelago – like going abroad. The area is, to those travellers, everything Honshu is not, and glossy travel brochures about Hokkaidô emphasise this difference. Phrases such as "enjoy magnificent nature," "all-you-can-eat seafood," "exotic landscape," and "outdoor volcanic hot-spring bath" accompany colourful photographs promoting this northernmost island of the Japanese archipelago. The catch-phrase used by the Hokkaidô tourism association in order to promote tourism in the early 1990s was "the earth is a genius." This is significant when compared with the catch-phrases of other prefectures in which the emphasis is on the presence of people.[20] In the grand narrative that the middlemen of tourism – such as travel agencies and the tourism association – have put forward of Hokkaidô, the Ainu fit perfectly. In the emphasis on Hokkaidô's "nature," the Ainu play an important role, along with the mountains, rivers, waterfalls, foxes, deer and bears. Such naturalisation of the Ainu is pervasive in the Japanese media as well, as can be seen in Ainu images in anime and magazines. An example that has caused much controversy in certain circles recently is a video game called "Samurai Spirit," an extremely popular game whose main characters are a female Ainu warrior and her sister. These characters also appear in anime magazines, which are largely pornographic; the episodes reinforce the Ainu's image as barbaric (one scene shows the Ainu warrior smiling, holding the severed head of an enemy) and as part of nature (in another setting, the sister is raped by a bear).[21]

The association of nature with the Ainu is not something initiated by Wajin middlemen in recent years. Hokkaidô Social Work noted in 1935 that "Along with snow and bears, it is the Ainu, regarded as a primitive race, that are thought of as the special characteristics of Hokkaidô."[22] As early as the late nineteenth century, the existence of the Ainu came to be acknowledged as an integral "prop" in the Hokkaidô landscape. The image of the "primitive" ways of the Ainu in the wilds of Hokkaidô was an important commodity to the Wajin colonisers who were already benefiting from natural resources that exist in the northern island. Thus, at the time when Ainu tourism was in its nascent phase in the late nineteenth century, tourism, which offered glimpses into the "savage" lives of the Ainu, was an integral factor in images of Hokkaidô perpetuated by the mainstream media of the time.[23]

An increase in the number of visitors to Hokkaidô resulted in the formation of tourist centres in Shiraoi and Chikabumi during the Taisho period (1912–1926). It was also at this time that regional differences with regard to the transmission of Ainu culture became apparent.[24] With the "Ainu boom" of the 1950s and 1960s, instigated by the economic development in Japan and by social trends such as the literary work, *Whistle of Kotan*, the movie made from it, and the hit song "Night of Iomante," the commoditisation of the Ainu and the existence of Ainu tourist villages as an integral part of Hokkaidô tourism was complete.[25] "Ainu products" – such as the woodcarvings of bears, often with salmon in their mouths, pairs of Ainu figures wearing Ainu traditional clothing made of elm bark (*attushi*), Ainu patterns embroidered on headbands and carved on wooden trays – were also important factors in this formula. The above Ainu souvenirs have their share of the Hokkaidô souvenir market today, along with other popular souvenirs such as fresh seafood, dairy products and vegetables. Such souvenirs are not only sold in Ainu tourist centres, but also at stores throughout Hokkaidô. Those products, along with the other products of nature that can be bought in Hokkaidô, still reinforce the image of Hokkaidô as somehow more abundant in natural resources, including the Ainu.

There are four Ainu communities that are significant for their renown and the number of visitors they attract. Each has a unique history and characteristics. The most famous tourist centre is Shiraoi Poroto Kotan, situated on Poroto Lake on the southern coast of Hokkaidô and conveniently located near Chitose airport, which is close to Sapporo, the capital of Hokkaidô. During the Meiji period (1868–1912), Shiraoi was visited by members of the Imperial family, including the Meiji emperor, who made his visit in 1881, as well as by domestic and foreign researchers and visitors.[26] Poroto Kotan consists of the Ainu Museum, a reconstructed Ainu village, and a structure with souvenir shops at the entrance. At the village, people entertain tourists with dances, songs and performances of "Bear Festivals."[27]

At Akan, in the eastern part of Hokkaidô, approximately 200 Ainu entertain 1,600,000 tourists a year.[28] Located on the edge of the Lake Akan resort area, this tourist village consists of streets lined with souvenir stores, with the main street leading to an Ainu house (*chise*), where people perform dances and music at regularly scheduled times. After the performance, the dancers advertise products which can be purchased in the shops lining the streets. According to an Ainu man I talked to, one of the reasons Akan is very successful is its location on the edge of the famous hotspring baths of Lake Akan.

Kawamura Kaneto Ainu Kinenkan (Memorial Hall) and the surrounding souvenir shops are at the centre of Asahikawa tourist village, near Chikabumi, located in the eastern half of interior Hokkaidô.[29] The memorial hall contains a small collection of Ainu objects, as well as a room with a stage on which Ainu dances take place. Outside the hall are a reconstructed house, a cage for bear cubs (*heperset*), and a storage house (*pu*).

Nibutani, in the southern part of Hokkaidô along the Saru River, is not a village fabricated for tourists but rather a town where approximately 80 percent of the population is Ainu. This is the largest concentration of Ainu in Hokkaidô, and the only place in the country where the Ainu are in a majority. Despite its remote location, in the estimate of an Ainu activist in Nibutani whom I interviewed, Nibutani has become a tourist destination hosting around 20,000 visitors in the summer. Scholars have noted that many of the traditions have been well preserved due to Nibutani's interior location, and many students and scholars go there in order to study the language and traditional aspects of the culture.[30]

Tourism and the Ainu

Before discussing the various ways in which the Ainu have been influenced by and through ethnic tourism, it is necessary to call attention to the effects of tourism that are generally perceived as negative, and to the overwhelmingly negative attitudes towards tourism that permeate the Ainu population. Ainu tourist centres are seen by many people as one of the numerous ways in which the Wajin have controlled the Ainu, producing stereotypical images of the Ainu and thus reinforcing prejudice. Moreover, as one of the most vital sources of constructing images of the Ainu, museums are an important factor in tourism. My observations of ten mainstream museums in Hokkaidô showed that the majority of them displayed only Ainu "traditions" and emphasised the "primitive" aspects of their culture, ignoring the long history of oppression of the Ainu by the Wajin, as well as the contemporary problems the Ainu face. The Wajin has succeeded in reshaping the Ainu through such exhibits in mainstream museums.

Questions as to who truly benefits economically from the revenue brought in by tourism cannot be ignored. Many of the facilities that result from tourism, such as hotels, are of little direct benefit to the indigenous population; most of the money spent in the tourist areas leaves the host society because the industry is dominated by outsiders.[31] Some Wajin middlemen, such as travel agencies, take advantage of Ainu tourism, often appropriating Ainu or Ainu-like words to sell Hokkaidô products and souvenirs. Those who benefit from the wealth brought in by tourists are frequently not the tourees themselves.[32]

Many Ainu have been vocal in expressing their opinions against tourism, including Kayano Shigeru, a former member of the National Diet and unquestionably Japan's most famous Ainu. Kayano looks back upon his years singing and dancing in traditional costume for tourists as a humiliating experience, "a phenomenon of ethnic oppression in a world of tourism."[33] During many years of oppression and discrimination, many Ainu willingly lost their culture and traditions in an effort to disassociate themselves from anything Ainu and "pass" as Wajin. Those who are involved with tourism are often looked down upon by fellow Ainu, and many Ainu people do not like to have the term "Kankô-Ainu" (Ainu involved in tourism), attributed to them. According to a curator at the Ainu Museum, this is because people involved in tourism are accused by other Ainu of "selling Ainu" and making a show of themselves. The curator spoke of an incident in 1974 when the town mayor of Shiraoi was stabbed by a young man who protested that the town of Shiraoi was commoditising and selling the Ainu. In another interview, an Ainu man who owns a restaurant in a tourist village and is a member of the village's tourism association, said that when he was growing up, he had little respect for his father's occupation of woodcarving Ainu crafts for tourists. Although he is currently well established in the community, he said that if he had the choice, he would get out of the village and do something else.

However, Ainu and tourism are concepts that are often associated with one another in Japanese society. Many Japanese consider tourism as the primary occupation in which Ainu people are, or can be, engaged. In a study conducted in 1980, 42.6 percent of university students living in Tokyo answered "tourism" to the question: "Which occupation do you think Ainu people are engaged in now?" The same study revealed that students living in Tokyo learned about Ainu culture mostly through the media and tourism; approximately a quarter of the students learned about the Ainu solely through tourism and tourism-related goods and services.[34] Although one hopes that attitudes concerning the Ainu, and minorities in general, have changed dramatically since then, such findings are not surprising in a country in which, until recently, tourist villages were the only domain where the Ainu were permitted to practice their culture. In an interview, an Ainu shop owner in Akan said that about 10 to 20 percent of the Wajin tourists tend to think that the Ainu live as they did centuries ago, and questions by some Wajin to Ainu working at tourist villages include "Do you go to the mountains to chase bears in your free time?" "My, your Japanese is very good. Where did you learn how to speak that well?" "Do you pay taxes?" and "What do Ainu people eat?"[35]

Despite the strong feelings some people have expressed against ethnic tourism, it has had and continues to have a profound impact on the Ainu. Tourism in Hokkaidô has resulted in numerous changes for the Ainu economically, socially, culturally and politically. Economically, tourism has given some Ainu a means of survival. Politically, tourism has helped increase Ainu visibility in Japanese society. Culturally, tourism has resulted in creative responses by the Ainu, and people involved with tourism have played an active role in the maintenance, dissemination, revival and development of Ainu culture and language. At the same time that tourism has influenced the Ainu in diverse ways, they have actively adapted to, or modified, their ways of living, to accommodate to, and make the best use of, tourism.

First, tourism brings food to the Ainu living in some areas of Hokkaidô, especially those in tourist villages. Kayano wrote that he started making Ainu woodcarvings in the late 1940s, and by the late 1950s, he earned more money than by working as a wage labourer in the mountains.[36] A survey conducted by the Hokkaidô Prefectural Office showed that 5.2 percent of the Ainu population are involved in manufacturing folk arts, while 8.2 percent are involved in their sales.[37] Thus, approximately 13 percent of the Ainu make a living out of tourism. Without the vast number of tourists flocking to their tourist centres, Ainu residents would have to find some other

economic base for survival. Moreover, tourist art is "precisely what constitutes the livelihood and daily production of Ainu workers" in tourist centres, making tourism an aspect of the modern Ainu that cannot be ignored.[38]

Second, tourism has played an important role in conserving and maintaining certain aspects of traditional Ainu culture. The Japanese government established and promoted Ainu tourism precisely at the time when the destruction of Ainu traditional life and Ainu impoverishment were at their worst. From the 1890s onwards, through the acts of middlemen – the government arranging for people such as the Meiji emperor and government officials to visit Hokkaidô to observe the Ainu people, their performances, and their production of art, and railway companies organising and sending groups off on Hokkaidô tours – Ainu villages came to be organised as tourist attractions. At the same time, the government was denying the rights of the Ainu and their traditions, depicting them as an inferior race who had been conquered and would soon disappear was an important tool used to emphasise the success of the modern Japanese nation.[39] While tourism has often been criticised for commoditising Ainu "traditional culture" by reproducing and diffusing stereotypes and fabricated images of the Ainu, ironically, the Ainu's performance and staging of certain aspects of their traditions – rituals, dances, songs and arts – for tourism has helped maintain core aspects of Ainu culture.[40] If it had not been for places like Shiraoi, where the Ainu were forced to "perform Ainu" and stage traditional rituals for the benefit of visitors (yarase),[41] many aspects of the culture would not have been recorded or practiced today.

Third, tourism is educational. Many people in tourist villages acknowledge the value tourism has in cross-cultural education and recognise the need to enlighten the general public through various activities promoting Ainu causes. An Ainu man working at a tourist centre has been quoted as saying that a tourist site with an educational viewpoint can be the foundation for an environment of respect for different cultures and ethnic groups, which would benefit both Wajin and Ainu.[42] More than being merely sites for entertainment, tourist villages have taken on the role of educating Japanese society. The Ainu Museum at Shiraoi has been particularly active in this outreach. According to a curator I interviewed, the museum has published over thirty books and pamphlets on the Ainu. An Ainu man in Asahikawa observed that there has been an increase in the number of high school students on field trips to Asahikawa since 1993. He told me that teachers request him to talk to students about the Ainu's history and about contemporary issues. An Ainu activist living in Nibutani said he gives talks to up to thirty school groups a year, almost all of which are from Honshu. In his talks, he emphasises the Ainu's existence in modern Japanese society, and encourages students to learn more about the Ainu culture and people.

Fourth, tourism has given rise to creative responses in the Ainu culture, influencing its cultural development. During the 1950s and 1960s, for example, festivals in which Ainu men and women in traditional clothes perform rituals were created in tourist centres in order to attract more tourists. Such festivals include the Marimo Festival (Festival of *aegagropila*, fresh-water algae found in Lake Akan) at Akan and the Poroto Lake Festival in Shiraoi. Moreover, a growing number of musicians are creating new music by mixing together Ainu and non-Ainu musical elements. Toyooka Masanori, known as Attui, according to an Ainu activist in Nibutani I interviewed, incorporates traditional Ainu music into jazz, while Kanô Oki, known as Oki, plays reggae-style music and traditional Ainu songs with an Ainu instrument, the *tonkori*.[43]

Finally, tourism can have political consequences by increasing Ainu visibility within Japanese society. One of the most important outcomes of Ainu tourism is the attention it has brought to the Ainu people. Although this is perceived by some as negative attention, such as the perpetuation of stereotypes, there have been more positive outcomes. A museum curator in Obihiro noted that there was an increase in interest in Ainu issues in 1993, the United Nations International Year of Indigenous People. Many students, interested in writing papers on the Ainu, visited tourist centres and museums to learn more about the indigenous people

of Japan. Attention gained through tourism can be focused on the urgent political and social issues facing the Ainu today. For example, a few years before the Ainu New Law was passed, in the Asahikawa tourist centre I observed a poster displaying some information on the law and a petition for its passing that visitors could sign.

Tourism, Ainu Cultural Expressions, and Ainu Ethnic Identities

As seen above, involvement in tourism has had various impacts upon the Ainu, economically, culturally and politically. Tourist centres act as an important venue of Ainu cultural expression, thereby playing a vital role in the preservation, practice and revival of certain aspects of Ainu culture and providing a place where cross-cultural education is facilitated. Thus, Ainu tourist villages and those who are involved with them are vital to the representation of the Ainu in Japanese society today. Consequently, tourism has been, and continues to be, a venue through which Ainu ethnic identities are represented, formulated and reinforced, and examining tourism is integral to the understanding of Ainu ethnic identities. Active involvement in tourism and expressions of Ainu cultural traditions have resulted in the consolidation of a collective Ainu identity for cultural, social and political purposes. By providing a safe sphere in which Ainu social interactions take place, tourist villages have also played a vital role in the formulation of diverse individual Ainu identities.

Ainu tourist centres provide an important venue for Ainu cultural expression, through performances of art, songs and dances. This is because tourist centres are among the few places in Japanese society in which Ainu traditional culture is still being practiced. As Sjöberg noted:

> Japan considers a practicable maintenance of Ainu customs outside the tourist arena to be unrealistic and severely circumscribes the efforts of the Ainu to celebrate, revive and preserve the customs of the past.[44]

As a result of over a hundred years of Wajin assimilation policies and discriminatory attitudes, Ainu material and spiritual cultures had been thoroughly affected. It was only through tourism that they could express themselves, although admittedly such expressions were extremely limited and the aspects of culture initially emphasised were in accordance with the commercial interests of the Wajin.

Learning more about their own culture by being involved with such cultural expressions has helped many Ainu reestablish their own identity. For example, a souvenir shop owner in Shiraoi told me she has been studying traditional aspects of Ainu material culture over the years she has had her shop, and plans to use the knowledge to make traditional goods such as bags woven from bark (*saranip*), headbands embroidered with traditional patterns (*matampus*), and Jews-harps made of bamboo (*mukkur*) to sell in her shop. Doing this would enable her to assert her Ainu identity. Similarly, an Ainu souvenir shop owner in Akan told me that during the winter, when the number of tourists decreases, he makes clothing out of nettle (*iragusa*). He does this because he recognises it as an important skill in traditional Ainu culture.

Art produced for tourists can be seen as not only for commercial profit, but it can be manipulated by the Ainu to make statements regarding their identity, as well as for their own cultural satisfaction. The products, then, are distinctive markers of a re-created ethnic identity stimulated by touristic encounters. Tourist art can be seen as reflecting a creative adaptation to the changed world in which the Ainu now live. By being involved in the commercialisation of such art, Wajin tourists also play an active and creative role in stimulating a renewal of pride, the preservation of culture and a renewed consciousness of the Ainu's ethnic heritage.[45]

An example of Ainu identity expression through tourist art can be seen in woodcarving (*kibori*). Carving on wood – such as carving patterns on sheaths of swords and figures on ritual tools such as a wooden staff with curled shavings used for religious altars (*inaw*) or prayer sticks (*iku-pasuy*) – had been an important custom for Ainu men, and it is a skill which has been perfected by the Ainu as a result of tourism. Traditionally, carving on wood embodied religious and social meanings, deeply rooted in the society and inseparable from Ainu ethnicity.[46] As early as the Edo period (1603–1868), Ainu men carved traditional patterns on wooden products to be sold or traded with the Wajin.[47] According to an Ainu shop owner in Akan, during the "Ainu boom," the shelves of his shop were constantly empty, and woodcarvers could not produce enough items to meet demand. Currently, woodcarvings available in stores include Japanese cranes, salmon and foxes. Woodcarvings of owls and Ainu fairy-like beings (*korpokkur*), and small items such as jewellery, are popular souvenir items today. It can be seen that, today, the custom of woodcarving exists in tourist centres as an art, symbolising a culture that is alive and being handed down to the younger generations in a renewed expression of Ainu identity.

Serving as a venue of Ainu cultural expression and identity, the tourist arena has also helped the Ainu consolidate a collective cultural identity. Being a touree is a means through which a sense of shared aesthetic and collective identity emerges:

> [Tourist centres] have become places where the Ainu, by "putting themselves on show," express their group or collective identity. These villages have become places where the conscious reconstruction of an Ainu identity is noticeable. In a way it emphasises the distinctive content of Ainu ethnicity for the tourists and the larger public who are invited not only to buy Ainu products, but see how they are made[48]

For the Ainu, tourist centres and Ainu art sold in souvenir shops have a dual meaning: not only are they a link to the nostalgic past, they are symbols of the Ainu and the Ainu alone. Their villages and the things contained within – such as the Ainu traditional house and the woodcarvings – are symbols of themselves. Publicly performing dances and rituals in tourist villages not only acts to reaffirm and further develop aspects of culture, it also acts to hold a group of people together in a common culture.[49] Tourism has played an important role in conserving and maintaining certain aspects of traditional culture because the Ainu were forced to "perform Ainu" for the benefit of those who visited tourist villages, and to satisfy their photographic appetites.

Ainu men and women involved with tourism not only perform for tourists, but also engage in other traditional Ainu practices. Currently, Ainu who are involved in tourism are at the heart of the recent movement towards the preservation, revival and development of Ainu culture, actively setting up venues where Ainu cultural traditions can be practised and displayed in order to ensure a future for the Ainu culture and people. For example, the first annual Hokkaidô Ainu Festival was organised by the Ainu tourist association in Asahikawa in 1963, where events included cultural conferences, Yukar reciting, Iomante and dances. Ainu participants in the festival numbered more than 200, with the number of spectators for Iomante reported to have been over 20,000. One Ainu participant noted that a positive outcome for this festival, at least for the older generations, was the opportunity for many Ainu to get together.[50] Members of the Ainu community in Shiraoi established the Shiraoi Institute for the Preservation of Ainu Culture in 1976. The annual Ainu Cultural Festival was begun in 1989, with traditional dances and speeches performed and woodcarvings and embroidery exhibited.[51]

Museums in Hokkaidô and throughout Japan that store and display Ainu artefacts have also played an important role in tourism and the conservation of material culture. Some curators recognise this to be the most important role, if not the sole mission, of museums. For example, a curator at the Tokyo National Museum told me that in order for a culture to grow, it is necessary to "go back to the old and traditional ways"; museums play an important role in this process. In the current movement of cultural transmission and cultural outreach, museums are the main resource to which the Ainu can turn in order to obtain information on their traditional culture. Museums also give the Ainu opportunities to reconstruct and recreate Ainu cultural artefacts for exhibits. Kayano wrote about getting a group of Ainu together to make a traditional Ainu house, clothing, dishes and weavings for the exhibits at the National Museum of Ethnology.[52] Through museums, the culture is not only conserved

but also handed down to the younger generations.

Members of tourist villages are committed to educating and engaging the Ainu who are not involved with tourism in their cultural practices through events such as those described above. An Ainu activist in Nibutani told me that a group from Akan has gone to nearby towns where there are large Ainu populations to teach dances and other aspects of traditional culture. Ainu language classes, originally started by Kayano, take place at some tourist villages, and have been taken up by Hokkaidô Utari Kyôkai[53] with the help of the Japanese government since 1987. While Nibutani is the heart of Ainu language classes, members at Shiraoi promote traditional dances, and the Ainu at Akan are in the process of reviving Yukar reciting. Other Ainu cultural classes which centre around tourist villages include dance, crafts and woodcarving.

Not only do tourist villages function as information centres fostering an awareness of Ainu identity, they also serve a social function. This is because for the Ainu involved in tourism, their commitment is a social one:

> . . . the tourist villages can be viewed as centres, or market places, where not only material needs are fulfilled but also and mainly, social and cultural ones. The centres may therefore, in their present disguise, be looked upon as based on shared feelings of mutual understanding and friendship, which emanate from a conscious sense of "belonging" and are consolidated by joint participation in a common culture. The tourist villages also function as a sort of public sphere for the Ainu.[54]

Tourist villages serve as a place to which many Ainu resort, as a safe place to be. Two Ainu men, one in Nibutani and another in Akan, told me stories of Ainu who grow up in tourist villages and then go to Sapporo to find jobs. Most of them come back to their villages; both men said it is unclear whether the big city is too harsh for these Ainu, or if their tourist village is simply comfortable, a place where there is a sense of belonging. Even for those Ainu who are not directly involved with the tourism industry, tourism has had a profound effect. As a Wajin scholar noted, going to tourist centres was an important factor that encouraged such Ainu to re-examine who they are, marking the beginning of their reaffirmation of ethnic identity.[55]

The sense of Ainu unity and solidarity produced by tourism has resulted in the formation of a political and unified identity vis-à-vis the Wajin. For example, different groups within the Ainu were brought together in one group for tourist villages, forcing them to overcome differences among themselves. A Wajin scholar noted in an interview that this reinforced Ainu ethnic identity, forming a broader Ainu identity and opening the way for cultural self-expression. An example of such a grouping is in Akan. According to an Ainu man in Nibutani I talked to, Akan was established after the Second World War by Ainu brought together from various towns in eastern Hokkaidô.

Cultural symbols of Ainu identity, which are increasingly used by the Ainu in political campaigns,[56] are those which have been disseminated throughout Japanese society through tourist villages and souvenirs. The emphasis on the Ainu's co-existence with nature is such an example. Many prominent Ainu promote an image of Ainu-the-nature-preserver, in opposition to Wajin-the-nature-destroyer, whenever they speak in public. A Wajin scholar I interviewed suggested that the emphasis on the Ainu's co-existence with nature is a political tool and an important way for them to obtain the attention of the Wajin. This is because Japan, like other countries in the world, has begun to be conscious about environmental problems and people have started to look at indigenous people's ways of living to learn from their experience. Thus, Ainu identity expressions can be political:

> Tourist production and display has become a central process in the conscious reconstruction of Ainu identity. It emphasizes the distinctive content of Ainu ethnicity for Japanese tourists in a context in which such specificity is officially interpreted as a mere variation of Japanese culture and not a separate identity. The presentation of Ainu selfhood is a political

instrument in the constitution of that selfhood.[57]

Expeditions to different places within and outside of Japan to perform Ainu dances, and efforts by Ainu groups to interact with other indigenous groups, such as those in Europe and Russia, and to exchange rituals and festivals, can also be viewed as part of the effort towards the consolidation of a unified and political Ainu identity. For example, members of Shiraoi Poroto Kotan went to England in 1995 to dance at the opening of the first Ainu exhibition in the United Kingdom, at the Museum of Mankind in London.[58] As of 1997, they had made four trips overseas, including ones to Finland and Taiwan.[59] A group based in Akan called Kamuiturano Kyokai, founded in 1985, went on a tour of Japan in 1996, promoting intercultural meetings, holding workshops, singing and performing Ainu dances.[60] An Ainu man in Akan told me of Yukar-za, an Akan-based group founded in 1968, which performs plays based on Yukar and has travelled to Europe and Asia for cultural performances.

Moreover, Native American and First Nations groups often visit Hokkaidô for cultural exchanges. Scholars have noted that global activism by indigenous groups, from the 1980s onwards in particular, has had a significant impact on the Ainu as a group. Interactions with other indigenous groups have resulted in movements among the Ainu to recognise the importance of their traditions, to revive certain aspects of their culture, and to revise the representations of Ainu through tourism. Such movements are also reflected in the establishment of museums in Ainu tourist villages such as the Ainu Museum in Shiraoi and the Ainu Cultural Museum in Nibutani, the only two museums in Japan that present the Ainu from their own point of view.[61] Furthermore, an Ainu activist in Nibutani told me that exchanges with other native populations around the world initiated the Ainu's participation at the International Conference of Indigenous People in Geneva in 1987. Other examples of interactions include trips to China to obtain recognition of the Ainu as an ethnic minority by the Chinese government and participation in international conferences. I have seen members of the Ainu interacting with First Nations groups, such as the Kwakwaka'wakw and the Stó:lo of the Northwest Coast of Canada.[62] This is one means the Ainu are using to obtain the international attention they need to receive recognition from the government and from Japanese society. As some Ainu have pointed out, the Japanese government has a weak spot for foreign pressure, and although the major objective of inter-indigenous cultural exchange is to promote Ainu culture and establish connections with other indigenous groups, another objective is to make allies who might encourage foreign pressure on the government.

Towards the Future

Tourism has played a vital role in the affirmation of the Ainu's unique ethnicity by being an important venue through which they could express themselves, and by being an integral part of the Ainu social sphere. Participation in tourism has also resulted in the formation of a unified and collective Ainu cultural and political identity. As can be seen from the above, Ainu ethnic tourism is an important aspect of their contemporary culture and society.

In recent years, the Ainu have become more active participants in tourism. No longer are they passive indigenous people who are used by the Wajin for show. They are increasingly taking the initiative in the staging of their performances, in order to benefit more from their involvement with tourism. One factor contributing to this change in the nature of the Ainu's participation in tourism may be the designation of Ainu traditional dances as important intangible cultural treasure (*Jûyô Mukei Bunkazai*) by the Japanese government in 1984. A curator who had worked at the Ainu Museum noted that the official recognition from the government changed the attitudes of many of the dancers at Shiraoi. They became professionals who took pride in their performance and strove to perfect their dances. Another factor in this change may be the Ainu's involvement in the worldwide movement among indigenous peoples, which has

resulted in increased recognition of indigenous cultures. Whatever the causes may be, active involvement in tourism will make it possible for the Ainu to appeal to tourists and express their unique identity. Instead of merely conforming to and confirming Wajin tourists' image of the Ainu as savage beings who live in the forests, it is possible for the Ainu involved with tourism to enlighten the Wajin and work towards rectifying the stereotypes. By taking more ownership of their own cultural expressions, the Ainu have moved away from a forced and imposed culture-showing through tourism to creation of Ainu ethnic pride. Such Ainu ethnic identities and pride cultivated through tourism can serve the younger generations, who shoulder the future and the political, social, and cultural movements of the Ainu. As an Ainu man who works at a tourist village emphasised, a united Ainu identity is vital to ensure a future for the Ainu.

Tourism reflects Wajin social attitudes towards the Ainu and Ainu ethnic identities. The production of the "Ainu" through tourism is co-authored by the Ainu and Wajin; both tourists and tourees are involved in the formation of Ainu identities. At the same time Wajin tourists admire the Ainu culture through tourism, the existence of tourism itself is an unconscious means for Wajin to take advantage of, exploit and cheapen Ainu culture. Through Wajin middlemen and the eyes of Wajin tourists, Ainu performances are interpreted to fit the stereotypic image Japanese society has created. Museums play a role in reinforcing some of those images. Yet some Ainu also use this stereotypic image to their own advantage. Although commoditisation of Ainu culture through tourism can lead to modification and reshaping of the culture, at the same time, it reinvigorates and reinvents the culture. It can facilitate the preservation, transmission and development of a cultural tradition, which is linked to Ainu pride. Tourism also provides employment. Cross-cultural education, increasing visibility, formation of a unified and political Ainu ethnic identity and formation of diverse individual Ainu identities as a result of tourism can be used as important tools with which to promote the current political agendas of the Ainu.

As an important venue of self-expression, and especially as a place where the Wajin can interact with the Ainu in the Ainu domain, tourist villages hold opportunities to make substantial changes and help carve out paths for future generations. As a product of Japanese colonialist and assimilationist policies and the historical relationship between the Wajin and Ainu, tourism is emblematic of the current relations between them. Further exploration into the topic of Ainu ethnic tourism will prove invaluable in research of the Ainu of the past, present, and future.

NOTES

Unless otherwise noted, all the translations from Japanese works are my own, and all interviews with Ainu and Wajin men and women were conducted in Japanese. All Ainu words in this text are of the *Saru* dialect and phonetically alphabetised according to the usage in *Kayano Shigeru no Ainu go Jiten*, ed. Kayano Shigeru.

1   The law regarding the promotion of Ainu culture and the dissemination and development of knowledge about Ainu traditions is also generally known as *Ainu Shimpô* (Ainu New Law). For portrayal of the new law in the mainstream media, see "Ainu Shimpô Seiritsu (Ainu New Law Enacted)," *Hokkaidô Shimbun*, 8 May 1997; "Ainu Shimpô Mirai e (Towards the Future with Ainu New Law)," *Hokkaidô Shimbun*, 8 May 1997; and "Minzoku Bunka Zenkoku he Hasshin (Ethnic Culture to be Transmitted across the Country)," *Asahi Shimbun* 9 May 1997. Hokkaidô Former Aborigines Protection Act, commonly known as *Kyûdojin Hogohô*, was put into force in 1899. This law was enacted with the intention of saving the Ainu from the destitute lives they were leading, a result of thirty years of assimilation policies put into effect with Hokkaidô's official incorporation into Japan in 1869. For more on the law, see Kazuyoshi Ôtsuka, *Ainu – Kaihin to Mizube no Tami (Ainu, Those Who Live by the Water)* (Tokyo: Shinjuku-shobô, 1995). Siddle noted in "The Ainu: Construction of an Image," in *Diversity in Japanese Culture and Language*, ed. J. C. Maher and G.

Macdonald (London: Kegan Paul International, 1995), that Kyudojin Hogohô was instrumental in institutionalising the authorities' paternalistic view of the Ainu as "former" aboriginals.

2   The term *Kankô Kotan* (*Kankô* means "tourism" in Japanese and *Kotan* means "village," or "community," in the Ainu language) is translated in this paper as "tourist villages" and "tourist centres." The term refers to a community in which a substantial portion of the revenue comes from tourism, and which is often created for the sole purpose of accommodating tourists.

3   The word *Wajin* is used here to indicate the mainstream Japanese, in contrast to the Ainu. This term is used primarily by Wajin themselves to differentiate themselves from minority groups in Japan, ethnic or otherwise, such as the Ainu, Okinawans, and Burakumin. Most Ainu use *shisamu* or *shamo* to indicate the Japanese people from Honshû.

4   "Shisamu: Muchi ga Umu Sabetsu Imanao (Wajin: Prejudice Born from Ignorance Prevails Today)," *Asahi Shimbun*, 19 March 1993.

5   Chris Taylor, et al., eds., *Lonely Planet: Japan* (Hawthorn: Lonely Planet Publications, 1981), 31. When former Prime Minister Nakasone remarked in 1986 that "Japan is a mono-ethnic country," his comment went unnoticed by the Japanese media but received much criticism in the US and from the Ainu. For more on the controversy surrounding Nakasone's comments, see Takaaki Mizuno, "Ainu, the Invisible Minority," *Japan Quarterly* (Apr–June 1987), pp. 143–48.

6   Although it is important to acknowledge that Ainu ethnic tourism has had a profound impact on the Wajin in many ways, and Wajin identities have been negotiated through contact with the Ainu in tourist centres, this paper will not address such matters.

7   The few papers on the topic include: Takeshi Higashimura, "'Kankô Ainu' ni miru Wajin no Ainu Minzoku Sabetsu (Ainu Discrimination as Seen through Ainu Tourism)," *Kaiho Shakaigaku* vol. 9 (1995): pp. 65–85; Tokuhei Narita and Kohei Hanazaki, eds., *Kindaika no Naka no Ainu Sabetsu no Kozo (The*

Structure of Ainu Discrimination in the Process of Modernization) (Tokyo: Akashi-shoten, 1985); Kazuyoshi Ôtsuka, "Ainu ni okeru Kankô no Yakuwari: Dôkaseisaku to Kankôseisaku no Sôkoku (The Role of Tourism for the Ainu: Conflict between Assimilation and Tourism Policies)," in *Nijusseiki ni okeru Shominzoku bunka no Dentô to Henyô 3: Kankô no Nijusseiki (Ethnic Cultures in the 20th Century, Their Traditions and Changes: Tourism of the 20th Century)*, ed. S. Ishimori (Tokyo: Domesu Shuppan, 1996), pp. 102–22; Reiko Saitô, "Hoppô Minzoku Bunka Kenkyu ni okeru Kankojinruigakuteki Shiten (1): Edo-Taisho-ki ni okeru Ainu no Baai (Author's English title: The Study of Tourist Arts in Ethnographic Records (1): In reference to the Ainu from the Edo era to the Taisho era)," *Hokkaidôristu Hoppôminzoku Hakubutsukan Kenkyû Kiyô (Research Bulletin of the Hokkaidô Museum of Northern Peoples)* vol. 3 (1994), pp. 139–60; and "Gendai Shakai ni okeru Ainu no Kôgei no Arikata: Kankô wo tôshita Kenkyû ni Mukete (Author's English title: Ainu Crafts in Contemporary Hokkaidô: An Overview for the Study of Acculturation and Cultural Mobilization through Tourism)," *Hokkaidôristu Hoppôminzoku Hakubutsukan Kenkyû Kiyo (Research Bulletin of the Hokkaidô Museum of Northern Peoples)* vol. 5 (1996), pp. 103–14.

8 Pierre L. van den Berghe and Charles F. Keyes, "Tourism and Re-Created Ethnicity," *Annals of Tourism Research* vol. 11 (1984), p. 343.

9 Davydd J. Greenwood, "Culture by the Pound: An Anthropological Perspective on Tourism as Cultural Commoditization," in *Hosts and Guests*, ed. V.L. Smith (Philadelphia: University of Pennsylvania Press, 1989), p. 171.

10 Benita J. Howell, "Weighing the Risks and Rewards of Involvement in Cultural Conservation and Heritage Tourism," *Human Organization* vol. 53, no. 2 (1994), pp. 150–59; and H. Michael Erisman, "Tourism and Cultural Dependency in the West Indies," *Annals of Tourism Research* vol. 10 (1983), pp. 337–61; Greenwood, "Culture by the Pound."

11 Erisman, "Tourism and Cultural Dependency."

12 Greenwood, "Culture by the Pound"; Howell, "Weighing the Risks and Rewards"; and John Urry, *The Tourist Gaze – Leisure and Travel in Contemporary Societies* (London: SAGE publications, 1990).

13 Simpson, "Tourism and Tradition," p. 171.

14 Erik Cohen, "Authenticity and Commoditization in Tourism," *Annals of Tourism Research* vol. 15 (1988), pp. 379–80.

15 Eric Hobsbawm and Terence Ranger eds., *The Invention of Culture* (Cambridge: Cambridge University Press, 1983). This book offset a large number of studies focusing on the various "invented traditions" that exist in societies and cultures around the world. Hobsbawm writes that invented traditions are based on "factitious" ties to the past and are fabrications to construe some aspects of life as remaining unchanged in the confusion and chaos of modernisation. He encourages anthropologists to make clear distinctions between "invented" and "old" traditional practices. Criticisms of "invention of tradition" include Richard Handler and Jocelyn Linnekin, "Tradition, Genuine or *Spurious*," *Journal of American Folklore* vol. 97, no. 385 (1984), pp. 273–89; and Jean Jackson, "Is There a Way to Talk about Making Culture without Making Enemies?" *Dialectical Anthropology* vol. 14 (1989), pp. 127–43. They contend that such studies assume that "old" traditions are static, unchanging, and unadaptable to change.

16 Cohen, "Authenticity and Commoditization in Tourism."

17 Van den Berghe and Keyes, "Tourism and Re-Created Ethnicity," pp. 343–47.

18 Sôrifu, Nihon Seifu (The Prime Minister's Office), ed., *Kankô Hakusho (White Paper on Tourism)*, (Tokyo: Ôkurashô, 1998), pp. 11–28, 68.

19 Nihon Kankô Kyôkai (Tourism Association of Japan), *Todôfuken Kankô Hakusho (Prefectural White Paper on Tourism)*, (Tokyo: Nihon Kankô Kyôkai, 1991), p. 63.

20 For example, Akita prefecture's "True Hearts of Akita" (*Magokoro Akita*), Gunma's "Warm Hearts of Gunma" (*Honobono Gunma*), and Ehime's "Smiles of Ehime" (*Egao no Ehime*). For all the other prefectures, see Nihon Kankô Kyôkai, *Todôfuken Kankô Hakusho*, p. 37.

21 For more on this topic, see Nishiura Hiroki, *Ainu, Ima ni Ikiru (Ainu, Who Live in the Present)*, (Tokyo: Shinsen-sha, 1997), pp. 96–123.

22 Cited in Richard Siddle, *Race, Resistance and the Ainu of Japan* (London: Routledge, 1996).

23 Ôtsuka, "Ainu ni okeru Kankô no Yakuwari."

24 Saitô, "Hoppô Minzoku Bunka Kenkyu"; Siddle, *Race, Resistance and the Ainu of Japan.*

25 Ôtsuka, "Ainu ni okeru Kankô no yakuwari." *Kotan no Kuchibue* is a novel published in 1957 by Nobuo Ishimori, a writer of children's books, about an Ainu boy and his sister. This book has been praised as one of the greatest works for children in the post-war period. *Iomante no Yoru*, which told of a beautiful Ainu girl, was a song by Itô Kunio that became a hit in the 1960s.

26 Saitô, "Hoppô Minzoku Bunka Kenkyu." This paper examines Ainu ethnic identities and relations vis-à-vis the Wajin and thus will not focus on foreign tourists who visit Hokkaidô and Ainu tourist villages, since the nature of the relations between the tourist and the touree are different For accounts of, and guides for, foreign visitors to Hokkaidô, see Siddle, *Race, Resistance and the Ainu of Japan*; Kyosuke Kindaiti (sic.), *Ainu Life and Legends* (Tokyo: Japan Tourist Bureau, 1941); Isabella Bird, *Unbeaten Tracks in Japan: An Account of Travels in the Interior Including Visits to the Aborigines of Yezo and the Shrine of Nikko* (Rutland: C.E. Tuttle Co., 1973); and Narita and Hanazaki, "Kindaika no Naka no Ainu Sabetsu."

27 An important aspect of Ainu spirituality which is well-known is *Iomante*, a ritual which involves the slaying of a bear, by which it is sent back to the world of gods. For more on the ritual, see Ainu Minzoku Hakubutsukan (Ainu Museum), ed., *Ainu Bunka no Kisochishiki (Basic Information on Ainu Culture)* (Tokyo: Sôfûkan, 1993), 142–43. Dances taken from the ritual performed in tourist villages are often called "Bear Festival" (*Kuma-Matsuri*).

28 "Kotan: Kankôchi de Saguru Kôryû no Michi (Kotan: Ways of Cultural Exchange Explored in Tourist Centres)," *Asahi Shimbun*, 18 March 1993.

29 Born in 1893 near Asahikawa, Kawamura Kaneto was an Ainu surveying engineer who, in the later years of his life, settled in Asahikawa, where he established the memorial hall in order to enlighten tourists. Since Kaneto's death, his efforts have been taken over by his son, Kenichi. For more on Kaneto, see "Ainu Sokuryôgishi 'Kaneto' (Kaneto, Ainu Survey Engineer)," series 1–5, *Asahi Shimbun*, 22–26 April 1997.

30 Ôtsuka, *Ainu-Kaihin to Mizube no Tami.* According to Kayano Shigeru in *Ainu no Ishibumi* (Tokyo: Asahi Shimbun-sha, 1990) (English translation: *Our Land was a Forest: An Ainu Memoir,* (Boulder, Colorado: Westview Press, 1994)), *Yukar* (collection of Ainu epic poems) notes that the Sam River is where *Okikurmikamuy* (the god who taught the Ainu subsistence methods and culture) lived and thus the area surrounding the river is the birthplace of Ainu culture.

31 Urry, *The Tourist Gaze,* and Erisman, "Tourism and Cultural Dependency."

32 *Asahi Shimbun*, "Kotan." For more discussions on the negative effects of tourism on the Ainu, see Higashimura, "'Kankô Ainu' ni Miru Sabetsu"; and Narita and Hanazaki, eds., *Kindaika no Naka no Ainu Sabetsu.*

33 Quoted in Sandra A. Niessen, "The Ainu in Mimpaku: A Representation of Japan's Indigenous People at the National Museum of Ethnology," *Museum Anthropology* vol. 18, no. 3 (1994), p. 21. Kayano Shigeru is a man who has dedicated his life to gaining recognition for Ainu culture, and to the resurgence of Ainu identity. He was the first Ainu to become a member of the Japanese Diet, and exerted much influence in the political realm, most notably in the passing of the Ainu New Law in 1997. Author of more than twenty-five books on the Ainu, including four textbooks and a Japanese–Ainu dictionary, Kayano, along with his wife, has appeared and performed in countless public arenas, including museums, television programmes and academic conferences.

34 Narita and Hanazaki, *Kindaika no Naka no Ainu Sabetsu*, pp. 232–33, 292–93.

35 Also "Kotan," *Asahi Shimbun.*

36   Kayano, *Ainu no Ishibumi.*
37   Hokkaidô Chô, "Hokkaidô Utari Seikatsu Jittai Chosa," p. 5, 15. Moreover, approximately 10 percent of the Ainu are involved in agriculture, 25 percent in fishing, and 30 percent are seasonal or wage labourers, mainly in construction.
38   John C. Maher, Book review of *European Studies on Ainu Language and Culture,* ed. Josef Kreiner in *Monumenta Nipponica* (1993) 49(3), pp. 385–87.
39   Ôtsuka, "Ainu ni Okeru Kankô no Yakuwari."
40   Ôtsuka, "Ainu ni Okeru Kankô no Yakuwari."
41   *Yarase,* "doing it for show," is similar in concept to what Dean MacCannell termed "staged authenticity" in *The Tourist: A New Theory of the Leisure Class* (New York: Schocken Books, 1976). For a brief discussion of *yarase* in Ainu tourism, see Kinase Takashi, "Ainu wo Meguru Gensetsu no Seijigaku (Author's English title: Politics of Discourse around the Ainu)," unpublished M.A. thesis, Tokyo University, 1995.
42   "Kotan," *Asahi Shimbun.*
43   "Ainu Dentô Gakki Dokugakude 'Saihakken' (Ainu Traditional Instruments 'Ridiscovered' through Self-teaching)," *Nihon Keizai Shimbun* 31 January 2000.
44   Katarina Sjöberg, *The Return of the Ainu: Cultural Mobilization and the Practice of Ethnicity in Japan* (New York: Routledge, 1993), p. xi.
45   Nelson H. H. Graburn, "The Evolution of Tourist Aits," *Annals of Tourism Research* vol. 11 (1984), pp. 393–419; and van den Berghe and Keyes, "Tourism and Re-Created Ethnicity."
46   Yamakawa Tsutomu, *Ainu Minzoku Bunka-shi eno Shiron* (*Essays on Ainu Cultural History*) (Tokyo: Mirai-sha, 1980).
47   Saitô "Hoppô Minzoku Bunka Kenkyû"; and Ôtsuka, *Ainu–Kaihin to Mizube no Tami.*
48   Sjöberg, *The Return of the Ainu,* p. 17.
49   Greenwood, "Culture by the Pound."
50   Narita and Hanazaki, *Kindaika no Naka no Ainu Sabetsu,* pp. 232–33, 292–93; and Higashimura, "'Kankô Ainu.'"
51   Ainu Minzoku Hakubutsukan, ed., *Ainu Bunka no Kisochishiki.*

52   Kayano, *Ainu no Ishibumi.*
53   According to the Ainu Association of Hokkaidô "Brochure on the Ainu People," Hokkaidô Utari Kyôkai – the largest organization of Ainu people, consisting of Ainu who reside in Hokkaidô – was established in 1946 as *Hokkaidô Ainu Kyokai.* The name was changed in 1961 when some people objected to the use of "Ainu" because "Ainu" had been, and still is, used in discriminatory ways and they did not feel comfortable with it. *Utari* in the Ainu language means "fellow" or "friend." In 1995, the association consisted of 15,968 members in 4,167 households, an estimated 67 percent of the total Ainu population. Also see Kaizawa Tadashi, *Ainu Waga Jinsei* (*Ainu, My Life*) (Tokyo: Iwanami-shoten, 1993), pp. 77–79.
54   Sjöberg, *The Return of the Ainu,* pp. 13, 17.
55   Yamakawa Tsutomu, ed., *Asu wo Tsukuru Ainu Minzoku* (*Ainu, Who Build the Future*) (Tokyo: Mirai-sha, 1988).
56   Siddle, *Race, Resistance and the Ainu.*
57   Johnathan Friedman, *Being in the World: Globalization and Localization* (Featherstone, 1990), p. 321.
58   I was in Cambridge, England, in the summer of 1995 and was able to see the exhibition. According to the curators, the exhibition was a minor triumph, considering the small space and small budget; there was a lot of press coverage, showing a booming interest in the Ainu in England. Although the exhibit was originally planned for six months, it was extended twice and went on until the summer of 1996.
59   "Shiraoi Ainu Minzoku Hakubutsukan 11 gatsu, Taiwan Kôen e (Shiraoi Ainu Museum Expedition to Taiwan in November)," *Muroran Mimpô* (*Newspaper of Muroran*), 3 April 1997.
60   "Ainu Bunka Zenkoku e (Ainu Culture to All of Japan)," *Asahi Shimbun,* 11 December 1995. According to Kayano Shigeru, ed., *Kayano Shigeru no Ainu go Jiten* (*Kayano Shigeru's Ainu Language Dictionary*) (Tokyo: Sunseido, 1996), *Kamuiturano* means "together with gods."
61   Ôtsuka, "Ainu ni okeru Kankô no Yakuwari."
62   Such interactions are described in David Suzuki and Keibo Oiwa, *The Japan We Never Knew: A Journey of Discovery*

(Toronto: Stoddart, 1996); in Mieko Chikkup, *Kaze no Megumi: Ainu Minzoku no Bunka to Jinken* (*Blessing of the Wind: Culture and Muman Rights of the Ainu*) (Tokyo: Ochanomizu Shobô, 1991); and in "'Kyôsei no Tsubasa' wo Ainu kara Sekai e (From Ainu to the World: 'Wing of Coexistence')," Kômei vol. 385 (1994), pp. 116–23. For a discussion on the Ainu's participation in the world-wide movement of indigenous peoples, and the commonalities between the Ainu and other indigenous peoples in terms of the experience of colonisation, the recent "cultural renaissance," political mobilisation and engagement in the "politics of memory," see Siddle, *Race, Resistance and the Ainu*, pp. 19–25, 185–86.

19

What They Came With: Carnival and the Persistence of African Performance Aesthetics in the Diaspora

Esiaba Irobi

In this article, I want to address Paul Gilroy's (1993) misleading discourse at the end of *The Black Atlantic* where he asserts that the significance and meaning of survivals of indigenous African performance forms in the diaspora got "irrevocably sundered from their origins" because of the "temporal and ontological rupture of the middle passage" and, therefore, challenge scholars of Black expressive vernacular cultures "to delve into the specific dynamics of this *severance*" (p. 222). I will argue that the indigenous African forms were not severed or sundered but were rather transformed, syncretized, or creolized in the African diaspora. I will also illustrate, with vivid examples from both Africa and the Brave New World, how what really survived and have persisted are the significance, meaning, semiology, performance theories, ontological framework, and most

important, functionality of these African-derived forms. My thesis, totally antithetical to Gilroy's, will juxtapose Igbo/West African festival theater aesthetics from the continent with Carnival performance aesthetics in the African diaspora, namely, Britain, Trinidad, the United States, and Canada, to show the similarities in significance and meaning between festivals on the continent and carnivals in the diaspora and, therefore, establish a theory of translocation, continuity, and self-redefinition instead of one of "sundering," "disjunctive temporality," and "severance" (p. 223). I also hope that my argument and illustrations in the entire essay will help to illuminate why and how Paul Gilroy's intellectual position is not only reductive but also politically dangerous in the 21st century because it is symptomatic of a hermeneutics of containment still used by the

Esiaba Irobi, "What They Came With: Carnival and the Persistence of African Performance Aesthetics in the Diaspora," pp. 896–913 from *Journal of Black Studies* 37(6), 2007.

The Anthropology of Performance: A Reader, First Edition. Edited by Frank J. Korom.

Western academy in its analysis and evaluation of the significance and importance of Africa's contributions to modernity and the contemporary world.

Phenomenology and the Theory of Translocation

To understand what the Africans who left the continent from 1441 to 1865 came with to the United States and other parts of the New World, we first need to understand what phenomenology means not only from Hegel's, Husserl's, Sartre's, or Maurice Merleau-Ponty's points of view but also from an African and African Diasporic perspective. This is important because phenomenology emphasizes "the engagement in lived experience between the individual consciousness and reality as *sensory* and *mental* phenomena" (Fortier, 2002, p. 41). The whole tradition of African festival and ritual theater, we must bear in mind, with all its complex music, drum language, dance, architecture, songs, spectacle, spatial configurations, choreography, and masking, has always been transferred from generation to generation, before and after slavery, phenomenologically, such as through the intelligence of the human body, not videos, films, or typographic literacy (e.g., journals, notebooks, or dramatic literature; see Gottschild, 2003, p. 15). The discourse of phenomenology therefore offers us the latitude to compare the European understanding of the somatogenic capabilities of the human body with an African and African Diasporic episteme of the same phenomenon.

Phenomenology – I don't have space and time to trace its Western intellectual history from Hegel through Husserl to Jean-Paul Sartre – posits that there is the possibility of a more authentic way for humans to exist in the world, one that brings them in fuller touch with things and themselves and that ultimately gives access to truth and even a spiritual realm (Fortier, 2002, p. 41). Maurice Merleau-Ponty redefined this understanding of phenomenology by stating that perception is an embodied experience. Against the abstract emptiness of the Cartesian cogito, "I think, therefore I am," Merleau-Ponty argued that "to be a body is to be tied to a certain world; . . . our body is not primarily in space: it is of it" (Lechte, 1994, p. 30). What this means, according to Merleau-Ponty, is that perception in itself does not exist without a specific context or situation whose sole basis is the human body. In other words, "the perceiving mind is an incarnated mind" and "the very imbrication of the perceiving organism and its surrounding is what lies at the basis of perception" (p. 30). In summary, what Merleau-Ponty and the other European philosophers are trying to say is that the ultimate source, site, and center of perception and signification, physical or transcendent, is the human body.

Africans, funnily enough, knew this all along. Centuries before Hegel, Husserl, Jean-Paul Sartre, and Maurice Merleau-Ponty were born, African cultures were existential spaces where life was and still remains an intensely ritualized and performed activity. Because the ontology of most African peoples is primarily spiritual, the physical body incorporates, at one level, habit memory through which functional activities such as climbing, sculpting, handwork, gestures, prostrations, and styles of walking are created and mastered. At the secondary modeling level (i.e., the more complex, metalingual system of communication), African societies consciously fashion a corporeal semiology through which the body becomes the symbolic repository of transcendent and expressive as well as philosophical ideas associated with religion, worship, the divine, ritual ceremony, celebration, war, weddings, funerals, royalty, politics, and so on. Most of these ideas and concepts are structured and expressed through mime, music, and dance. The Ashanti of Ghana have a highly stylized dance called *Kete*, which is reserved only for members of the royal family. Captured and sold into slavery, members of the royal family, or other Ashantis who had watched and metabolized the dance through their bodies, were still able to replicate aspects of the dance through the memory of their bodies even after they lost their verbal, vernacular languages. Vestiges of the dance, even if hybridized in the New World, remain an embodied and performative aesthetic for "rememorying" where the Ghanaian captives came from into slavery. The dance, as a semiotic device, becomes a performance of a half-remembered history and identity. It is important to note that even after most African peoples lost their languages because of seasoning in the New World, phrases and fragments of their dances remained and survived as choreographic and phenomenological vocabularies of their original identity and cultural history. Black women in Suriname, South America, have a heartrending African song, fleshed out by dance, which they sang and danced to after the humiliating toil on the slave plantations. The song says, "We may have been reduced to servants and serfs here-/but we are still proud and dance with our heads held high/because we come from a proud and dignified people." The dance movements are regal with gentle sways of an upright torso, eagle-like lifting of the hands, and a smile that breaks through the mask of pain on the women's faces.

In *How Societies Remember*, Paul Connerton (1989) contextualizes what I have described above phenomenologically when he says that in all cultures, much of the choreography of authority is expressed through the body. Within this choreography, he argues, there is an identifiable range of repertoires through which many postural performances become meaningful by registering meaningful inflections of the upright gesture. "Such inflections recall a pattern of authority to performers and observers. . . . Culturally specific postural performances provide us with a mnemonics of the body" (p. 74). Anybody who has seen the Yoruba *Ege* dance, Igbo *Ese* dance, or Kalahari *Alagba* dance drama will agree that the African concept of choreography is much more sophisticated than the examples that Connerton gives in his book, most of which, unfortunately, are drawn from Europe. This leads us to observe that, perhaps, Western postpositivist history, particularly the valorization of the printed word and cryptographic literacy over other forms of communication, seems to have drastically affected the way Western scholars understand and value the power of the body as a site of multiple discourses for sculpting history, memory, identity, and culture. Jamake Highwater (1982), a Native American scholar, has discussed this in detail in his very incisive book, *The Primal Mind*. David Abram (1996) and Diane

Ackerman (1990) have rejected the Western tendency to explain the quotidian quiddity of life through the intellect and abstract reasoning. Their books, *The Spell of the Sensuous* and *A Natural History of the Senses*, respectively, emphasize that human beings apprehend life and the world most powerfully through the senses. We can therefore argue that dance, and the somatogenic power of the body, may have been highly undervalued in the West largely because of the West's own history: the Judeo-Christian stigmatizing of the body as the swamp of sin; and the industrial revolution that industrialized many European societies, as well as the bodies of the people, cutting them away from communal, ritual, festive, and agrarian practices from which most indigenous dances, theaters, and carnivals flower.

On the African continent and in many parts of the African diaspora, dance, accompanied by music, represents the supreme art, the art par excellence. This is because dance, as a form of kinaesthetic literacy, is the primary medium for coding the perception of our outer and inner worlds, our transcendent worlds, our spiritual history, and the memory of that complex history. The body is the major conduit of artistic expression, whether it is a painting, a dance, a book like *The Black Atlantic*, sculpting, or performing. The medium is immaterial. The ultimate source of signification is the human body. It is therefore because the body is the primary instrument for incubating, articulating, and expressing all ideas as well as transporting all art, be it music, drama, literature, electronic messages, theater, festival, or carnival, that I want to argue that it is through phenomenology and kinaesthetic literacy (i.e., the use of the medium of the body as a site of cultural signification) that crucial aspects of indigenous African festival theater were translocated to the New World. These fragments of performative texts were then deployed by diasporized Africans to negotiate the creation of hybrid and syncretic forms that are now called African American or Caribbean or South American carnival texts or "anti-texts," as Paul Gilroy derogatorily prefers to call them. In this negotiation, the African aspects became the basic performative currency for resisting total incorporation or seasoning into European or native South/North American identities, signs, and modes of representation.

What makes Carnival even more remarkable, in light of our discussion that the body has a memory and can be a site of resistance through performance, is that it is an eloquent example of the transcendent expressed through spectacle, procession, colors, music, dance, and most important, the physical movement of the body. Bakhtin, who has had the last word on carnival in the West for a long time, thinks that "carnival . . . embraces lowness. Degradation, debasement, the body and all functions – but particularly defecation, urination, copulation – are part and parcel of [carnival's] ambivalence" (Lechte, 1994, pp. 7–12). Yes, of course, carnival incorporates but also transcends these easy European-derived definitions of the phenomenon. Carnival participation and responses by onlookers in the African Diaspora, even White British policemen who do not usually smile at Black people in Britain, is sentient (i.e., produces a physical response and is therefore transcendent), that is, healing in terms of interpersonal and racial relationships within given hegemonic societies. Carnival therefore illustrates that transcendence, the word most associated with phenomenology, in the Western academy, is more easily achievable as a bodily and performative experience than as an intellectual or logocentric engagement.

This is all so evident in different parts of the African Diaspora where Carnival, a hybridized derivative of African festival and ritual theater, has come to represent a performative retheorizing of individualism and alienation – the twin ethos and punishment of Western capitalist ontology. Africans, translocated to the West Indies, Britain, North America, Canada, and South America, have consistently used carnival performance to defy, mock, reject, interrogate, and deconstruct individualism and Western naturalistic, closed-door, mouse-tongue-of-a-stage, middle-class theater for centuries. They have been able to do this because Carnival opens up spaces for communality and mass participation despite societal differences in terms of class, race, color, income, intellectual pretensions, or the memories from the lacerations of history. In recent years, Carnival has become an act of incorporation and atonement.

It has become a ritual of purgation and regeneration, cleansing the blood and sores of slaves and serfs from sidewalks in Europe, the Caribbean, and the Americas. Politically, Carnival has come to represent a collective and dynamic process of subjectivity and creativity that enables Africans in the Diaspora to engage, rethink, redefine themselves, and act out the contradictions of their histories. Through the elaborate pre-performance processes of building masks, costumes, and musical arrangements, choreography practices, composing new tunes, and sculpting masks, props, and floats, the actants and participants of Carnival literally, performatively and philosophically, transcend themselves. They enter into a realm of imaginative and experiential possibilities often denied them by their everyday social, economic, political, and religious reality. Carnival thus becomes the festive and secular variation of the more serious and cultic traditions of ritual performances translocated from Africa such as Candomble, Santeria, Lucumi, Orisha worship, Macumba, the Haitian omphor, Abakua, and so on.

Hollis Liverpool (1998) has contextualized how people of African descent redefined Carnival experience in Trinidad. In his essay, "Origins of Rituals and Customs in the Trinidad Carnival: African or European?," he traces the beginnings of carnival to the Egyptians of Africa who, thousands of years ago, held Carnival festivities in celebration of the fertility of the earth and women, as well as the replenishments of their foodstocks (p. 26). Making clear distinctions between the carnival traditions of the Spaniards, the English, the French, and the free coloreds on the island of Trinidad, Liverpool significantly points out how the complexion and dynamism as well as aesthetic and performative dimensions of Carnival changed radically once the Africans took over the artform, changing it from a consolidation of class distinctions to a dissolution of class, a street theater that took over the entire city, streets, and festive areas of the plantations from which the Africans had just been emancipated as slaves. By 1881, the Africans had so totally revolutionized carnival that the Whites, who used their own limited notion of the liberating potential of carnival to practice apartheid, had joined in the celebration and were now dancing African bamboula, gouiba, and calinda dances and even parodying or pretending to be Africans as part of their own performance. Today, Carnival has spread to other islands in the Caribbean and even migrated to North America and Europe. In Britain, for example, Carnival has spread from Nottinghill Gate, where it still remains the longest street festival in Europe, to other cities in England including Birmingham, Wolverhampton, Leeds, Leicester, Luton, and Manchester, where it continually draws participating multicultural audiences that range from 20,000 to 2 million in each city. In the United States, Carnival takes place in 21 cities including New York, where it attracts 2 million participants yearly. In Canada, this African-derived form of collective theater has become a cultural institution in Calgary, Edmonton, Montreal, Ottawa, Vancouver, Winnipeg, and Toronto, where the participants each year total 1 million people (Nurse, 2004, pp. 245–253). It is important to remark that this popular, mass street theater that has invaded and conquered both postmodern Europe and North America is a translocation and reinvention of the indigenous African festival theaters – an example of which we will see in detail below – complete with masquerades, extraordinary costumes, intoxicating music, and suggestive, insinuating, liberating dancing. Its appeal lies in the great release it gives to the body politic through participation, dressing up, and dancing. More corporeal, Rabelaisian, open, and collective than the European traditions or variations mentioned above, Carnival has a double-faced template. It reinforces the concealed spiritual, more esoteric, and religious concerns of the culture that produces it and strengthens its notions of identity, communality, liminality, and continuity. At the same time, as in the African context, it reveals and revels in the more playful dimensions of the society's psyche, invests richly in the spectacular, what Walter Benjamin calls the "exhibitionistic" side to art, which includes clowning, ribaldry, irreverent activities, raising the leg, playing the devil, stick fighting, and symbolic gender reversals that make psychic and sexual liberation and catharsis possible. In all its undertaking, the human body remains the ultimate arbiter of signs and information as well as the major phenomenological instrument for this process of historicizing the complexity of African diasporic subjectivity. A Guyanese, Afro-British poet, Grace Nichols (1983), puts this diasporic transformational phenomenon beautifully when she says, "I have crossed an ocean/I have lost my tongue-/from the root of the old one/a new one has sprung." Carnival, as we can see, is a bridge, a continuum, a collective performative aesthetic that manifests both an African and African diasporic need and facility for self-redefinition. The impulse and aesthetic impetus comes from the continent and, like seeds, replicates its parent stalk with adventitious variations or mutations on a new geography and history. A coconut that falls from a coconut tree and floats from the shores of Accra across the Atlantic to the Caribbean and sprouts in Jamaica is still a coconut, despite the sea change. I will now use the Omabe festival theater of Nsukka in Northern Igbo land of contemporary Nigeria to highlight the similarities between the sign systems, dynamics, structures, and worldview of African festival performance and their translocated derivatives in the diaspora.

Semiological Similarities between African Festivals and Diasporic Carnivals

Omabe, as festival drama, represents the African ingenuity for theatricalizing abstract, spiritual, ontological, and historical concepts into performative forms that make these concepts accessible, memorable, and in fact, retainable, to the entirety of the population of any given African society. The Omabe performance functions primarily as the coda of a collective, political identity as well as a creative device for ensuring the continuity of the festive and theatrical art form. It is theater history written on the body as a performance text, not anti-text, as Gilroy misrepresents the phenomenon in *The Black Atlantic*. The central theatrical action in Omabe festival drama, which has been practiced for more than a thousand years in Nsukka, Nigeria, involves the extremely colorful and choreographed descent of the spirits of dead ancestors from behind the Omabe hills, their abode and resting place. The spirits, who represent different lineages in Nsukka, are magnificently costumed as leopards and appear in hundreds as masquerade characters. Sometimes, the exposed parts of their bodies are rubbed with honey so that they glisten in the sun as if wet. There are, however, a few ugly, disruptive animal characters such as the civet cat and the hyena, but these are outshone by the beauty and grace of the leopards who display their feline distinction through the Omabe gait and dance in response to Omabe music. There are young and old Omabe – the age ranges differ because, in the Nsukka-Igbo worldview, the spirit world mirrors the human world. But what is breathtaking is the massive appearance of hundreds of Omabe, in fluid formations, on the brow of the hill in the setting sun amid gunshots, songs, chants, and ululations from the crowd below. The visual beauty of this spectacle has been described by Ossie Enekwe (1987) as "poetry in motion." These ethereal presences in glinting appliqué material are coming to commune and stay with the living, who flank the hillside in thousands for one whole year, during which they (the Omabe) will replenish the population, economic wealth, and agricultural harvest of the community as part of the dream of faith that powers the existential ontology of the festival. After 11 months, in another communal festival drama, the dead will depart. Thus, their movement from the hills to the marketplace, the public and occult center of the community, is highly symbolic because the Nsukka Igbo are actually ritualizing an abstract concept, a myth, an idealized future, through theater and performance.

The festival, under which the dramatic activities unfold, signals the temporal divisions in the ecological, hence occupational, world of the Nsukka-Igbo. It is the marker or watershed between the season of dryness and the season of plenty or feasting. The outing is usually preceded by a period of peace in the community during which enmity and disagreements are reconciled. Commensality or the sharing of food among friends and relatives plays a very important role in the festival. Prior to the drama, young male children are initiated into the Omabe cult, an exercise that is a form of census within the community and also an induction into the political hierarchy of the society and the civic responsibilities of the younger generation. Most of these educational values are, however, encoded in the artistic forms and iconographies preserved and administered by the older members of the Omabe cult. On Eke (the name of a market day of the week) nights, the same masquerades, muffling their voices, expose the injustices perpetrated on the poor and the weak by the powerful and rich throughout the past year. Thus, we begin to see how participation in every aspect of the festival drama and its accompanying social activities for the rest of the year is a reflection of the organic and communal nature of the theater-making process among the Nsukka-Igbo of Nigeria. Because the super-objective of the festival drama is to allow the populace to experience the myth of its origin and well-being through communal performance, it is important to observe that by participating, every member of the community leases out his or her individuality to the political status quo. The festival myth, as we can see, serves the ideology of the moment and is used for political control and social restructuring. The drama also has "psychotherapeutic" value in the sense that the myth of the return of the Omabe ancestors serves as a way of dealing with the phenomenon of death and its accompanying traumas.

Omabe, on the other hand, is a collective creation. Male dancers, choreographers, musicians, and all Omabe initiates are drawn from various segments of the community to celebrate and reinforce the Nsukka-Igbo people's worldview and perception of themselves as they "perform" themselves. It is this collective involvement, we can argue, that gives the performance its mythic and epic structure, a synthesis of all the artforms – sculpture, music, drum language, dance, mythic language, poetry, costume, body painting, incantations, and so on – whose cumulative effect on the senses opens up the subconscious and makes ritual efficacy or transformation possible. The collective ethos also demands that there must be space within the plot of the performance for the community or non-Omabe cult members to experience or participate, even if peripherally, in the myth that regulates their lives. The link between authorship and participation is therefore clear. When a people feel a sense of ownership and belonging and participation to the theatrical process, the performance will embody and validate their experiences and cement their sense of community.

Myth in African and African Diasporic Festival/Carnival Performance

More revealing, perhaps, is that the myth of Omabe and its employment as a performative metanarrative highlights the crucial difference between a Western (contemporary) use or understanding of the word *myth* and the indigenous African conception of the same word. For although admitting that African myth possesses the traditional form of a narrative, this narrative is not just a simple story, a relation of past events, but a system and mode of knowledge that can become, and indeed usually does become, the structure of a plot (Laroche, 1974, p. 45). As Maximilien Laroche has observed, myth in an oral culture, before being a narrative fixed by writing, is the spoken word, the facial expression, the gesture that defines the event within the individual heart. It unites the sacred and the historic, expresses a world order, is situated within a religious framework, and possesses a situational character (i.e., it is a socioeconomic product, an ideological superstructure inseparable from its social structure). It ties together the everyday, the ephemeral, to the atemporal, the metaphysical. Myth, then, is not simply narrative, something static or fixed, but action (p. 45). And poignant to our argument about the continuity, not severance, of African ontologies and performance forms in the diaspora, Maximilien Laroche, who is Haitian, explains very articulately the logic and process of transforming African myths and their performative aesthetics into Haitian myths. He argues that to speak of the evolution of African myth into Haitian myth is to speak of a process by which the African, as he became Haitian, was able to retain the essential nature of his heritage and at the same time renew it.

"Or rather adapt it, for although he held on to his ancestral myths he nevertheless gave them a new application, a new meaning, *one not different front the old but one capable of serving a similar function within the framework of a new situation*" (p. 45; italics added).

Laroche, we must observe, does not use a grandiose phrase like "temporal and ontological rupture" or "irrevocably sundered," neither does he present an essentialist or racialized Africentric discourse, which is what agitates Paul Gilroy and his postmodern sensibilities. Rather, Laroche's discourse, like Paul Carter Harrison's in *Totem Voices* (1989) and *The Drama of Nommo* (1973), is a discourse of continuity, hybridization, and syncreticism. It echoes, as well as precedes, Stuart Hall, who keeps reminding us that identity is not a fixed thing but an evolving, synthetic, and omnivorous process that draws or rather selects from available aesthetic and ontological constructs to perform or manifest its ever-evolving, protean self. As a comparative perspective, the actor/audience configuration in Omabe, the picture of a collective mass yet spatially reverential to the masked figures, is an expression of solidarity, of identity, of history, of – even arguably – the authenticity of a particular people's approach to art within a wider cultural and national framework. It indicates the conceptual and experiential sources of Black expressive vernacular performances in the diaspora, particularly in Carnivals in Britain, the Caribbean, and South and North America.

In a semiotic sense, the appearance and descent of the mass of Omabe masquerades from the hills to the market square and the acting out of the Omabe myth – accompanied by Omabe music, dance, mime, costume, and so on during the performance – highlight what Aston and Savona have referred to as the polysemic nature of the theater. It exemplifies the tendency of Igbo/African indigenous theater to draw on "a number of sign-systems which do not operate in a linear mode but in a complex and simultaneously operating network unfolding in time and place" (Aston & Savona, 1991, p. 116). It also shows various literacies at work. We can say the same about African-derived Carnival in Brazil, Canada, Trinidad, or St. Lucia. As the Omabe vividly illustrates, in indigenous (i.e., preslavery, precolonial) Igbo festival and ritual theater, massing, processions, use of colors, music, collective dancing, and bonding through bodily contact predominate. The philosophy that theater is a form of communal therapy whereby the society rewires the threads of human relationship that have been broken in the course of the year is very well-known by the entire community. Just as well, the theory that festival theater is a ritual that allows us to enter into a state of consciousness that brings us into spiritual contact with eternal concepts like community, nationhood, democracy, collectivity, history, metaphysics, and worldview is common lore. Even children who start participating in these performances in the womb and on their mothers' backs know that participation renews in us the strength to face the world by awakening in the individual the understanding that he or she is not alone but contains multitudes. The entire community is propelled by the collective mechanics of the festival to perform a philosophy of life that is totally antithetical to Descartes's "I think, therefore I am!" African community performance is an antithetical albeit transcendent concept: "We are, therefore I am!" A close examination of Carnival in London, Brooklyn, Toronto, Bahia, Rio, Trinidad, New Orleans, New York, and Canada will reveal similarities in structure, function, polysemy, aesthetics, and most important, ontology and functionality.

Collective memory in premodern societies was forged through song, myth, poetry, dance, drum language, processions, mime, and drama and expressed through the umbrella of festival and ritual performances: initiations, rites of passage, and naming, wedding, and funeral ceremonies. The primary function of these festivals and rituals, at one level, is to reify and imbue historical values with recognizable meaning – as in a wedding ceremony or a war dance. At the secondary level, they serve as processes for recalling and preserving the aesthetic used to structure the idea, experience, or cultural value being expressed into a text for reenactment. This is why and how the Africans who were translocated to North America were able to resist Europe's foremost attempts at globalizing them. As O. E. Uya (1992) puts it, despite its chains and whips, its great

anxieties and fears, the bondsmen (and women in North America) refused to become slaves to their environments. "They created viable cultures which reflected their *African Aboriginal values* as well as their American environment. Slavery despite its cruelties and the assumptions of the white masters and intellectual descendants, failed to reduce blacks to mere chattel" (pp. 128–194; italics added). Quoting Martin Brewer, Uya goes on to say that probably no people have been so completely the bearers of tradition as the African slave immigrants. They carried in their minds and hearts a treasure of complete "musical forms, dramatic speech, and imaginative stories, which they perpetuated through vital acts of self expression. Wherever slaves were ultimately placed they established an enclave of African culture that flourished in spite of environmental disadvantages" (pp. 128–194). Each performance, as we can see, served as an occasion for recall, reiteration, reinvention, and resisting the capitalist agenda of slavery that was to globalize the Africans into what the West wanted them to be: chattel slaves.

Conclusion: Carnival as an Encyclopedia of Other Literacies

Literacy, as we have inherited from the Western tradition of education, is cast in a cryptographic or typographic form. To be literate means to be able to read and write in a particular form of gnosis, logocentric gnosis, with a specific orthographic or calligraphic structure, origin, and history. But suppose we shift our examples of literacy to sculpture, dance, music, attire, gesture, dreams, space, and tattoos? What emerges is a new definition of literacy that resides in semiotic intelligence. We are faced with iconographic literacy: What would the Omabe mean or represent to Paul Gilroy without my analysis? Can he read it? If he cannot decode the messages encoded in Omabe's metalanguages, will the Nsukka-Igbo creators of this extremely complex festival and ritual theater, cultic and carnivalesque at the same time, not see Paul Gilroy as a cultural and semiotic illiterate? In other words, most non-Western cultures express themselves through kinaesthetic, proxemic, sonic, calligraphic, iconographic, olfactory, linguistic, tactile, and other literacies, as I have illustrated with the Omabe Festival Drama and Carnivals in the African Diaspora. Failure to decode them – with the pretence that the Plato to Postmodernism paradigm is all there is to knowledge – is only a manifestation of how, in the Western academy, ignorance continues to wear the mask of arrogance. The tendency to refer to African diasporica vernacular expressive forms as anti-texts refracts not just a conservative kind of theoretical intelligence but one that is fascistic as well. It fails to acknowledge the centrality of what Africans and working-class African diasporic populations have contributed to modernity and global popular culture through music, sports, dance, fashion, sermons, ritual worship, spirituality, theater, and Carnival. Look at how rap has morphed from Black noise to global noise! Significantly, Michael Bristol (1985) has observed in his book, *Carnival and Theatre*, that "the social and political life of the theatre as a public gathering place has an importance of its own over and above the more exclusively literary interest of texts and the contemplation of their meaning" (p. 3).

It is difficult to disagree with Michael Bristol because Diana Taylor reminds us in her book, *Hauntology of Performance* (cited in Schechner, 2002), that in the Western Hemisphere during the past 500 years, "both writing and embodied performance have often worked together to layer the historical memories that constitute community. Enacted mnemonic rituals and documented records, might retain what the other 'forgot.' These epistemes are mutually constituting" (p. 271). She then remarks significantly that *"written documents have repeatedly announced the disappearance of performance. Writing has served as a strategy for repudiating and foreclosing the very embodiedness it claims to describe"* (p. 271; italics added). Then, pointedly, as if referring to Paul Gilroy's reduction of African and African diasporic (i.e., Black performance) texts to the term *anti-texts*, Diana Taylor poignantly asks (cited in Schechner, 2002),

What is at risk, in thinking about embodied knowledge and performance as that which

disappears? Whose memories "disappear" if only archival knowledge is valorized? These questions can be addressed by challenging the psycho analytical claim – from Freud to Derrida – that writing alone preserves memory. *Such a challenge is particularly decisive to understanding colonial domination and erasure.* (p. 271; italics added)

Performance, she concludes, "is both for the strong as well as the weak." It underwrites strategies as well as tactics, banquet as well as carnival.

I have gone through this semiological archeology about literacy to make it clear that the Africans who were translocated to the Brave New World left Africa with indigenous theories of performance, notions, and philosophies of theatrical semiosis, political organization, economics, worship, and social memory, which they used as weapons of intervention and currencies for negotiation against a Western renaissance and humanistic vision that enslaved them for five centuries. These indigenous forms that they carried like breasts beneath the chains on their necks served as cultural talisman, restitutive sources, and regenerative structures for the innovative reinvention of their selves, identities, and humanity as they "trespassed on the human race," as Toni Morrison (1987) phrases it in *Beloved*. The Africans' success in creating hybridized and syncretized cultic and popular performance forms is a pointer to the sophistication, complexity, and resilience of these forms as we see even today in the African-derived carnivals and rituals of Brazil, New Orleans, Cuba, Britain, Oman in the Middle East, and everywhere else that Africans have been translocated to, willingly and unwillingly, within the past 500 years. I hope that the totality of my argument above puts paid to the question: What was there before the Europeans arrived? And what exactly did the Africans come with to the Brave New World? I also believe that the article has deflated the fallacy at the heart of Gilroy's (1993) hypothesis at the end of *The Black Atlantic* when he argues that "the modern world represents a break with the past, not in the sense that premodern, traditional Africanisms don't survive its institutions, but because the significance and meaning of these survivals get irrevocably sundered from their origins" (p. 223). The significance and meanings of the Africanisms were not sundered or severed as a result of the ineffable terrors of slavery, but they were driven underground in some parts of the African diaspora like the United States by the persecuting project of Protestantism, whereas in the Caribbean and South America, with its predominantly Catholic penchant for festivities and celebrations of saints, these same Africanisms were deployed subversively for the continuation of hybridized and syncretized African religious worship, social, political, and performative traditions in the Brave New World.

REFERENCES

Abram, D. 1996. *The spell of the sensuous*. New York: Random House.

Ackerman, D. 1990. *A natural history of the senses*. New York: Random House.

Aston, E., & Savona, G. 1991. *Theatre as sign system: A semiotics of text and performance*. London: Routledge.

Bristol, M. 1985. *Carnival and theatre*. New York: Methuen.

Connerton, P. 1989. *How societies remember*. Cambridge: Cambridge University Press.

Enekwe, O. 1987. *Igbo masks: The oneness of ritual and theatre*. Lagos: Nigeria Magazine.

Fortier, M. 2002. *Theatre/theory: An introduction*. London: Routledge.

Gilroy, P. 1993. *The Black Atlantic*. Boston: Harvard University Press.

Gottschild, B. 2003. *The Black dancing body: A geography from Coon*. New York: Palgrave Macmillan.

Harrison, P.C. 1973. *The drama of Nommo*. New York: Grove Press.

Harrison, P.C. 1989. *Totem voices*. New York: Grove Press.

Highwater, J. 1982. *The primal mind*. New York: Meridian.

Laroche, M. 1974 "The myth of the zombi." *Exile and tradition*. London: Heinemann.

Lechte, J. 1994. *Fifty key contemporary thinkers*. London: Routledge.

Liverpool, H. 1998. Origins of rituals and customs in the Trinidad carnival: African or European? *The Drama Review*, 42(3), 24–37.

Morrison, T. 1987. *Beloved*. New York: Picador.

Nichols, G. 1983. *I is a long memoried woman*. London: Karnak House.

Nurse, K. 2004. Globalization in reverse: Diaspora and the export of Trinidad carnival. In M. C. Riggio (Ed.), *Carnival: Culture in action – the Trinidad experience*. New York: Routledge.

Schechner, R. 2002. *Performance studies: An introduction*. New York: Routledge.

Uya, O.E. 1992. *African diaspora: And the Black experience in the New World slavery*. New York: Third Press.

20

Global Breakdancing and the Intercultural Body

Halifu Osumare

The experiences and perceptions of the body are to a great extent immune to the objective, analytic description that technology prefers; they can be hinted at in poetry and art, but they always constitute a real and inexhaustible resource against narrow rationality.
— Jonathan Benthall, *The Body Electric*

When I arrived at nine o'clock, the deejay was spinning "trip hop" style disks in the "chill room" upstairs until the formal dance show was supposed to start at ten o'clock downstairs.[1] Critical mass is important: the event did not begin until midnight; size of crowd and group energy are the determining factors for starting time in hip hop culture. Eventually, the audience of about two hundred consisted of black, white, Asian, Hawaiian, military, and civilian patrons who were mostly in their late twenties. "What's up, y'all? Y'all ready for the show?" asked Jamal, Honolulu hip hop promoter and emcee, to open the event.

Jamal proceeded to read from a script about the beginnings of American society's acceptance of "African American culture in the 1920s Jazz Age," putting what was about to happen in historical context and giving the event an informative purpose. This scripted narration of hip hop's historical context at a club event reflected an interest in specific African American origins of the pop culture form expressed by many global hip hop leaders. Thus began "Urban Movement," a November 1998 b-boy (breakdance) event produced at the Wave Waikiki nightclub in Honolulu, on the island of Oahu. What followed was a demonstration of the current-day variations of hip hop dance that began in the 1970s with virtuosic athletic b-boying or b-girling and "popping," the phenomenal muscular control of the rapid-fire rhythmic isolations. Urban Movement provided several hip hop enactments that illuminated what I investigate in this essay – the interdependence of performance and performativity as dual forces in global breakdancing.

Hip hop culture has come to constitute a major force in the contemporary American popular culture market, while simultaneously proliferating as an "underground" international network of loosely connected hip hop

Halifu Osumare, "Global Breakdancing and the Intercultural Body," pp. 30–45 from *Dance Research Journal* 34(2), 2002.

communities. African American music and dance have always been bought and sold according to the exigencies of a global supply-and-demand, capitalist marketplace. However, today's global reach of hip hop culture expands to ever-widening cultural spheres at a speed like never before. Whereas seventy years ago the Theater Owners' Booking Agency could find audiences for Whitey's Lindy Hoppers only in the United States or Europe, today Rock Steady Crew's co-founder, Crazy Legs, can profitably tour Japan and Southeast Asia. In these new international sites, local audiences and performers absorb African American cultural forms, scripting their own embodied spin on them.

In what follows, I argue that transnational hip hop culture expands upon its basis in African American performance and poses new challenges to the once clear-cut paradigm of cultural appropriation of black dance and music by European-Americans. I explore the intricacies of resulting cultural appropriative dimensions of hip hop's global trajectory by investigating today's hip hop generation in the Hawaiian Islands, where I conducted field research throughout 1998 and 1999. While Hawai'i is, of course, a part of the United States, its local culture is heavily inflected by its geographical location in, and historical relation to, the Pacific region. I will bring into focus intercultural *enactments* of Hawai'i-based hip hop professionals and high-school-age consumers of hip hop culture.

By enactments I mean those acts that bring forth, through the body, what has been previously invisible, submerged in the psyche. These enactments can take form through two major processes: performance and performativity. The differentiation between performance and performativity has been discussed in diverse scholarly disciplines, such as philosophy (Jacques Derrida 1978, 2000), gender studies and linguistics (Judith Butler 1990a, 1990b), and performance studies (Anthony Kubiak 1998). These theoretical analyses of performance and performativity often explicitly insinuate embodied social praxis, and can be helpful in investigating the process of grafting of expressive physical characteristics by one culture onto another. Because bodily social

practices can be made more visible through dance, when I interrogate cultural appropriation through breakdance, I must consider hip hop expressive style that includes body language, that is, attitudinal dispositions made visible through posturing and gesturing. Furthermore, such an analysis must situate itself within the larger discussion of a hip hop culture that exists sometimes in conjunction with, but often in opposition to, the more obvious big business production of rap music.

In this essay, I view *performance*, and specifically dance performance, as a series of bodily enactments that bring conscious intent and purpose to the physical execution of rhythmically patterned movement. These performances often have resonance with codified, learned systems of movement practices and specific dance styles that encompass gestures that represent implicit sociocultural values. In relation to performance, I define *performativity* as an often unconscious but meaningful series of bodily postures, gestures, and movements that implicitly signify and mark a sense of social identity or identities in everyday pedestrian activity.[2] The performativity of gestures and body language constitutes the manner in which we understand ourselves through our bodies, literally through the muscular and skeletal structure as well as semiotically and metaphorically. Peformativity might be understood as the bodily methodology by which we project our sense of ourselves into the world, while performance is the technique of embodying innovations on historicized movement styles and their attendant cultural values that represent particular collectivities.

Using this model, I examine enactments of hip hop culture among youth in Hawai'i to view the bodily "text" of appropriation. In doing so, I explore breakdancing as a clear example of movement that, in the words of dance scholar Jane Desmond, is "primary, not secondary social text" (Desmond 1997, 31). In the process of conducting my research, a salutary embodied intertext was revealed to me that I call the "Intercultural Body." I explore the Intercultural Body as a tangible result of the globalization of American pop culture in general and hip hop subculture in particular.

Hip Hop's Global Proliferation

Hip hop culture, now nearly thirty years old, greatly facilitates the proliferation of a global youth dance phenomenon that has affected nearly every country on the map. What started in the South Bronx in the mid-1970s among African American and Jamaican-born deejays as party music, using new turntable technology with booming base sounds in the percussive "breaks" of the recorded songs, has become the latest saga in the ongoing exportation of black American culture; and what began as acrobatic and highly syncopated breakdancing to those musical break beats among Bronx Puerto Ricans is now being expanded upon in an international conversation of danced text.

The global reach of hip hop culture has spawned both a conscious and an unconscious cultural dialogue within societies far removed from its origins. Local emcees (rappers) in the major capital cities of Asia, South America, and Africa may attempt exact imitations of Dr. Dre's early gangsta rap style, but eventually they must mature into rap styles that address their own local issues, sung often in indigenous languages that draw on other oral-based traditions (Perkins, 1996). In dance, the highly skilled moves of Rock Steady Crew, for example, are both mimicked and expanded upon by local movement communities throughout Europe, Canada, Polynesia, and anywhere penetrated by either MTV or Rock Steady Crew's network of international chapters. The following extensive quote from a Hawai'i-born Japanese and African American b-boy named Justin Alladin (better known in Honolulu hip hop circles as TeN) documents the growing international encoded dance language that b-boying has become:

When I was last in Japan, there were two kids battling. One kid came in and cut the other off before he was finished, and so they walked around in a circle looking at each other. And all of a sudden they jumped like this, boom, together, at the same time, knowing exactly what they were doing. It was the "Brooklyn rock." Do you know what a "Brooklyn rock" is? No, I can barely do it. These two kids, one from Japan, one from Hawai'i, never met each other before, got to the park not even an hour

before, just started dancing, and cannot communicate [verbally] with each other. They walked in the circle, jumped at the right time together and landed at the same time together, and started Brooklyn rocking together. That is international communication. That is people of the same culture.

That is the difference between someone really from hip hop and someone from commercialized hip hop. A person in commercialized hip hop cannot do that, does not know what that is, don't know anything about it, and could not do it to save their life. That's just [the difference in authenticity] on the dancing level. The same difference exists on the emcee level, on the deejay level, on the [aerosol] art level. That part about them knowing what to do is what you [I, the interviewer] are talking about: how traditions are passed on. Who passed it on? They didn't go to school. They lived it, you know. That's their life, so they know it. They have the same values. That kid knows that he cut the other kid off, and he should not have done that. That's why they jumped into the Brooklyn rock. They knew and they were ready for it. They knew what a [hip hop] battle was.

(Alladin 1999)

Indeed, breakdance has traditionally taken place in an improvisational circle, allowing each soloist to demonstrate his or her skills while encoding gestural messages into the executed movement phrases. These messages often comment with bravura on other dancers' perceived lack of skill, while extolling one's own prowess as a performer. Breakdance "battles" originally took place in lined-up opposing "gangs" facing each other. They executed the original uprock, or Brooklyn rock, that was used in TeN's Tokyo b-boy circle to settle the dispute over the breach in b-boy protocol. Classic examples of this early breaking culture were immortalized in the subway scene between New Year City Breakers and Rock Steady Crew in the 1983 film *Beat Street*, and in the highway underpass gang scene in the 1984 *Breakin' II*. That breakdancing originated as a creative dance alternative to actual gang violence, as well as party moves in the percussive breaks of the early 1970s hip hop mix of funk, soul, disco, and salsa music, allows it to claim a discursive foundation as a particularized dance form of the signifying tradition so prevalent in African American popular culture (Gottschild 1996; Gates 1988).

Breakdancing, as an embodied and particularized signifying tradition, became a global phenomenon during the current era of late capitalism. The significance of global economic trends that dictate behavior from the individual to the national levels cannot be overemphasized. The transnational subculture to which TeN refers goes beyond barriers of language and is proliferating through several processes. The era of late capitalism has several interconnected trajectories: increased personal international travel; major multinational corporations as purveyors of popular culture (e.g., Time-Warner, Microsoft, Viacom, the major record companies such as Columbia, Warner Brothers, Arista, BMG, and others with their European and Asian divisions); and the increased economic interdependency of nation states. Global capital and evolving hip hop subculture exist as parallel, yet intertwined, forces in this increasingly complex era. Before I probe the simultaneous dynamics of the popular culture industry and the circulation of hip hop culture through its underground, I would like to use the Urban Movement Honolulu event – a collective enactment – to demonstrate dimensions of both sociocultural dynamics as they intersect.

Urban Movement in Hawai'i

The Waikiki hip hop event Urban Movement, a short description of which started this essay, was a grassroots-organized, narrated, five-group performance that situated hip hop as a vivid example of danced text. Urban Movement linked four styles of contemporary hip hop dance, while the whole event demonstrated what hip hop scholar Tricia Rose calls the reimagination and "symbolic appropriation of urban space through sampling, attitude, dance, style, and sound effects" (Rose 1994, 22).

Hawai'i, as a cultural crossroads of East and West, is an important site of hip hop's transnationalism. With eight-five percent of the state of Hawaii's multiethnic population living on Oahu, along with several United States military bases, and the big tourist "machine" of Waikiki Beach, the cultural dynamics of any performance in Honolulu becomes a multilayered, multicultural event.

Continuing with my description of the event, the first dance group to perform was the Evolution Dancers, a six-member "street dance" girl group, predominantly of Asian descent. They were clad in baggy black and red sweat clothes and were accompanied by an Asian drag queen in a blue satin nightgown, a platinum wig, and athletic shoes and socks. The girls strutted with panache and rhythmically isolated their torsos, á la Janet Jackson, in perfect sync to the fast-thumping techno music. A shifting straightline choreographic floor pattern dominated, with syncopated body movements in interesting contrapuntal juxtaposition to the music. The drag queen vamped in front of the changing first line of dancers, taunting the audience with voguing, a disco style of rhythmic dance posing that originated in black male gay clubs of the 1970s. The Evolution Dancers represented a commercialized hip hop style that is more typically exhibited on MTV and BET behind current-day rap stars, and is not considered "real" hip hop dance by those who "live" hip hop underground subculture. It was meaningful that the Evolution Dancers were included by the b-boys who organized Urban Movement, for it reflected the power that commercialized MTV hip hop dance choreography has attained in the public presentation of so-called "underground" hip hop events. The Evolution Dancers, however, were just the warm-up act.

Next, Josiah, a slight and nimble "local" guy of primarily Caucasian descent, cut loose with his freestyling "house" dance.[3] Having come of dance age in the late 1980s era of the "running man" and "the smurf" fad dances, Josiah combined an eclectic array of highly individualized moves involving breaking floorwork with popping and locking, reinterpreted into Josiah-speak. He demonstrated a smooth rag-doll style of moving within the small dance-floor space that was circumscribed by a mesmerized crowd. Josiah's style seamlessly conjoined an MTV cut-and-paste *pastiche* with a personal, improvised freestyle virtuosity that juxtaposed the three major hip hop styles: breaking, popping, and locking (Figure 20.1).

At the same time, Josiah's embodied sense of self-expression was entirely his own. He simultaneously blended a perfected underground dance style with moves promulgated by the pop culture industry along with his personal local style. His danced text was a lens through which several layers of the global hip hop phenomenon were made visible.

After Josiah's solo, Skill-Roy and Strategy, two members of the Hawai'i Chapter of Rock Steady Crew, followed with more traditional b-boying. Their breaking style represents the "new school" that includes faster footwork and swifter, lower-to-the-ground directional turns than did the early days of b-boying. Following the entrance into the dance circle, four basic sections of b-boying are the tools of good improvisation: (1) uprocking (standing footwork of rapid weight shifts); (2) six-stepping (feet and hands working together

while crouched close to the floor); (3) improvised acrobatics containing a myriad of spins and flips; and (4) an ending "freeze" pose. It is the repeated juxtaposition of the second and third sections that mark the "new school." The third section, which may contain traditional moves such as "flares" (spinning on the back with legs above the head), the "turtle" (rhythmical hopping on both hands while the rest of the body is suspended close to the floor), one-handed hand spins, or back flips, is interspersed throughout the entire rhythmic improvised mix. This combination renders a more *danced* emphasis along with the acrobatic b-boy style. The new school takes greater inspiration from the subtle textures of the music than does the more athletic-focused old school breaking.

Breakdancing is embodied text just as rap music is oral poetry. Dance as narrative that indicates, identifies, imagines, and subverts normative social narratives in the context of hip hop culture was elucidated early on by Sally Banes's description of the potential of the freeze in b-boying in *Fresh Hip Hop, Don't Stop*:

Figure 20.1 *Josiah in b-boy circle executing a highly personalized house-style of hip hop dance. (Photo by Halifu Osumare, 1999)*

> Another important set of motifs in the freeze section was the exploration of body states in a subjunctive mode – things not as they are, but as they might be – comparing and contrasting youthful male vitality with its range of opposites: women, animals (dogs, horses, mules), babies, old age, injury and illness . . . and death.[4]
>
> (Banes 1985, 97)

The innovative freezes executed in Urban Movement testified to the eloquent articulation of both direct (text) and subtle (subtext) nuances through dance.

The democracy of the b-boy circle demonstrates how the individualism of dance styles, styles that *speak*, works together with good b-boy form, all rendering a cool Africanist aesthetic (Gottschild 1996).[5] All b-boys or b-girls take their turn soloing as the energy builds. Each new dancer knows the etiquette of just the right moment to enter the circle when the previous dancer executes his or her final freeze. This was the particular danced social process of good form and cultural etiquette to which b-boy TeN alluded. In true Africanist expressive style, it is the collective energy of the circle to which each individual has contributed that is evaluated as success or failure. Therefore, this communal aesthetic promotes a particular kind of socialization. Part of that socializing process in the global era of hip hop culture is the development of an Intercultural Body that is represented both similarly and differently in various parts of the globe. I turn now to the dynamics of performativity and its implications in an intercultural context.

Performing Race: Performativity as Complex Embodiment

Clearly, breakdance is a dance genre requiring tremendous skill and extensive practice. As an improvised dance form, it is a conscious willing of the body to represent personal and cultural identity. The conscious signifying involved in hip hop performance, however, takes place within a larger breakdance repertory that scripts sometimes unconscious but assimilated messages – what I earlier termed performativity. Further, this complex bodily language is created through improvisation, in which moment-by-moment choices are made that allow performativity and performance to merge. As we observed in the case of Josiah, these performance decisions represent the agency that the dancer practices in order to mediate the vicissitudes of global pop culture influences in relation to his or her individual personality. A perplexing question, however, remains: how *exactly* does the mix of conscious and unconscious cultural referencing inflect the way we understand these expressions in relation to the notion of appropriation?

In order to further understand hip hop's particularized cultural appropriation in Hawai'i, I conducted a high school study on the extent of hip hop culture among youth on the island of Hawai'i.[6] Pahoa High School, in the rural village of Pahoa, is about fifteen miles south of Hilo on the Big Island of Hawai'i. Pahoa's population is only about 1,300 people, located in the district of Puna whose population is approximately 28,000. The demography includes Caucasian, Filipino, Japanese, and Hawaiian mixtures, with African Americans representing less than one percent of the population. It is from this population of Puna that the Pahoa High students are drawn.[7]

Within three classrooms at Pahoa High, grades ten through twelve, I conducted group interviews with students. They were given a choice of designating class spokespersons or using a group response approach; all classes unanimously chose the group response approach. The collective voice format created an interactive environment that encouraged collaborative, and sometimes contradictory, answers to questions that included their taste in music, the influence of media and the marketplace, and cultural identity and social turf, as well as ethnic and class issues.

Although Pahoa is relatively small in size, the high school students' responses qualified Pahoa Village as what I call a "hip hop diaspora" site. An affirmation of the importance of rap music and hip hop style became the dominant finding in my research. Rap lyrics have even lodged themselves in the students' discourse of identity and self-image. The "N" word, for example, is pervasive among the Pahoa youth. When I asked them what they meant when they referred to each other by using the "N" word, responses such as "It's like my homey" emerged. Realizing that the use of this word carries a dangerous history, one Pahoa male quickly added the hip hop revisionist distinction that is reflected in the spelling of the word: "We not putting nobody down; it's just like 'What's up, nigga?'" The last statement was made with "black" hip hop body language, complete with tilted head and the arm pushing backward by his side for emphasis. Although not surprised at the use of the word, I was taken aback at the obvious internalizing of the *attitude* behind the word that could be read in bodily gestures that came all too naturally. This was performativity in action – an enactment of identity that was not indigenous, but assumed, yet not contrived.

Black music, dance, and style traditionally generated from the black working class (e.g., blues, jazz, rhythm and blues) have long been cultural image definers of America. Norman Mailer's essay "The White Negro" captured the American appropriative dynamic as a part of the 1950s-era Beat generation and white jazz buffs.[8] Presently, this cultural trend has vastly expanded through the expediency of global technology. The new kind of American rebel with, or without, a cause – the gangsta rapper – is promulgated by high-paid Madison Avenue advertising executives and MTV programmers to young hip hoppers globally. What is more, in the late capitalist era, the entire process happens stunningly easily at the level of the body. Recording artists, for example, are packaged with image-setting body language, wardrobe, and dance moves to match iconic marketing representations that are as much a part of the international marketing of a new compact disc as the music itself. Global hip hop "heads" begin to imitate the slick mack-daddy image of dancer-singer Usher, the playa-pimp image of rapper Jay-Z, or the thug image of the late Tupac Shakur, all as American cool.

On the other hand, I found other evidence demonstrating that indigenous culture is also important. The Pahoa High students acknowledged contemporary Hawaiian music, often sung in the Hawaiian language, as also giving them significant listening pleasure. Local youths' identification with rap music and the hip hop lifestyle reflects the hegemony of United States mainland pop music promulgated by MTV. Yet it became obvious to me that contemporary Hawaiian musicians, who themselves participate in contemporary global culture's intertextualization of musical styles, ensure that the Hawaiian side of the equation stays vital and relevant for today's youth in Hawai'i. Against the rubric of the imported hip hop vernacular, continuing Polynesian-Asian indigenous styles are also embodied in gesture and posturing, such as martial arts gestures and local Hawaiian gaits. The synthesis of globally proliferating popular culture body styles with local movement predilections that have been present for centuries forms what I call the Intercultural Body. It is to this concept I now turn.

Hip Hop's Two-Pronged Bodily Text

As mentioned earlier, feminist theorist Judith Butler has been one of the most prolific scholars in conceptualizing and explicating the multiple dimensions of performativity. She has used the concept to explore how gender is performed (Butler 1990a), as well as to investigate contextual speech acts (Butler 1997). Butler's theories can be directly applied to physical enactments as performed text or bodily speech acts. In her essay "Performativity's Social Magic" she interrogates performativity from the perspective of Pierre Bourdieu's concept of *habitus*. Habitus is the accumulation of cultural and individual learned patterns that are unconsciously enacted. But what Bourdieu calls "the field," the various social domains in which the individual has to interact, influences habitus. The most important of the social domains of the field is the economic marketplace. Butler explains:

> Practice presupposes belief where belief is generated by the *habitus* and, specifically, the dispositions out of which the habitus is composed. And yet, as a necessary counter to this apparently subjectivistic account of practice, Bourdieu argues that a set of fields and, indeed, the market as ultimate field will inform and limit practices from an objective direction.
>
> (Butler 1996, 30)

Butler's use of Bourdieu's "habitus and field" is a compelling model through which to view the processes by which global hip hop youths construct their performed identities. My fieldwork revealed that Hawai'i's local styles of bodily posturing and practices, developing out of almost two hundred years of Polynesians' and Asians' social and biological mixing on Hawai'i's sugarcane and pineapple plantations, is meeting headlong with the bodily practices that are generic to today's MTV and BET generation. Movement styles generated out of Hawai'i's multicultural past as habitus are profoundly impacted by the virtual space of the Internet, the trendsetting bodily images of the print media, and the youth-oriented popular culture of satellite-projected music videos.

The resulting Intercultural Body is dramatically illustrated through the prism of what I call hip hop's two-pronged bodily text. The breakdancer's use of his or her own individual body language is mandatory if the improviser, in the moment, is going to "keep it real" within the b-boy circle. Everyday bodily gestures, drawn from the habitus and the field, become embodied social identity, forming the often unconscious performativity of social practice. When these embodied habits are situated within the act of dancing in the b-boy circle, the dual process of performance and performativity merge. Such social praxis demonstrates performance and performativity as two components of enacted bodily text through the prism of hip hop dance. The body language of ordinary life of a hip hop practitioner projects encoded cues that allow other b-boys or b-girls to literally recognize him/her, in the manner that TeN's Japan example demonstrated.

Dance theorist Randy Martin tellingly articulates the importance of dance as social practice when he explains that "Dance is best understood as a kind of embodied practice that makes manifest how movement comes to be by momentarily concentrating and elaborating in one place forces drawn from beyond a given performance setting" (Martin 1998, 5). Social process, reflective of history, politics, economics, and intercultural dynamics, can be drawn into the center of the b-boy circle with a well-articulated breakdance solo. But, as Martin reminds us, "it cannot presume to be the [theoretical] scene itself" (Martin 1998, 5).

The improvisatory breakdance circle allows both performativity, determined by both habitus and field, to connect with performance, the movement skills of the recognized subculture. In hip hop, it is the Africanist aesthetic of polyrhythmic isolations, narrative gesture, signifying, and, most importantly, improvisation that facilitates the movement-by-movement mix. The Intercultural Body, in the increasingly complex historical moment of economic and cultural exchange, emanates as a natural flow from embodied cultural practices that have as their center the objectified "black" body. The MTV-generated externalized "black" body is another revision of the historical minstrel image, and is promoted by the field of the marketplace as it has been historically. In the era of globalization, the objectified "black" body is now combined with indigenous bodily practices from the local habitus. Yet the entire

amalgam is allowed to fuse through a particularization of the age-old African aesthetic.

The *skills* needed for the Africanist aesthetic in breakdancing extend a path of enculturation that was originally opened during the Atlantic slave trade. Emerging social practices, with the Africanist aesthetic as integrating principle, eventually formed what Paul Gilroy calls the black Atlantic (Gilroy 1993). However, unlike the Du Boisian double-consciousness of nineteenth- and twentieth-century black and white social practices and migrations that Gilroy explores, the cultural multiplicity of the globally defined twenty-first century offers more polyvalent possibilities, such as the commingling of the black Atlantic and the yellow Pacific. Contemporary hip hop culture allows us a vision of how intercultural processes can push us beyond the social construction and objectification of "race" inculcated over the last three hundred years.

Hawaiian b-boys, for example, do not employ *studied* and *conscious* African dance elements in their b-boying and house styles. However, Asian martial arts *are* viewed as important cultural source material. Martin emphasizes the component cultural characteristics of dance styles that render habitus more intelligible:

> The constituent features of any given dance work include technical proclivities and aesthetic sensibilities that elaborate and depend on aspects of physical culture and prevailing ideologies. While dance is neither language nor politics, it is clarified and qualified through these means.
>
> (Martin 1998, 5)

Hawaiians are just beginning to understand the inherent African aesthetic principles at play in hip hop dance, so unconsciously exhibited in demonstrations like Urban Movement.

African American emcees also appropriate other global cultural influences. On the other side of the Afro-Asian equation, New York's well-known Wu Tang Clan, as their name indicates, consciously place a high value on the strength, discipline, and brotherhood of kung fu that was proliferated through Hong Kong-produced martial arts B-movies. Bruce

Lee flicks, for example, became a 1980s and early 1990s staple on Saturday-morning television, and therefore a part of the socialization process of many young black rappers growing up in New York and Los Angeles. Twenty-first-century hip hop culture, therefore, becomes a potpourri of cultural practices informed by the intersection of habita of indigenous cultures that have been mediated by the field according to the exigencies of the global capitalist marketplace.

Hip Hop Postmodernity: Dimensions of Late Capitalism and Cultural Studies

Hip hop functions as a central site of the ongoing battle in popular culture between marketplace hegemony and subculture counter-hegemony, a central tenet of British-initiated Cultural Studies as an academic discipline. How economics and subculture co-optation work together to create marketable popular culture style is a central connection in Cultural Studies analyses. As a neo-Marxian theoretical framework that first examined punk culture as a part of working-class Britain, it has generated its American academic adherents. A Cultural Studies approach helps to explain how popular culture is absolutely crucial to the era of late capitalism. Fredric Jameson's *Postmodernism, or The Cultural Logic of Late Capitalism* is a neo-Marxian economic understanding of postmodernity. Jameson's seminal text, as such, investigates the shift in the American cultural *Zeitgeist* and economic emphasis since the 1960s that, in turn, has affected the world. Postmodernity followed the era of modernity and, according to Jameson, it is not "the cultural dominant of a wholly new social order . . . but only the reflex and the concomitant of yet another systemic modification of capitalism itself" (Jameson 1992, xii).[9]

The popular culture industries – Hollywood, MTV, the recording industry, and much of the Internet – facilitate the interdependency of pop culture and economics as the crux of the postmodern era. Therefore, Jameson's concept of late capitalism "is not merely an emphasis on the emergence of new forms of business organization (multinationals, transnational) beyond the monopoly stage, but above all, the vision of a world capitalist system fundamentally distinct from the older imperialism, which was little more than a rivalry between the various colonial powers" (Jameson 1992, xvii–xix).[10]

This new form of "benign" imperialism that pop culture multinational corporations have become has further defined the transnational underground hip hop movement. In true counterhegemonic subculture stance, underground hip hop positions itself in proprietary opposition to the commercialization of rap music and hip hop dance. Yet, in reality, global pop culture commerce and the network of hip hop's subculture communities both socialize youth and affect their bodily identities, and therefore hip hop enactments in every part of the globe. Hip hop's underground has formed its own habitus, in a sense, which seeks to protect itself from the all-encompassing field of late capitalism in the postmodern era. Transnational hip hop culture has become a primary site for the working out of the dynamics of habitus and the field, with the body as a fundamental locus of the battle. Whether in Tokyo, Buenos Aires, Dakar, New York, or Honolulu, both ancient and contemporary identities are mapped into the muscles and manipulated by the agency and creativity of the hip hop dancer. Furthermore, hip hop culture's dialectic of global and local – as well as its complicity with, and aesthetic and contextual resistance to, late capitalism's hegemony – all point to it as a complex sign of the postmodern era.

Conclusions

Global breakdance offers poignant answers to Butler's question about the relationship between habitus and the field in the age of postmodernism. For the hip hop generation, a generation indoctrinated by MTV as well as by local styles, these interdependent processes are facilitated through the central Africanist aesthetic of improvisation. Dance improvisation allows for the minute-by-minute negotiation of personal and collective identity – the playing of the many rhythms of the self. MTV may very well be exporting virtualized and racialized body imagery, advanced out of America's invidious history of the enactments of the black body since nineteenth-century minstrelsy. But the original hip hop street dance form is also being kept alive in vital global breakdance communities of the hip hop underground. These communities' leaders, like TeN, travel and circulate myriad personal variations on b-boying, thereby establishing a counter-hegemonic international language as different bodily dialects of the same b-boy language. International competitions are held in Japan, Germany, New York, and other global sites with participants from every continent. It is in these international sites of underground hip hop, less mediated by American pop culture big business, that the Intercultural Body is flourishing.

My conception of the Intercultural Body is by no means the first theoretical paradigm of global hybrid dance. Just as MTV's "pop-up" windows complicate the choreographic screen, several theoretical explanations seem to pop out of this dance scenario, helping to capture the increasing global and cross-cultural complexity of hip hop dance. Randy Martin's theory of the "composite body" places the discussion of intertextuality clearly within an embodied context that is positioned within the multicultural United States itself:

In particular, hip hop moves are constituted across very different kinds of space laminated together to configure a composite body. While the electronic media provide a mapped virtual space in which bodies can circulate, these composite bodies always seem to be getting away, disappearing in the moment of reception only to reappear in altered form in that virtuality. . . . For multiculturalism as a critical perspective rather than a government policy, the composite body allows us to focus on how difference is associated among those assembled in the nation, rather than being forced to sort out one body from another.

(Martin 1998, 109–110)

Although Martin's composite body concept may invoke visions of a "cybernetic hybrid," a caveat that he disclaims, I prefer the term Intercultural Body, which posits the human form as part of a sentient being interacting in sociocultural space.

Other differences also separate our conceptions. Martin is concerned with "popular culture situated in, and figurative of, a certain multicultural and national context . . . [where] persons who attach themselves to practical instances (songs, video dance or fitness clubs) never actually meet except in the present scene of writing where I attempt to imagine their connection" (Martin 1998, 110–111). I am interested in experiencing the Intercultural Body in the act of producing itself during live enactments containing the improvised dancing body situated in the larger frames of ethnicity, indigenous cultures, and global popular culture. Where Martin focuses on contrived sites of the field like music videos and aerobics studios, I try to bring into focus the complexities of street or underground club sites that are removed from the gaze of the television camera or appropriating multimillion dollar venues.

Viewed within this context, global breakdancing is a potentially subversive means of culturally transgressing the nation-state, as well as transcending the controlling and racializing aspects of capitalism. The Intercultural Body is where "natural" appropriation can take place on the street and in the clubs by practitioners of all nationalities drawn by the powerful improvisatory Africanist aesthetic. Yet these same b-boys and b-girls are allowed to "keep it real" by negotiating through movement their personal and indigenous cultural identities.

Hip hop makes evident how habitus and the field exist simultaneously to shape individual identity. Alongside this personal, and potentially subversive, agency, b-boying and hip hop culture is also dispersed in innovative ways by the virtuality of a cut-and-paste potpourri of global culture promulgated by cable television and satellite broadcasts. However, it is also disseminated by disparate breakdance communities, the members of which are negotiating their complex identities in the moment through their bodies within the dynamic and energetic b-boy/b-girl circle. In the words of Schatzki and Natter, "The very existence and perpetuation of society amounts largely to the existence and reproduction of sociocultural bodies" (Schatzki and Natter 1996, 3). Global break-dancing is producing sociocultural bodies moving in often subversive ways. Their movement transcends nation-states and generates a global Intercultural Body that we are only beginning to fathom.

NOTES

1 Trip hop is a style of rap music originating in England that is more laid-back, cool, and, some perceive, more reflective than the majority of American rap. Trip hop's existence testifies to the globalization of rap music, in that some international sites have adapted the genre to their own cultural sensibilities. Two of trip hop's major proponents are the Bristol group Massive Attack, and their spin-off soloist, Tricky (AKA Adrian Thaws).

2 Judith Butler's use of performativity differs from my usage here in that she emphasizes bodily enactments as "fabrications" of identity to explicate her notion of the fictitious nature of a gender essence (*Gender Trouble*, 1990, Chapter 2, "Bodily Inscriptions, Performative Subversions"). In my investigation of performativity as unconscious gesture to explain performed culture that combines these gestures of the self with practiced dance, I am not concerned about fictitiously constructed elements of ethnicity or culture of a given people, as she is with gender. I take it for granted that culture, and for sure "race," are learned processes and are therefore conceived through various manufactured practices that come to represent a group. What most concerns me here, however, is how the individual creates with inherited (yet often unconscious) body languages to negotiate his/her identity in conjunction with inculcated dance styles of the marketplace through the improvising, dancing body.

3 House dancing is done to house music, a derivative of techno music that originated in Europe and became popular at rave events in the US House music is driven by a strong thumping bass beat. House dancing does not necessarily lend itself to the acrobatic break dance style, but rather utilizes some b-boy moves with a more upright dance style.

4 For the most complete theoretical text on the language-like semantic features of dance see Judith Lynne Hanna, *To Dance is Human: A Theory of Nonverbal Communication*, 2nd edn. (Chicago: The University of Chicago Press), 1987.

5 Brenda Dixon Gottschild explains that principles such as Embracing the Conflict, Polycentrism/Polyrhythm, High-Affect Juxtaposition, Ephebism or youthfulness, and the Aesthetic of the Cool, all add up to a process-based aesthetic that originated in various African cultures and has been revised and re-encoded throughout the Americas. All of these principles are significantly evident in hip hop culture.

6 I would like to thank the Hawai'i Committee for the Humanities for their belief in the timeliness of my research and for providing me with an individual grant to conduct my research project titled "Hip Hop Youth Culture: Local Hawaiians and African Americans in Dialogue." Also, my gratitude is extended to the Pahoa High School administrators and faculty for their support and cooperation.

7 Big Island population figures are taken from the 1996 County of Hawaii Data Book, Department of Research and Development, June, 1997.

8 Norman Mailer's "The White Negro," about the beatnik generation and its participation in bebop jazz era, was first published in *Dissent* IV (Spring): 1957.

9 Modernity originated for European Americans during the Gilded Age of the late nineteenth century and for African Americans, as Houston Baker argues, during the New Negro Renaissance of the 1920s. Periodization, though often binding us to the Western conception of time as a linear, fixed progression, is useful for understanding the cultural and political dynamics at the beginning of hip hop in the Bronx. It is also important to understanding hip hop's subsequent development into an often mind-boggling global display by the end of the twentieth century.

I am well aware that there have been other ways of periodizing modernity and postmodernity. Some scholars, for example, date modernity from the Renaissance of the sixteenth century and others place its beginnings in the Enlightenment of the eighteenth century. However, for my contemporary purposes, Jameson's positioning of modernity in the nineteenth century, from the industrial age through World War II, allows me to periodize hip hop culture within a cultural time frame relevant to it.

10 Jameson does not discount Marx's own engagement of the "world market" in the *Grundrisse*, nor does he ignore Wallerstein's "world system" as other possible explanations of the current phase of capitalism. However, he emphasizes a particular understanding of late capitalism that "turn[s] on this matter of internationalization and how it is to be described" (xix).

REFERENCES

Alladin, Justin. 1999. Personal interview. March 28.

Banes, Sally. 1985. "Breaking." In *Fresh Hip Hop Don't Stop*. Edited by Nelson George, 79–111. New York: Random House.

Butler, Judith. 1990a. *Gender Trouble: Feminism and the Subversion of Identity*. New York: Routledge.

Butler, Judith and Joan W. Scott, eds. 1990b. *Feminists Theorize the Political*. New York: Routledge.

Butler, Judith. 1996. "Performativity's Social Magic." In *The Social and Political Body*. Edited by Theodore R. Schatzki and Wolfgang Natter, 29–48. New York: Guilford Press.

Butler, Judith. 1997. *Excitable Speech: A Politics of the Performative*. New York: Routledge.

Desmond, Jane C. 1997. "Embodying Difference: Issues in Dance and Cultural Studies." In *Meaning in Motion: New Cultural Studies of Dance*. Edited by Jane C. Desmond, 29–54. Durham, NC: Duke University Press.

Derrida, Jacques. 1978. *Writing and Difference*. Chicago: University of Chicago Press.

Derrida, Jacques. 2000. *Revenge of the Aesthetic: The Place of Literature in Theory Today*. Berkeley: University of California Press.

Gates, Jr., Henry Louis. 1988. *The Signifying Monkey: A Theory of African-American Literary Criticism*. New York: Oxford University Press.

Gilroy, Paul. 1993. *The Black Atlantic: Modernity and Double Consciousness*. Cambridge, MA: Harvard University Press.

Gottschild, Brenda Dixon. 1996. *Digging the Africanist Presence in American Performance: Dance and Other Contexts*. Westport, CT: Greenwood Press.

Hanna, Judith Lynne. 1987. *To Dance is Human: A Theory of Nonverbal Communication*. 2nd edn. Chicago: University of Chicago Press.

Jameson, Fredric. 1992. *Postmodernism, or, The Cultural Logic of Late Capitalism*. Durham, NC: Duke University Press.

Kubiak, Anthony. 1998. "Splitting the Difference: Performance and Its Double in American Culture." *The Drama Review* 42(4): 91–114.

Mailer, Norman. 1959. "The White Negro." In *Advertisements for Myself* 337–358. New York: Putnam.

Martin, Randy. 1998. *Critical Moves: Dance Studies in Theory & Politics*. Durham, NC: Duke University Press.

Perkins, William Eric. 1996. "Youth Global Village: An Epilogue." In *Droppin' Science: Critical Essays on Rap Music and Hip Hop Culture*. Edited by William Eric Perkins, 258–273. Philadelphia: Temple University Press.

Rose, Tricia. 1994. *Black Noise: Rap Music and Black Culture in Contemporary America*. Middletown, CT: Wesleyan University Press.

Schatzki, Theodore R. and Wolfgang Natter. 1996. "Sociocultural Bodies, Bodies Sociopolitical." In *The Social and Political Body*. Edited by Theodore R. Schatzki and Wolfgang Natter, 1–28. New York: Guilford Press.

Further Readings

The readings included in the following bibliography are by no means comprehensive, but they are intended both to supplement the sources cited in the Introduction and to complement the readings selected for this volume. Some key themes that thus emerge are the relationship between politics and performance; ritualistic performances, such as rites of passage; the formulation of indigenous genres; public spectacles and identity formation; oral history; the impact of tourism; the cultural role of sports; mass-mediated performances; and the role that globalization and transnationalism play in the creation of new and innovative modes of expressive culture.

Abercrombie, N. and B. Longhurst
  1998. *Audiences: A Sociological Theory of Performance and Imagination*. Thousand Oaks, CA: Sage Publishing, Inc.
Abrahams, R.D.
  1969. The Complex Relations of Simple Forms. *Genre* 2(2): 104–128.
Abrahams, R.D.
  1970. A Performance-Centered Approach to Gossip. *Man* 5(2): 290–301.
Abrahams, R.D.
  1982. Storytelling Events: Wake Amusements and the Structure of Nonsense on St. Vincent. *Journal of American Folklore* 95(378): 389–414.
Abrahams, R.D.
  1983. *The Man-of-Words in the West Indies: Performance and the Emergence of Creole Culture*. Baltimore, MD: Johns Hopkins University Press.
Abu-Lughod, L.
  1986a. Modest Women, Subversive Poems: The Politics of Love in an Egyptian Bedouin Society. *Bulletin. British Society for Middle Eastern Studies* 13(2): 159–168.
Abu-Lughod, L.
  1986b. *Veiled Sentiments: Honor and Poetry in a Bedouin Society*. Berkeley: University of California Press.

The Anthropology of Performance: A Reader, First Edition. Edited by Frank J. Korom.
© 2013 John Wiley & Sons, Inc. Published 2013 by John Wiley & Sons, Inc.

Alexander, J.C.
   2004. Cultural Pragmatics: Social Performance Between Ritual and Strategy. *Sociological Theory* 22(4): 527–573.
Ali, S.M.
   2010. *Arabic Literary Salons in the Islamic Middle Ages: Poetry, Public Performance, and the Presentation of the Past*. Notre Dame, IN: University of Notre Dame Press.
Allen, C.J. and N. Garner
   1996. *Condor Qatay: Anthropology in Performance*. Long Grove, IL: Waveland Press.
Appadurai, A.
   1988. How to Make a National Cuisine: Cookbooks in Contemporary India. *Comparative Studies in Society and History* 30(1): 3–24.
Arnoldi, Mary Jo
   1995. *Playing with Time: Art and Performance in Central Mali*. Bloomington: Indiana University Press.
Babcock, B.A.
   1988. At Home, No Womens are Storytellers: Potteries, Stories, and Politics in Cochiti Pueblo. *Journal of the Southwest* 30(3): 356–389.
Babiracki, C.M.
   2008. Between Life History and Performance: Sundari Devi and the Art of Allusion. *Ethnomusicology* 52(1): 1–30.
Bank, R.K.
   2002. Representing History: Performing the Columbian Exposition. *Theatre Journal* 54(4): 589–606.
Banks, G.
   1995. Peruvian Pots, Crafts and Foreigners. *Journal of Museum Ethnography* 7: 1–16.
Barber, K.
   2003. Text and Performance in Africa. *Bulletin of the School of Oriental and African Studies* 66(3): 324–333.
Bauman, R.
   1975. Verbal Art as Performance. *American Anthropologist* 77: 290–312.
Bauman, R., *ed.*
   1977. *Verbal Art as Performance*. Rowley, MA: Newbury House Publishers.
Bauman, R.
   1986. *Story, Performance and Event: Contextual Studies of Oral Narrative*. New York: Cambridge University Press.
Bauman, R. and C.L. Briggs
   1990. Poetics and Performance as Critical Perspectives on Language and Social Life. *Annual Review of Anthropology* 19: 59–88.
Beeman, W.O.
   1993. The Anthropology of Theater and Spectacle. *Annual Review of Anthropology* 22: 369–393.
Becker, A.L.
   1983. Biography of a Sentence: A Burmese Proverb. In: *Text, Play, and Story: The Construction and Reconstruction of Self and Society*. E.M. Bruner, ed., pp. 135–155. Washington, DC: American Ethnological Society.
Bell, C.
   1987. Ritualization of Texts and the Textualization of Ritual in the Codification of Taoist Liturgy. *History of Religions* 27: 366–392.
Bell, D.
   2002. Person and Place: Making Meaning of the Art of Australian Indigenous Women. *Feminist Studies* 28(1): 95–127.

Ben-Amos, D.
  1993. "Context" in Context. *Western Folklore* 52: 209–226.
Ben-Amos, D.
  1998. A Performer-Centered Study of Narration. *Anthropos* 4(6): 556–558.
Ben-Amos, D. and K. Goldstein, *eds*.
  1975. *Folklore: Performance and Communication*. The Hague: Mouton.
Besnier, N.
  1989. Information Withholding as a Manipulative and Collusive Strategy in Nukulaelae
  Gossip. *Language in Society* 18(3): 315–341.
Besnier, N.
  1990. Language and Affect. *Annual Review of Anthropology* 19: 419–452.
Birdwhistell, R.
  1970. *Kinesics and Context*. Philadelphia: University of Pennsylvania Press.
Blackburn, S.H.
  1981. Oral Performance: Narrative and Ritual in a Tamil Tradition. *Journal of American
  Folklore* 94: 207–227.
Blackburn, S.H. and A.K. Ramanujan, eds.
  1986. *Another Harmony: New Essays on the Folklore of India*. Berkeley: University of
  California Press.
Blain, J. and R.J. Wallis
  2004. Sacred Sites/Contested Rites: Contemporary Pagan Engagements with the Past. *Journal of
  Material Culture* 9: 237–261.
Bloch, M.
  1974. Symbols, Song, Dance, and Features of Articulation: Is Religion an Extreme form
  of Traditional Authority? *European Journal of Sociology* 15(1): 54–81.
Blount, M.
  1992. The Preacherly Text: African American Poetry and Vernacular Performance. *Periodical
  of the Modern Language Association* 107(3): 582–593.
Bowen, J.R.
  1986. On the Political Construction of Tradition: *Gotong Royong* in Indonesia. *Journal of
  Asian Studies* 45(3): 545–561.
Boyarin, J.
  1993. Voices Around the Text: The Ethnography of Reading at Mesivta Tifereth Jerusalem. In:
  The Ethnography of Reading. J. Boyarin, ed., pp. 212–237. Berkeley: University of California
  Press.
Brenneis, D.
  1984. Grog and Gossip in Bhatgaon: Style and Substance in Fiji Indian Conversation. *American
  Ethnologist* 11: 487–506.
Brenneis, D.
  1986. Shared Territory: Audience, Indirection and Meaning. *Text* 6: 339–347.
Briggs, C.L.
  1985. Treasure Tales and Pedagogical Discourse in Mexicano New Mexico. *Journal of
  American Folklore* 98: 287–314.
Briggs, C.L.
  1985. The Pragmatics of Proverb Performances in New Mexican Spanish. *American Anthro-
  pologist* 87: 793–810.
Briggs, C.L.
  1988. *Competence in Performance: The Creativity of Tradition in Mexicano Verbal Art*.
  Philadelphia: University of Pennsylvania Press.
Briggs, C.L. and R. Bauman
  1992. Genre, Intertextuality and Social Power. *Journal of Linguistic Anthropology* 2: 131–172.

Bruner, E.M. and B. Girshenblatt-Gimblett
1994. Maasai on the Lawn: Tourist Realism in East Africa. *Cultural Anthropology* 9(4): 435–470.

Caraveli, A.
1982. The Song Beyond the Song: Aesthetics and Social Interaction in Greek Folk Song. *Journal of American Folklore* 95: 129–158.

Caravali, A.
1985. The Symbolic Village: Community Born in Performance. *Journal of American Folklore* 98: 259–286.

Caton, S.
1985. The Poetic Construction of Self. *Anthropological Quarterly* 58(4): 141–151.

Caton, S.
1993. Icons of the Person: Lacan's "Imago" in the Yemeni Male's Tribal Wedding. *Asian Folklore Studies* 52(2): 359–381.

Charlsey, S.
2004. Interpreting Untouchability: The Performance of Caste In Andhra Pradesh, South India. *Asian Folklore Studies* 63(2): 267–290.

Coleman, S.
1996. Words as Things: Language, Aesthetics and the Objectification of Protestant Evangelicalism. *Journal of Material Culture* 1(1): 107–128.

Combs-Shillings, M.E.
1989. *Sacred Performances: Islam, Sexuality, and Sacrifice*. New York: Columbia University Press.

Cornelissen, S.
2005. Producing and Imaging "Place" and "People": The Political Economy of South African International Tourist Representation. *Review of International Political Economy* 12(4): 674–699.

Cummings, W.
2003. Rethinking the Interaction of Orality and Literacy: Historical Discourse in Early Modern Makassar." *Journal of Asian Studies* 62(2): 531–551.

Dégh, L.
1969. *Folktales and Society: Story-Telling in a Hungarian Peasant Community*. Bloomington: Indiana University Press.

De Marinis, M.
1993. *The Semiotics of Performance*. Bloomington: Indiana University Press.

Denecke, W.
2004. Chinese Antiquity and Court Spectacle in Early "Kanshi. " *Journal of Japanese Studies* 30 (1): 97–122.

Dening, G.
1993. The Theatricality of History Making and the Paradoxes of Acting. *Cultural Anthropology* 8(1): 73–95.

Dening, G.
2002. Performing on the Beaches of the Mind: An Essay. *History and Theory* 41(1): 1–24.

Dexter, N.
1983. Folk Song Performance in the Caribbean. *Caribbean Quarterly* 29(1): 66–69.

Drewal, M.T.
1991. The State of Research on Performance in Africa. *African Studies Review* 34(3): 1–64.

Dubisch, J.
1996. Anthropology of Pilgrimage. *Etnofoor* 9(2): 66–77.

Duey, P.A.
1946. Vocal Art in Antiquity. *The Musical Quarterly* 32(3): 390–410.

Duranti, A.
1981. Speechmaking and the Organization of Discourse in a Samoan Fono. *Journal of the Polynesian Society* 90(3): 357–400.
Duranti, A.
1983. Samoan Speechmaking across Social Events: One Genre in and Out of a *Fono*. *Language in Society* 12: 1–22.
Duranti, A.
1990. Politics and Grammar: Agency in Samoan Political Discourse. *American Ethnologist* 17(4): 646–666.
Duranti, A. and D.L. Brennies, eds.
1986. The Audience as Co-Author. *Text* 6(3): 239–347.
Epskamp, K.
2003. Intercultural Puzzles, Richard Schechner and the Anthropology of Theatre in the 20th Century. *Anthropos* 98(2): 499–509.
Errington, F.
1987. Reflexivity Deflected: The Festival of Nations as an American Performance. *American Ethnologist* 14(4): 654–667.
Fabian, J.
1990. *Power and Performance: Ethnographic Explorations through Proverbial Wisdom and Theatre in Shoba, Zaire*. Madison: University of Wisconsin Press.
Feld, S. and A.A. Fox
1994. Music and Language. *Annual Review of Anthropology* 23: 25–53.
Fernandez, J.W.
1966. Unbelievably Subtle Words: Representation and Integration in the Sermons of an African Reformative Cult. *History of Religions* 6(1): 43–69.
Fernandez, J.W.
1972. Persuasions and Performances: Of the Beast in Every Body . . . And the Metaphors of Everyman. *Daedalus* 101(1): 39–60.
Fernandez, J.W.
1986. *Persuasions and Performances: The Play of Tropes in Culture*. Bloomington: Indiana University Press.
Finnegan, R.
1969. How to Do Things with Words: Performative Utterances among the Limba of Sierra Leone. *Man* 4: 537–552.
Finnegan, R.
1970. A Note on Oral Tradition and Historical Evidence. *History and Theory* 9(2): 195–201.
Flores, R.R.
1994. "Los Pastores" and the Gifting of Performance. *American Ethnologist* 21: 270–285.
Foley, J.M.
1995. *The Singer of Tales in Performance*. Bloomington: Indiana University Press.
Foster, M.
1989. It's Cookin' Now: A Performance Analysis of the Speech Events of a Black Teacher in an Urban Community College. *Language in Society* 18(1): 1–29.
Foster, R.J.
1991. Making National Cultures in the Global Ecumene. *Annual Review of Anthropology* 20: 235–260.
Frisbie, C.J.
1980. Ritual Drama in the Navajo House Blessing Ceremony. In: *Southwestern Indian Ritual Drama*. C.J. Frisbie, ed., pp. 161–198. Albuquerque: University of New Mexico Press.
Gatewood, J.B. *et al.*
2004. Battlefield Pilgrims at Gettysburg National Military Park. *Ethnology* 43(3): 193–216.

Geroian, C.R.
  2001. Performing the Museum. *Studies in Art Education* 42(3): 234–248.
Goldstein, D.M.
  1998. Performing National Culture in a Bolivian Migrant Community. *Ethnology* 37(2): 117–132.
Goldstein, D.M.
  2004. *The Spectacular City: Violence and Performance in Urban Bolivia*. Durham, NC: Duke University Press.
Goodwin, M.H.
  1980. "He-said-she-said": Formal Cultural Procedures for the Construction of a Gossip Dispute Activity. *American Ethnologist* 9: 76–96.
Goodwin, M.H.
  1985. The Serious Side of Jump Rope: Conversational Practices and Social Organization in the Frame of Play. *Journal of American Folklore* 98: 315–330.
Gouk, P.
  1996. Performing Practice: Music, Medicine and Natural Philosophy in Interregnum Oxford. *British Journal of the History of Science* 29: 257–288.
Grima, B.
  1992. *"The Misfortunes Which Have Befallen Me:" Paxtun Women's Life Stories*. Austin: University of Texas Press.
Gumperz, J.
  1982. *Discourse Strategies*. London: Cambridge University Press.
Guss, D.M.
  1993. The Selling of San Juan: The Performance of History in an Afro-Venezuelan Community. *American Ethnologist* 20(3): 451–473.
Guss, D.M.
  2000. *The Festive State: Race, Ethnicity, and Nationalism as a Cultural Performance*. Berkeley: University of California Press.
Hagedorn, K.J.
  2001. *Divine Utterances: The Performance of Afro-Cuban Santeria*. Washington, DC: Smithsonian Books.
Hanks, W.F.
  1987. Discourse Genres in a Theory of Practice. *American Ethnologist* 14: 668–692.
Hansen, K.T.
  2004. The World in Dress: Anthropological Perspectives on Clothing, Fashion, and Culture. *Annual Review of Anthropology* 33: 369–392.
Haring, L.
  1992. *Verbal Art in Madagascar: Performance in Historical Perspective*. Philadelphia: University of Pennsylvania Press.
Herman, B.
  1985. Time and Performance: Folk Houses in Delaware. In: *American Material Culture and Folklife*. S. Bronner, ed., pp. 155–175. Ann Arbor: UMI Resources Press.
Herzfeld, M.
  1985. *The Poetics of Manhood: Context and Identity in a Cretan Mountain Village*. Princeton, NJ: Princeton University Press.
Heselink, N.
  2012. *SamulNori: Contemporary Korean Drumming and the Rebirth of Itinerant Culture*. Chicago: University of Chicago Press.
Hirsch, Eric
  1990. From Bone to Betelnuts: Processes of Ritual Transformation and the Development of "National Culture" in Papua New Guinea. *Man (N.S.)* 25(1): 18–34.

Hirschfeld, L.A.
    1977. Art in Cunaland: Ideology and Cultural Adaptation. *Man (N.S.)* 12(1): 104–123.
Hitchcock, M.
    1995. The Indonesian Cultural Village Museum and Its Forbears. *Journal of Museum Eth-*
    nography 7: 17–24.
Hoelscher, S.
    2003. Making Place, Making Race: Performances of Whiteness in the Jim Crow South. *Annals*
    of the Association of American Geographers 93(3): 657–686.
Hymes, D.
    1974. *Foundations in Sociolinguistics: An Ethnographic Approach*. Philadelphia: University of
    Pennsylvania Press.
Hymes, D.
    1975a. Breakthrough into Performance. In: *Folklore: Performance and Communication*. D.
    Ben-Amos and K. Goldstein, eds., pp. 11–74. The Hague: Mouton.
Hymes, D.
    1975b. Folklore's Nature and the Sun's Myth. *Journal of American Folklore* 88: 346–369.
Hymes, D.
    1977. Discovering Oral Performance and measured Verse in American Indian Narrative. *New*
    Literary History 8(3): 431–457.
Jackson, J.B.
    2005. *Yuchi Ceremonial Life: Performance, Meaning, and Tradition in a Contemporary*
    American Indian Community. Lincoln: University of Nebraska Press.
Johnson, E.P.
    2003. *Appropriating Blackness: Performance and Politics of Authenticity*. Durham, NC: Duke
    University Press.
Joseph, Mary
    1999. *Nomadic Identities: The Performance of Citizenship*. Minneapolis: University of Min-
    nesota Press.
Kalcik, S.
    1975. . . . Like Ann's Gynecologist or the Time I Was Almost Raped. *Journal of American*
    Folklore 88(347): 3–11.
Kapchan, D.A.
    1996. *Gender in the Market: Moroccan Women and the Revoicing of Tradition*. Philadelphia:
    University of Pennsylvania Press.
Keane, W.
    1994. The Value of Words and the Meaning of Things in Eastern Indonesian Exchange. *Man*
    (N.S.) 29(3): 605–629.
Keane, W.
    1995. The Spoken House: Text, Act, and Object in Eastern Indonesia. *American Ethnologist* 22:
    102–124.
Keane, W.
    1997. Religious Language. *Annual Review of Anthropology* 26: 47–71.
Keber, E.Q.
    2002. *Representing Aztec Ritual: Performance, Text, and Image in the Work of Sahagun*.
    Boulder: University Press of Colorado.
Kelly, H.A.
    1979. Tragedy and the Performance of Tragedy in Late Roman Antiquity. *Traditio* 35:
    21–44.
Kligman, G.
    1984. The Rites of Women: Oral Poetry, Ideology, and the Socialization of Peasant Women in
    Contemporary Romania. *Journal of American Folklore* 97(384): 167–188.

Korom, F.J.
2003. *Muharram Performances in an Indo-Caribbean Diaspora*. Philadelphia: University of Pennsylvania Press.
Korom, F.J.
2006a. *Village of Painters: Narrative Scrolls from West Bengal*. Santa Fe: Museum of New Mexico Press.
Korom, F.J.
2006b. *South Asian Folklore: A Handbook*. Westport, CT: Greenwood Press.
Kratz, C.A.
1994. *Affecting Performance: Meaning, Movement, and Experience in Okiek Women's Initiation*. Washington, DC: Smithsonian Institution Press.
Kuiper, K. and D. Haggo
1984. Livestock Auctions, Oral Poetry, and Ordinary Language. *Language in Society* 13(2): 205–234.
Labov, W.
1972. Rules for Ritual Insults. In: *Rappin' and Stylin', Out.*, T. Kochman, ed., pp. 265–314. Urbana: University of Illinois Press.
Laderman, C. and M. Roseman, eds.
1995. *The Performance of Healing*. New York: Routledge.
LaFleur, W.
1979. Points of Departure: Comments on Religious Pilgrimage in Sri Lanka and Japan. *Journal of Asian Studies* 38(2): 271–281.
Lambek, M.
2000. The Anthropology of Religion and the Quarrel between Poetry and Philosophy. *Current Anthropology* 41(3): 309–320.
Limón. J.E.
1982. History, Chicano Joking, and the Varieties of Higher Education: Tradition and Performance as Critical Symbolic Action. *Journal of the Folklore Institute* 9: 141–166.
Limón, J.E.
1983. Legendry, Metafolklore, and Performance: A Mexican-American Example. *Western Folklore* 42: 191–208.
Little, K.
1993. Masochism, Spectacle, and the "Broken Mirror" Clown Entrée: A Note on the Anthropology of Performance in Postmodern Culture. *Cultural Anthropology* 8(1): 117–129.
Little, W.E.
2000. Home as a Place of Exhibition and Performance: Mayan Household Transformations in Guatemala. *Ethnology* 39(2): 163–181.
Logan, A.P.
1978. The Palio of Siena: Performance and Process. *Urban Anthropology* 7(1): 45–65.
Lord, A.
1953. Homer's Originality. *Transactions and Proceedings of the American Philological Association* 84: 124–134.
MacAloon, J.J.
1982. Double Vision: Olympic Games and American Culture. *The Kenyon Review* 4(1): 98–112.
MacAloon, J.J., ed.
1984. *Rite, Drama, Festival, Spectacle*. Philadelphia: Institute for the Study of Human Issues.
Mannheim, B.
1986. Popular Song and Popular Grammar, Poetry and Metalanguage. *Word* 37: 45–75.

Manning, F.E.
  1978. Carnival in Antigua: An Indigenous Festival in a Tourist Economy. *Anthropos* 73(1–2): 191–204.
Manning, F.E.
  1985. The Performance of Politics: Caribbean Music and the Anthropology of Victor Turner. *Anthropologica* (N.S.) 27(1–2): 39–53.
Markus, D.D.
  2000. Performing the Book: The Recital of Epic in First-Century CE Rome. *Classical Antiquity* 19(1): 138–179.
Matsuki, K.
  2000. Negotiation of Memory and Agency in Japanese Oral Narrative Accounts of Wartime Experiences. *Ethos* 29(4): 534–550.
Mendoza, Z.S.
  1998. Defining Folklore: Mestizo and Indigenous Identities on the Move. *Bulletin of Latin American Research* 17(2): 165–183.
Mills, M.A.
  1991. *Rhetoric and Politics in Afghan Traditional Storytelling*. Philadelphia: University of Pennsylvania Press.
More, M.T.
  1965–66. The Performance of Plainsong in the Later Middle Ages and the Sixteenth Century. *Proceedings of the Royal Musical Association* 92: 121–134.
Muana, P.K.
  1998. Beyond Frontiers: A Review of Analytical Paradigms in Folklore Studies. *Journal of African Cultural Studies* 11(1): 39–58.
Murck, A.
  2007. Golden Mangoes: The Life Cycle of a Cultural Revolution Symbol. *Archives of Asian Art* 57: 1–21.
Ness, S.A.
  1992. *Body, Movement, and Culture*. Philadelphia: University of Pennsylvania Press.
Noyes, D.
  2003. *Fire in the Placa: Catalan Festival Politics After Franco*. Philadelphia: University of Pennsylvania Press.
Orgel, S.
  1971. The Poetics of Spectacle. *New Literary History* 2(3): 367–399.
Pagliai, V.
  2002. Poetic Dialogues: Performance and Politics in the Tuscan "Contrasto." *Ethnology* 41(2): 135–154.
Parker, B.L.
  2006. Art, Culture and Authenticity in South African Music. *International Review of Aesthetics and Sociology of Music* 39(1): 57–71.
Passes, A.
  2004. The Place of Politics: Powerful Speech and Women Speakers in Everyday Pa'ikwené Life. *Journal of the Royal Anthropological Institute* 10(1): 1–18.
Peacock, J.
  1967. Anti-Dutch, Anti-Muslim Drama among the Surabaja Proletarians: A Description of Performances and Responses. *Indonesia* 4: 43–73.
Peñaloza, L.
  2001. Consuming the American West: Animating Cultural Meaning and Memory at a Stock Show and Rodeo. *Journal of Consumer Research* 28(3): 369–398.

Peterson, S.
   1988. Translating Experience and the Reading of a Story Cloth. *Journal of American Folklore*
   101(399): 6–22.
Picard, M.
   1990. "Cultural Tourism in Bali": Cultural Performances as Tourist Attraction. *Indonesia* 49:
   37–74.
Porcello, T. *et al.*
   2010. The Reorganization of the Sensory World. *Annual Review of Anthropology* 39: 51–66.
Port, M. van de
   1999. The Articulation of Soul: Gypsy Musicians and the Serbian Other. *Popular Music* 18(3):
   291–308.
Poveda, D. *et al.*
   2005. Religious Genres, Entextualization and Literacy in Gitano Children. *Language in Society*
   34(1): 87–115.
Raheja, G.G.
   1996. Caste, Colonialism, and the Speech of the Colonized: Entextualization and Disciplinary
   Control in India. *American Ethnologist* 23(3): 494–513.
Ramnarine, T.
   1998. Historical Representations, Performance Spaces, and Kinship Themes in Indian–Caribbean
   Popular Song Texts. *Asian Music* 30(1): 1–33.
Reed, S.A.
   1998. The Politics and Poetics of Dance. *Annual Review of Anthropology* 27: 503–532.
Retzleff, A.
   2003. Near Eastern Theatres in Late Antiquity. *Phoenix* 57(1-2): 115–138.
Reynolds, D.
   1994. Feathered Brides and Bridled Fertility: Architecture, Ritual, and Change in a Northern
   Egyptian Village. *Muqarnas* 11: 166–178.
Reynolds, D.
   1995. *Heroic Poets and Poetic Heroes: The Ethnography of Performance in an Arabic Oral
   Epic Tradition*. Ithaca, NY: Cornell University Press.
Román-Velázquez, P.
   1999. The Embodiment of Salsa: Musicians, Instruments and Performance of a Latin Style and
   Identity. *Popular Music* 18(1): 115–131.
Rosaldo, M.Z.
   1972. Metaphors and Folk Classification. *Southwestern Journal of Anthropology* 28(1):
   83–99.
Rosaldo, M.Z.
   1982. The Things We Do with Words: Ilongot Speech Acts and Speech Act Theory in
   Philosophy. *Language in Society* 11: 203–35.
Roseman, M.
   1983. The New Rican Village Artists in Control of the Image-Making Machinery. *Latin
   American Review* 4(1): 132–167.
Roseman, M.
   1988. The Pragmatics of Aesthetics: The Performance of Healing among the Senoi Temiar.
   Social Science Medicine 27: 811–818.
Roseman, M.
   1998. Singers of the Landscape: Song, History, and property Rights in the Malaysian Rain
   Forest. *American Anthropologist* 100(1): 106–121.
Sacks, H.
   1974. An Analysis of the Course of a Joke's Telling in Conversation. In: *Explorations in the*

Ethnography of Speaking. 2nd edn. R. Bauman and R. Sherzer, eds., pp. 337–353. Cambridge: Cambridge University Press.

Sanches, M. and B. Kirshenblatt-Gimblett
1975. Children's Traditional Speech Play and Child Language. In: *Speech Play.* B. Girshenblatt-Gimblett, ed., pp. 65–110. Philadelphia: University of Pennsylvania Press.

Sax, W.S.
1990. The Ramnagar Ramlila: Text, Performance, Pilgrimage. *History of Religions* 30(2): 129–153.

Sax, W.S.
2002. *Dancing the Self: Personhood and Performance in the Pandav Lila of Garhwal.* New York: Oxford University Press.

Scher, P.W.
2002. Copyright Heritage: Carnival and the State in Trinidad. *Anthropological Quarterly* 75(3): 453–484.

Scheub, H.
1970. The Technique of the Expansible Image in Xhosa "Ntsomi" Performance. *Research in African Literatures* 1(2): 119–146.

Scheub, H.
1987. Oral Poetry and History. *New Literary History* 18(3): 477–496.

Sharaby, R.
2006. The Bride's Henna Rituals: Symbols, Meanings, and Changes. *Nashim* 11: 11–42.

Sherzer, D. and J. Sherzer
1976. Mormaknamaloe: The Cuna Mola. In: *Ritual and Symbol in Native Central America.* P. Young and J. Howe, eds., pp. 23–42. University of Oregon Anthropological Papers, Number 9.

Sherzer, J.
1990. *Verbal Art in San Blas: Kuna Culture Through Its Discourse.* Cambridge: Cambridge University Press.

Shimoni, B.
2006. Cultural Borders, Hybridization, and a Sense of Boundaries in Thailand, Mexico, and Israel. *Journal of Anthropological Research* 62(2): 217–234.

Shuck, G.
2004. Conversational Performance and the Poetic Construction of an Ideology. *Language in Society* 33(2): 195–222.

Shukla-Bhatt, N.
2007. Performance as Translation: Mira in Gujarat. *International Journal of Hindu Studies* 11(3): 273–298.

Silverstein, M.
2005. The Poetics of Politics: "Theirs" and "Ours." *Journal of Anthropological Research* 61(1): 1–24.

Singer, M.
1963. The Radha Krishna "Bhajans" of Madras City. *History of Religions* 2(2): 183–226.

Slyomovics, S.
1987. *The Merchant of Art: An Egyptian Hilali Oral Epic Poet in Performance.* Berkeley: University of California Press.

Slyomovics, S.
1989. Cross-Cultural Dress and Tourist Performance in Egypt. *Performing Arts Journal* 11(3): 139–148.

Slyomovics, S.
2005. *The Performance of Human Rights in Morocco.* Philadelphia: University of Philadelphia Press.

Spencer, P.
   1986. *Society and the Dance: The Social Anthropology of Process and Performance.* New York: Cambridge University Press.

Stevenson, T.B. and A.B. Alaug
   2000. Football in Newly United Yemen: Rituals of Equity, Identity, and State Formation. *Journal of Anthropological Research* 56(4): 453–475.

Stillman, A.K.
   1996. Hawaiian Hula Competitions: Event, Repertoire, Performance, Tradition. *Journal of American Folklore* 109(434): 357–380.

Stronsa, A.
   2001. Anthropology of Tourism: Forging New Ground for Ecotourism and Other Alternatives. *Annual Review of Anthropology* 30: 261–283.

Suter, A.
   2003. Lament in Euripidies' "Trojan War. " *Mnemosyne* (Fourth Series) 56(1): 1–28.

Tambiah, S.
   1979. A Performative Approach to Ritual. *Proceedings of the British Academy* 65: 113–169.

Taussig, M.
   1993. *Mimesis and Alterity: A Particular History of the Senses.* New York: Routledge.

Teague, K.
   1995. Tourism, Anthropology and Museums: Representations of Nepalese Reality. *Journal of Museum Ethnography* 7: 41–62.

Tedlock, B. and D. Tedlock
   1985. Text and Textile: Language and Technology in the Arts of the Quiché Maya. *Journal of Anthropological Research* 41(2): 121–146.

Tedlock, D.
   1975. Learning to Listen: Oral History as Poetry. *Boundary* 23(3): 707–728.

Thomas, R.
   2003. Performance and Written Literature in Classical Greece. *Bulletin of the School of Oriental and African Studies* 66(3): 348–357.

Tuan, Y.F.
   1991. Language and the Making of Place: A Narrative-Descriptive Approach. *Annals of the Association of American Geographers* 81(4): 681–696.

Turner, V.
   1975. Symbolic Studies. *Annual Review of Anthropology* 4: 145–161.

Turner, V.
   1979. Frame, Flow and Reflection: Ritual and Drama as Public Liminality. *Japanese Journal of Religious Studies* 6(4): 465–499.

Upton, D.
   1979. Toward a Performance Theory of Vernacular Architecture: Early Tidewater Virginia as a Case Study. *Folklore Forum* 12: 173–198.

Urban, G.
   1988. Ritual Wailing in Amerindian Brazil. *American Anthropologist* 90: 385–400.

Vannini, P.
   2008. A Queen's Drowning: Material Culture, Drama, and the Performance of a Technological Accident. *Symbolic Interaction* 31(2): 155–188.

Webber, S.J.
   1991. *Romancing the Real: Folklore and Ethnographic Representation in North Africa.* Philadelphia: University of Pennsylvania Press.

Werbner, P.
   2002. *Imagined Diasporas among Manchester Muslims: The Public Performance of Pakistani Transnational Identity.* London: James Currey.